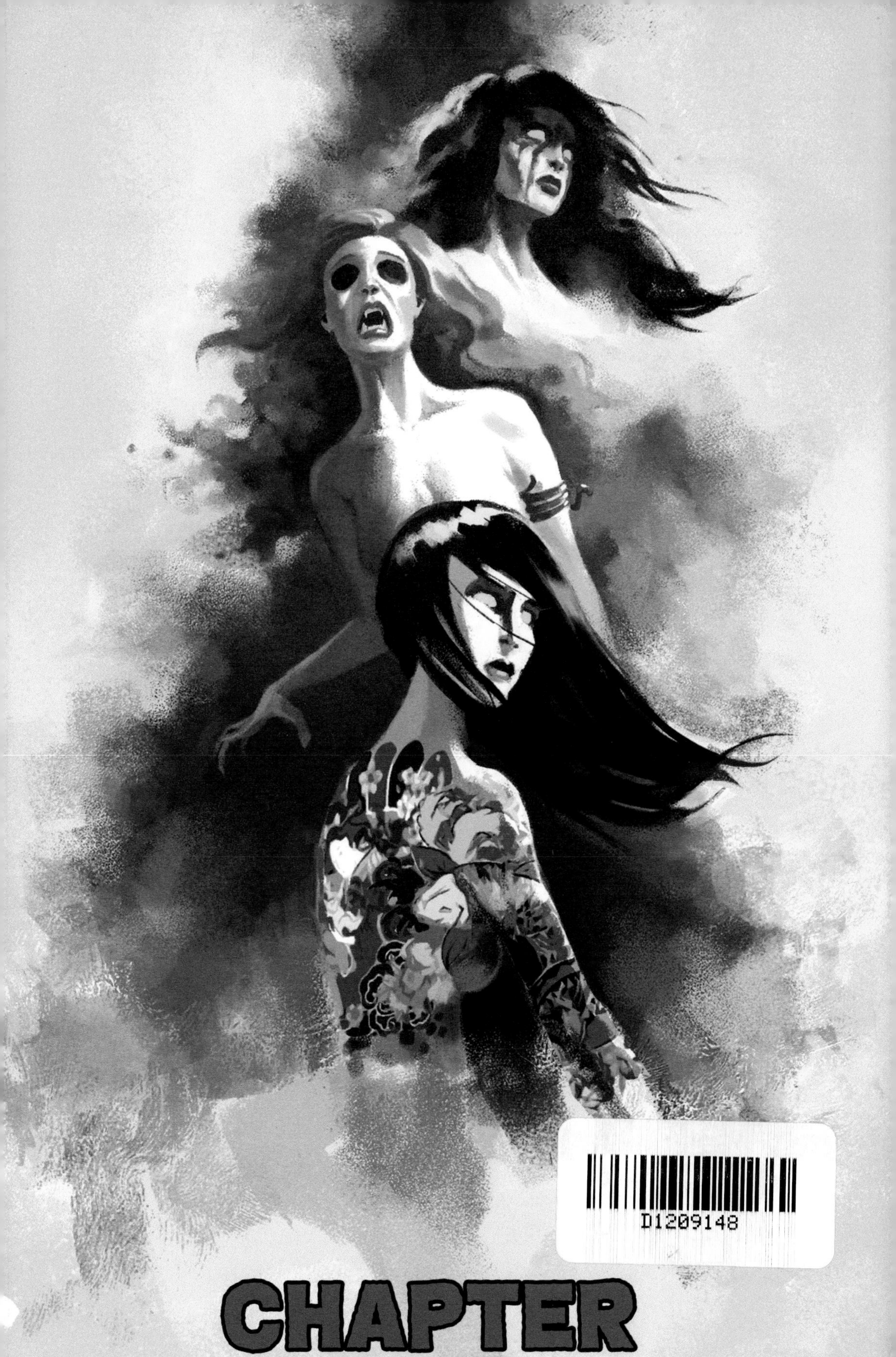

CHAPTER ONE

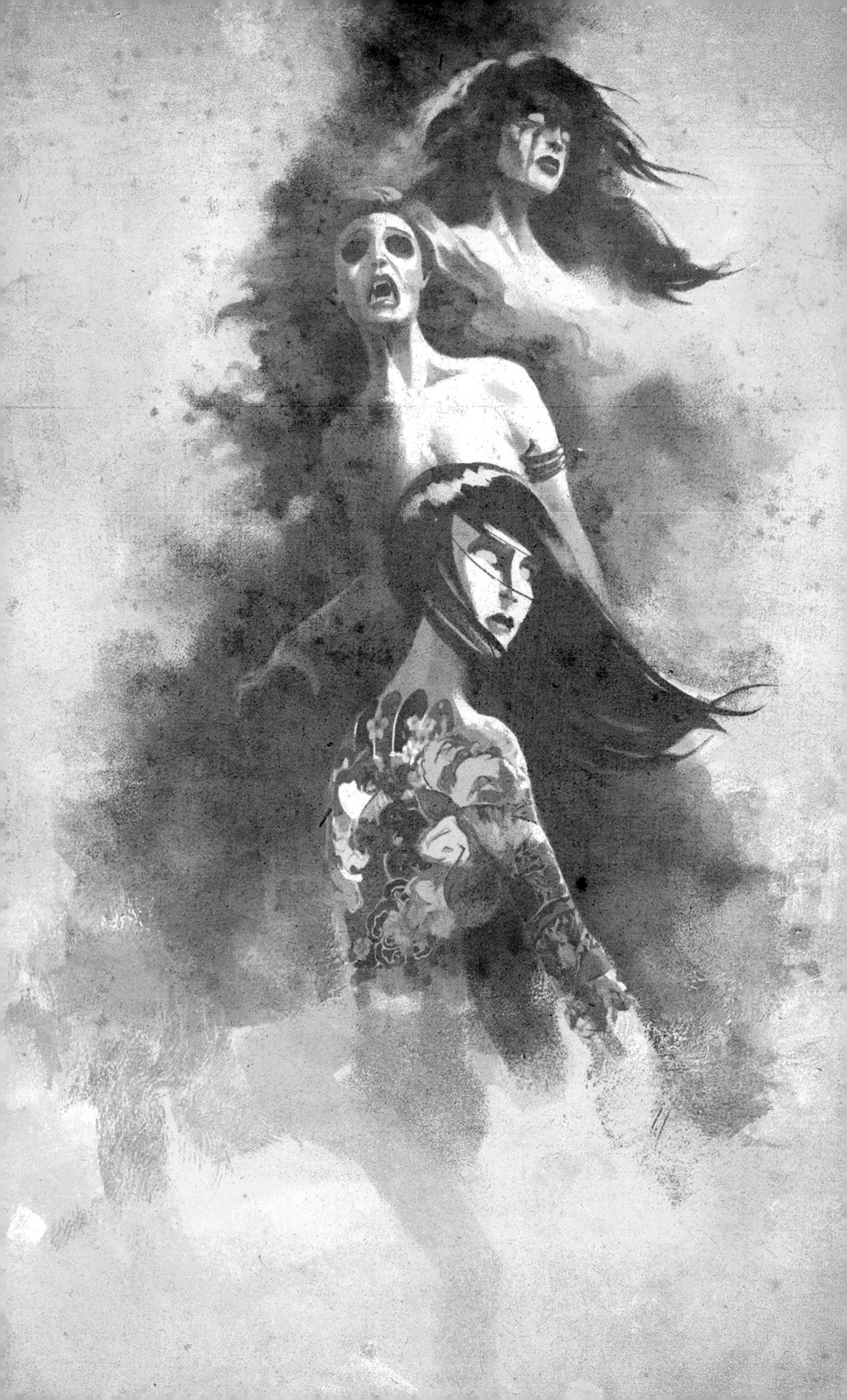

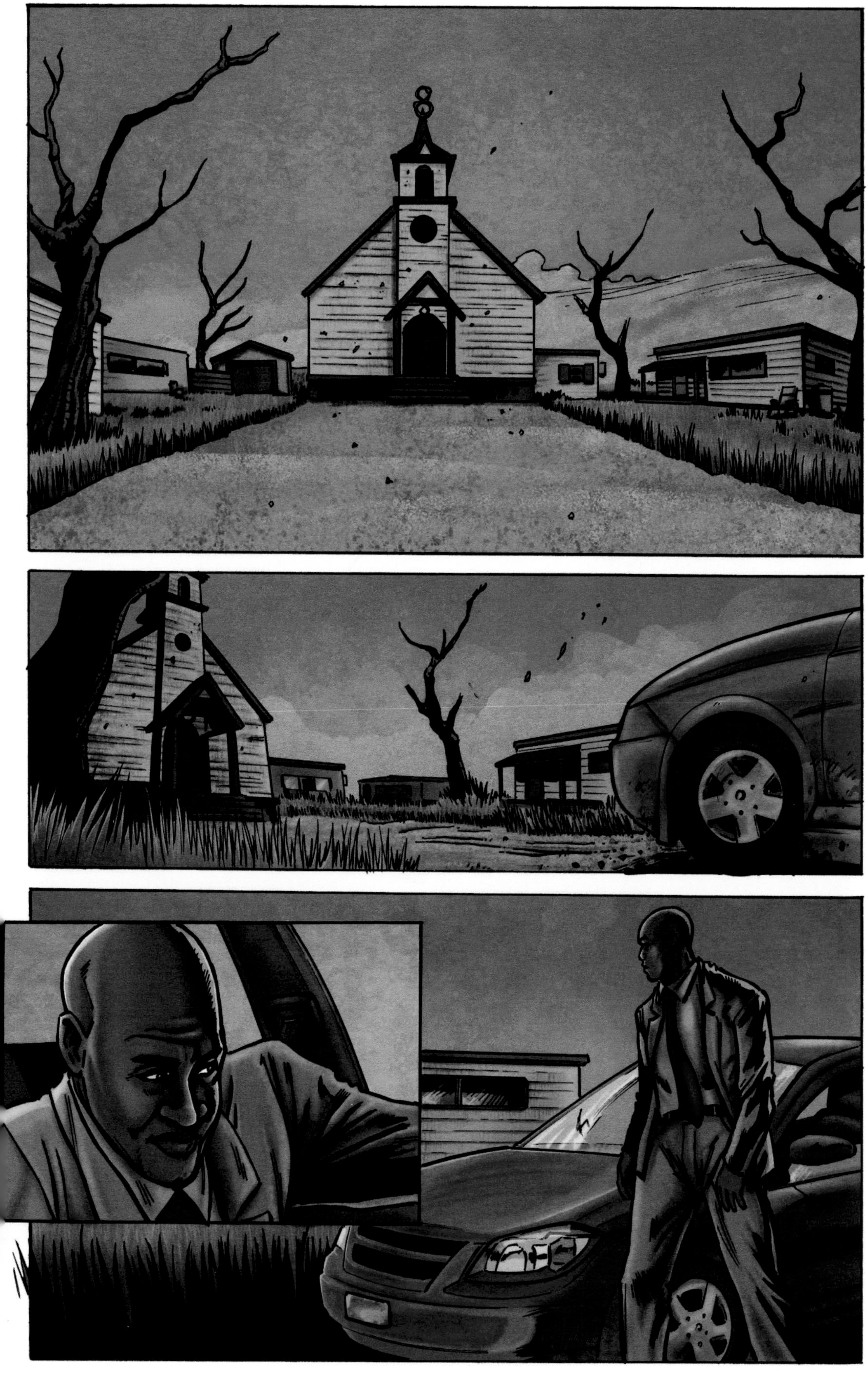

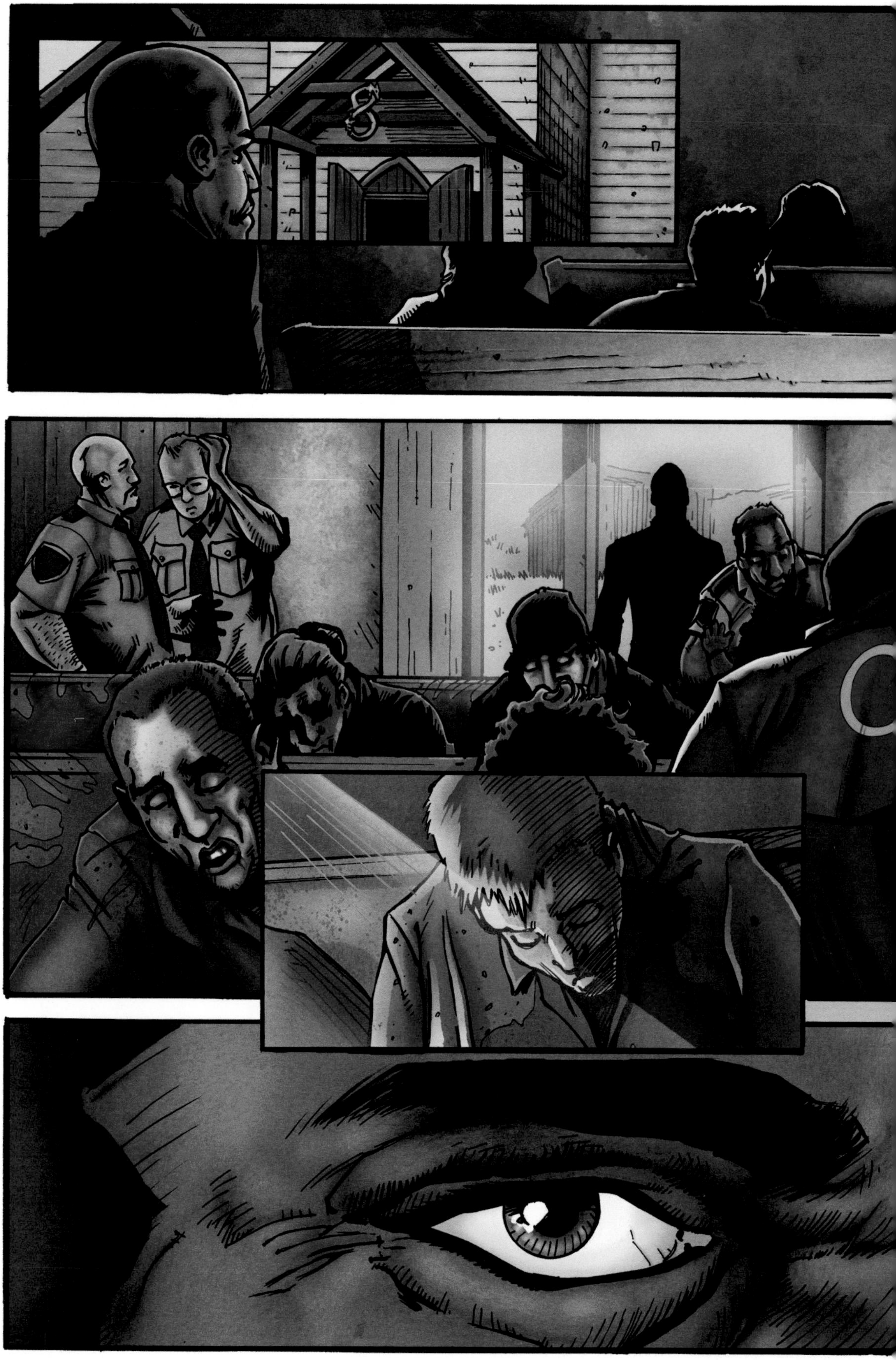

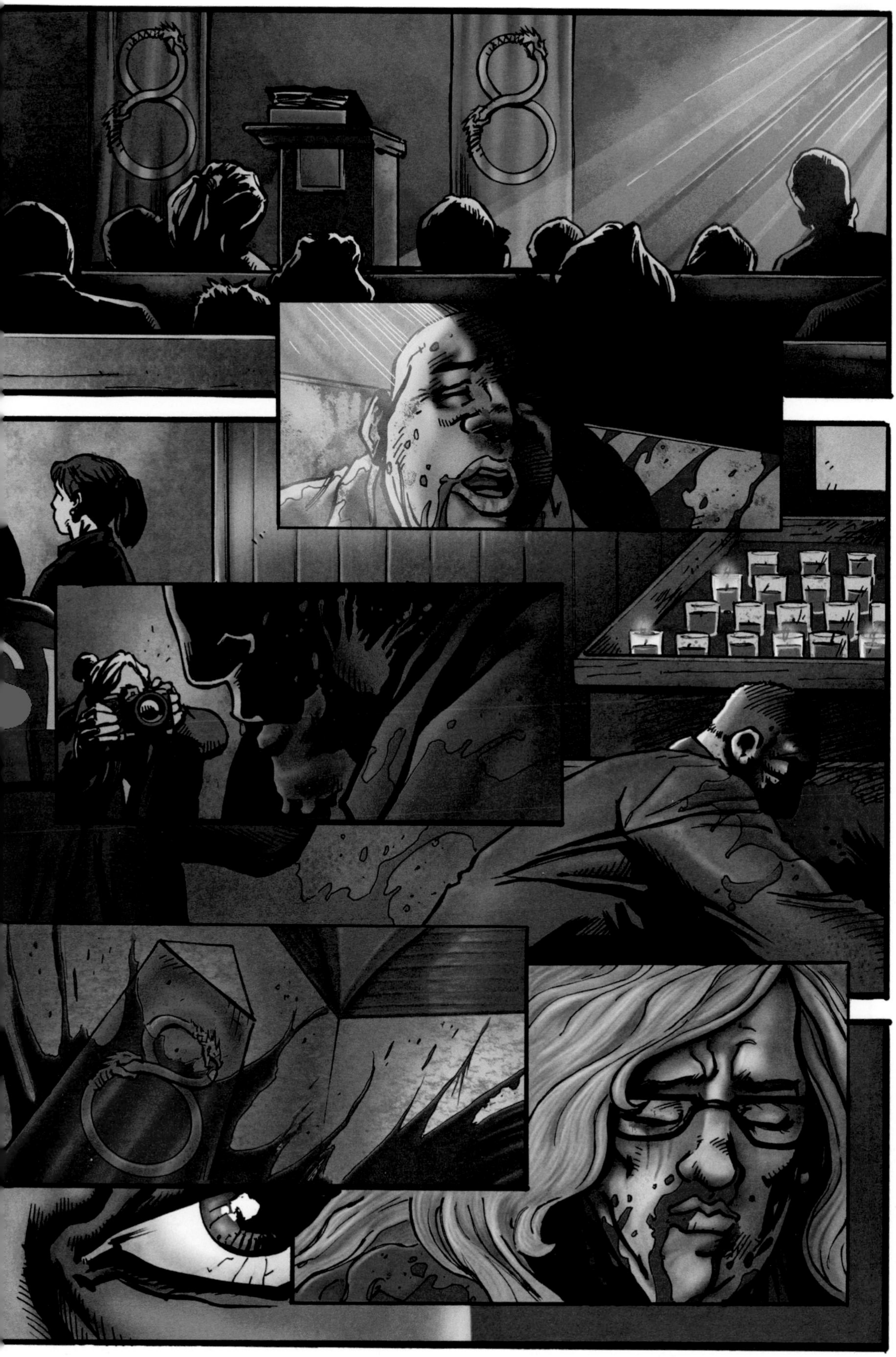

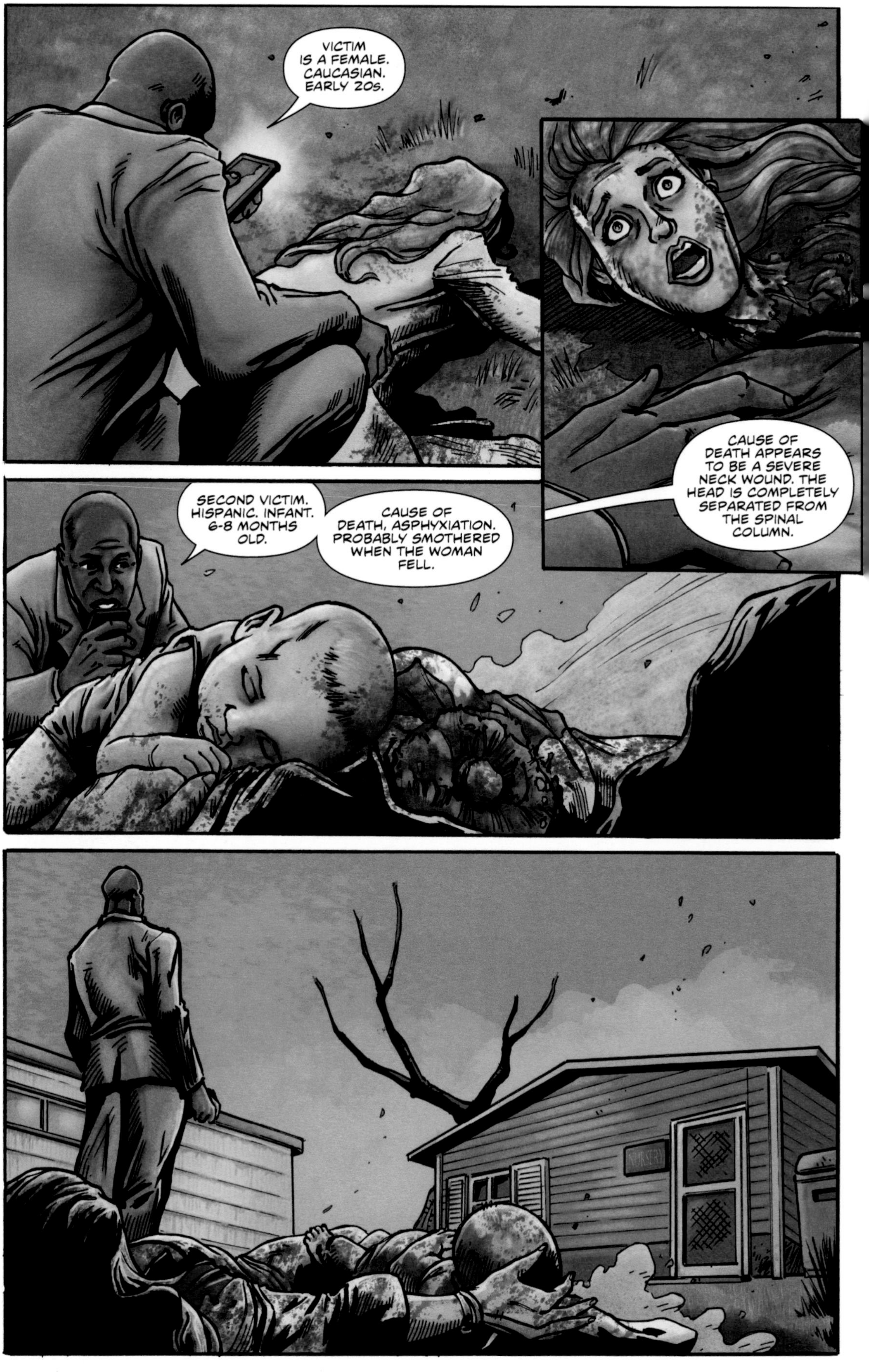
VICTIM IS A FEMALE. CAUCASIAN. EARLY 20S.
CAUSE OF DEATH APPEARS TO BE A SEVERE NECK WOUND. THE HEAD IS COMPLETELY SEPARATED FROM THE SPINAL COLUMN.
SECOND VICTIM. HISPANIC. INFANT. 6-8 MONTHS OLD.
CAUSE OF DEATH, ASPHYXIATION. PROBABLY SMOTHERED WHEN THE WOMAN FELL.

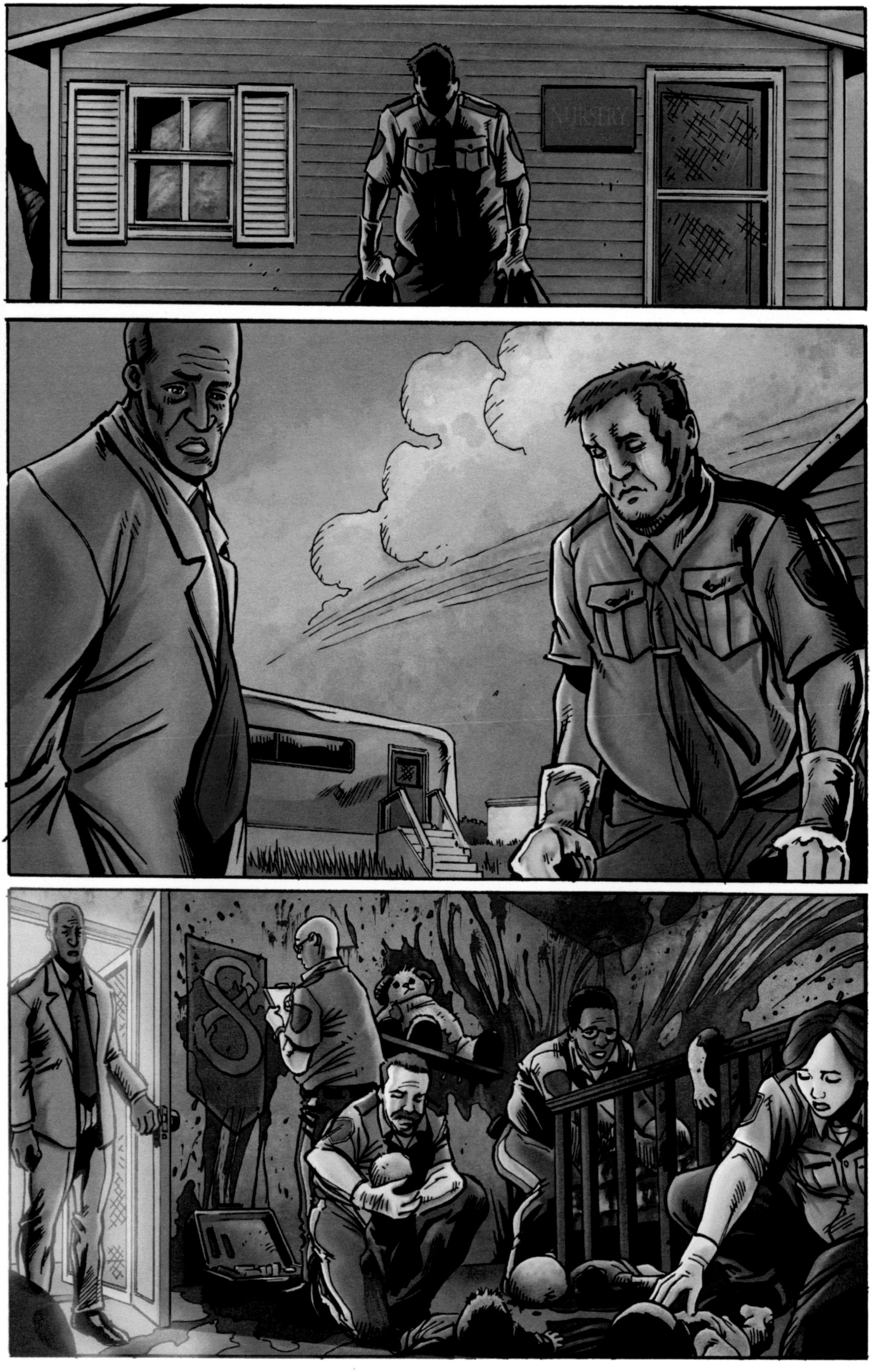
NURSERY

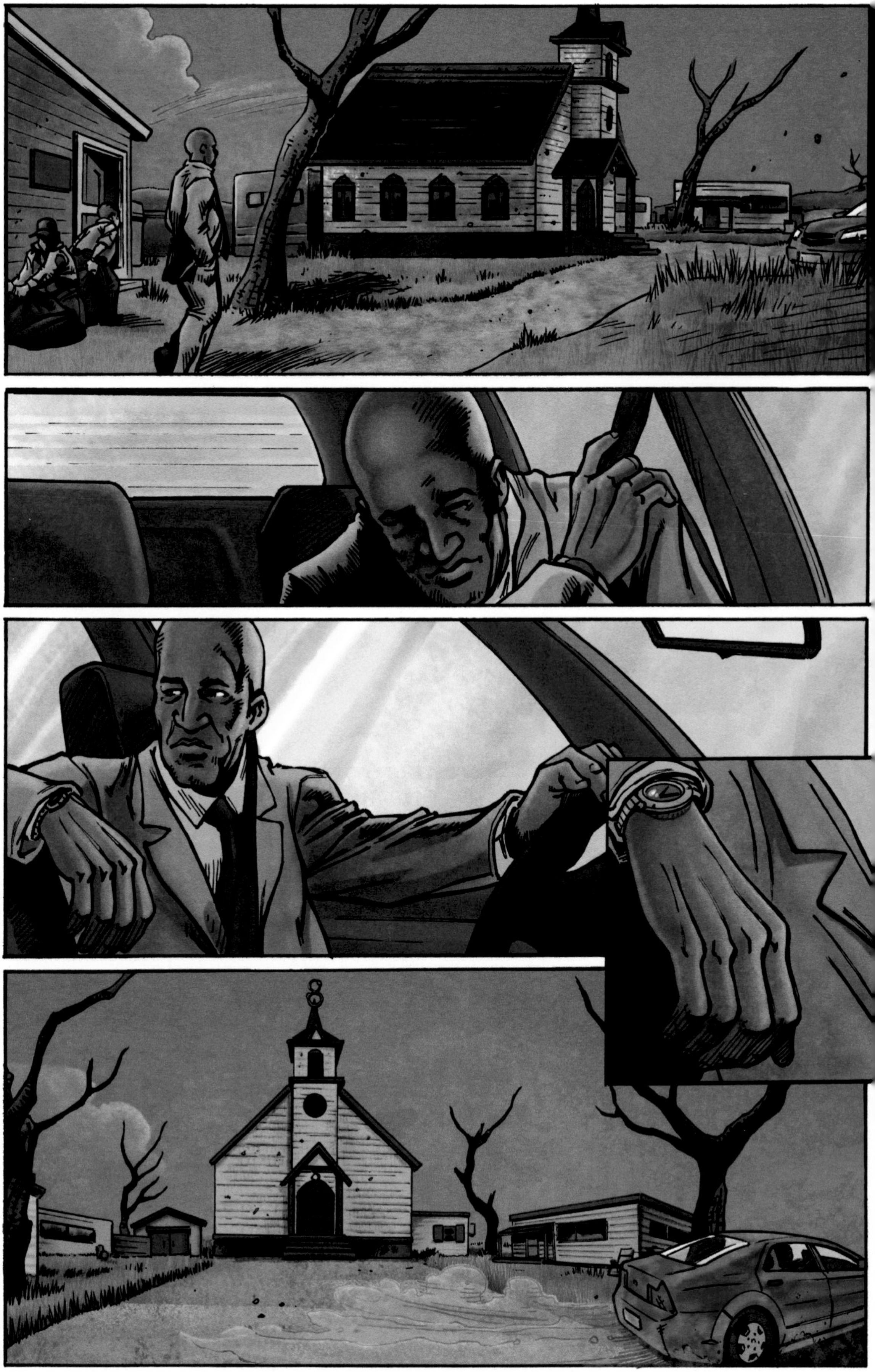

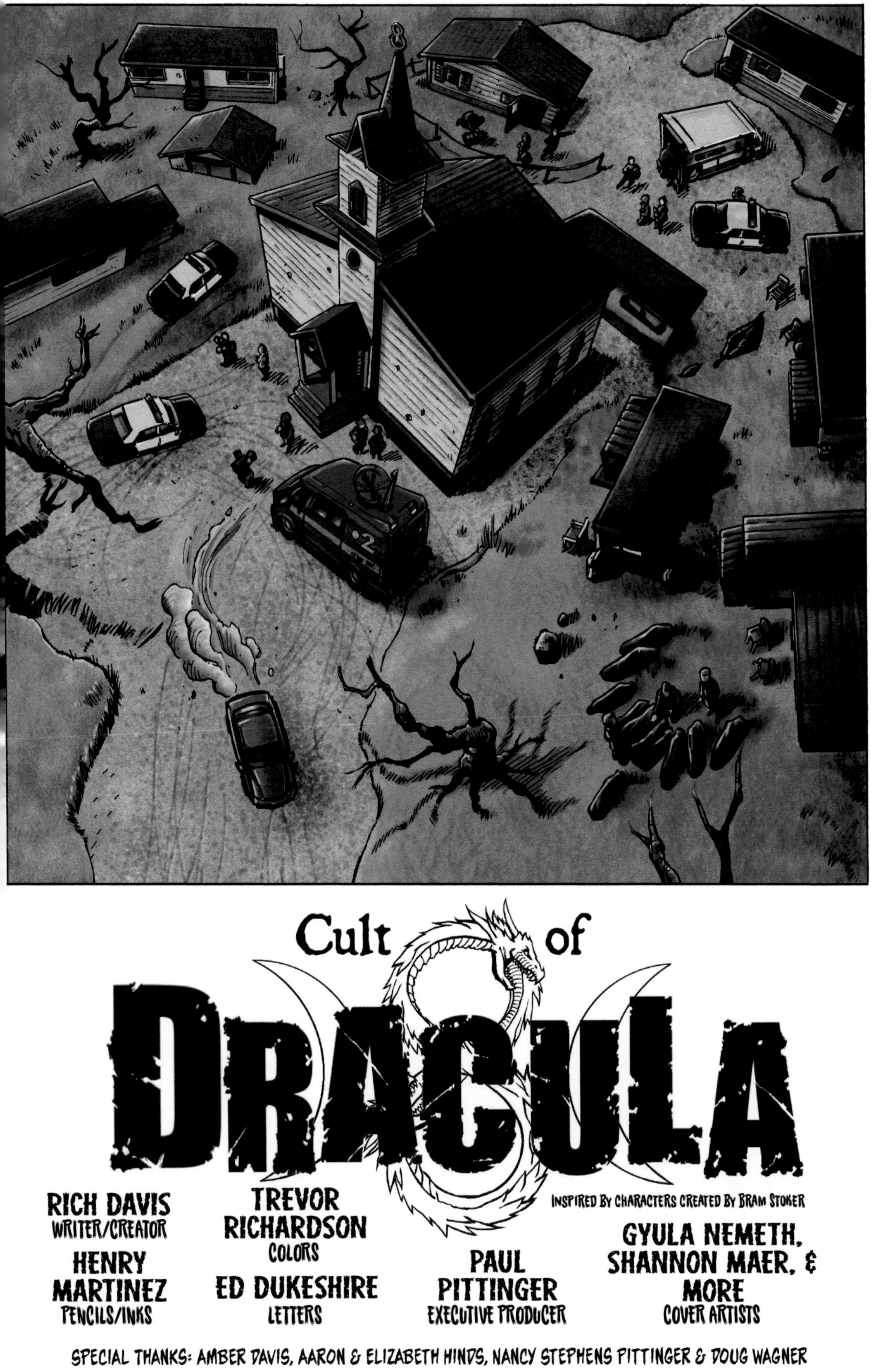

Cult of DRACULA

INSPIRED BY CHARACTERS CREATED BY BRAM STOKER

RICH DAVIS
WRITER/CREATOR

HENRY MARTINEZ
PENCILS/INKS

TREVOR RICHARDSON
COLORS

ED DUKESHIRE
LETTERS

PAUL PITTINGER
EXECUTIVE PRODUCER

GYULA NEMETH, SHANNON MAER, & MORE
COVER ARTISTS

SPECIAL THANKS: AMBER DAVIS, AARON & ELIZABETH HINDS, NANCY STEPHENS PITTINGER & DOUG WAGNER

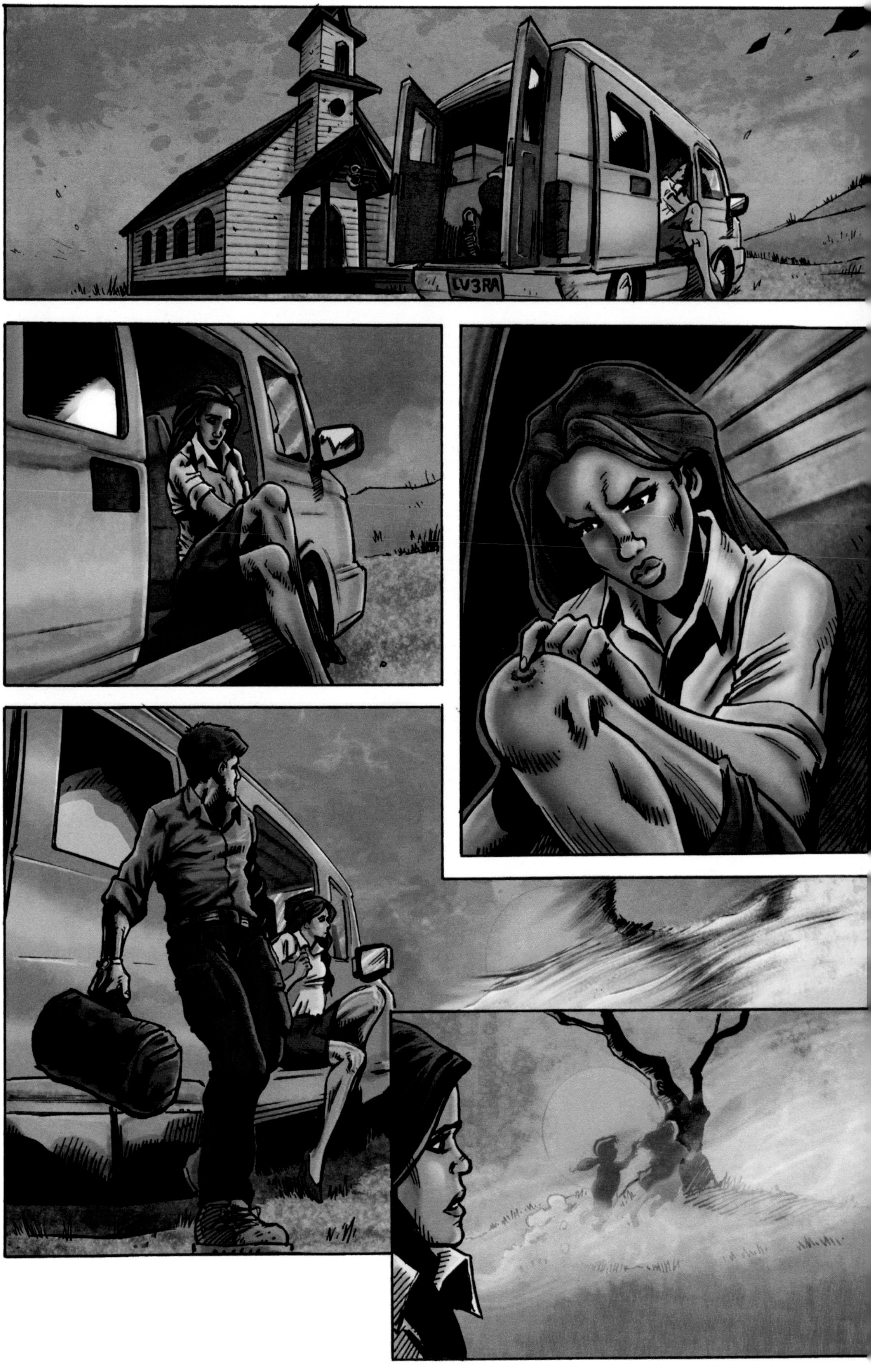
LV3RA

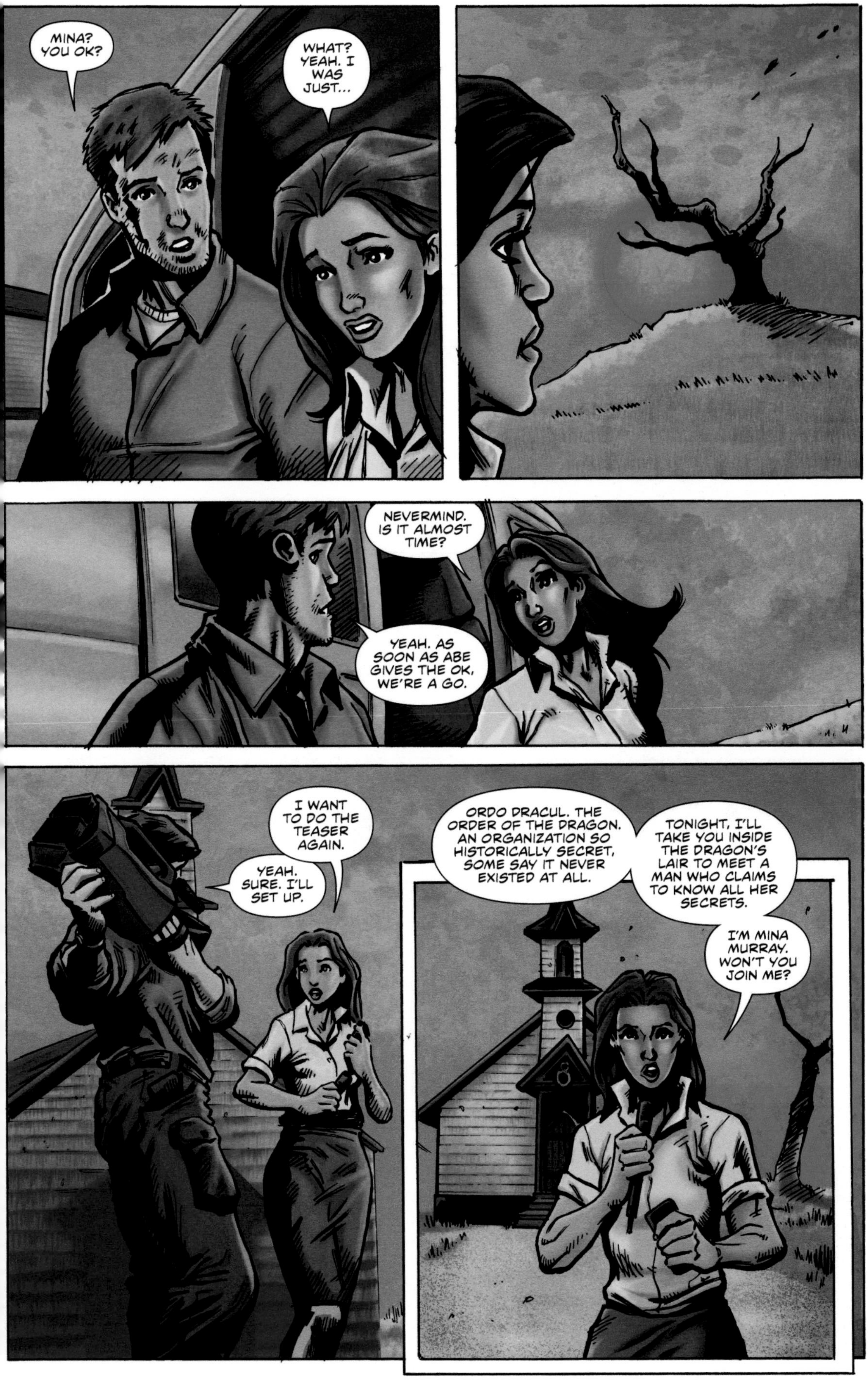
MINA? YOU OK?
WHAT? YEAH. I WAS JUST...
NEVERMIND. IS IT ALMOST TIME?
YEAH. AS SOON AS ABE GIVES THE OK, WE'RE A GO.
I WANT TO DO THE TEASER AGAIN.
YEAH. SURE. I'LL SET UP.
ORDO DRACUL. THE ORDER OF THE DRAGON. AN ORGANIZATION SO HISTORICALLY SECRET, SOME SAY IT NEVER EXISTED AT ALL.
TONIGHT, I'LL TAKE YOU INSIDE THE DRAGON'S LAIR TO MEET A MAN WHO CLAIMS TO KNOW ALL HER SECRETS.
I'M MINA MURRAY. WON'T YOU JOIN ME?

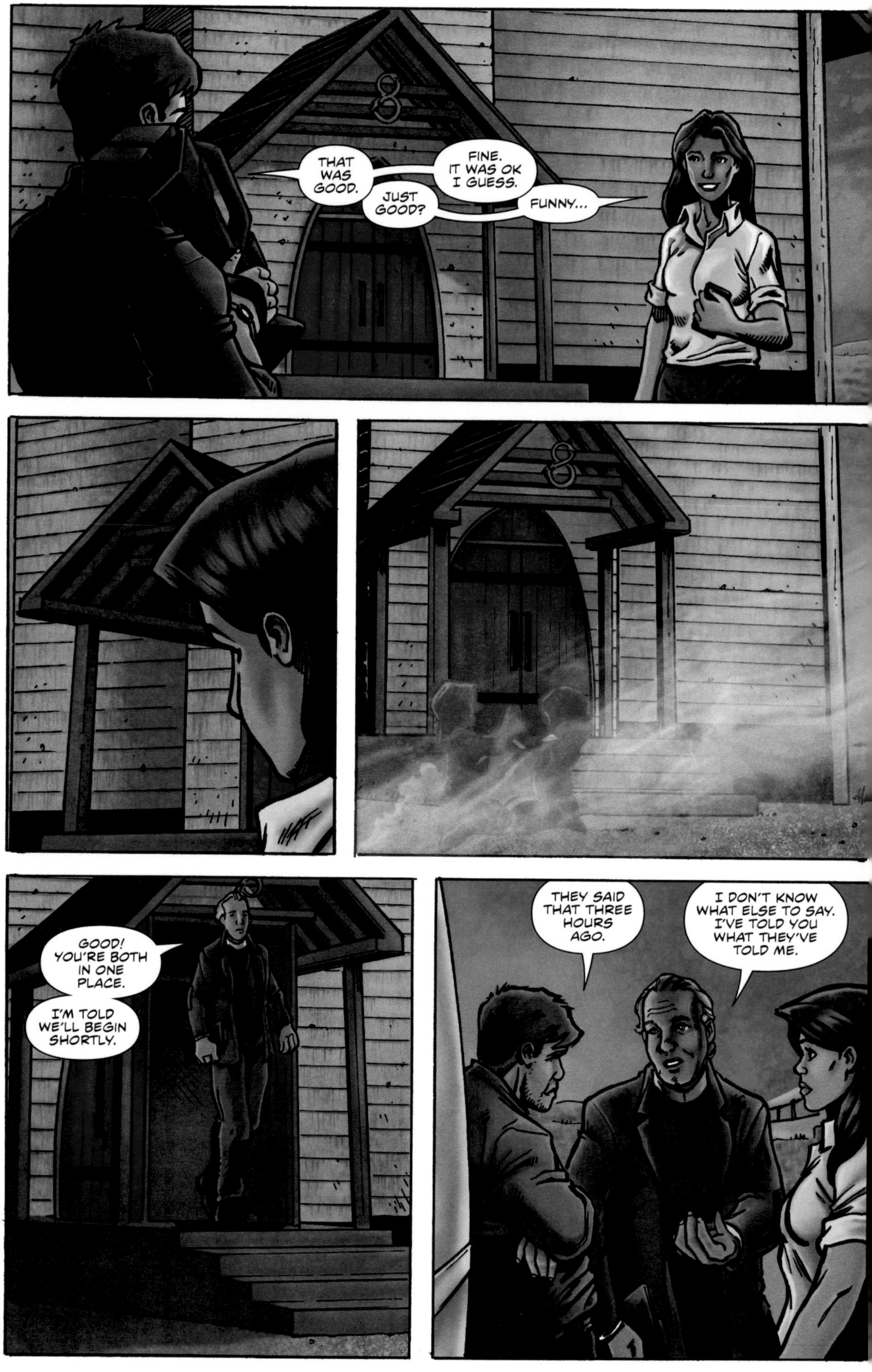
THAT WAS GOOD.
FINE. IT WAS OK I GUESS.
JUST GOOD?
FUNNY...
GOOD! YOU'RE BOTH IN ONE PLACE.
I'M TOLD WE'LL BEGIN SHORTLY.
THEY SAID THAT THREE HOURS AGO.
I DON'T KNOW WHAT ELSE TO SAY. I'VE TOLD YOU WHAT THEY'VE TOLD ME.

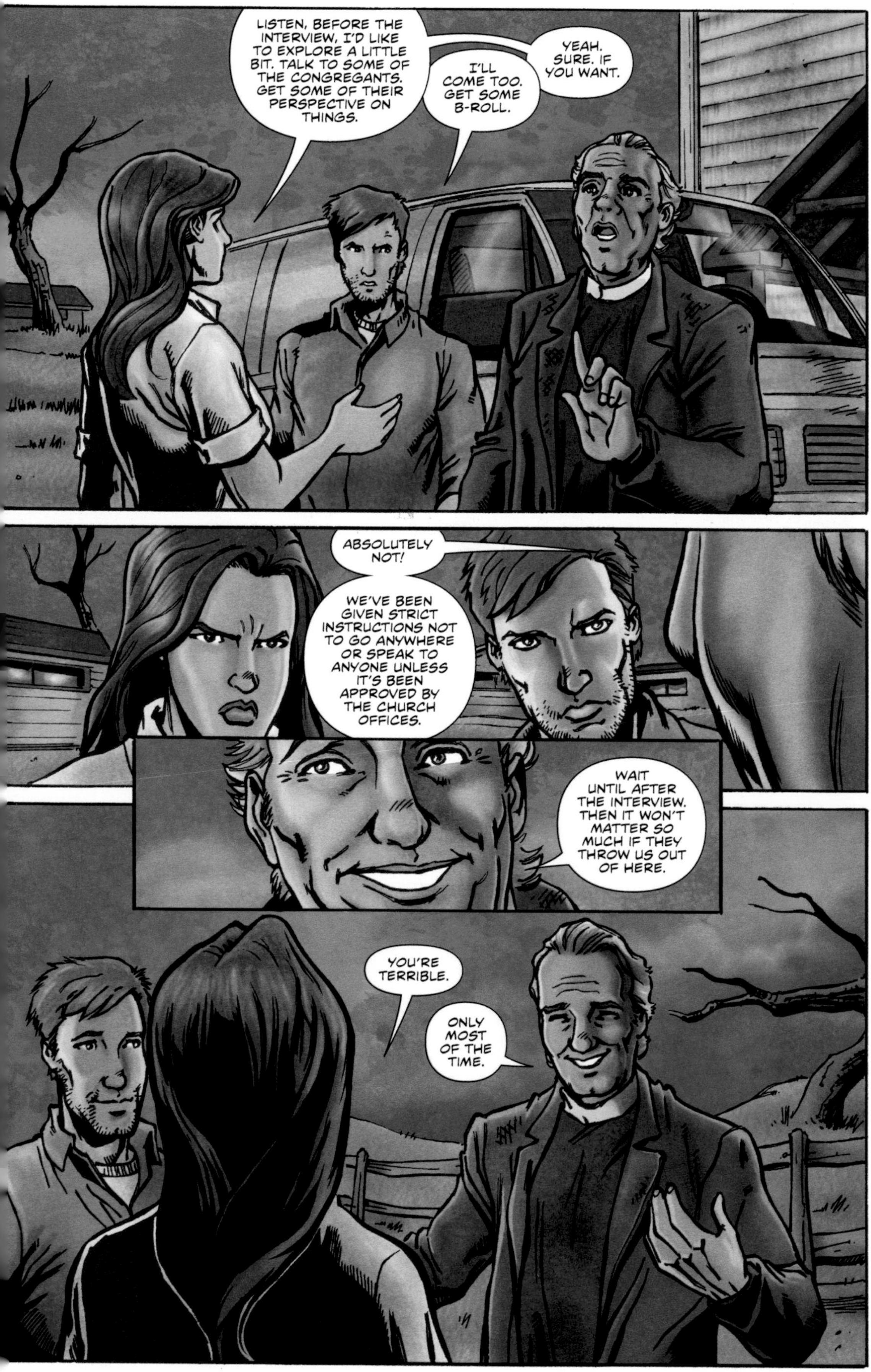
LISTEN, BEFORE THE INTERVIEW, I'D LIKE TO EXPLORE A LITTLE BIT. TALK TO SOME OF THE CONGREGANTS. GET SOME OF THEIR PERSPECTIVE ON THINGS.
I'LL COME TOO. GET SOME B-ROLL.
YEAH. SURE. IF YOU WANT.
ABSOLUTELY NOT!
WE'VE BEEN GIVEN STRICT INSTRUCTIONS NOT TO GO ANYWHERE OR SPEAK TO ANYONE UNLESS IT'S BEEN APPROVED BY THE CHURCH OFFICES.
WAIT UNTIL AFTER THE INTERVIEW. THEN IT WON'T MATTER SO MUCH IF THEY THROW US OUT OF HERE.
YOU'RE TERRIBLE.
ONLY MOST OF THE TIME.

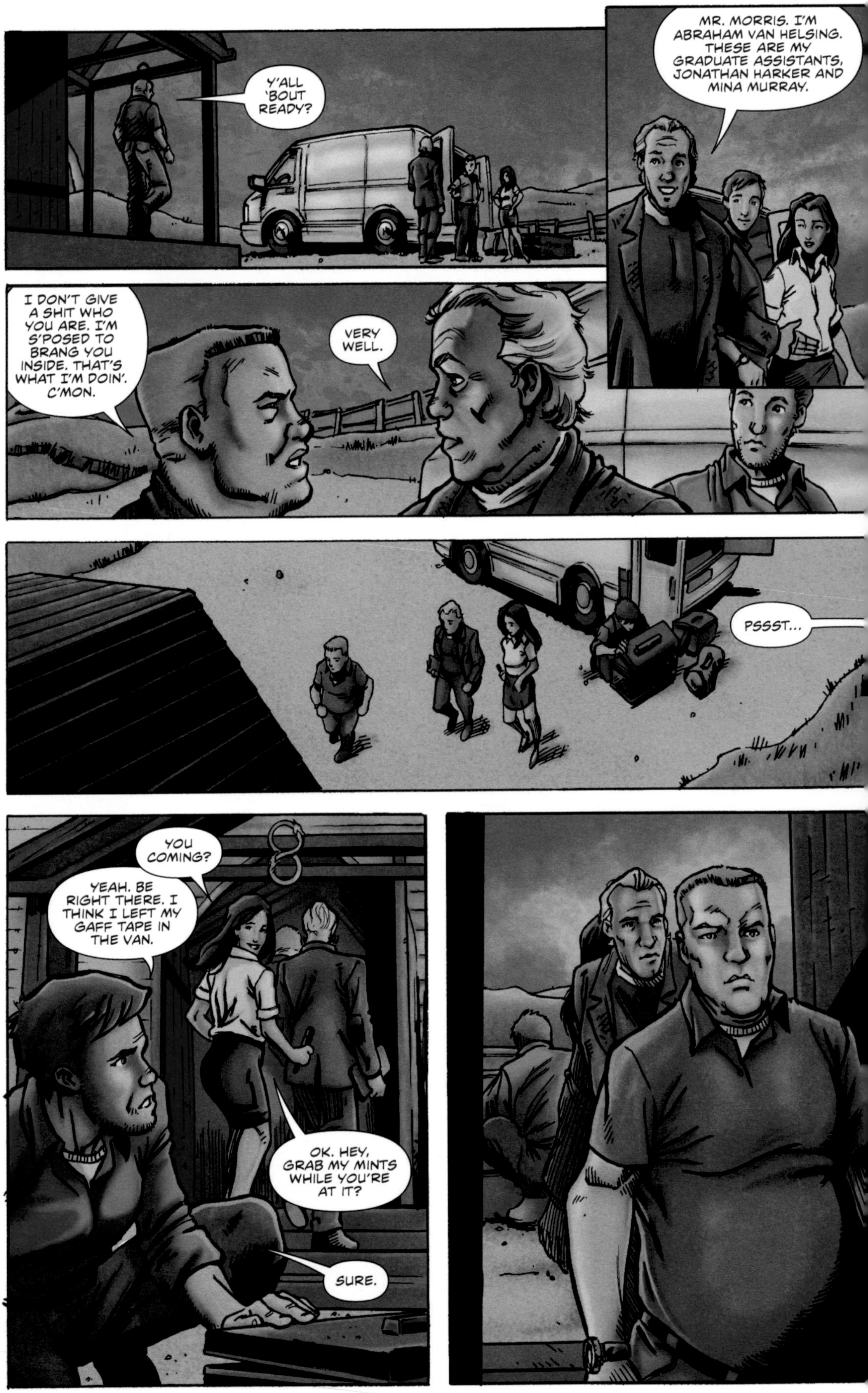
Y'ALL 'BOUT READY?
MR. MORRIS. I'M ABRAHAM VAN HELSING. THESE ARE MY GRADUATE ASSISTANTS, JONATHAN HARKER AND MINA MURRAY.
I DON'T GIVE A SHIT WHO YOU ARE. I'M S'POSED TO BRANG YOU INSIDE. THAT'S WHAT I'M DOIN'. C'MON.
VERY WELL.
PSSST...
YOU COMING?
YEAH. BE RIGHT THERE. I THINK I LEFT MY GAFF TAPE IN THE VAN.
OK. HEY, GRAB MY MINTS WHILE YOU'RE AT IT?
SURE.

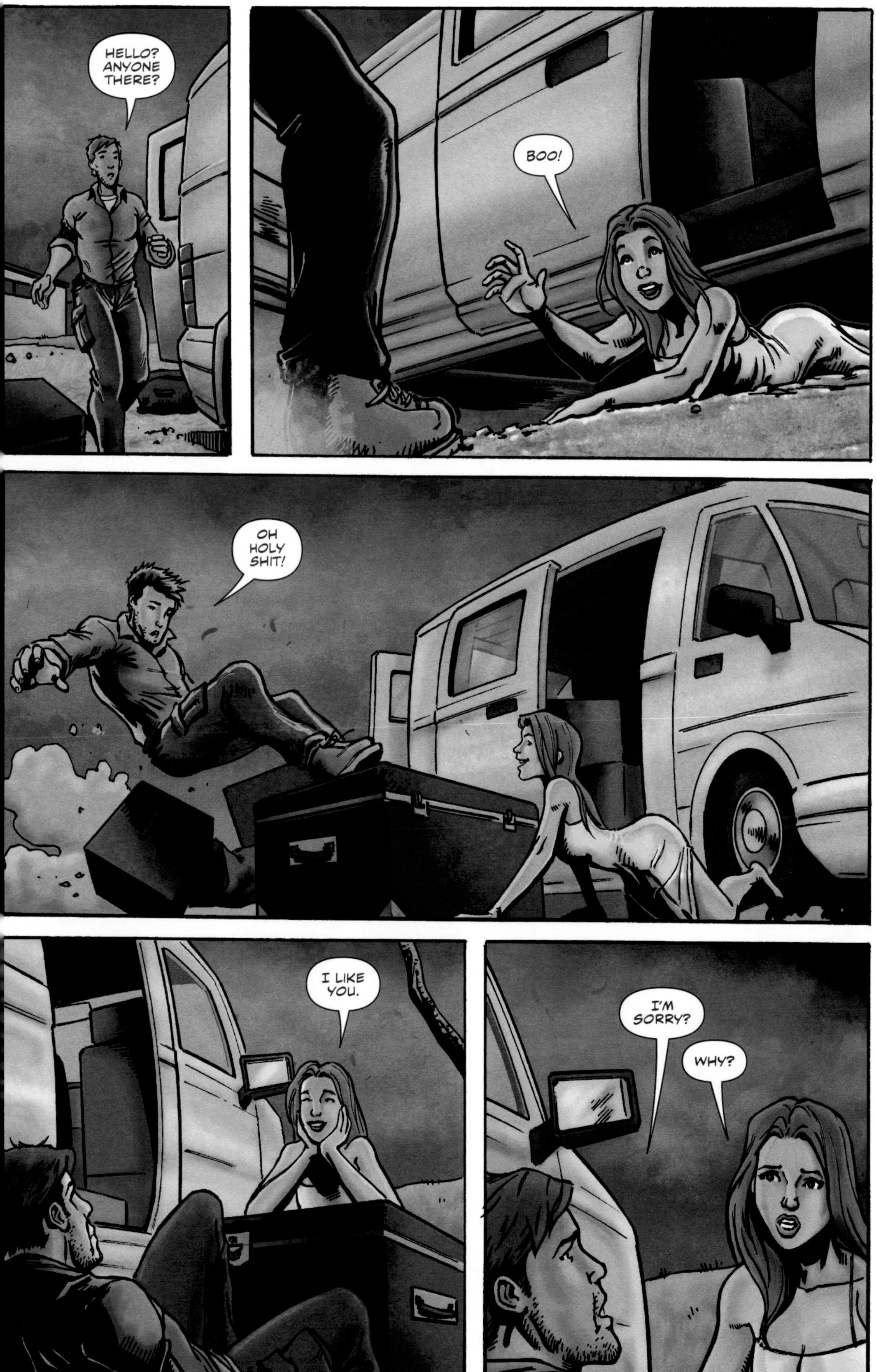
HELLO? ANYONE THERE?
BOO!
OH HOLY SHIT!
I LIKE YOU.
I'M SORRY?
WHY?

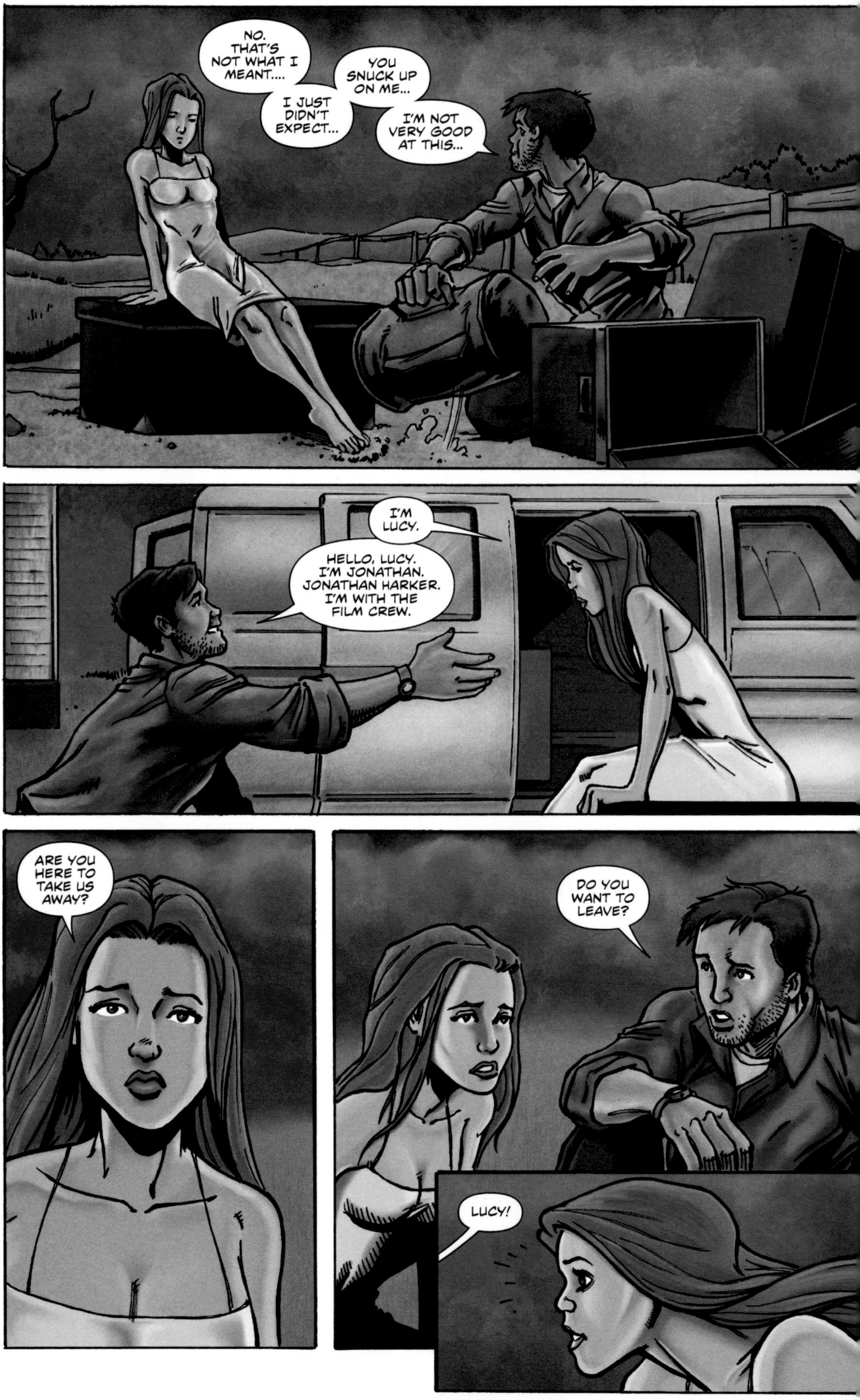
NO. THAT'S NOT WHAT I MEANT....
YOU SNUCK UP ON ME...
I JUST DIDN'T EXPECT...
I'M NOT VERY GOOD AT THIS...
I'M LUCY.
HELLO, LUCY. I'M JONATHAN. JONATHAN HARKER. I'M WITH THE FILM CREW.
ARE YOU HERE TO TAKE US AWAY?
DO YOU WANT TO LEAVE?
LUCY!

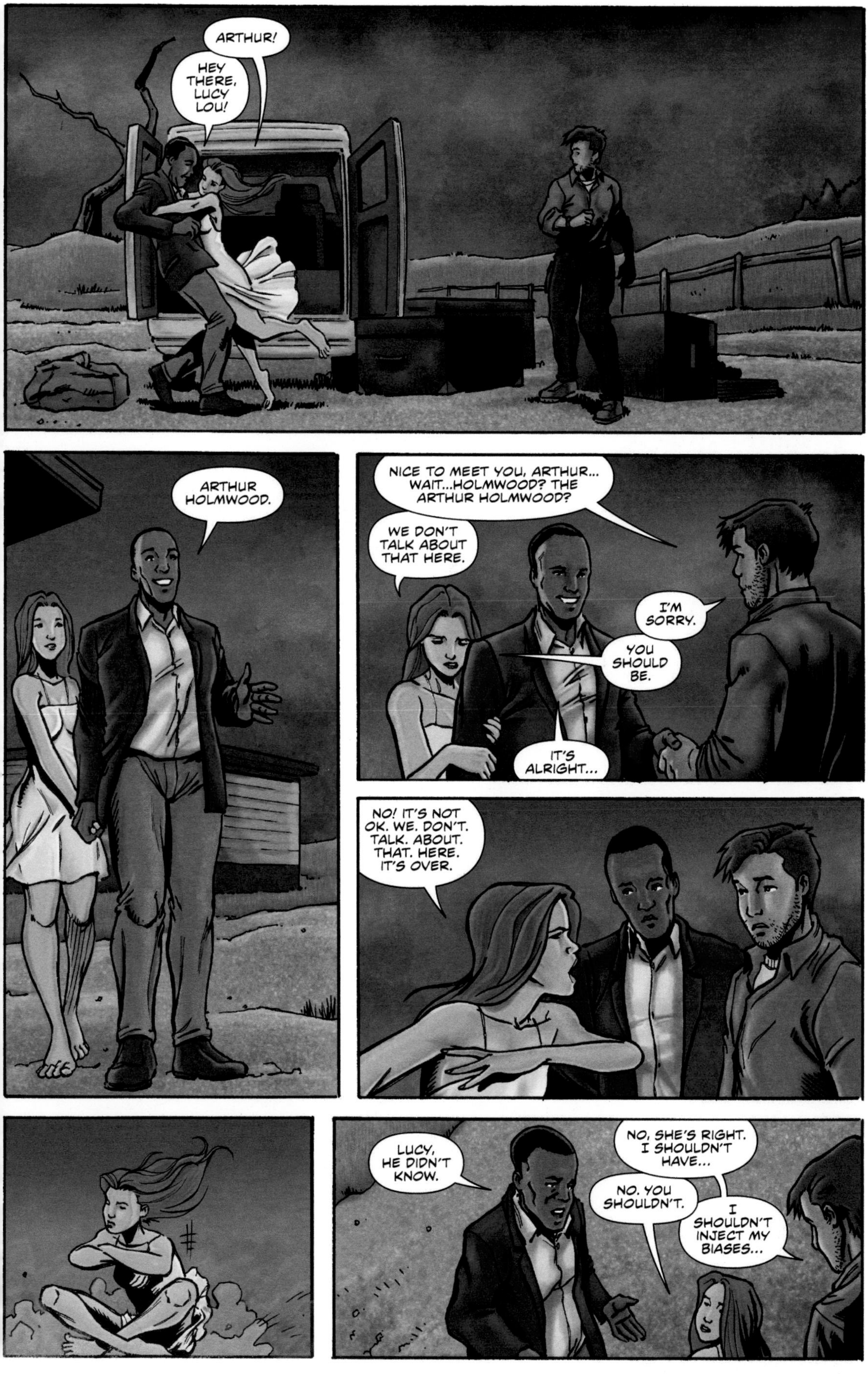
ARTHUR!
HEY THERE, LUCY LOU!
ARTHUR HOLMWOOD.
NICE TO MEET YOU, ARTHUR... WAIT...HOLMWOOD? THE ARTHUR HOLMWOOD?
WE DON'T TALK ABOUT THAT HERE.
I'M SORRY.
YOU SHOULD BE.
IT'S ALRIGHT...
NO! IT'S NOT OK. WE. DON'T. TALK. ABOUT. THAT. HERE. IT'S OVER.
LUCY, HE DIDN'T KNOW.
NO, SHE'S RIGHT. I SHOULDN'T HAVE...
NO. YOU SHOULDN'T.
I SHOULDN'T INJECT MY BIASES...

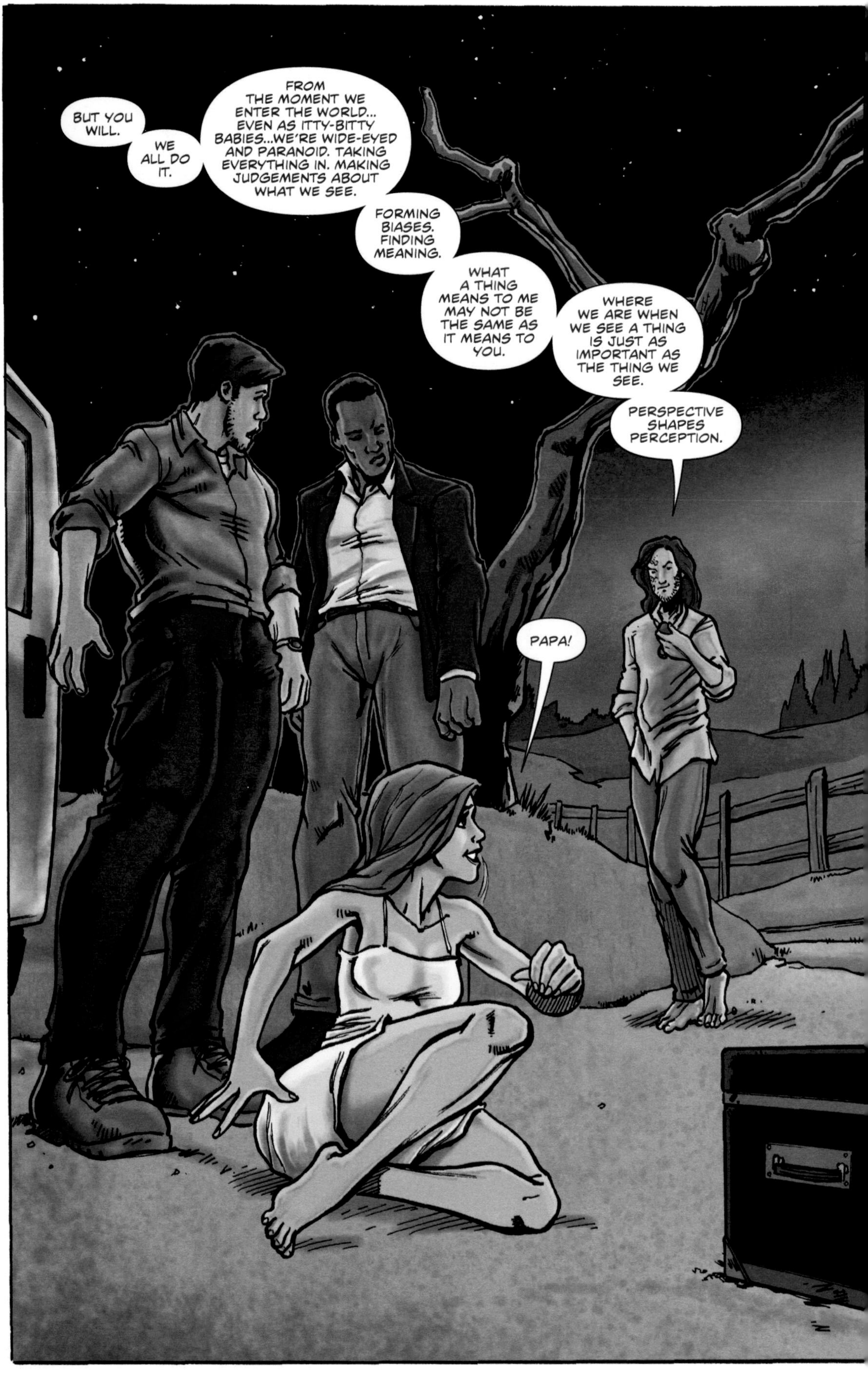
BUT YOU WILL.
WE ALL DO IT.
FROM THE MOMENT WE ENTER THE WORLD... EVEN AS ITTY-BITTY BABIES...WE'RE WIDE-EYED AND PARANOID. TAKING EVERYTHING IN. MAKING JUDGEMENTS ABOUT WHAT WE SEE.
FORMING BIASES. FINDING MEANING.
WHAT A THING MEANS TO ME MAY NOT BE THE SAME AS IT MEANS TO YOU.
WHERE WE ARE WHEN WE SEE A THING IS JUST AS IMPORTANT AS THE THING WE SEE.
PERSPECTIVE SHAPES PERCEPTION.
PAPA!

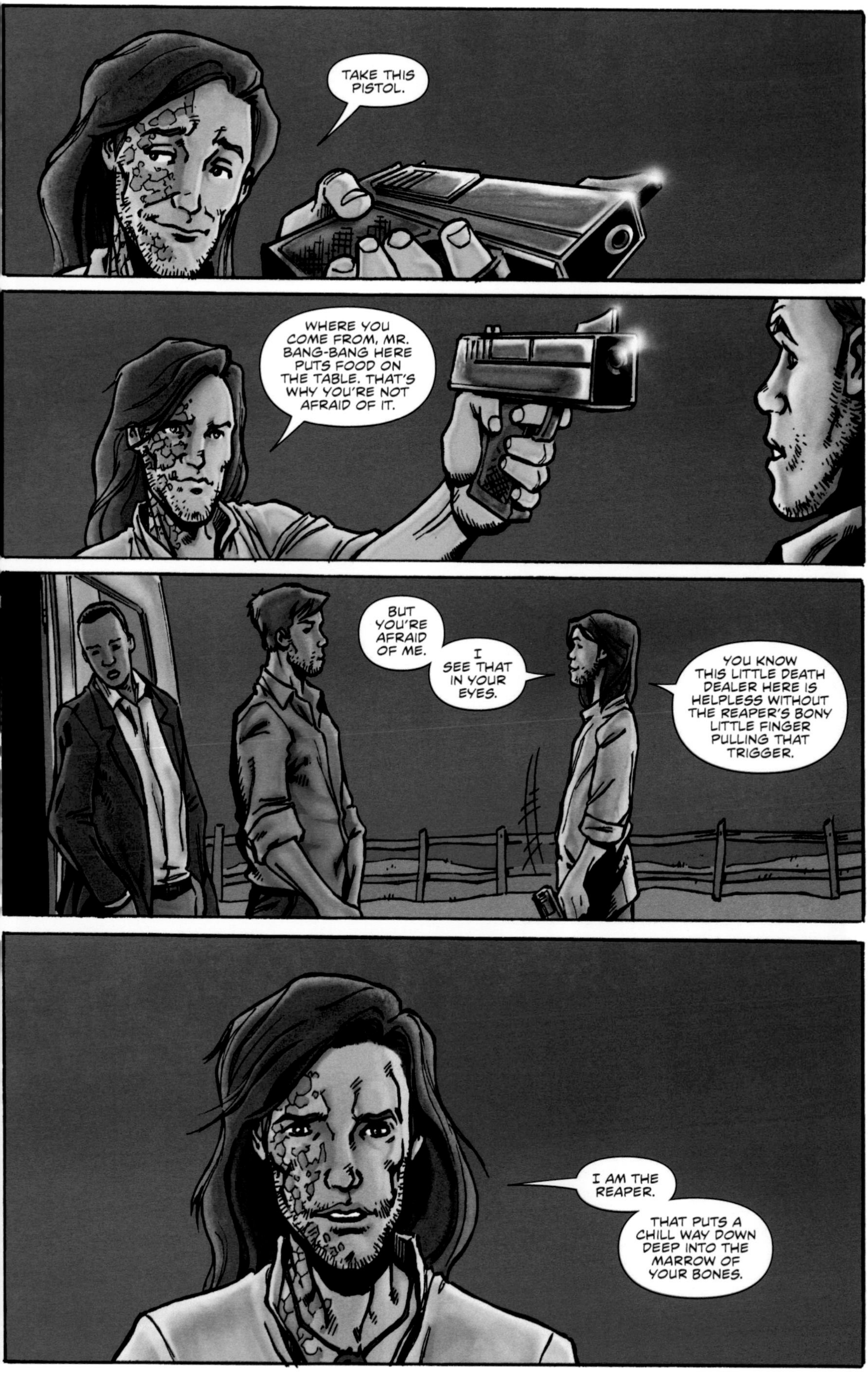
TAKE THIS PISTOL.
WHERE YOU COME FROM, MR. BANG-BANG HERE PUTS FOOD ON THE TABLE. THAT'S WHY YOU'RE NOT AFRAID OF IT.
BUT YOU'RE AFRAID OF ME.
I SEE THAT IN YOUR EYES.
YOU KNOW THIS LITTLE DEATH DEALER HERE IS HELPLESS WITHOUT THE REAPER'S BONY LITTLE FINGER PULLING THAT TRIGGER.
I AM THE REAPER.
THAT PUTS A CHILL WAY DOWN DEEP INTO THE MARROW OF YOUR BONES.

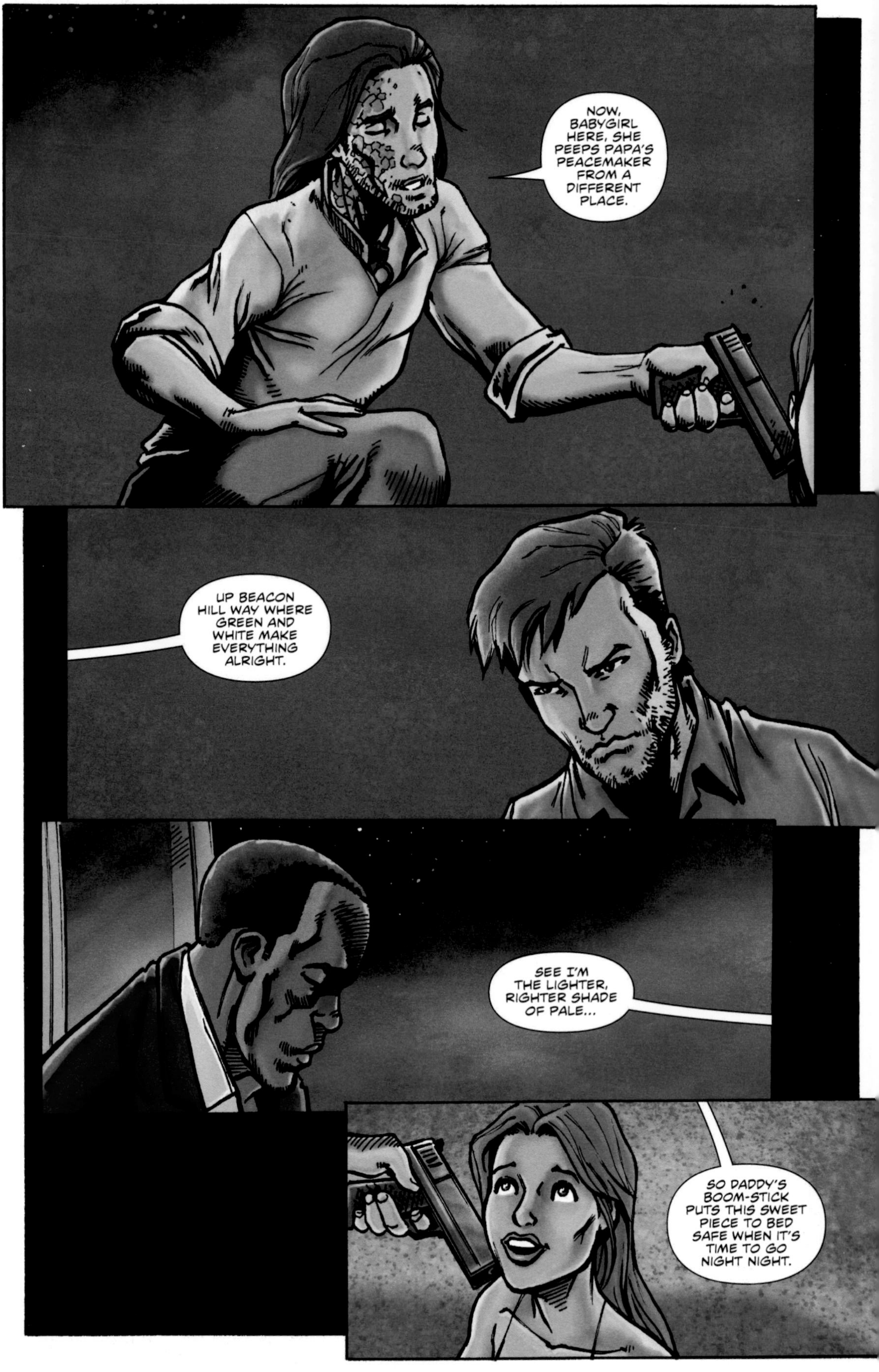
NOW, BABYGIRL HERE, SHE PEEPS PAPA'S PEACEMAKER FROM A DIFFERENT PLACE.
UP BEACON HILL WAY WHERE GREEN AND WHITE MAKE EVERYTHING ALRIGHT.
SEE I'M THE LIGHTER, RIGHTER SHADE OF PALE...
SO DADDY'S BOOM-STICK PUTS THIS SWEET PIECE TO BED SAFE WHEN IT'S TIME TO GO NIGHT NIGHT.

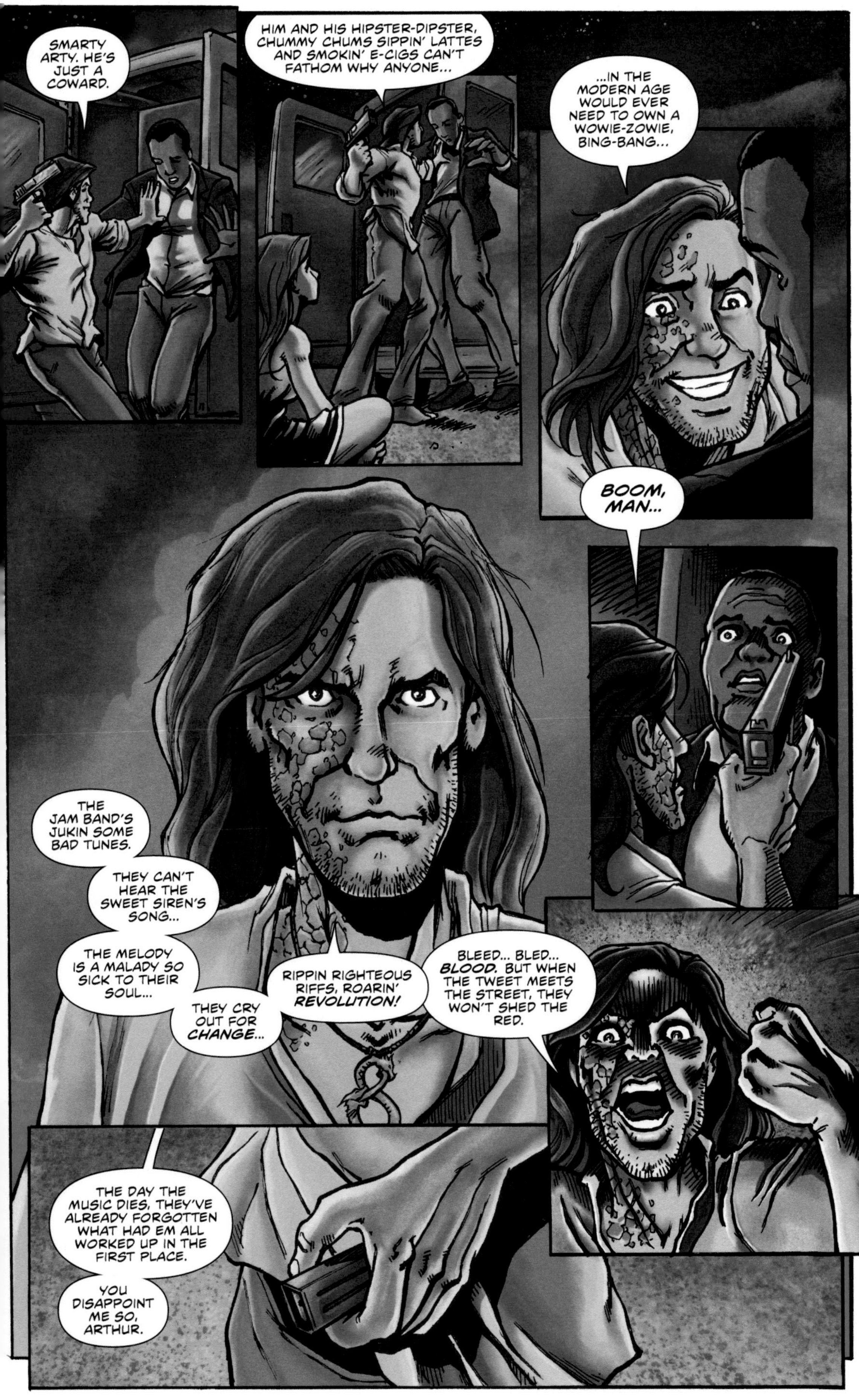

SMARTY ARTY. HE'S JUST A COWARD.
HIM AND HIS HIPSTER-DIPSTER, CHUMMY CHUMS SIPPIN' LATTES AND SMOKIN' E-CIGS CAN'T FATHOM WHY ANYONE...
...IN THE MODERN AGE WOULD EVER NEED TO OWN A WOWIE-ZOWIE, BING-BANG...
BOOM, MAN...
THE JAM BAND'S JUKIN SOME BAD TUNES.
THEY CAN'T HEAR THE SWEET SIREN'S SONG...
THE MELODY IS A MALADY SO SICK TO THEIR SOUL...
THEY CRY OUT FOR CHANGE...
RIPPIN RIGHTEOUS RIFFS, ROARIN' REVOLUTION!
BLEED... BLED... BLOOD. BUT WHEN THE TWEET MEETS THE STREET, THEY WON'T SHED THE RED.
THE DAY THE MUSIC DIES, THEY'VE ALREADY FORGOTTEN WHAT HAD EM ALL WORKED UP IN THE FIRST PLACE.
YOU DISAPPOINT ME SO, ARTHUR.

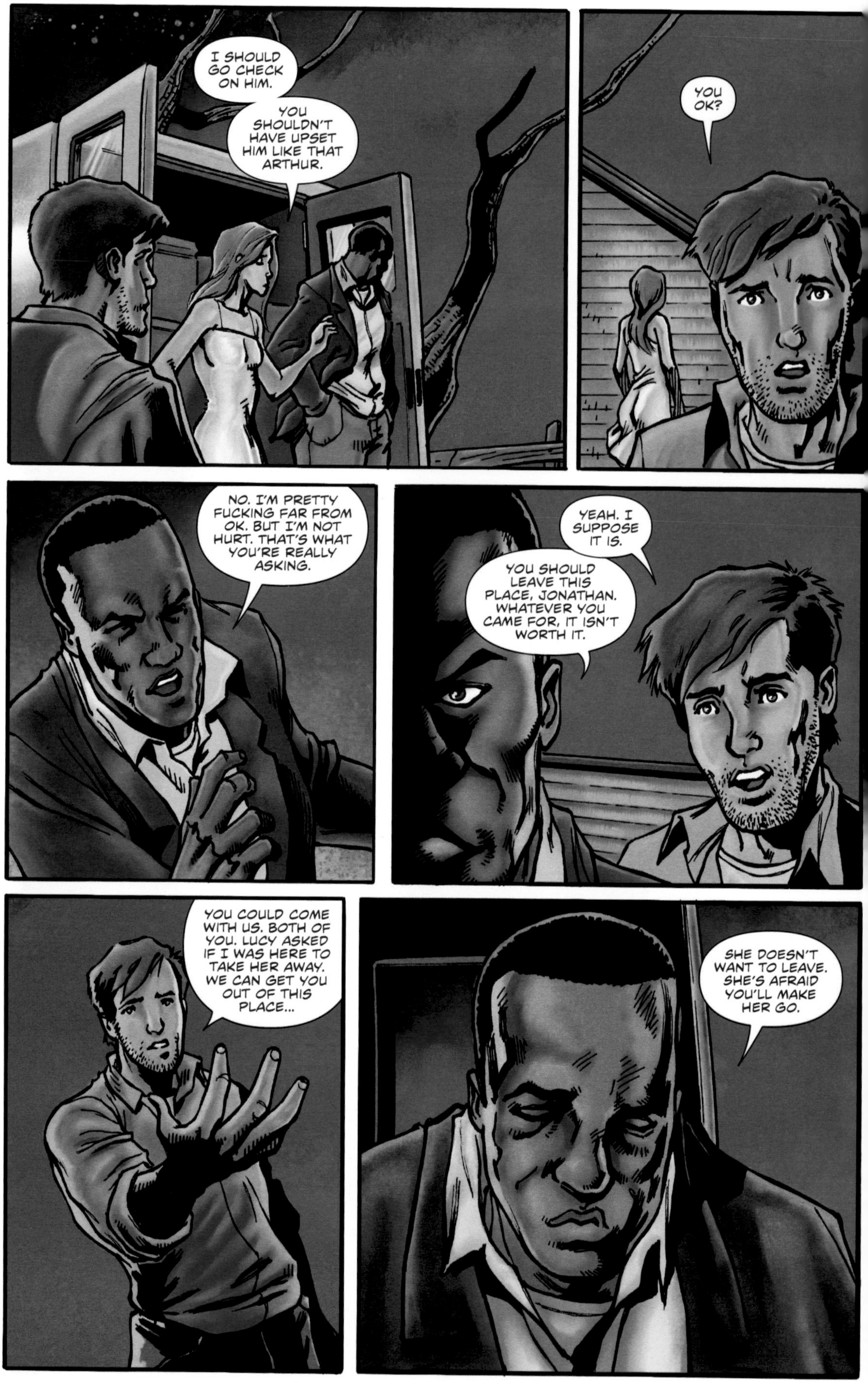
I SHOULD GO CHECK ON HIM.
YOU SHOULDN'T HAVE UPSET HIM LIKE THAT ARTHUR.
YOU OK?
NO. I'M PRETTY FUCKING FAR FROM OK. BUT I'M NOT HURT. THAT'S WHAT YOU'RE REALLY ASKING.
YEAH. I SUPPOSE IT IS.
YOU SHOULD LEAVE THIS PLACE, JONATHAN. WHATEVER YOU CAME FOR, IT ISN'T WORTH IT.
YOU COULD COME WITH US. BOTH OF YOU. LUCY ASKED IF I WAS HERE TO TAKE HER AWAY. WE CAN GET YOU OUT OF THIS PLACE...
SHE DOESN'T WANT TO LEAVE. SHE'S AFRAID YOU'LL MAKE HER GO.

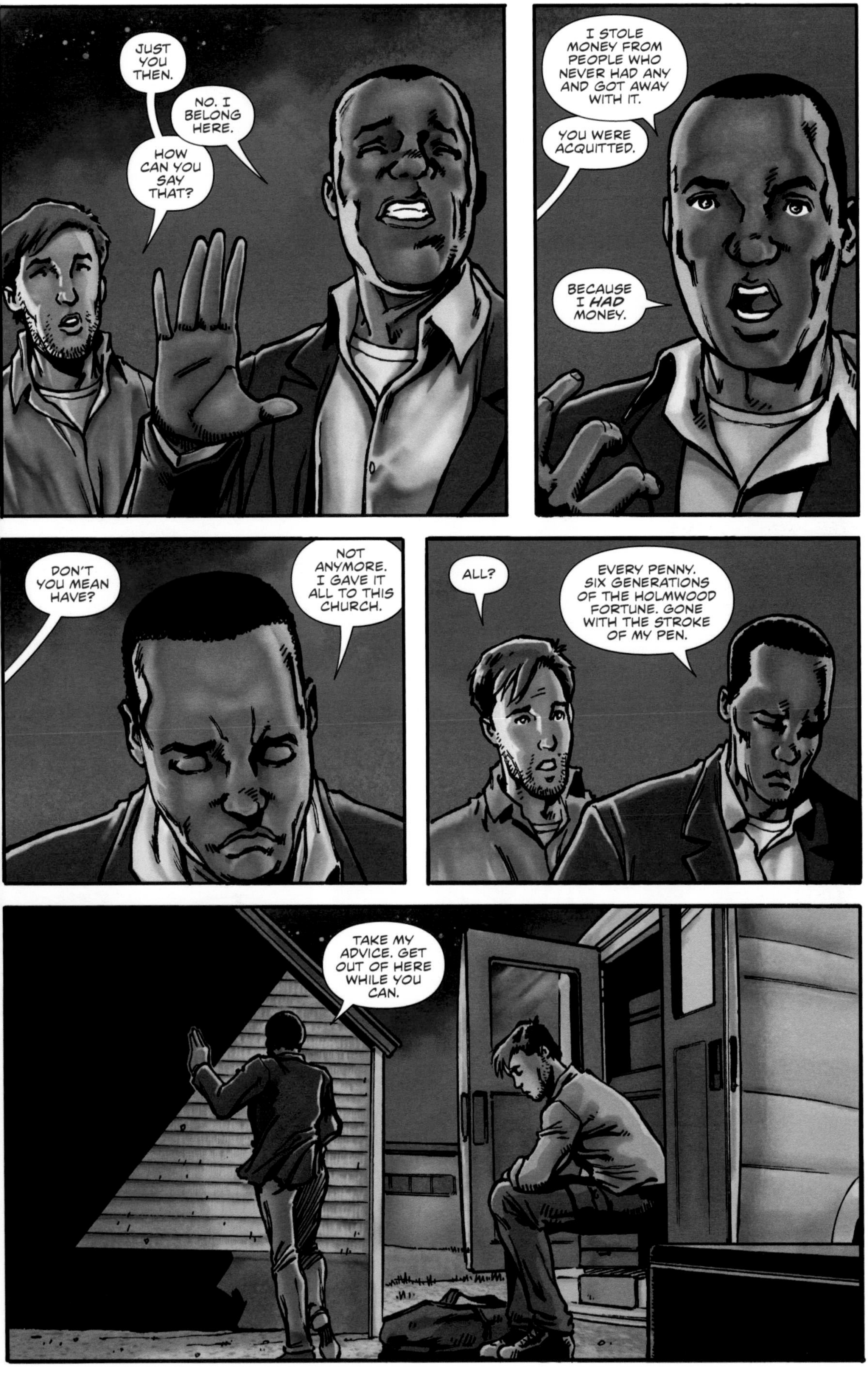
JUST YOU THEN.
NO. I BELONG HERE.
HOW CAN YOU SAY THAT?
I STOLE MONEY FROM PEOPLE WHO NEVER HAD ANY AND GOT AWAY WITH IT.
YOU WERE ACQUITTED.
BECAUSE I *HAD* MONEY.
DON'T YOU MEAN HAVE?
NOT ANYMORE. I GAVE IT ALL TO THIS CHURCH.
ALL?
EVERY PENNY. SIX GENERATIONS OF THE HOLMWOOD FORTUNE. GONE WITH THE STROKE OF MY PEN.
TAKE MY ADVICE. GET OUT OF HERE WHILE YOU CAN.

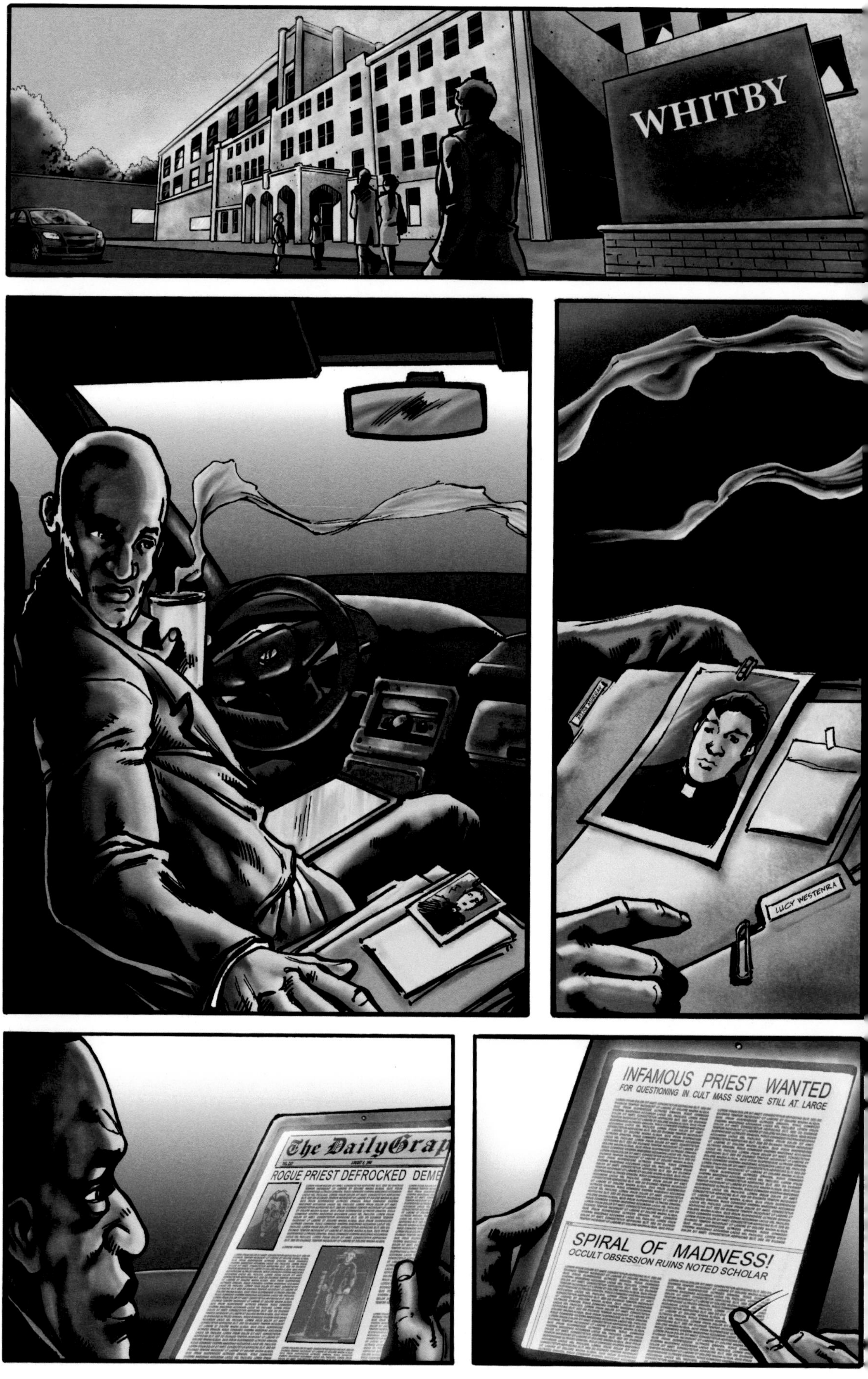
WHITBY
MINA MURRAY
LUCY WESTENRA
The DailyGrap
ROGUE PRIEST DEFROCKED DEME
INFAMOUS PRIEST WANTED
FOR QUESTIONING IN CULT MASS SUICIDE STILL AT LARGE
SPIRAL OF MADNESS!
OCCULT OBSESSION RUINS NOTED SCHOLAR

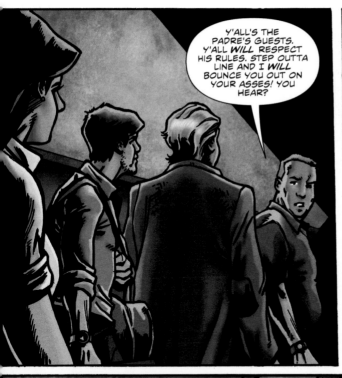

Y'ALL'S THE PADRE'S GUESTS. Y'ALL *WILL* RESPECT HIS RULES. STEP OUTTA LINE AND I *WILL* BOUNCE YOU OUT ON YOUR ASSES! YOU HEAR?

OF COURSE, MR. MORRIS.

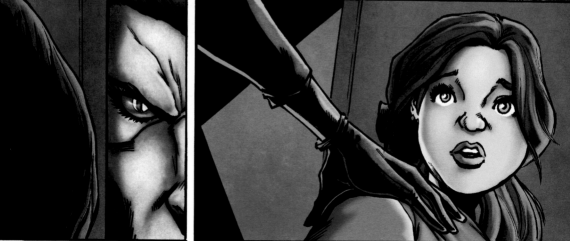

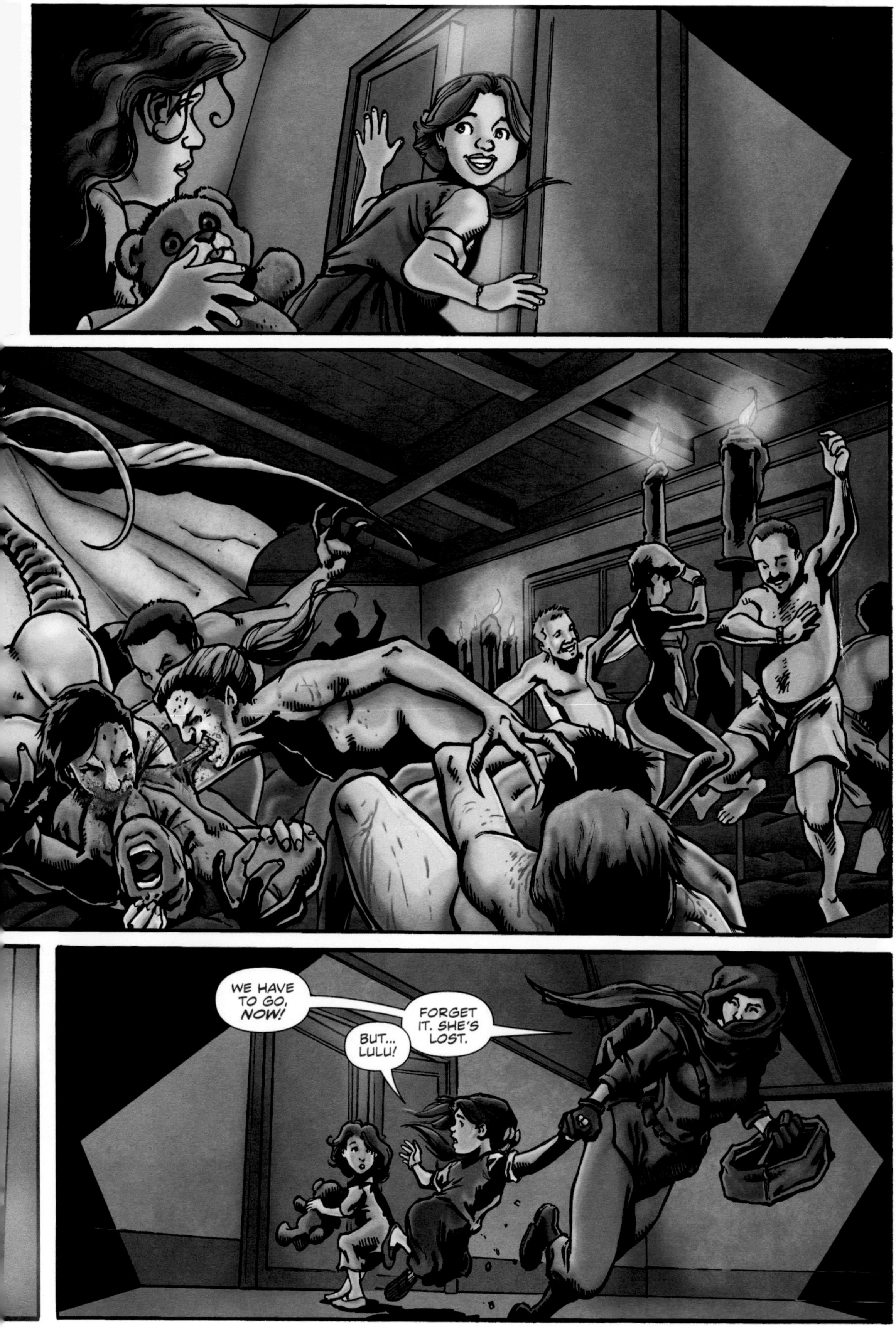
WE HAVE TO GO, NOW!
BUT... LULU!
FORGET IT. SHE'S LOST.

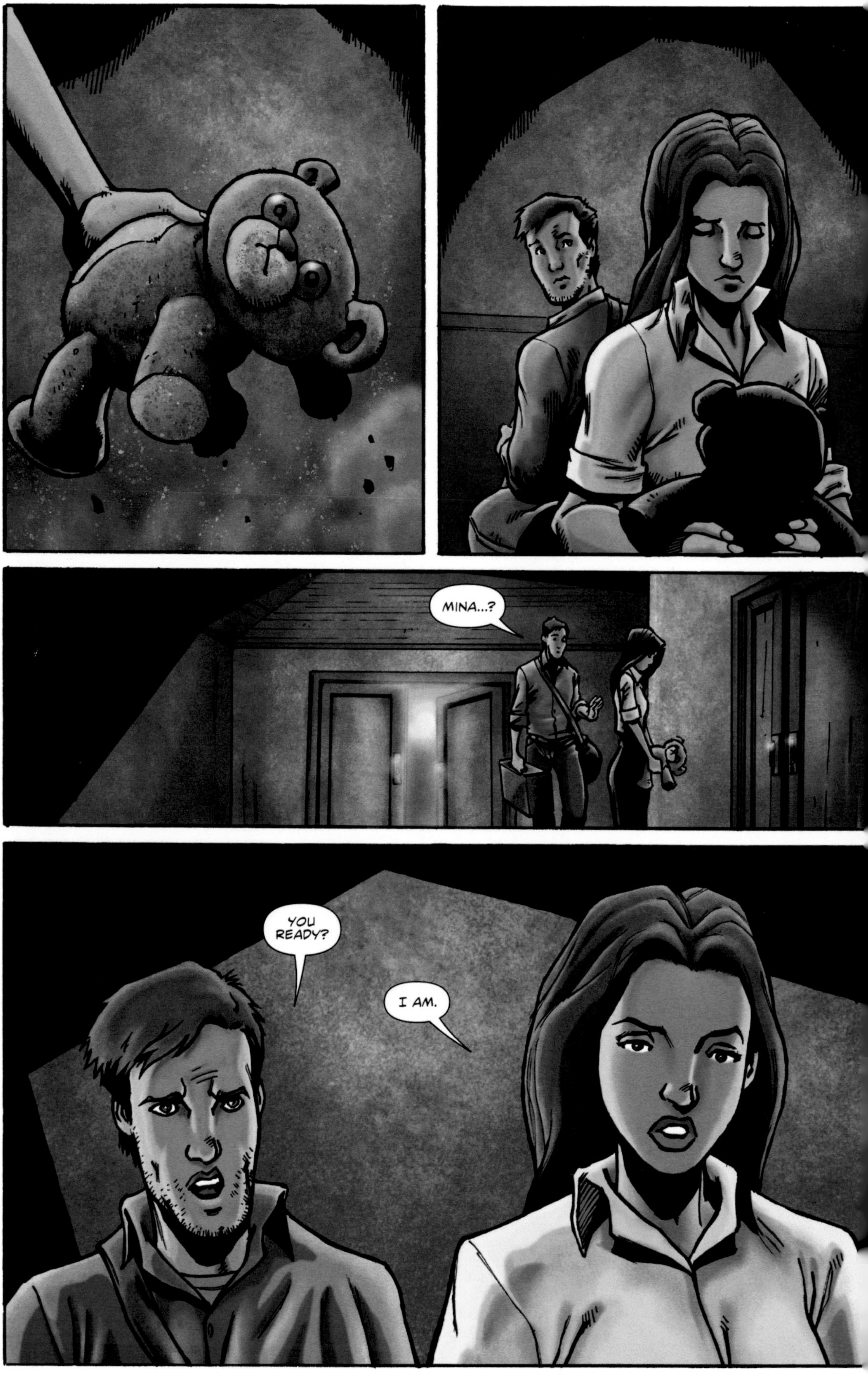
MINA...?
YOU READY?
I AM.

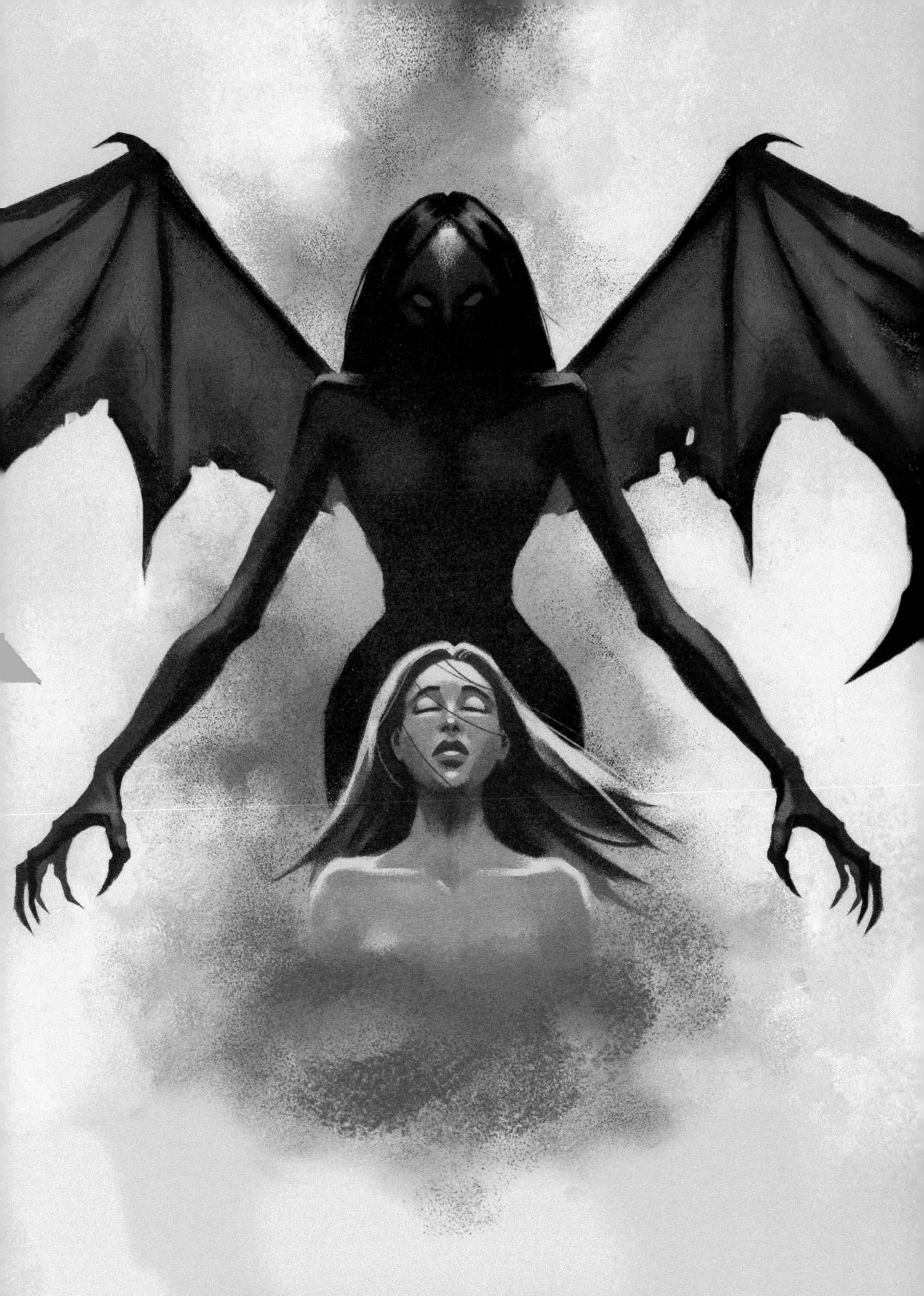

CHAPTER TWO

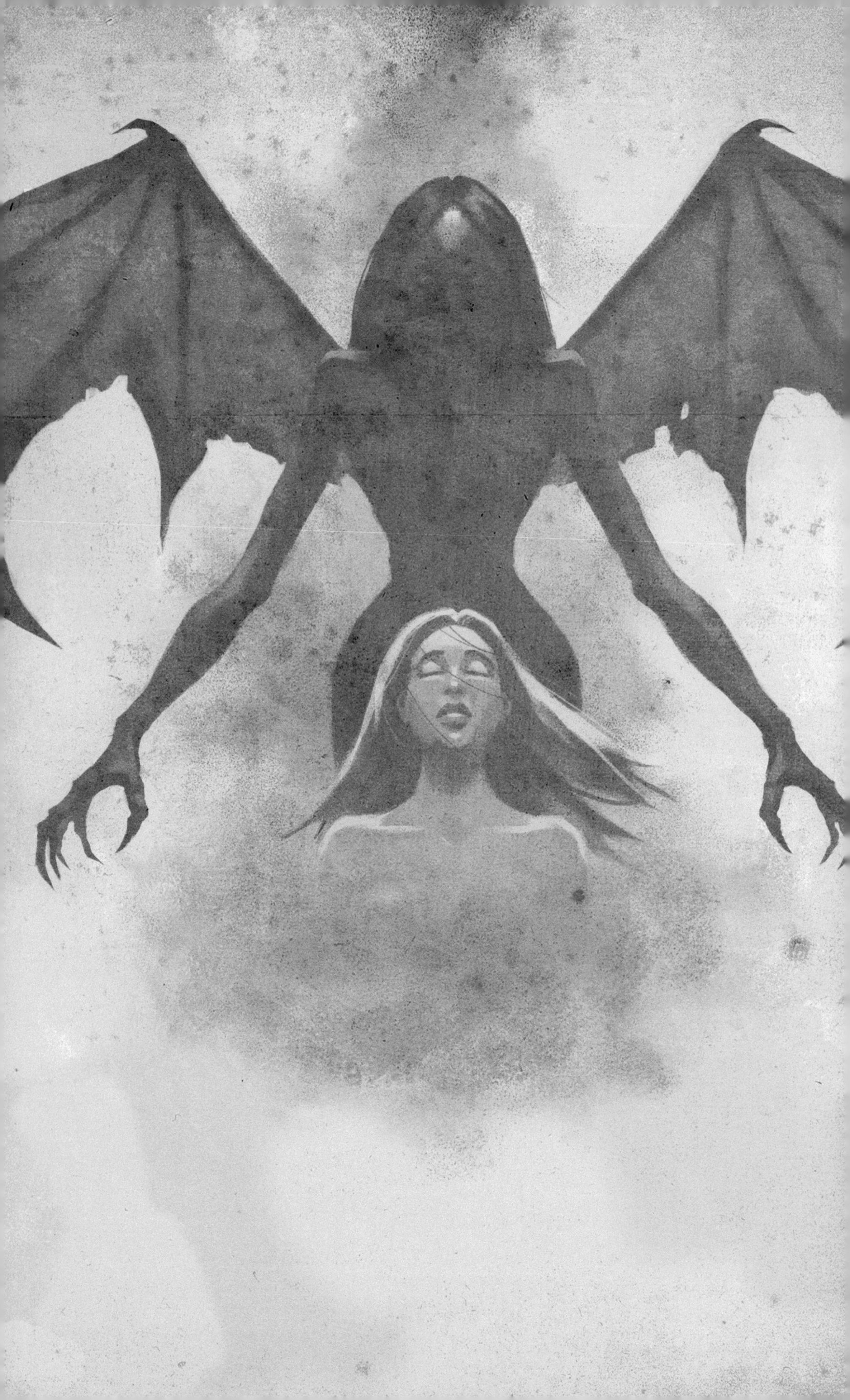

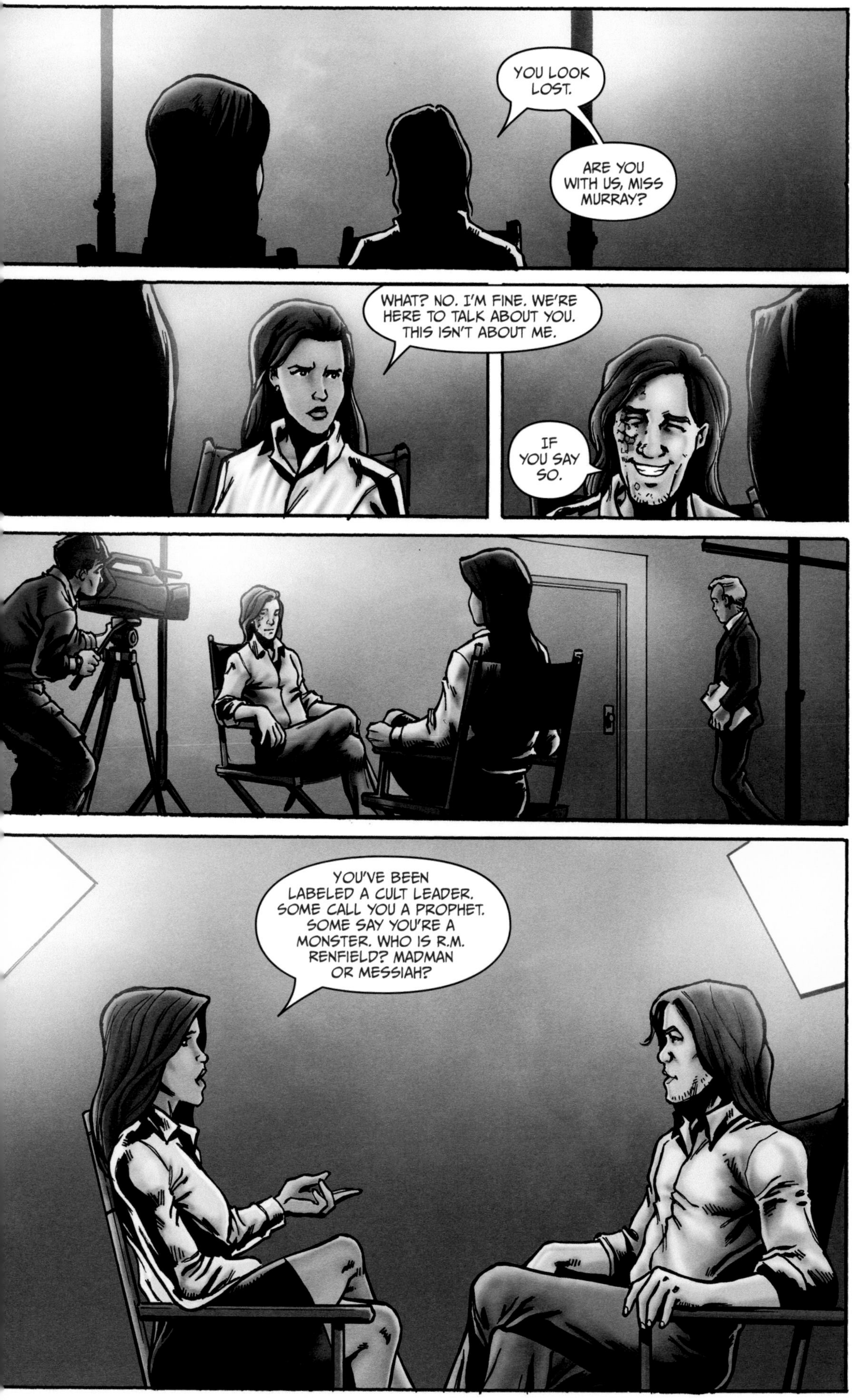
YOU LOOK LOST.
ARE YOU WITH US, MISS MURRAY?
WHAT? NO. I'M FINE. WE'RE HERE TO TALK ABOUT YOU. THIS ISN'T ABOUT ME.
IF YOU SAY SO.
YOU'VE BEEN LABELED A CULT LEADER. SOME CALL YOU A PROPHET. SOME SAY YOU'RE A MONSTER. WHO IS R.M. RENFIELD? MADMAN OR MESSIAH?

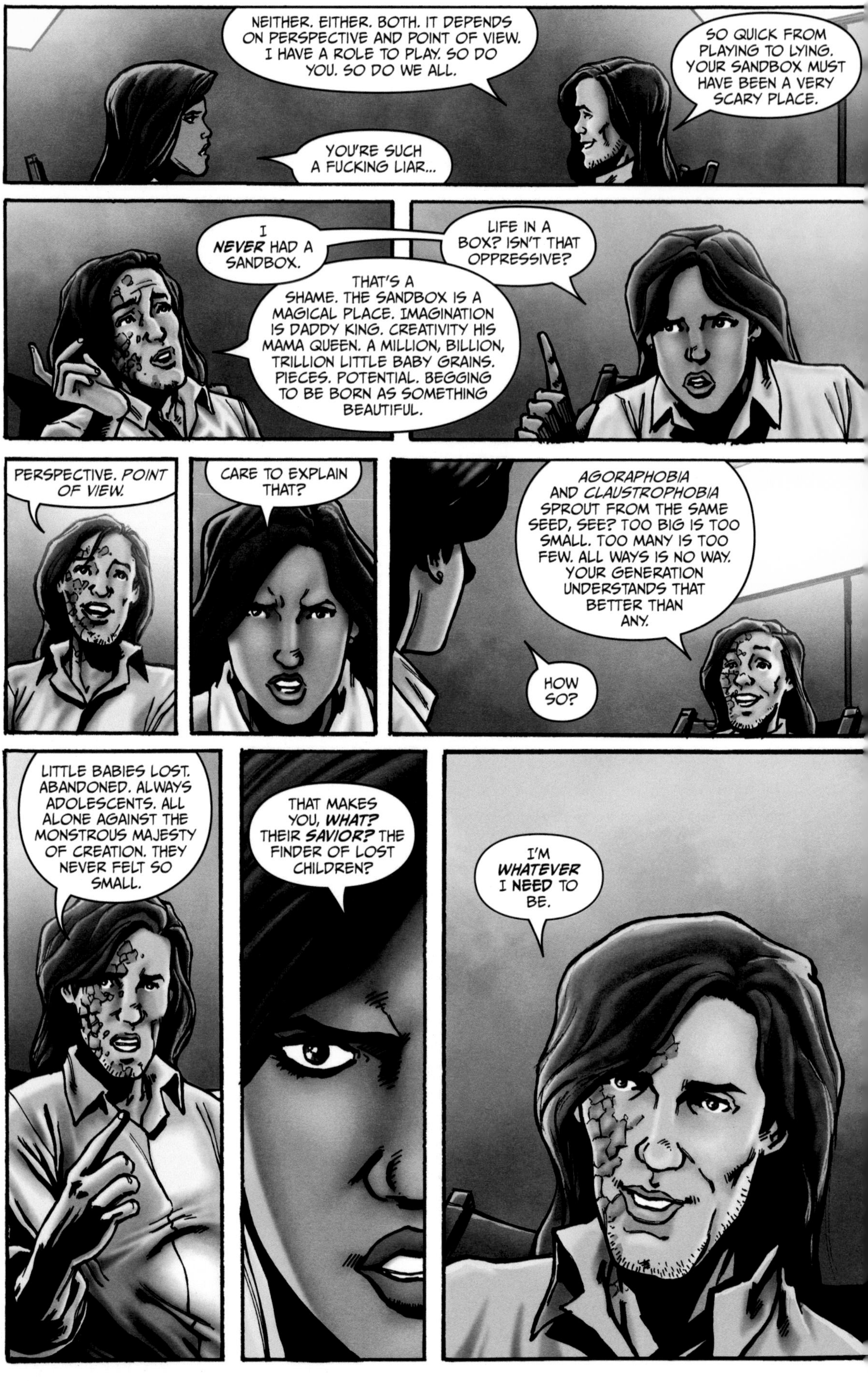
NEITHER. EITHER. BOTH. IT DEPENDS ON PERSPECTIVE AND POINT OF VIEW. I HAVE A ROLE TO PLAY. SO DO YOU. SO DO WE ALL.
YOU'RE SUCH A FUCKING LIAR...
SO QUICK FROM PLAYING TO LYING. YOUR SANDBOX MUST HAVE BEEN A VERY SCARY PLACE.
I NEVER HAD A SANDBOX.
THAT'S A SHAME. THE SANDBOX IS A MAGICAL PLACE. IMAGINATION IS DADDY KING. CREATIVITY HIS MAMA QUEEN. A MILLION, BILLION, TRILLION LITTLE BABY GRAINS. PIECES. POTENTIAL. BEGGING TO BE BORN AS SOMETHING BEAUTIFUL.
LIFE IN A BOX? ISN'T THAT OPPRESSIVE?
PERSPECTIVE. POINT OF VIEW.
CARE TO EXPLAIN THAT?
AGORAPHOBIA AND CLAUSTROPHOBIA SPROUT FROM THE SAME SEED, SEE? TOO BIG IS TOO SMALL. TOO MANY IS TOO FEW. ALL WAYS IS NO WAY. YOUR GENERATION UNDERSTANDS THAT BETTER THAN ANY.
HOW SO?
LITTLE BABIES LOST. ABANDONED. ALWAYS ADOLESCENTS. ALL ALONE AGAINST THE MONSTROUS MAJESTY OF CREATION. THEY NEVER FELT SO SMALL.
THAT MAKES YOU, WHAT? THEIR SAVIOR? THE FINDER OF LOST CHILDREN?
I'M WHATEVER I NEED TO BE.

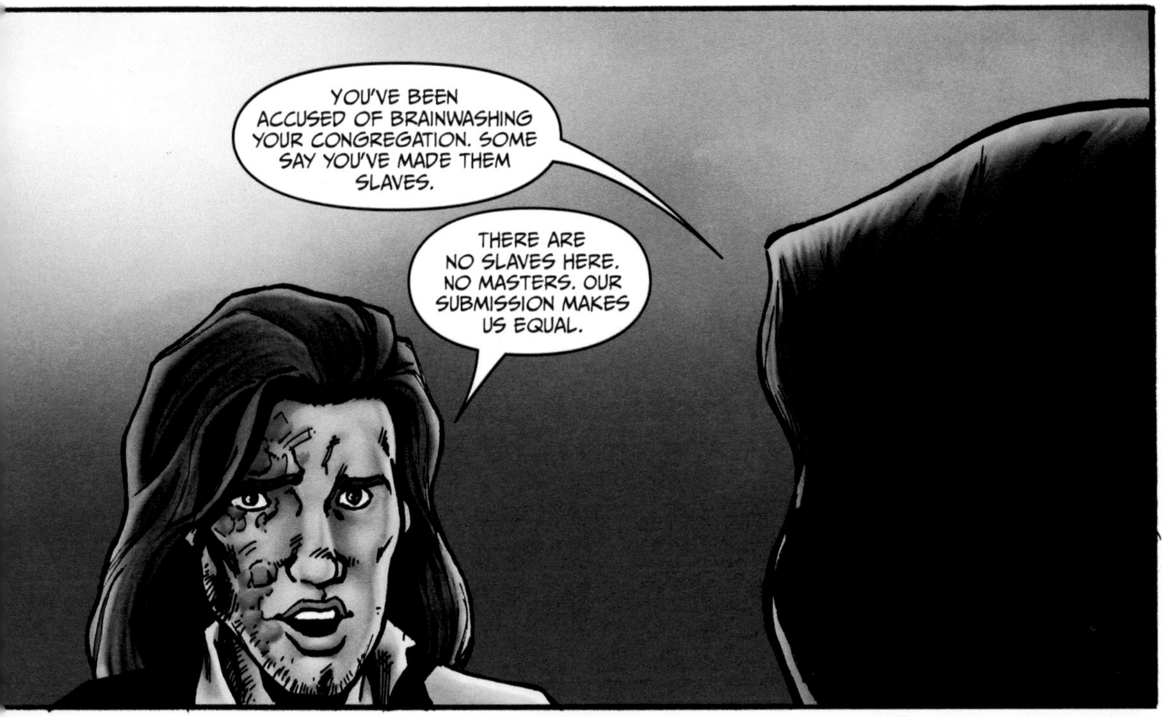
YOU'VE BEEN ACCUSED OF BRAINWASHING YOUR CONGREGATION. SOME SAY YOU'VE MADE THEM SLAVES.
THERE ARE NO SLAVES HERE. NO MASTERS. OUR SUBMISSION MAKES US EQUAL.

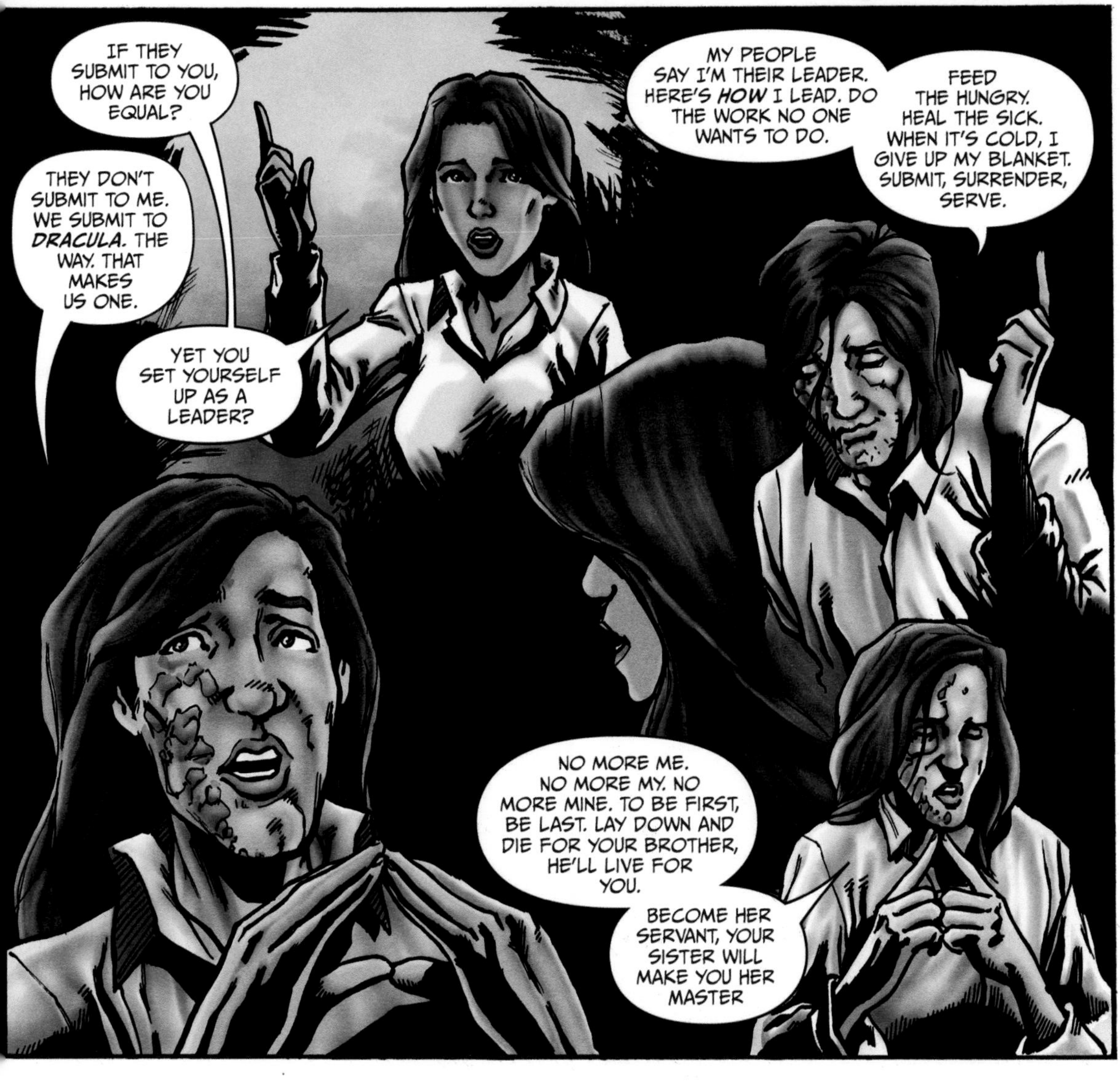
IF THEY SUBMIT TO YOU, HOW ARE YOU EQUAL?
THEY DON'T SUBMIT TO ME. WE SUBMIT TO *DRACULA.* THE WAY. THAT MAKES US ONE.
YET YOU SET YOURSELF UP AS A LEADER?
MY PEOPLE SAY I'M THEIR LEADER. HERE'S ***HOW*** I LEAD. DO THE WORK NO ONE WANTS TO DO.
FEED THE HUNGRY. HEAL THE SICK. WHEN IT'S COLD, I GIVE UP MY BLANKET. SUBMIT, SURRENDER, SERVE.
NO MORE ME. NO MORE MY. NO MORE MINE. TO BE FIRST, BE LAST. LAY DOWN AND DIE FOR YOUR BROTHER, HE'LL LIVE FOR YOU.
BECOME HER SERVANT, YOUR SISTER WILL MAKE YOU HER MASTER

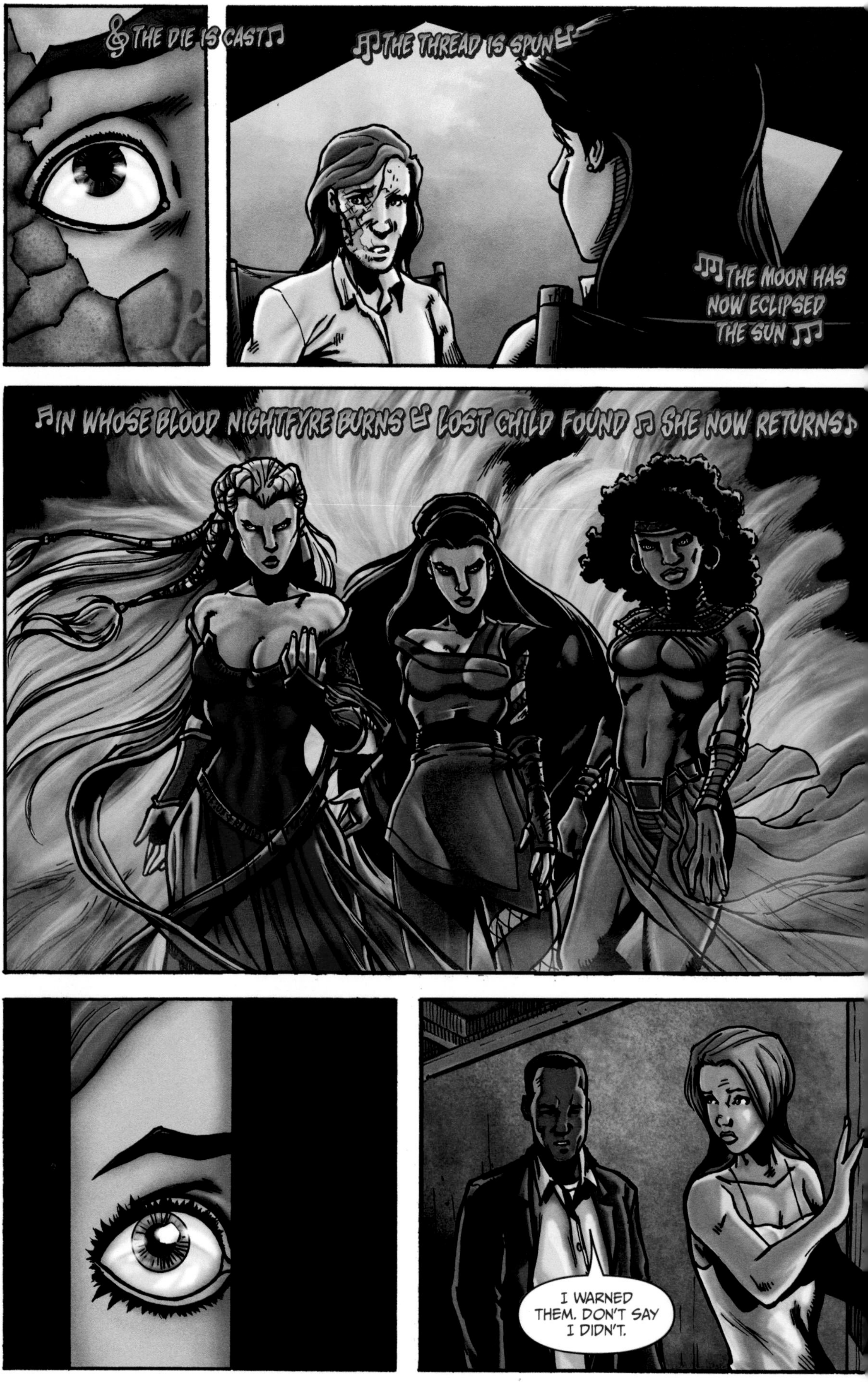
THE DIE IS CAST
THE THREAD IS SPUN
THE MOON HAS NOW ECLIPSED THE SUN
IN WHOSE BLOOD NIGHTFYRE BURNS
LOST CHILD FOUND
SHE NOW RETURNS
I WARNED THEM. DON'T SAY I DIDN'T.

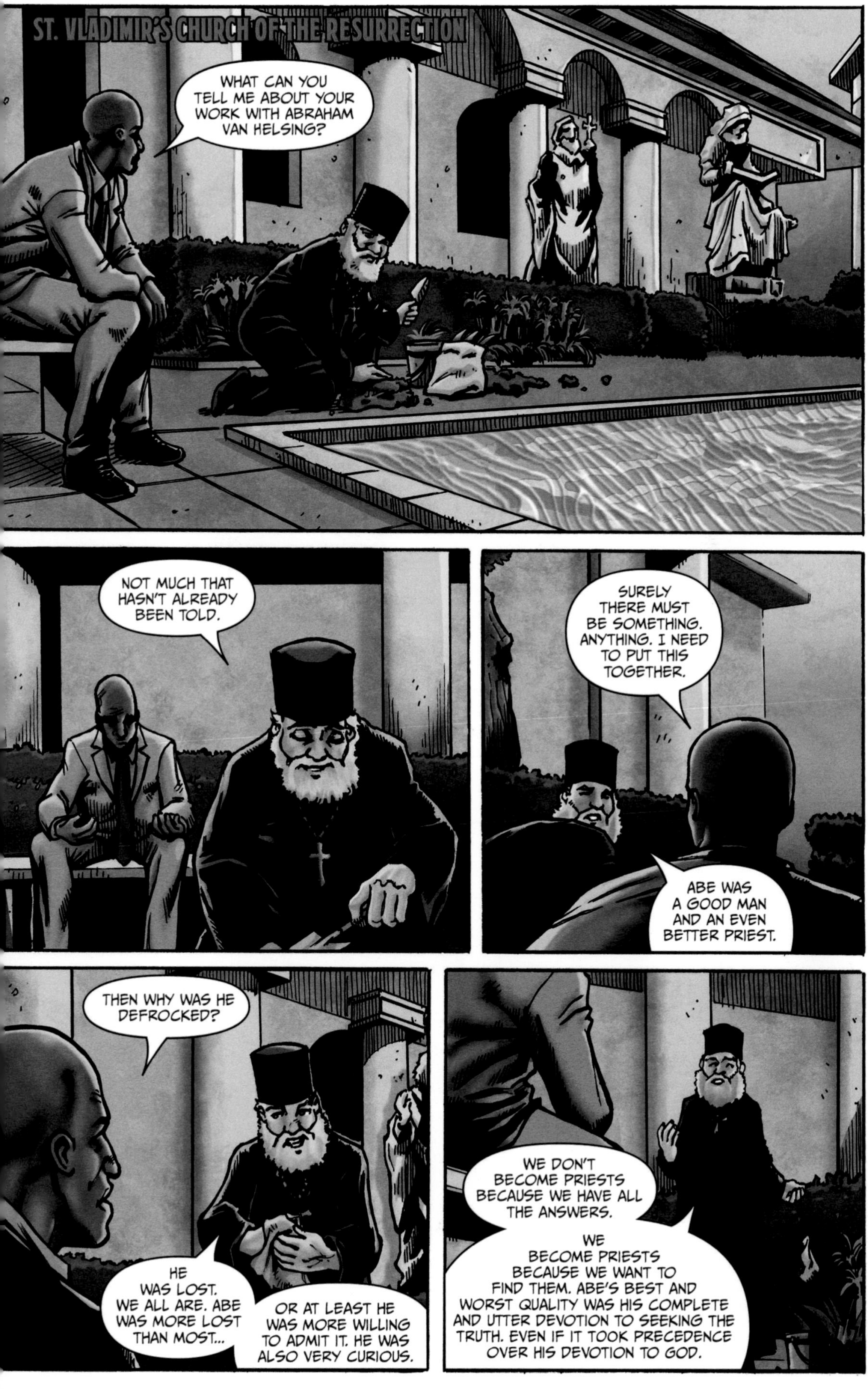
ST. VLADIMIR'S CHURCH OF THE RESURRECTION
WHAT CAN YOU TELL ME ABOUT YOUR WORK WITH ABRAHAM VAN HELSING?
NOT MUCH THAT HASN'T ALREADY BEEN TOLD.
SURELY THERE MUST BE SOMETHING. ANYTHING. I NEED TO PUT THIS TOGETHER.
ABE WAS A GOOD MAN AND AN EVEN BETTER PRIEST.
THEN WHY WAS HE DEFROCKED?
HE WAS LOST. WE ALL ARE. ABE WAS MORE LOST THAN MOST...
OR AT LEAST HE WAS MORE WILLING TO ADMIT IT. HE WAS ALSO VERY CURIOUS.
WE DON'T BECOME PRIESTS BECAUSE WE HAVE ALL THE ANSWERS.
WE BECOME PRIESTS BECAUSE WE WANT TO FIND THEM. ABE'S BEST AND WORST QUALITY WAS HIS COMPLETE AND UTTER DEVOTION TO SEEKING THE TRUTH. EVEN IF IT TOOK PRECEDENCE OVER HIS DEVOTION TO GOD.

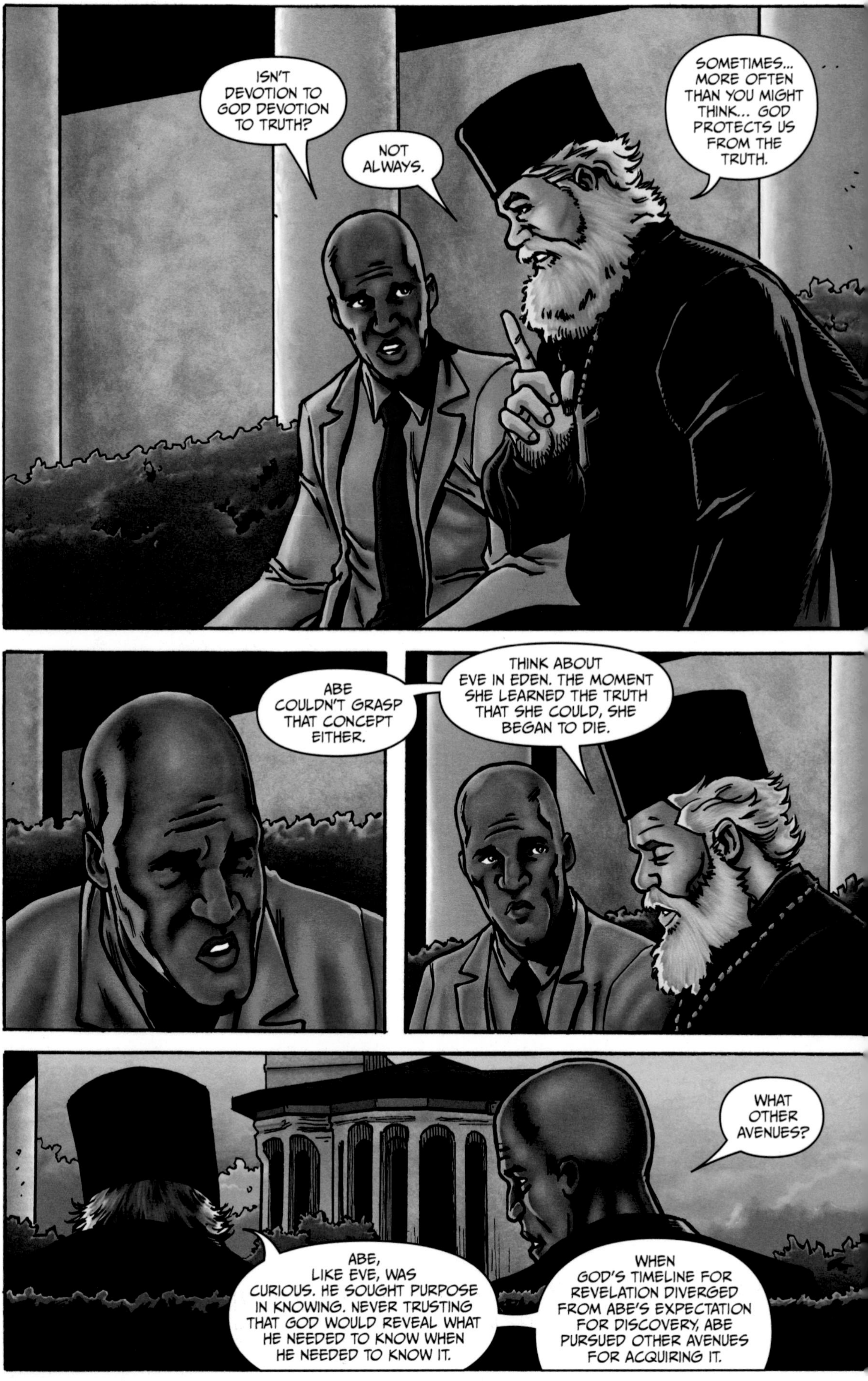
ISN'T DEVOTION TO GOD DEVOTION TO TRUTH?
NOT ALWAYS.
SOMETIMES... MORE OFTEN THAN YOU MIGHT THINK... GOD PROTECTS US FROM THE TRUTH.
ABE COULDN'T GRASP THAT CONCEPT EITHER.
THINK ABOUT EVE IN EDEN. THE MOMENT SHE LEARNED THE TRUTH THAT SHE COULD, SHE BEGAN TO DIE.
WHAT OTHER AVENUES?
ABE, LIKE EVE, WAS CURIOUS. HE SOUGHT PURPOSE IN KNOWING. NEVER TRUSTING THAT GOD WOULD REVEAL WHAT HE NEEDED TO KNOW WHEN HE NEEDED TO KNOW IT.
WHEN GOD'S TIMELINE FOR REVELATION DIVERGED FROM ABE'S EXPECTATION FOR DISCOVERY, ABE PURSUED OTHER AVENUES FOR ACQUIRING IT.

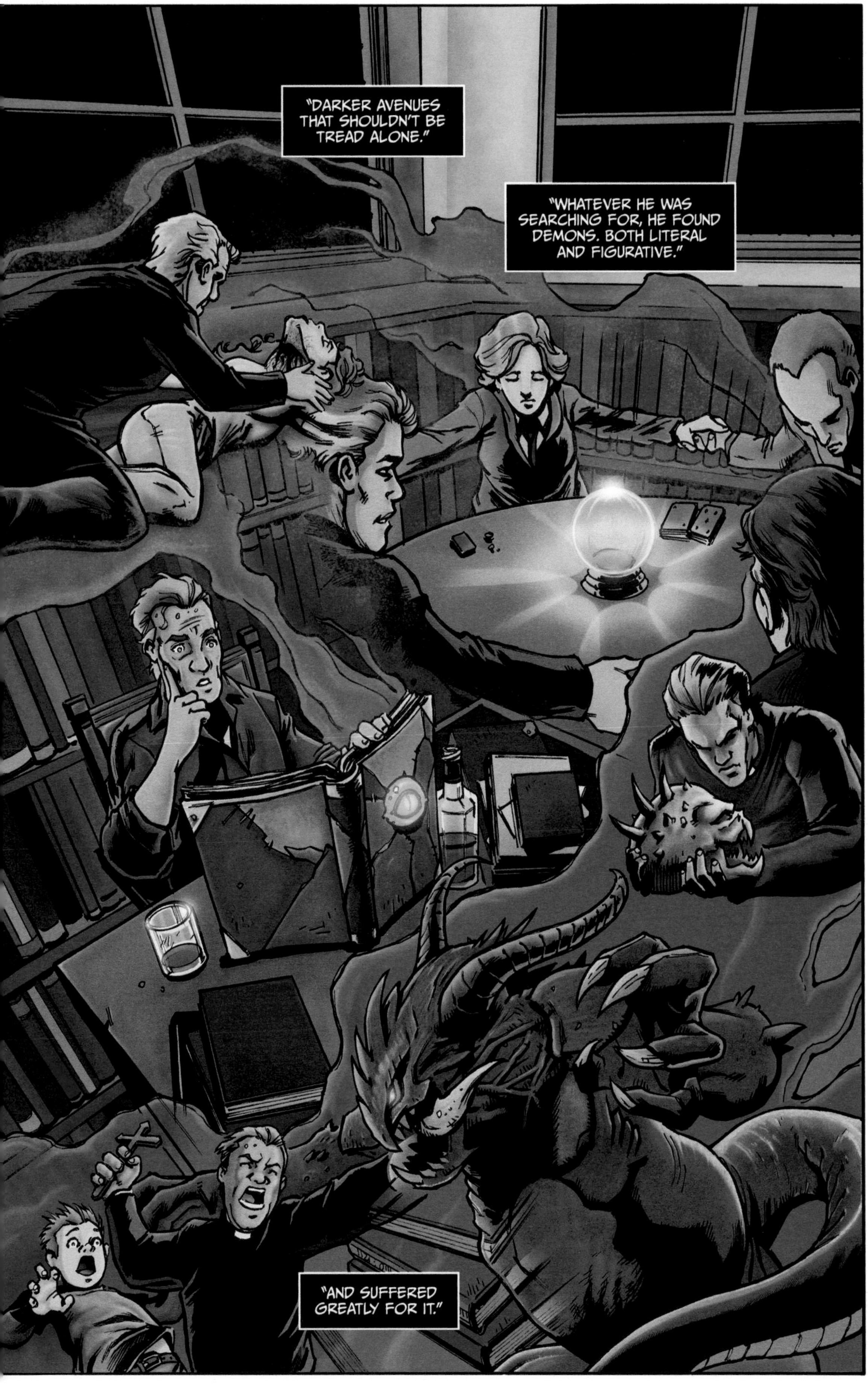
"DARKER AVENUES THAT SHOULDN'T BE TREAD ALONE."
"WHATEVER HE WAS SEARCHING FOR, HE FOUND DEMONS. BOTH LITERAL AND FIGURATIVE."
"AND SUFFERED GREATLY FOR IT."

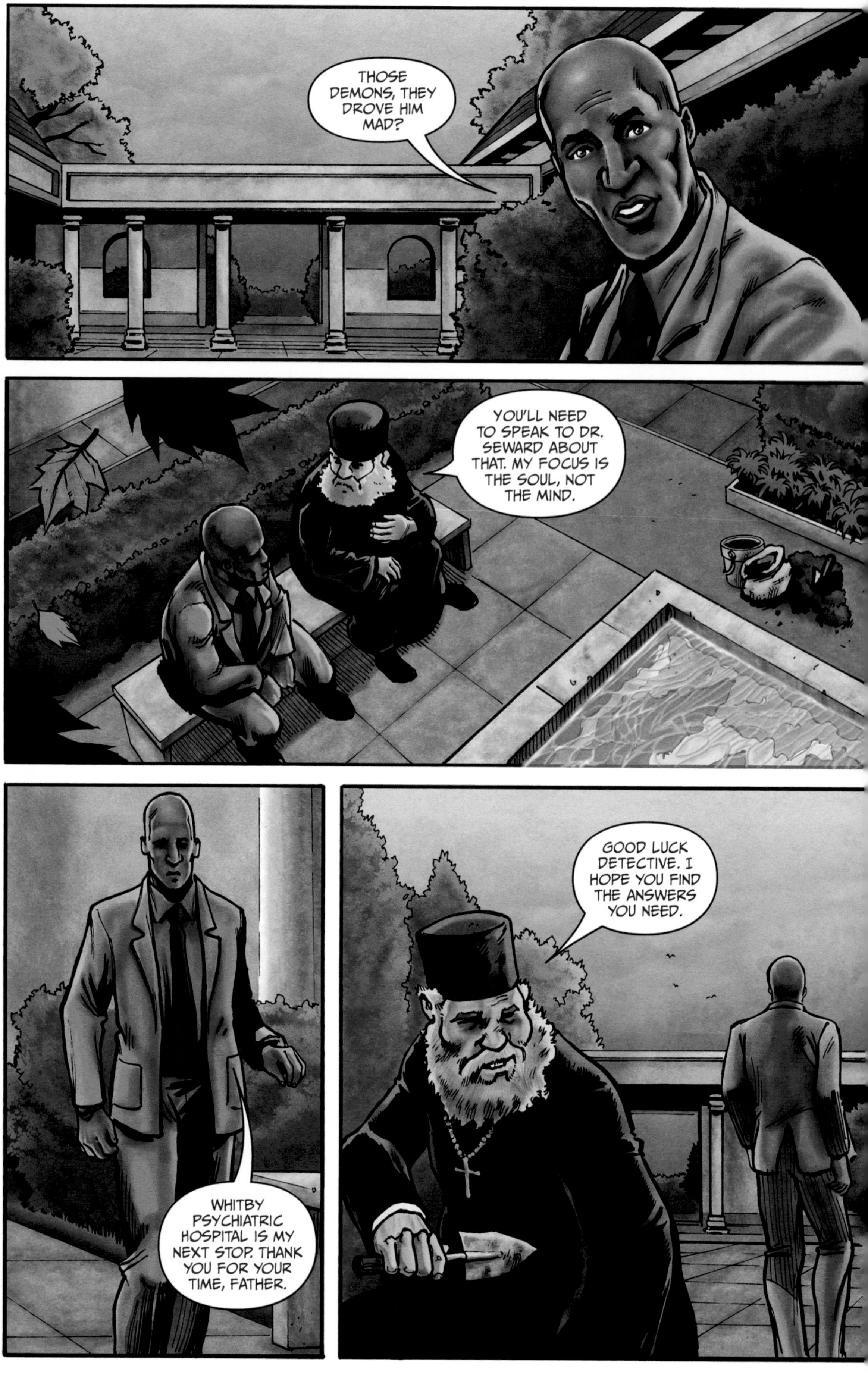
THOSE DEMONS, THEY DROVE HIM MAD?
YOU'LL NEED TO SPEAK TO DR. SEWARD ABOUT THAT. MY FOCUS IS THE SOUL, NOT THE MIND.
WHITBY PSYCHIATRIC HOSPITAL IS MY NEXT STOP. THANK YOU FOR YOUR TIME, FATHER.
GOOD LUCK DETECTIVE. I HOPE YOU FIND THE ANSWERS YOU NEED.

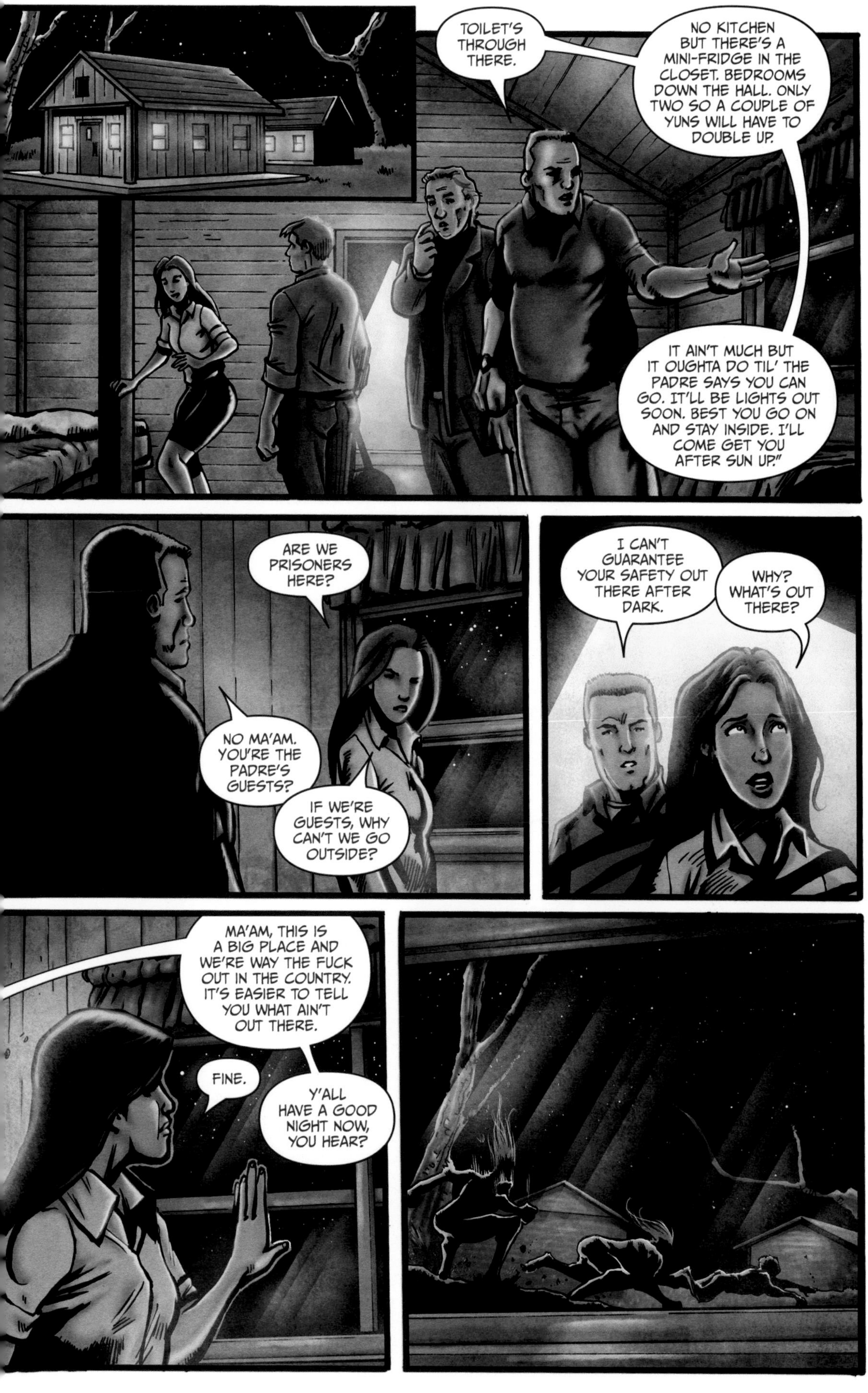
TOILET'S THROUGH THERE.
NO KITCHEN BUT THERE'S A MINI-FRIDGE IN THE CLOSET. BEDROOMS DOWN THE HALL. ONLY TWO SO A COUPLE OF YUNS WILL HAVE TO DOUBLE UP.
IT AIN'T MUCH BUT IT OUGHTA DO TIL' THE PADRE SAYS YOU CAN GO. IT'LL BE LIGHTS OUT SOON. BEST YOU GO ON AND STAY INSIDE. I'LL COME GET YOU AFTER SUN UP."
ARE WE PRISONERS HERE?
NO MA'AM. YOU'RE THE PADRE'S GUESTS?
IF WE'RE GUESTS, WHY CAN'T WE GO OUTSIDE?
I CAN'T GUARANTEE YOUR SAFETY OUT THERE AFTER DARK.
WHY? WHAT'S OUT THERE?
MA'AM, THIS IS A BIG PLACE AND WE'RE WAY THE FUCK OUT IN THE COUNTRY. IT'S EASIER TO TELL YOU WHAT AIN'T OUT THERE.
FINE.
Y'ALL HAVE A GOOD NIGHT NOW, YOU HEAR?

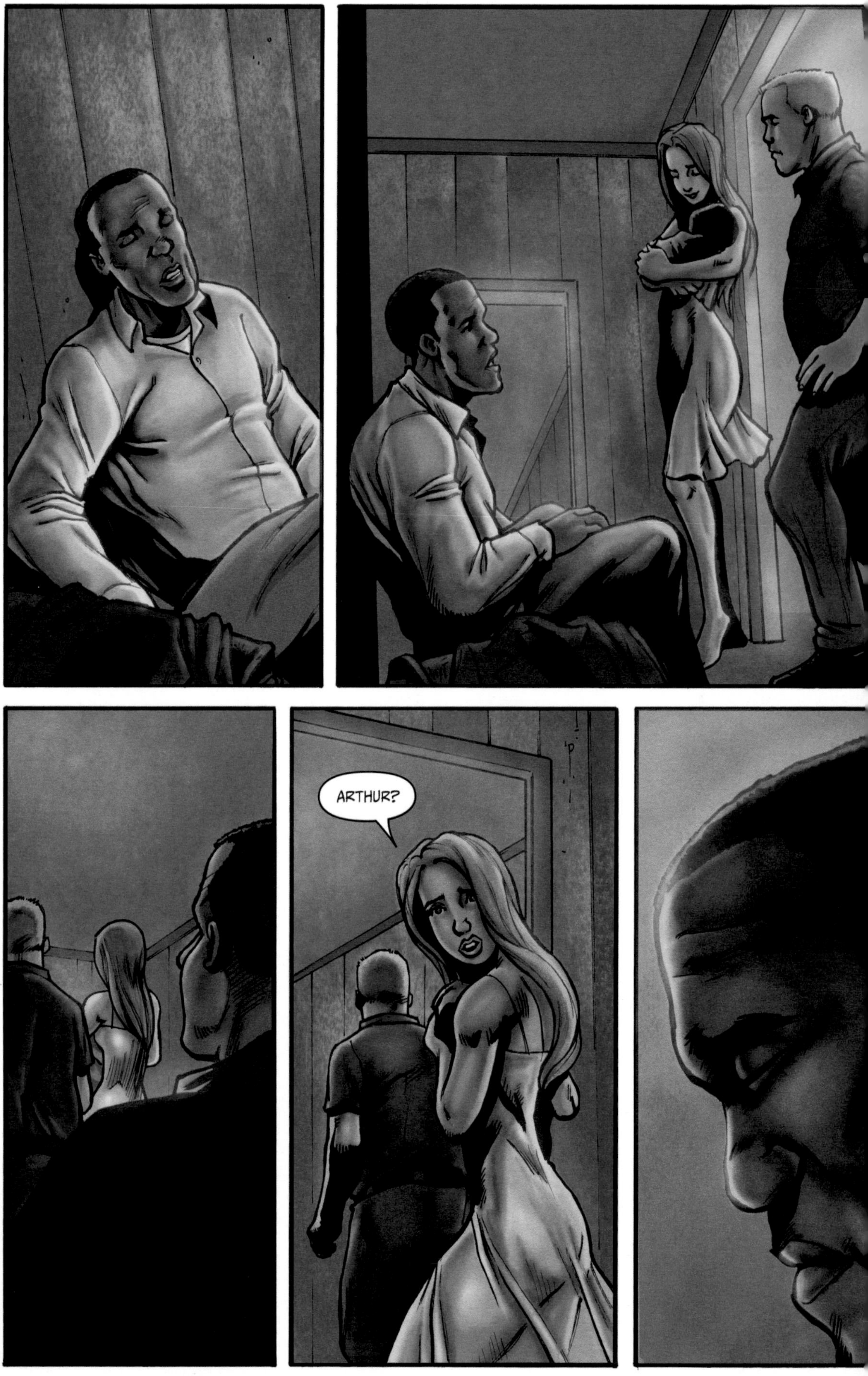
ARTHUR?

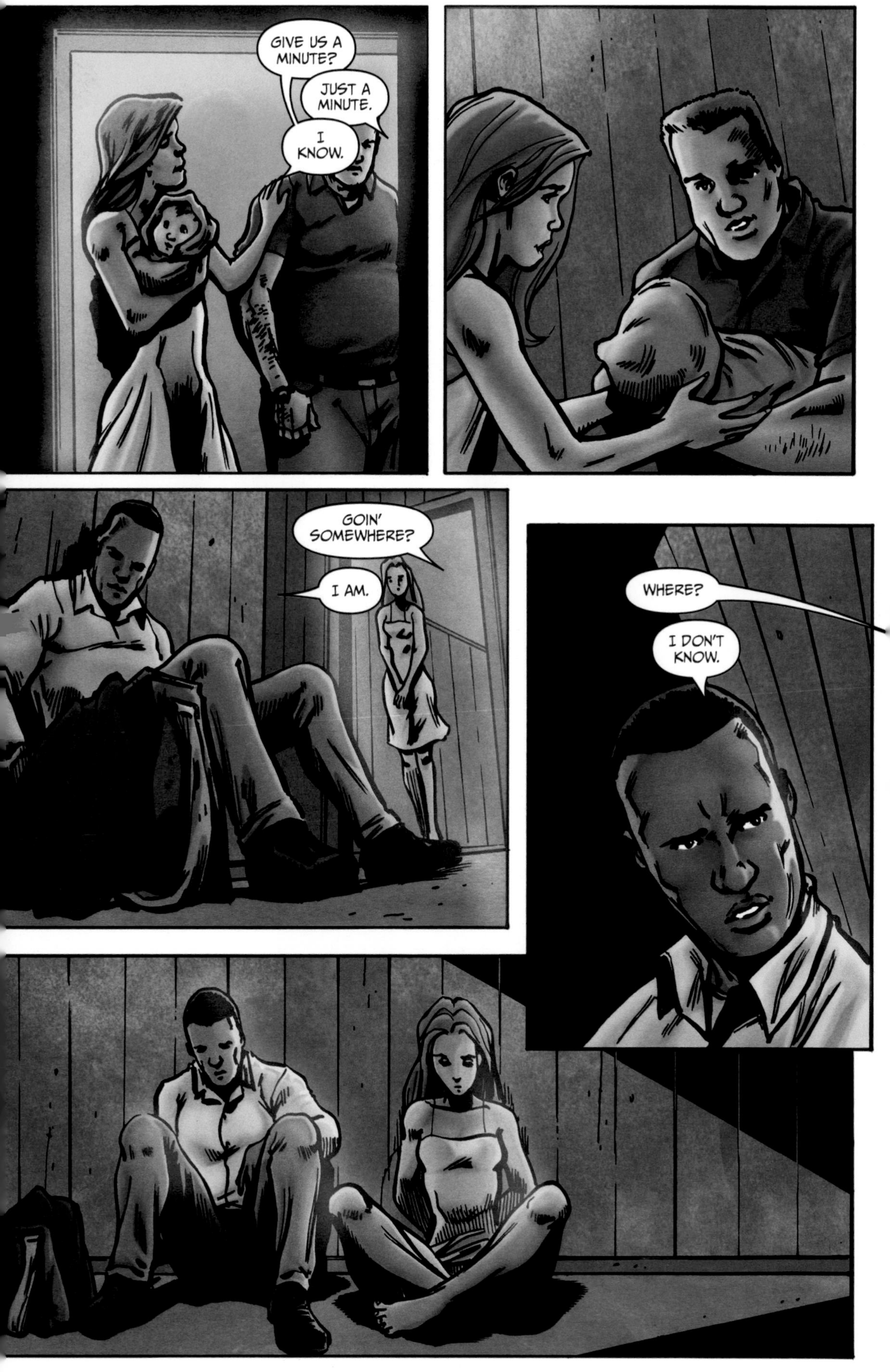
GIVE US A MINUTE?
JUST A MINUTE.
I KNOW.
GOIN' SOMEWHERE?
I AM.
WHERE?
I DON'T KNOW.

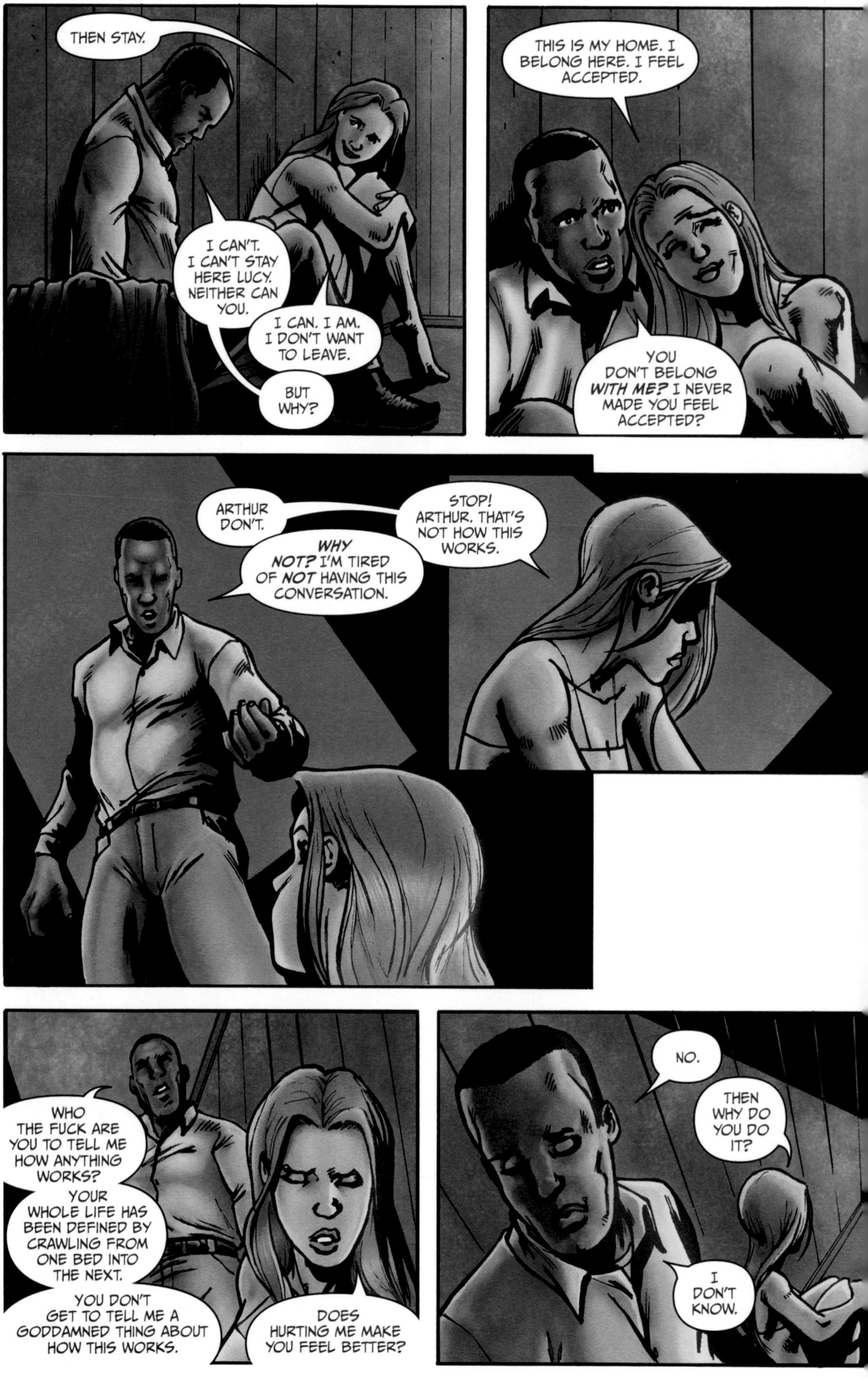
THEN STAY.
I CAN'T. I CAN'T STAY HERE LUCY. NEITHER CAN YOU.
I CAN. I AM. I DON'T WANT TO LEAVE.
BUT WHY?
THIS IS MY HOME. I BELONG HERE. I FEEL ACCEPTED.
YOU DON'T BELONG *WITH ME?* I NEVER MADE YOU FEEL ACCEPTED?
ARTHUR DON'T.
WHY NOT? I'M TIRED OF *NOT* HAVING THIS CONVERSATION.
STOP! ARTHUR. THAT'S NOT HOW THIS WORKS.
WHO THE FUCK ARE YOU TO TELL ME HOW ANYTHING WORKS?
YOUR WHOLE LIFE HAS BEEN DEFINED BY CRAWLING FROM ONE BED INTO THE NEXT.
YOU DON'T GET TO TELL ME A GODDAMNED THING ABOUT HOW THIS WORKS.
DOES HURTING ME MAKE YOU FEEL BETTER?
NO.
THEN WHY DO YOU DO IT?
I DON'T KNOW.

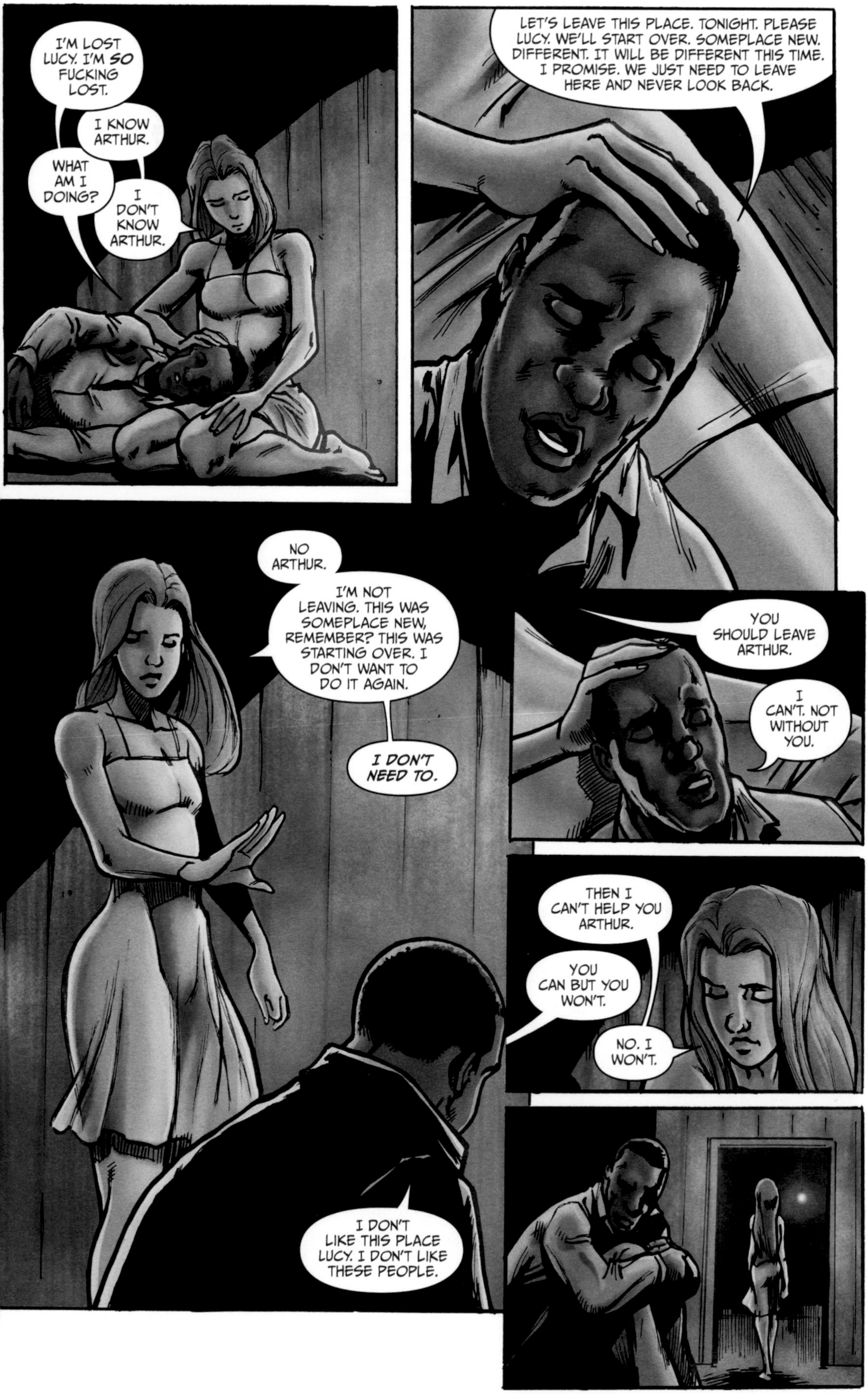
I'M LOST LUCY. I'M SO FUCKING LOST.
I KNOW ARTHUR.
WHAT AM I DOING?
I DON'T KNOW ARTHUR.
LET'S LEAVE THIS PLACE. TONIGHT. PLEASE LUCY. WE'LL START OVER. SOMEPLACE NEW. DIFFERENT. IT WILL BE DIFFERENT THIS TIME. I PROMISE. WE JUST NEED TO LEAVE HERE AND NEVER LOOK BACK.
NO ARTHUR.
I'M NOT LEAVING. THIS WAS SOMEPLACE NEW, REMEMBER? THIS WAS STARTING OVER. I DON'T WANT TO DO IT AGAIN.
I DON'T NEED TO.
I DON'T LIKE THIS PLACE LUCY. I DON'T LIKE THESE PEOPLE.
YOU SHOULD LEAVE ARTHUR.
I CAN'T. NOT WITHOUT YOU.
THEN I CAN'T HELP YOU ARTHUR.
YOU CAN BUT YOU WON'T.
NO. I WON'T.

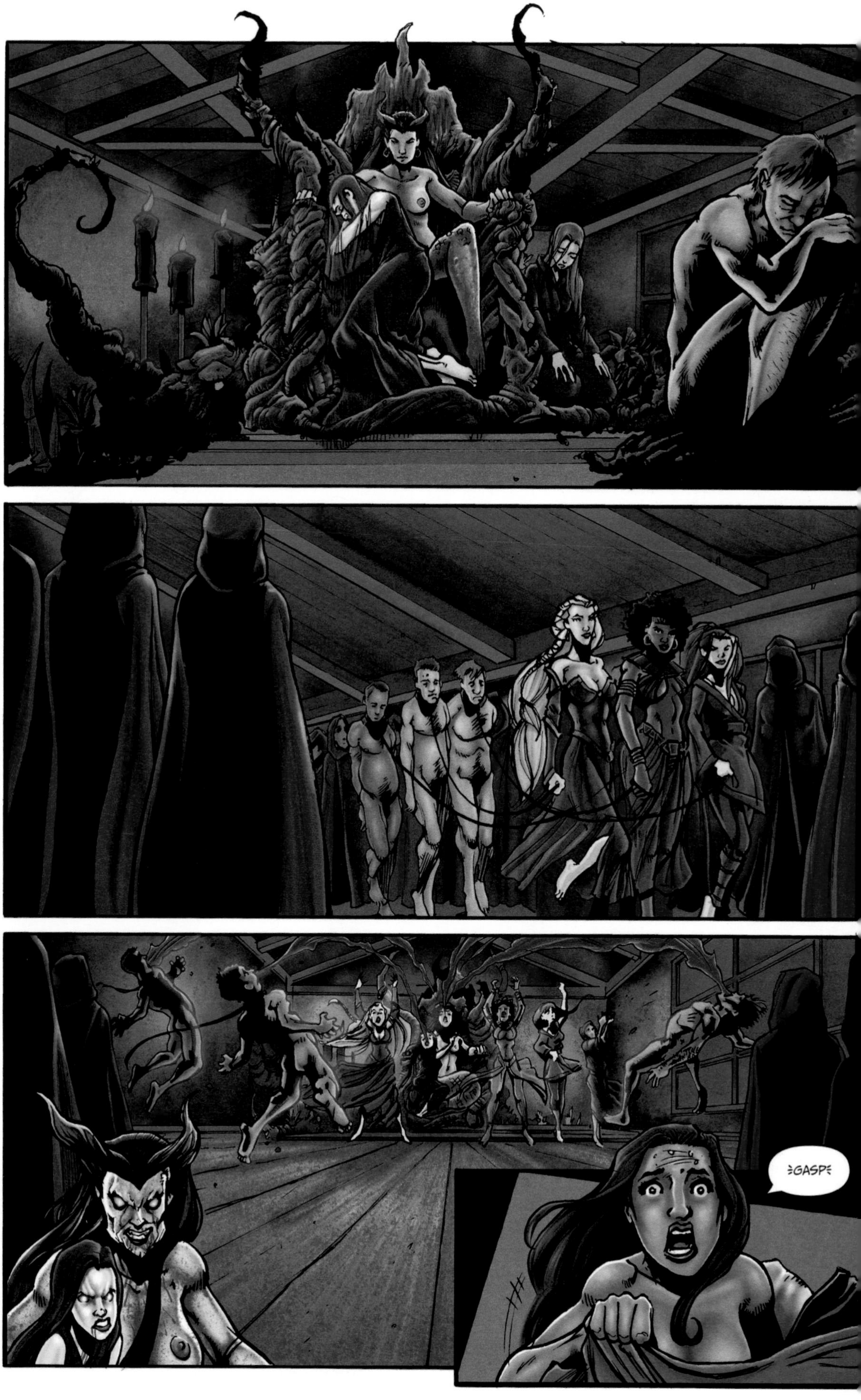
GASP

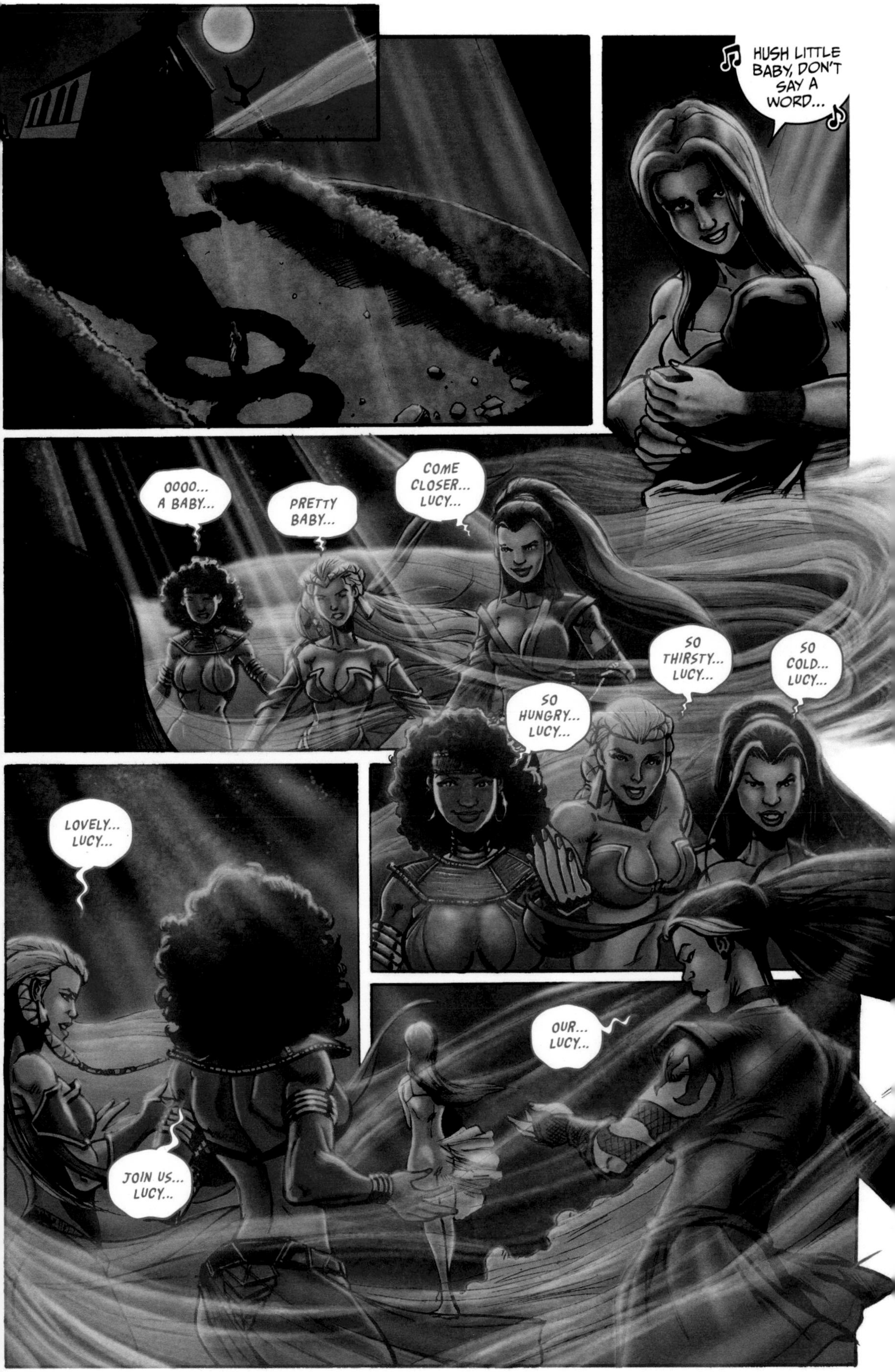
HUSH LITTLE BABY, DON'T SAY A WORD...
OOOO... A BABY...
PRETTY BABY...
COME CLOSER... LUCY...
SO HUNGRY... LUCY...
SO THIRSTY... LUCY...
SO COLD... LUCY...
LOVELY... LUCY...
JOIN US... LUCY...
OUR... LUCY...

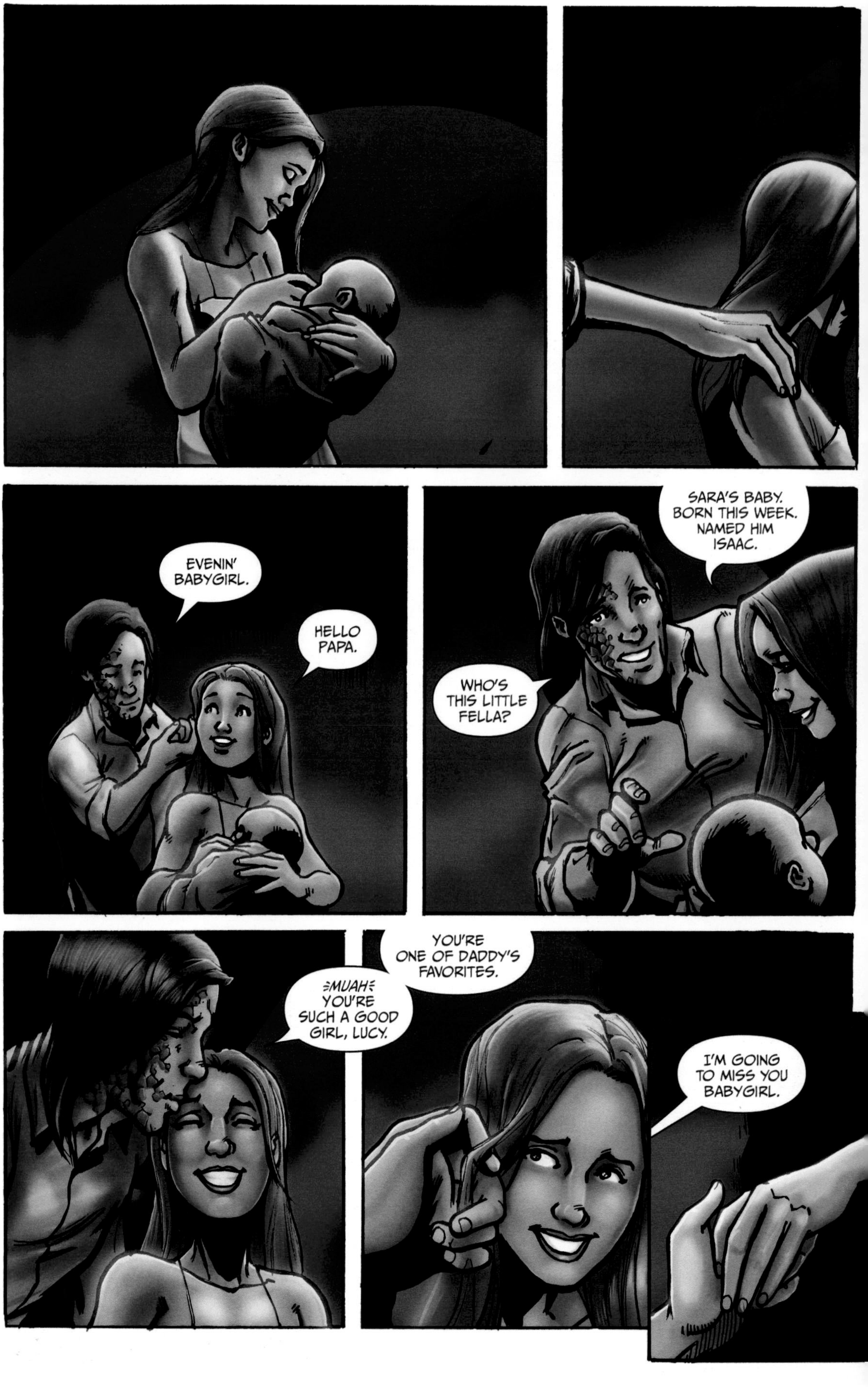

EVENIN' BABYGIRL.
HELLO PAPA.
SARA'S BABY. BORN THIS WEEK. NAMED HIM ISAAC.
WHO'S THIS LITTLE FELLA?
≶MUAH≷ YOU'RE SUCH A GOOD GIRL, LUCY.
YOU'RE ONE OF DADDY'S FAVORITES.
I'M GOING TO MISS YOU BABYGIRL.

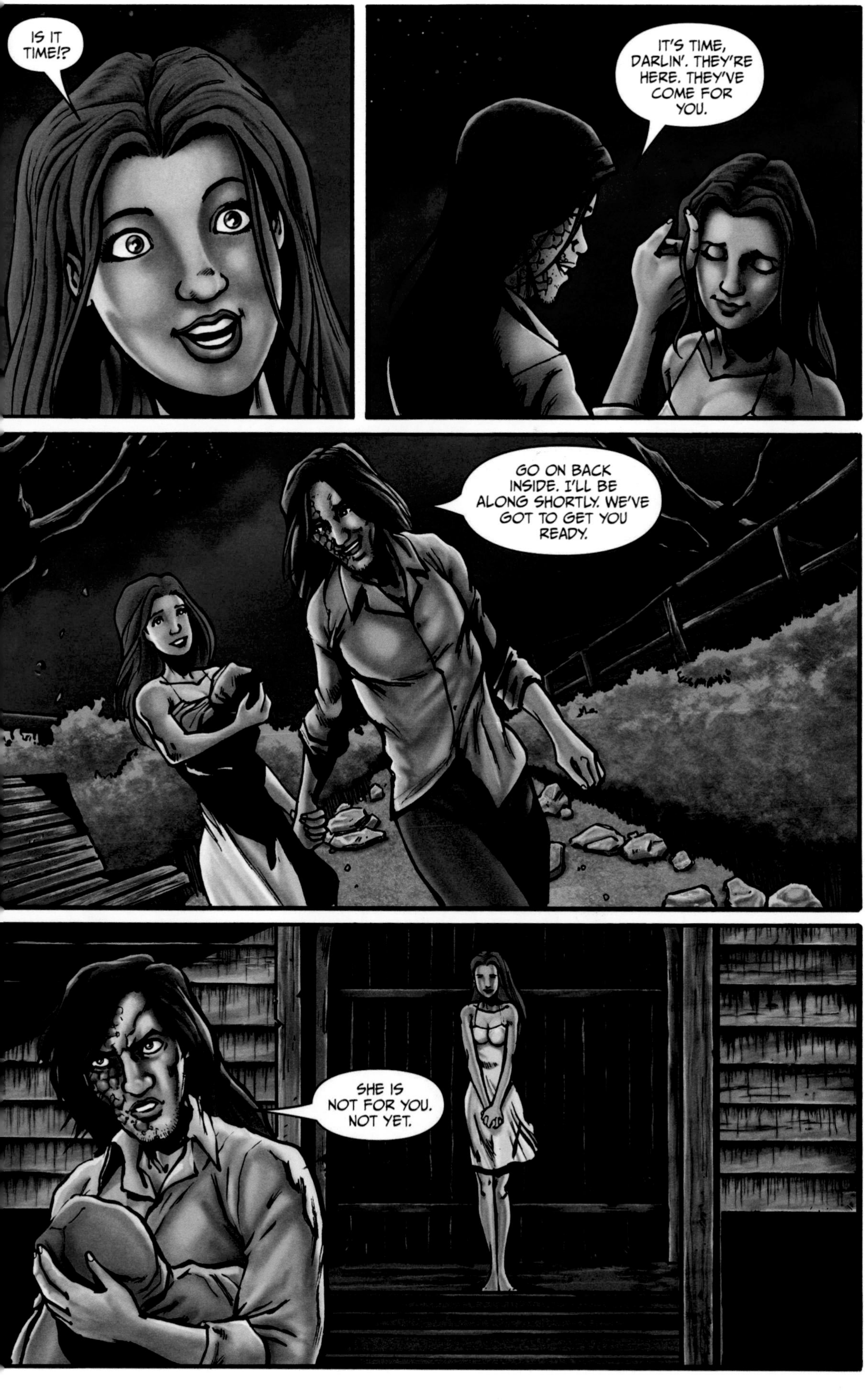
IS IT TIME!?
IT'S TIME, DARLIN'. THEY'RE HERE. THEY'VE COME FOR YOU.
GO ON BACK INSIDE. I'LL BE ALONG SHORTLY. WE'VE GOT TO GET YOU READY.
SHE IS NOT FOR YOU. NOT YET.

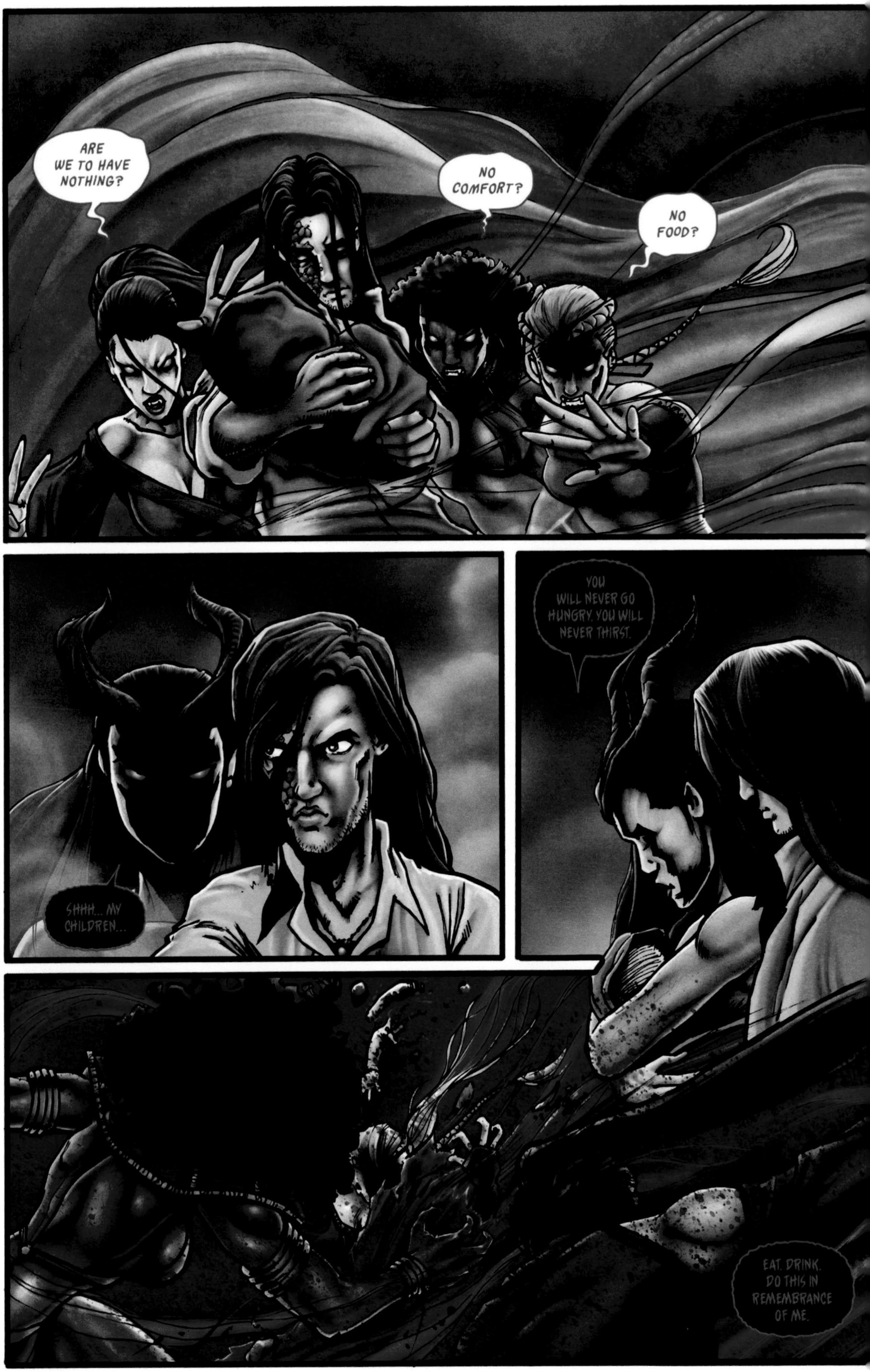
ARE WE TO HAVE NOTHING?
NO COMFORT?
NO FOOD?
SHHH... MY CHILDREN...
YOU WILL NEVER GO HUNGRY. YOU WILL NEVER THIRST.
EAT. DRINK. DO THIS IN REMEMBRANCE OF ME.

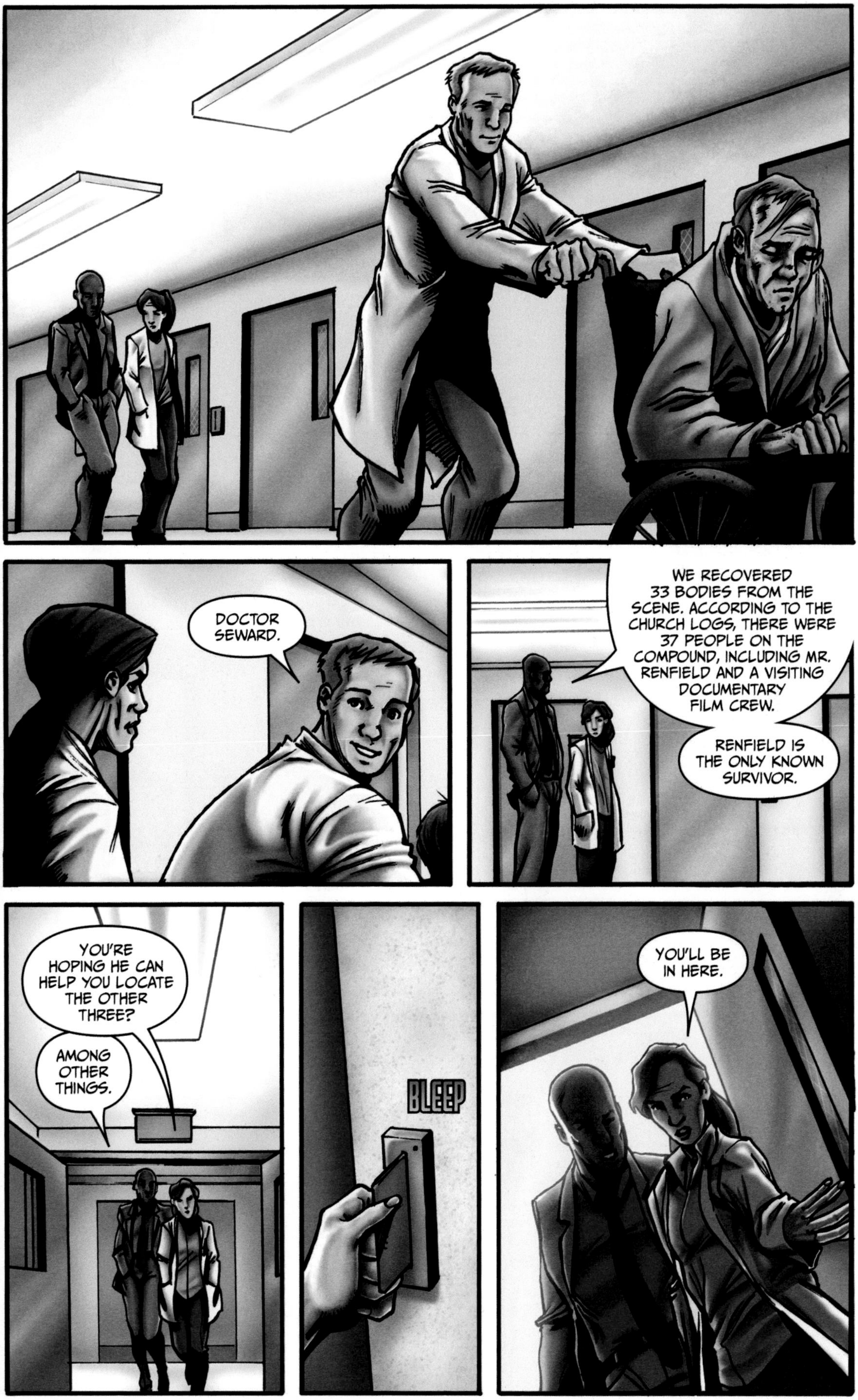
DOCTOR SEWARD.
WE RECOVERED 33 BODIES FROM THE SCENE. ACCORDING TO THE CHURCH LOGS, THERE WERE 37 PEOPLE ON THE COMPOUND, INCLUDING MR. RENFIELD AND A VISITING DOCUMENTARY FILM CREW.
RENFIELD IS THE ONLY KNOWN SURVIVOR.
YOU'RE HOPING HE CAN HELP YOU LOCATE THE OTHER THREE?
AMONG OTHER THINGS.
BLEEP
YOU'LL BE IN HERE.

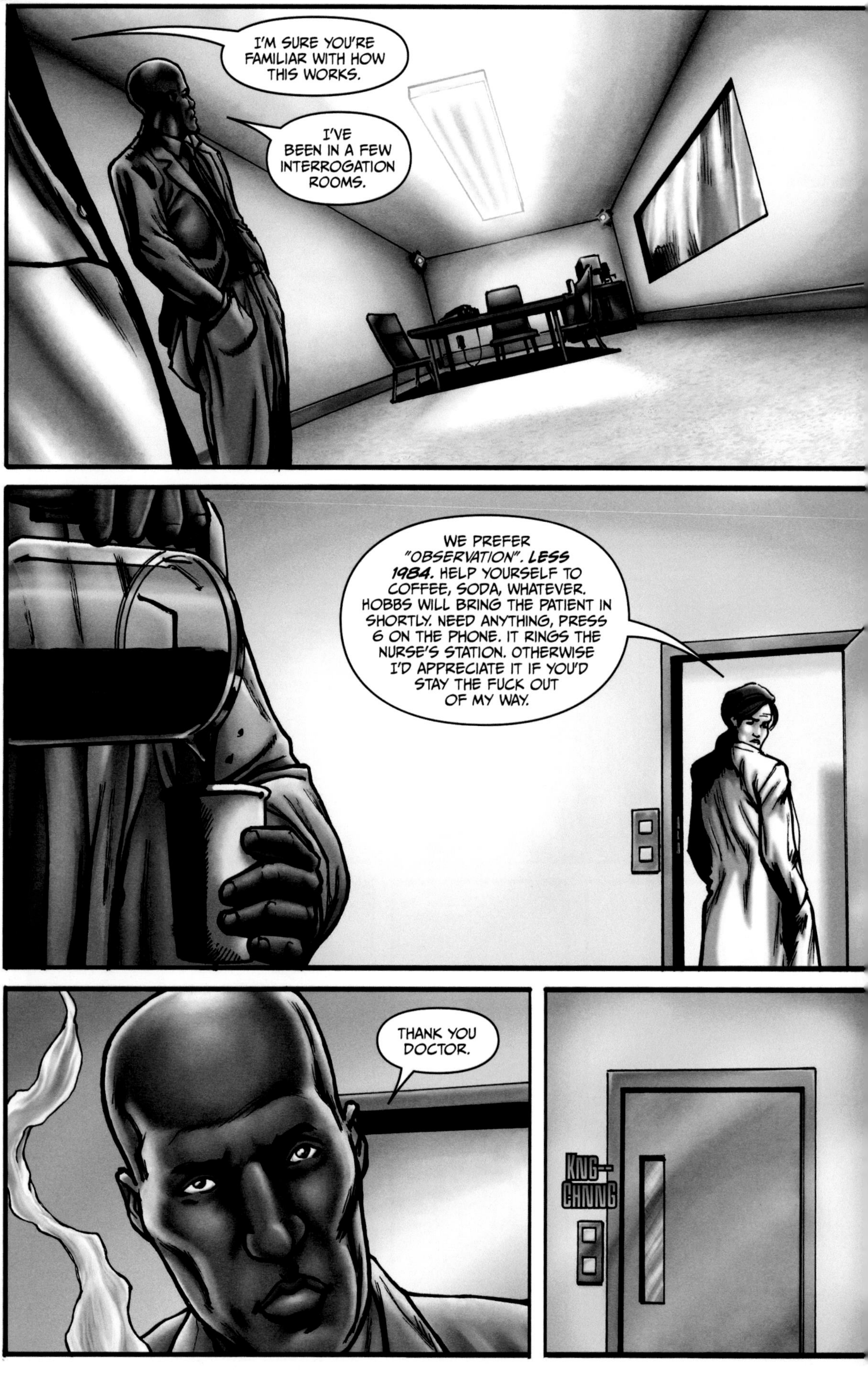
I'M SURE YOU'RE FAMILIAR WITH HOW THIS WORKS.
I'VE BEEN IN A FEW INTERROGATION ROOMS.
WE PREFER "OBSERVATION". LESS 1984. HELP YOURSELF TO COFFEE, SODA, WHATEVER. HOBBS WILL BRING THE PATIENT IN SHORTLY. NEED ANYTHING, PRESS 6 ON THE PHONE. IT RINGS THE NURSE'S STATION. OTHERWISE I'D APPRECIATE IT IF YOU'D STAY THE FUCK OUT OF MY WAY.
THANK YOU DOCTOR.
KNG-CHNNG

DO YOU HAVE A WILLING HEART?

YES.

DO YOU BELIEVE IN SHE WHO DIED AND WAS BURIED? SHE WHO CONQUERED DEATH AND ROSE FROM THE GRAVE?

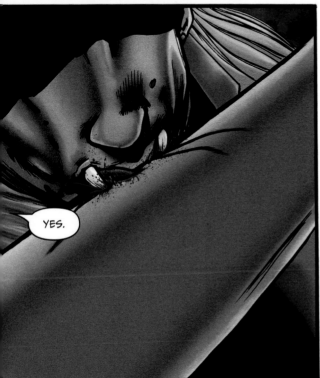

YES.

DO YOU BELIEVE IN THE POWER OF HER BLOOD TO GRANT LIFE EVERLASTING?

YES!!

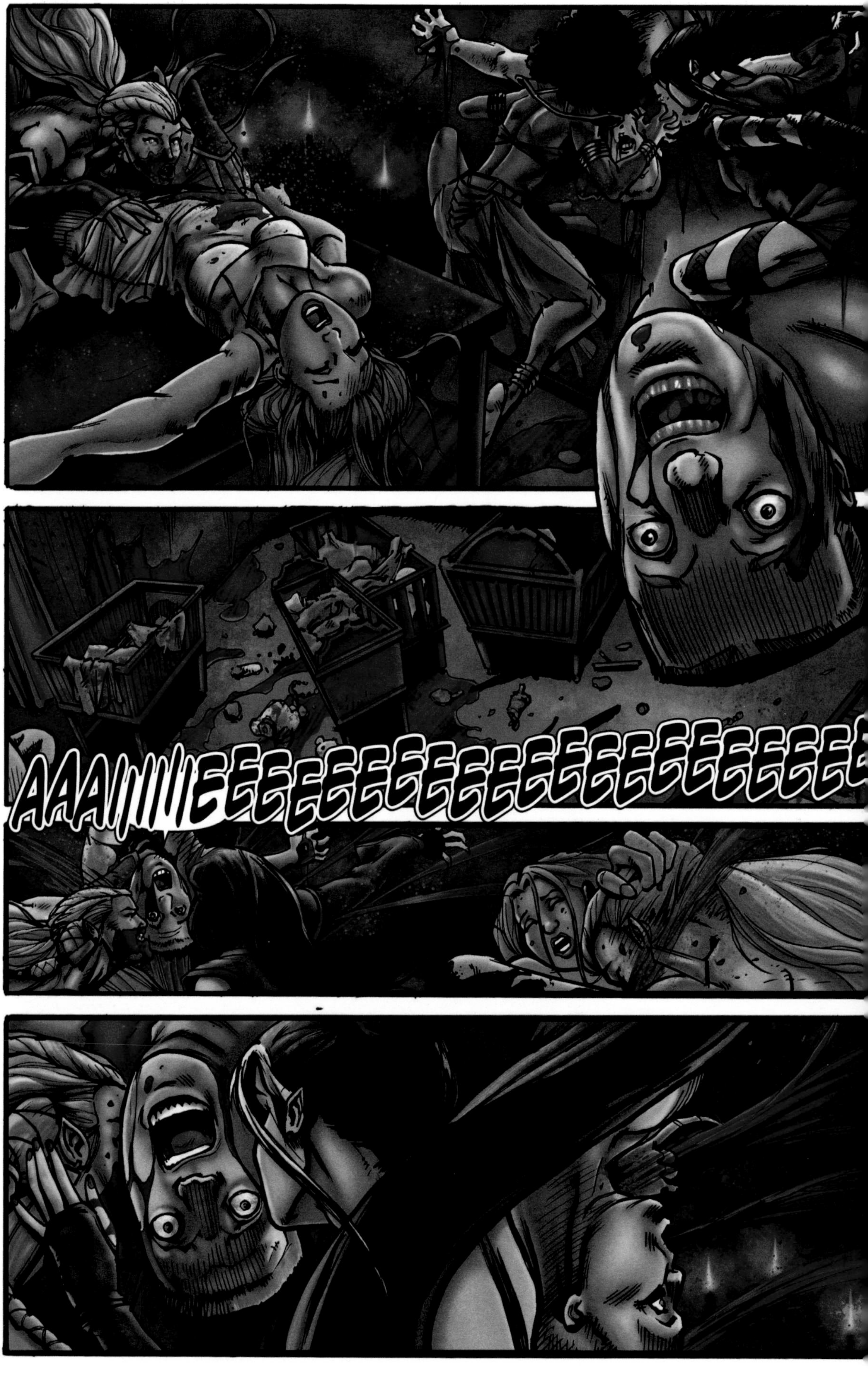
AAAIIIIIIEEEEEEEEEEEEEEEE

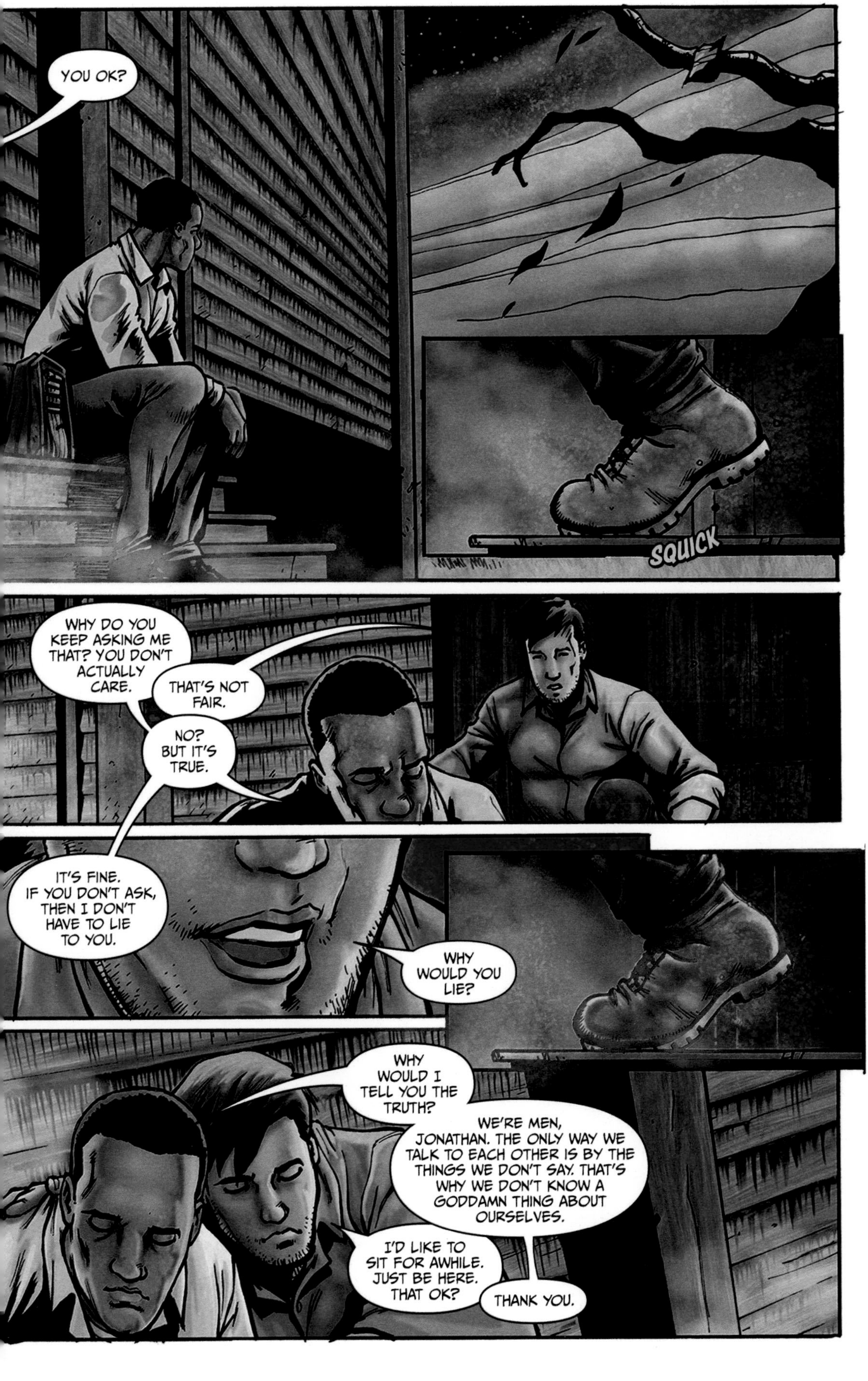

YOU OK?
SQUICK
WHY DO YOU KEEP ASKING ME THAT? YOU DON'T ACTUALLY CARE.
THAT'S NOT FAIR.
NO? BUT IT'S TRUE.
IT'S FINE. IF YOU DON'T ASK, THEN I DON'T HAVE TO LIE TO YOU.
WHY WOULD YOU LIE?
WHY WOULD I TELL YOU THE TRUTH?
WE'RE MEN, JONATHAN. THE ONLY WAY WE TALK TO EACH OTHER IS BY THE THINGS WE DON'T SAY. THAT'S WHY WE DON'T KNOW A GODDAMN THING ABOUT OURSELVES.
I'D LIKE TO SIT FOR AWHILE. JUST BE HERE. THAT OK?
THANK YOU.

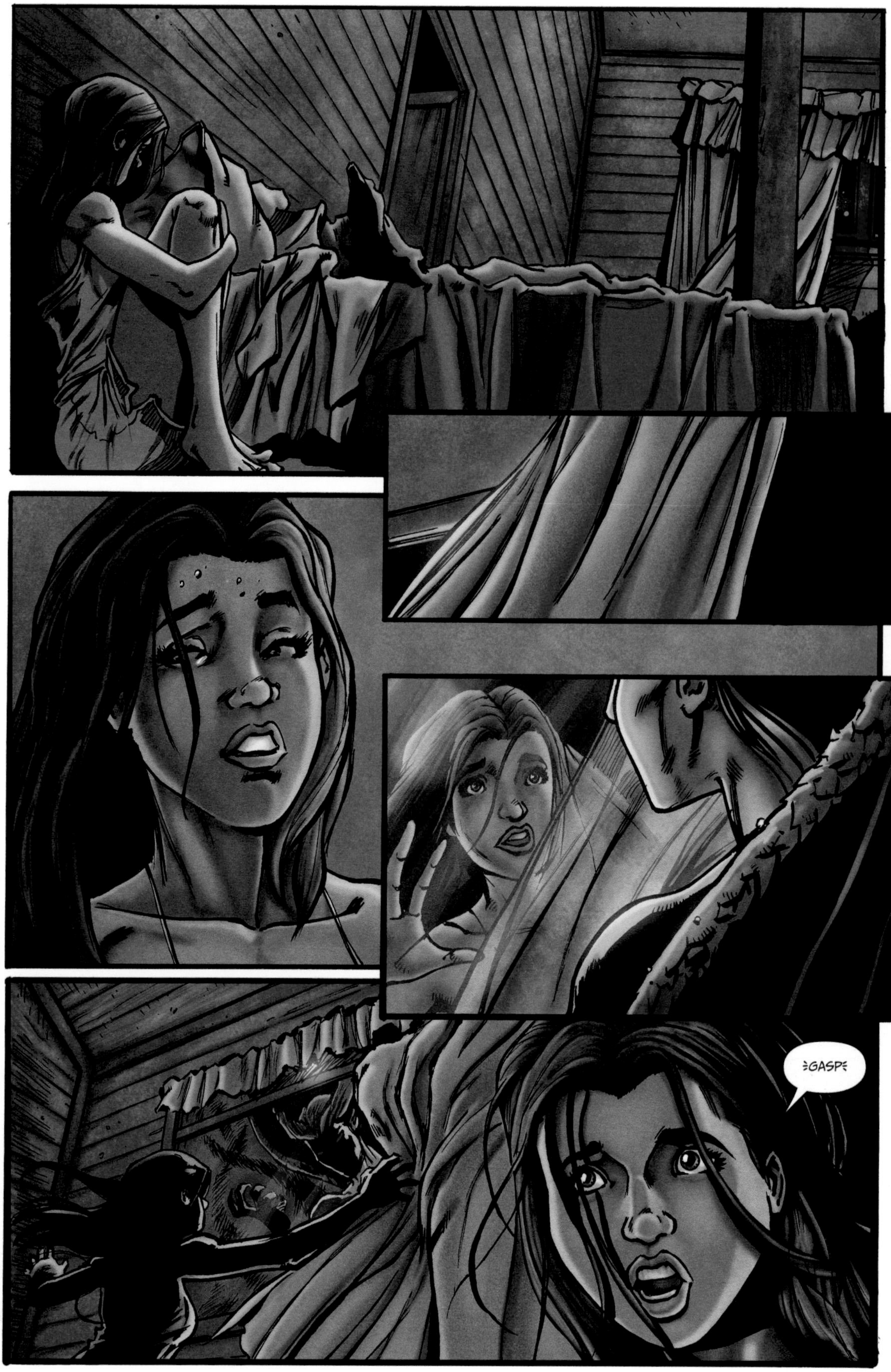
GASP

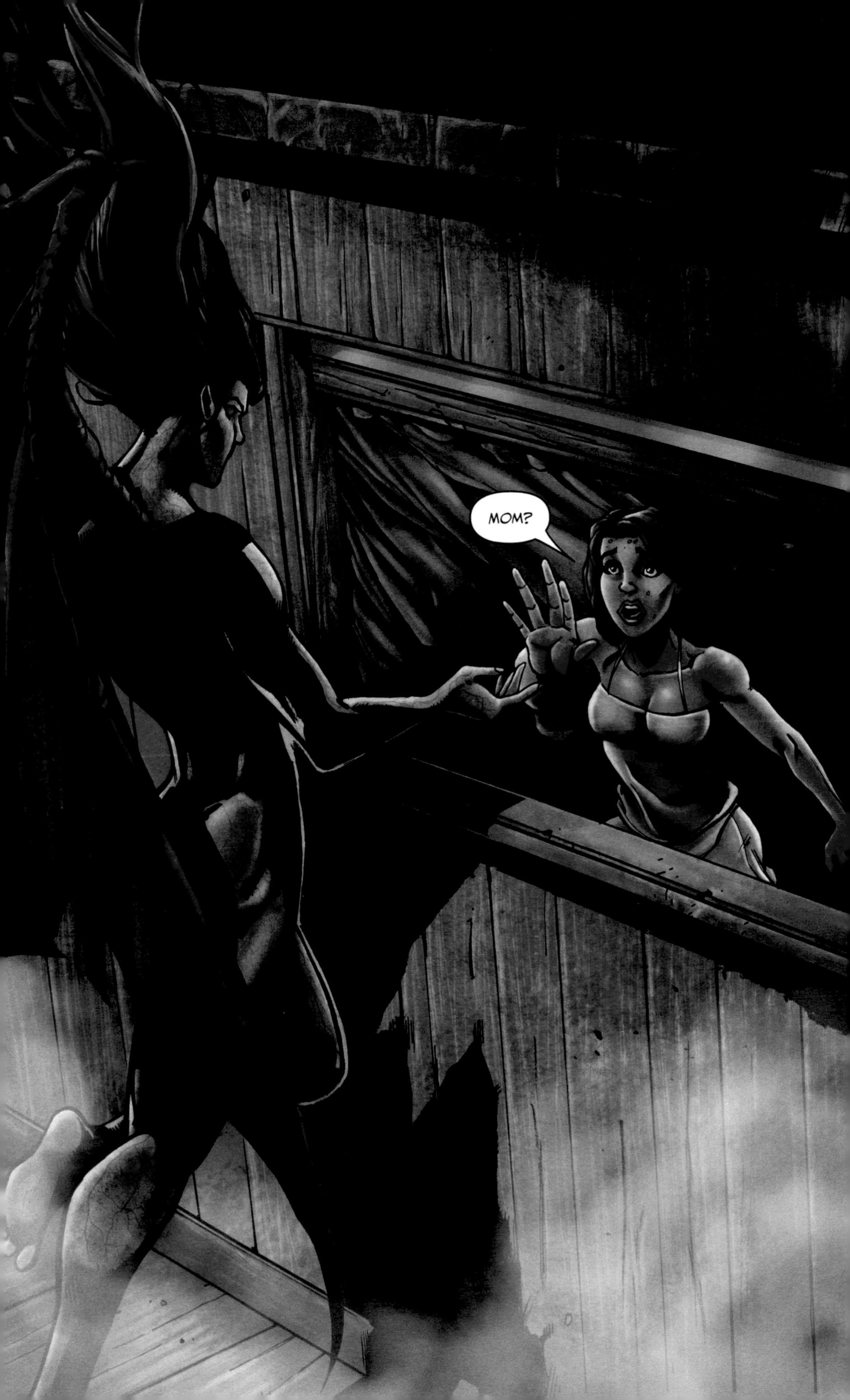
MOM?

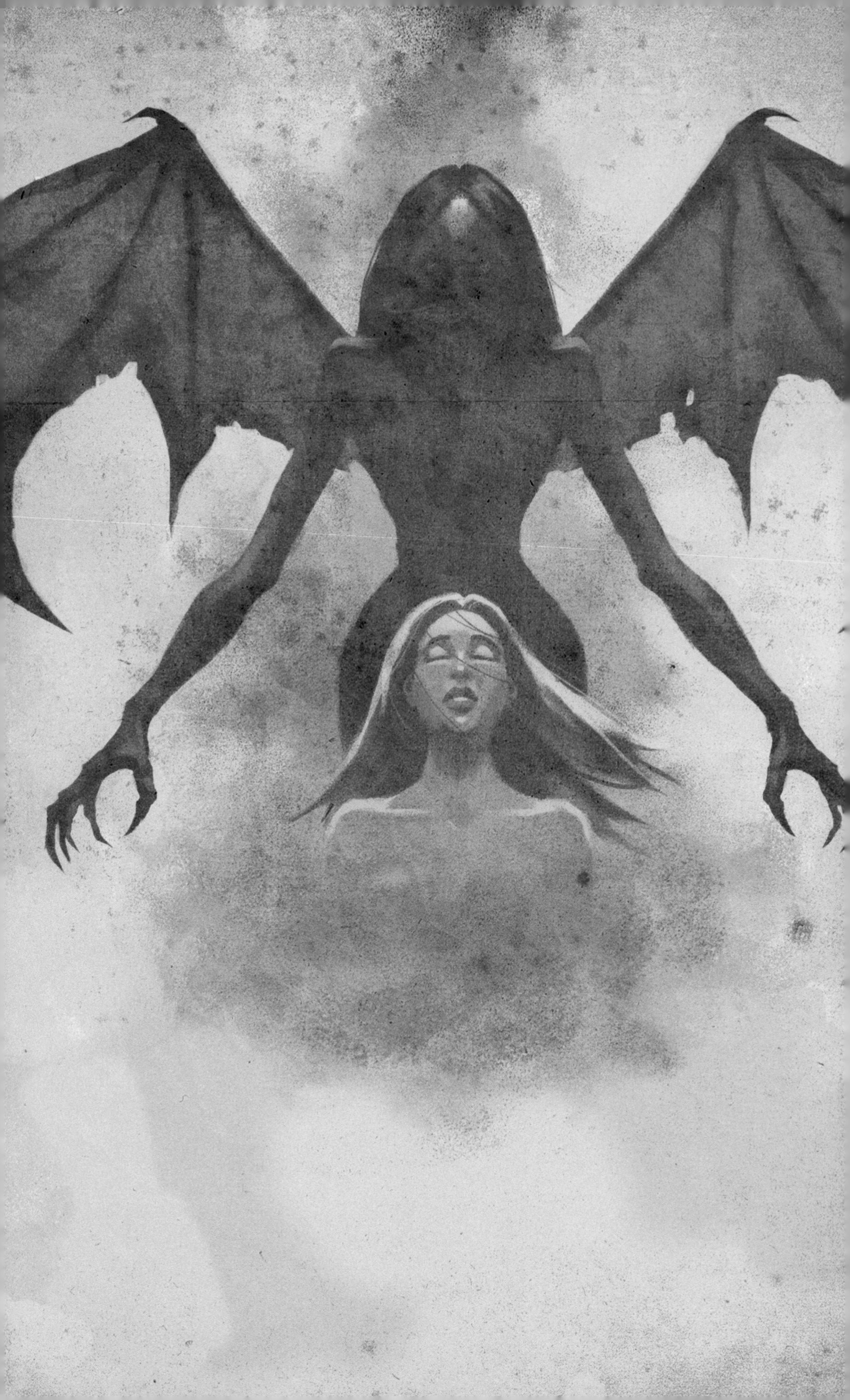

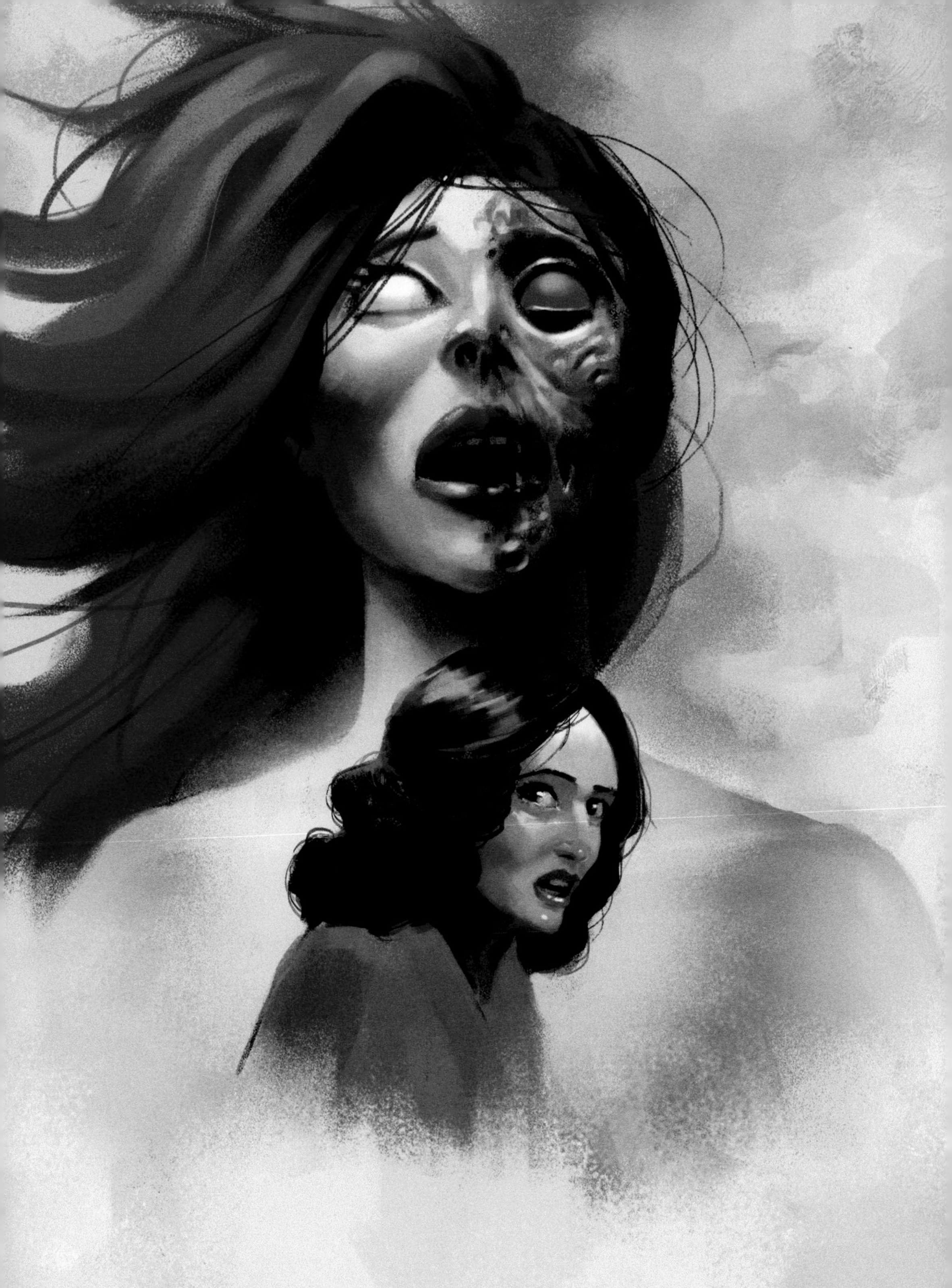

CHAPTER THREE

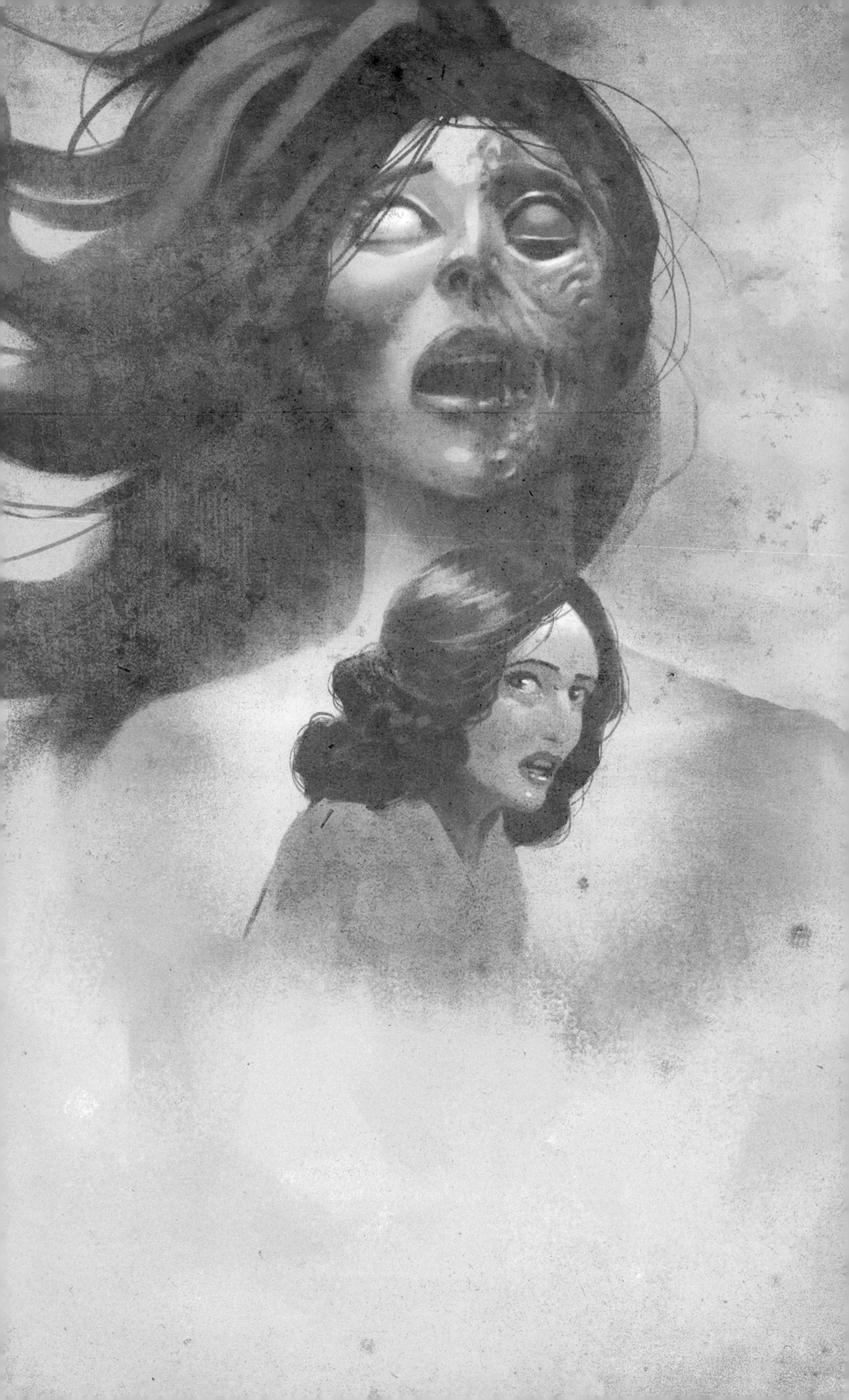

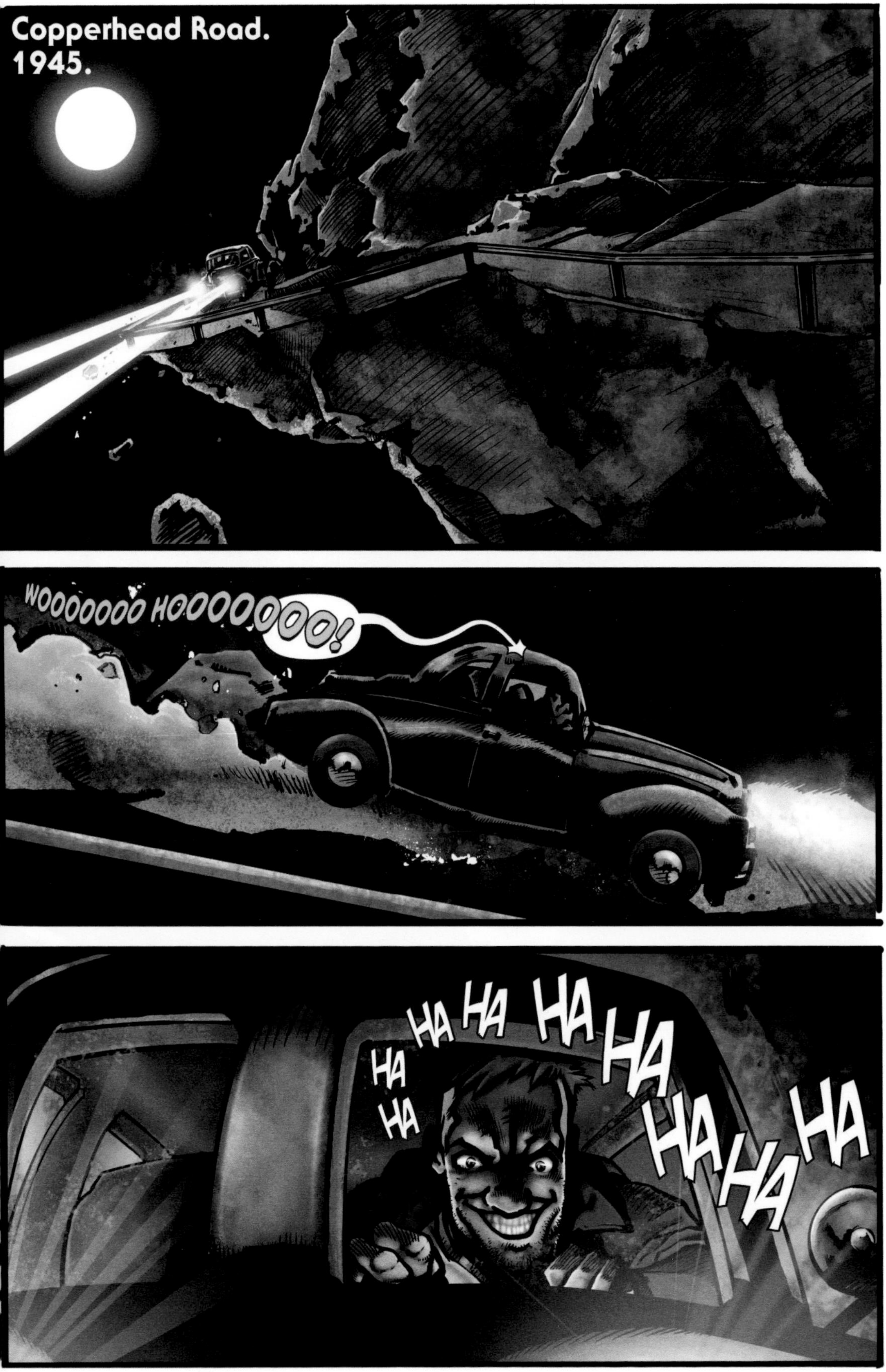
Copperhead Road.
1945.
WOOOOOOO HOOOOOOO!
HA HA HA HA HA HA HA HA HA

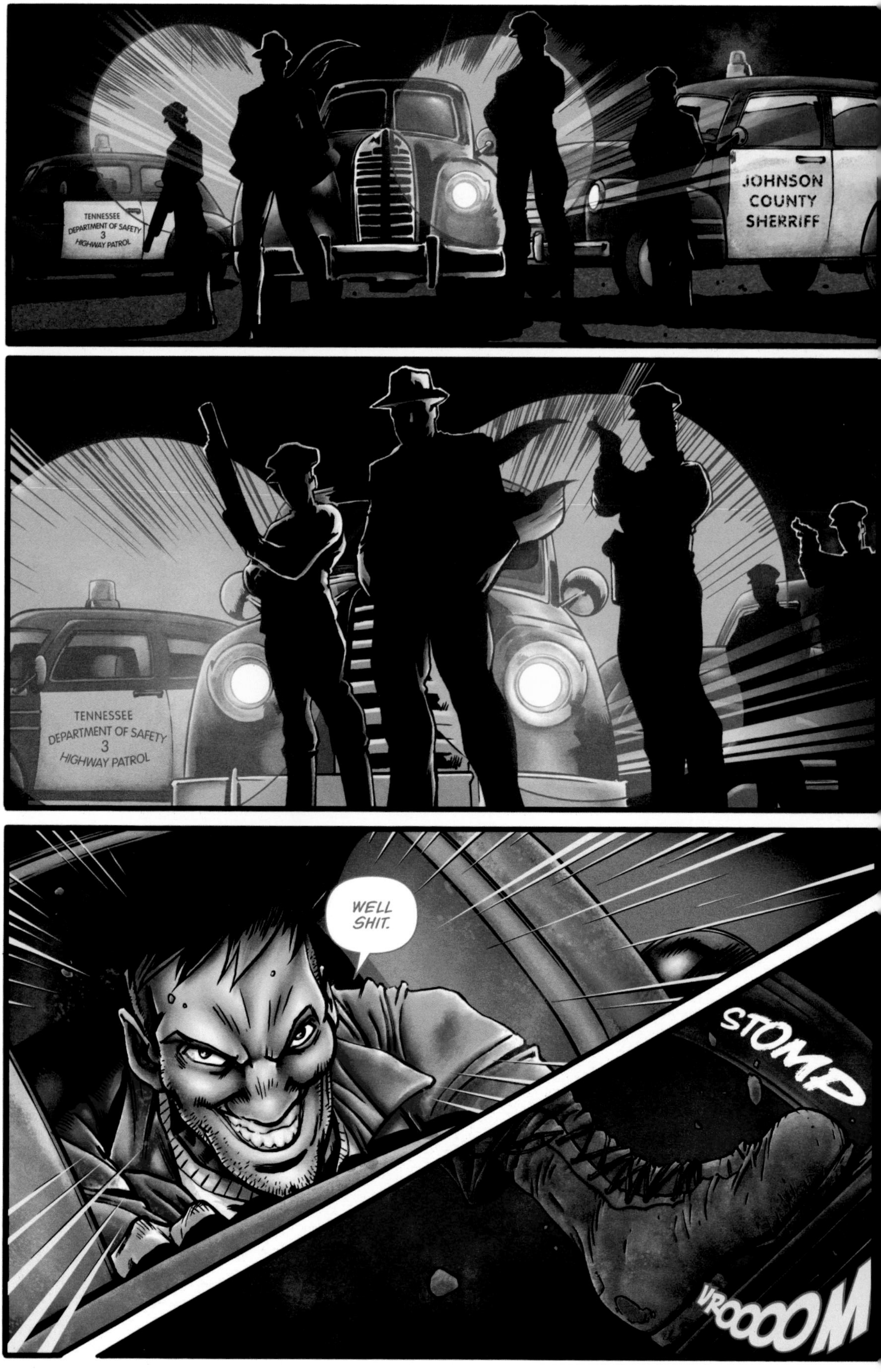
TENNESSEE DEPARTMENT OF SAFETY 3 HIGHWAY PATROL
JOHNSON COUNTY SHERRIFF
TENNESSEE DEPARTMENT OF SAFETY 3 HIGHWAY PATROL
WELL SHIT.
STOMP
VROOOOM

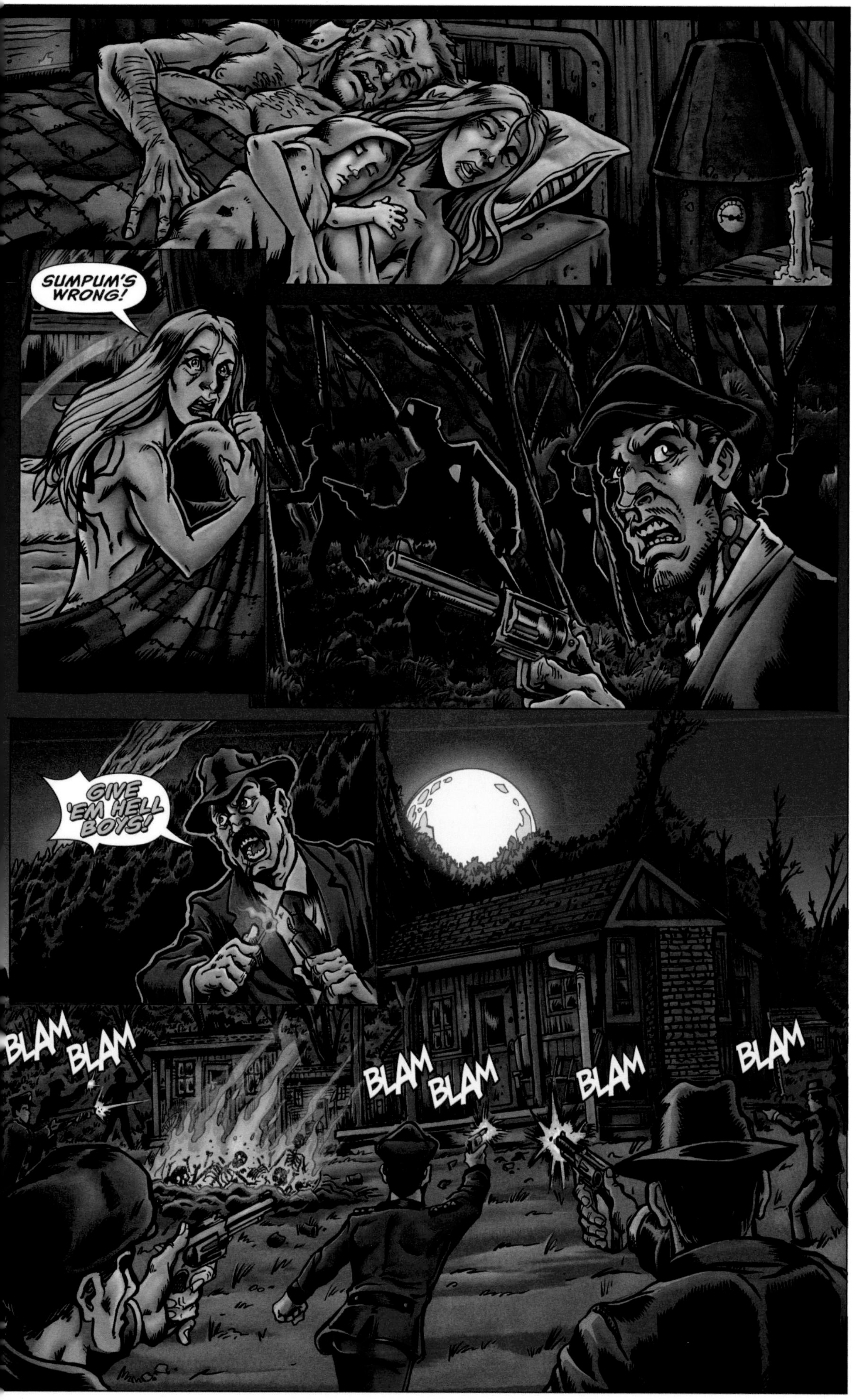
SUMPUM'S WRONG!
GIVE 'EM HELL BOYS!
BLAM
BLAM
BLAM
BLAM
BLAM
BLAM

BOOM

MÁTHAIR DRAC UL'A? CÉN FÁTH?*

*MOTHER DRACULA? WHY?
- SPOKEN IN THE HILL
FOLK DIALECT OF GAELIC.

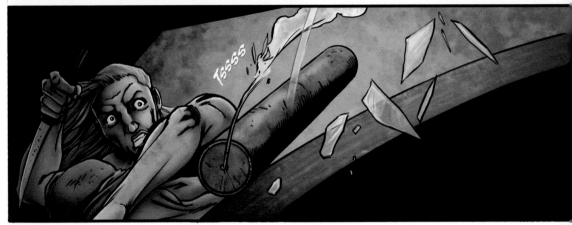

TSSSS

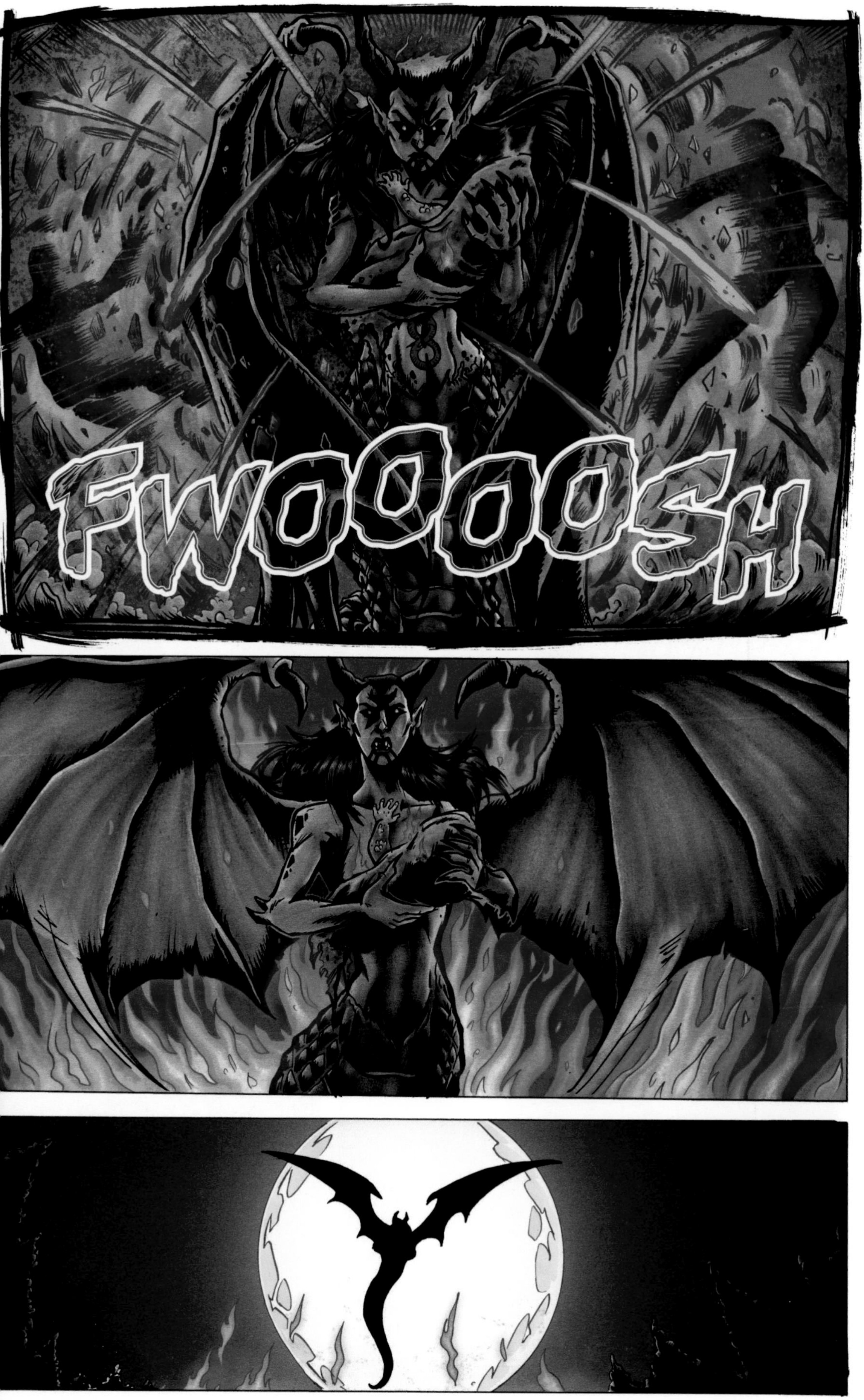
FWOOOOSH

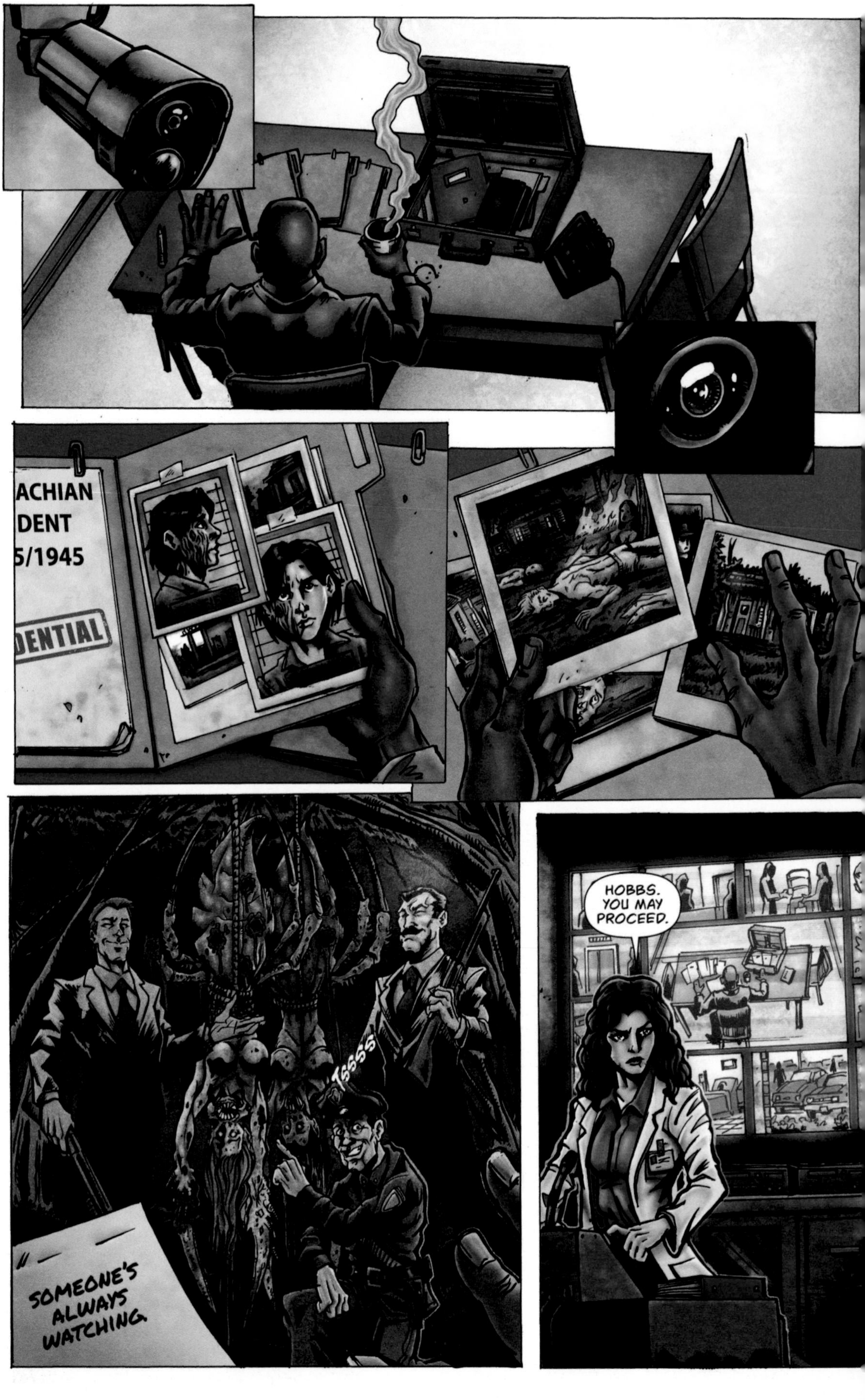
ACHIAN
DENT
5/1945
DENTIAL
HOBBS. YOU MAY PROCEED.
T5555
SOMEONE'S ALWAYS WATCHING.

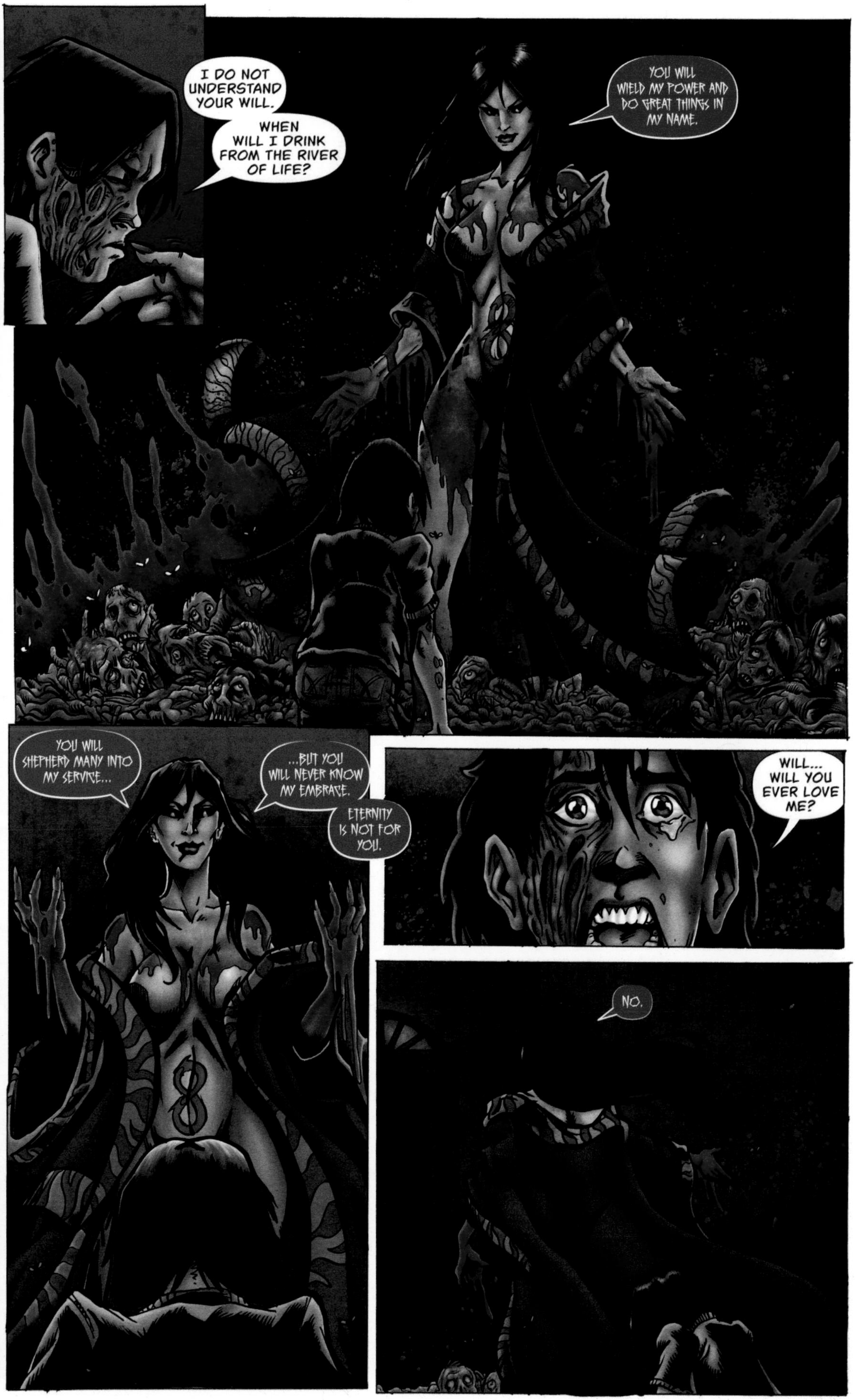
I DO NOT UNDERSTAND YOUR WILL.
WHEN WILL I DRINK FROM THE RIVER OF LIFE?
YOU WILL WIELD MY POWER AND DO GREAT THINGS IN MY NAME.
YOU WILL SHEPHERD MANY INTO MY SERVICE...
...BUT YOU WILL NEVER KNOW MY EMBRACE.
ETERNITY IS NOT FOR YOU.
WILL... WILL YOU EVER LOVE ME?
NO.

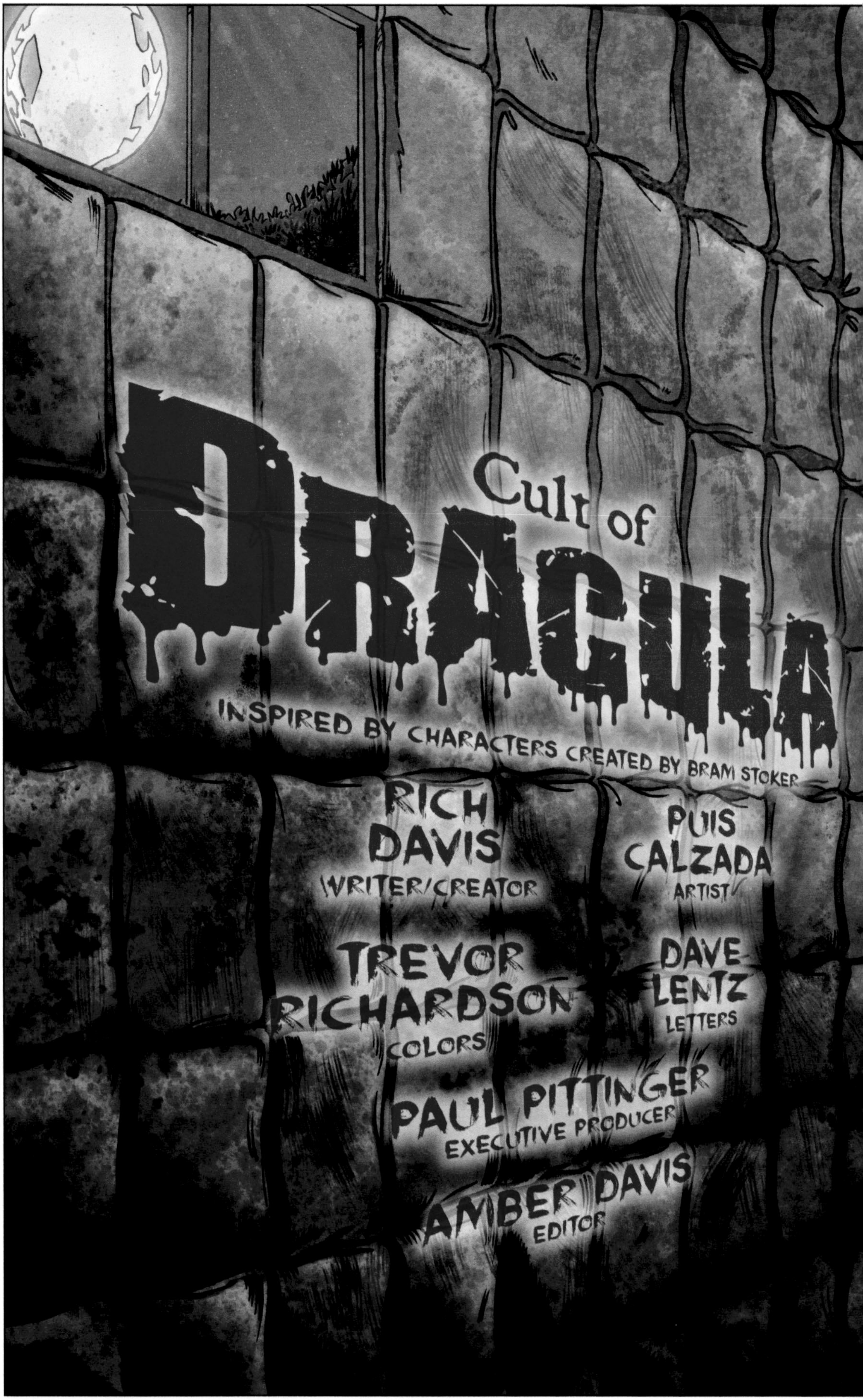
Cult of
DRACULA
INSPIRED BY CHARACTERS CREATED BY BRAM STOKER
RICH DAVIS
WRITER/CREATOR
PUIS CALZADA
ARTIST
TREVOR RICHARDSON
COLORS
DAVE LENTZ
LETTERS
PAUL PITTINGER
EXECUTIVE PRODUCER
AMBER DAVIS
EDITOR

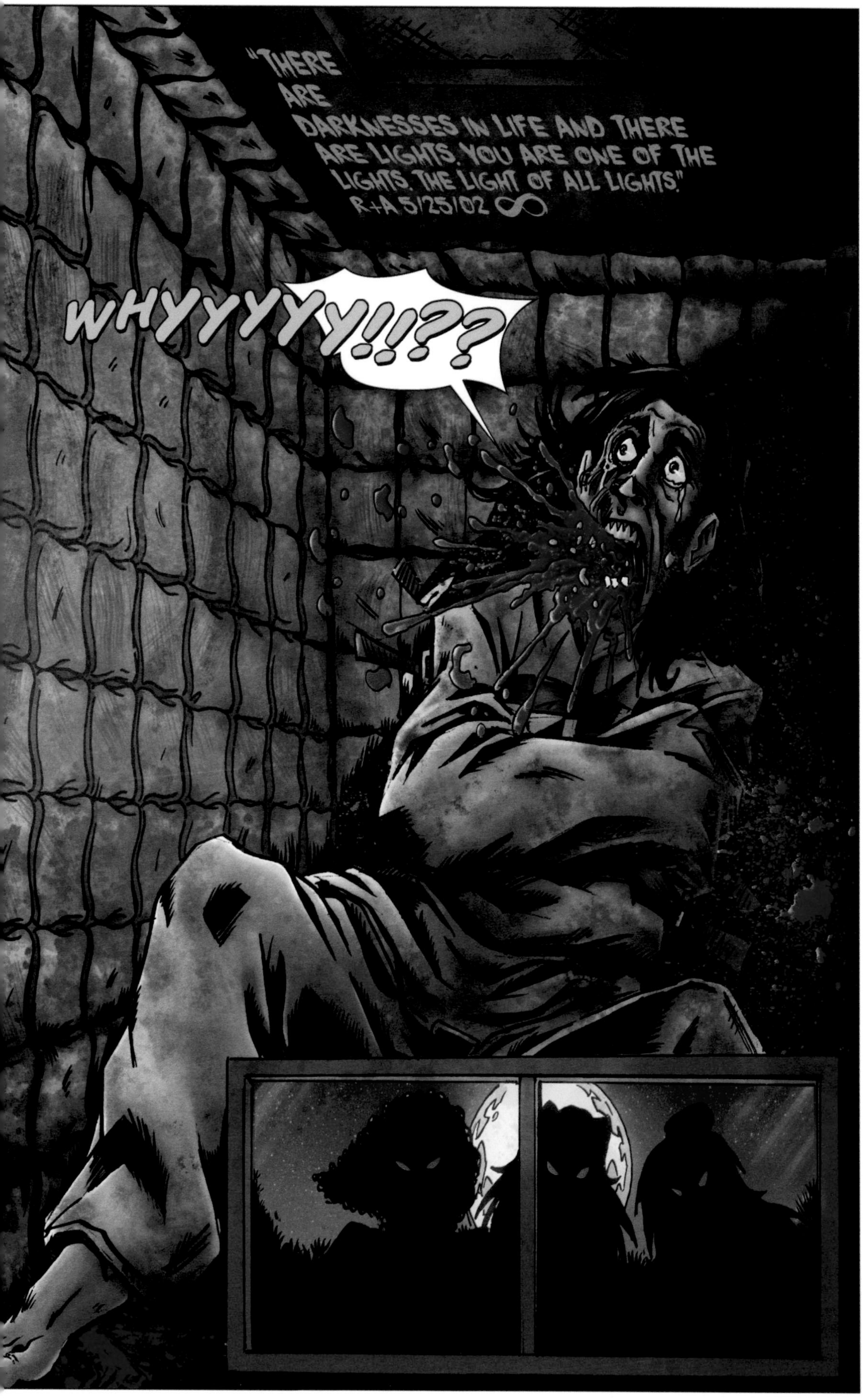
"THERE ARE DARKNESSES IN LIFE AND THERE ARE LIGHTS. YOU ARE ONE OF THE LIGHTS. THE LIGHT OF ALL LIGHTS."
R+A 5/25/02 ∞
WHYYYYYY!!!??

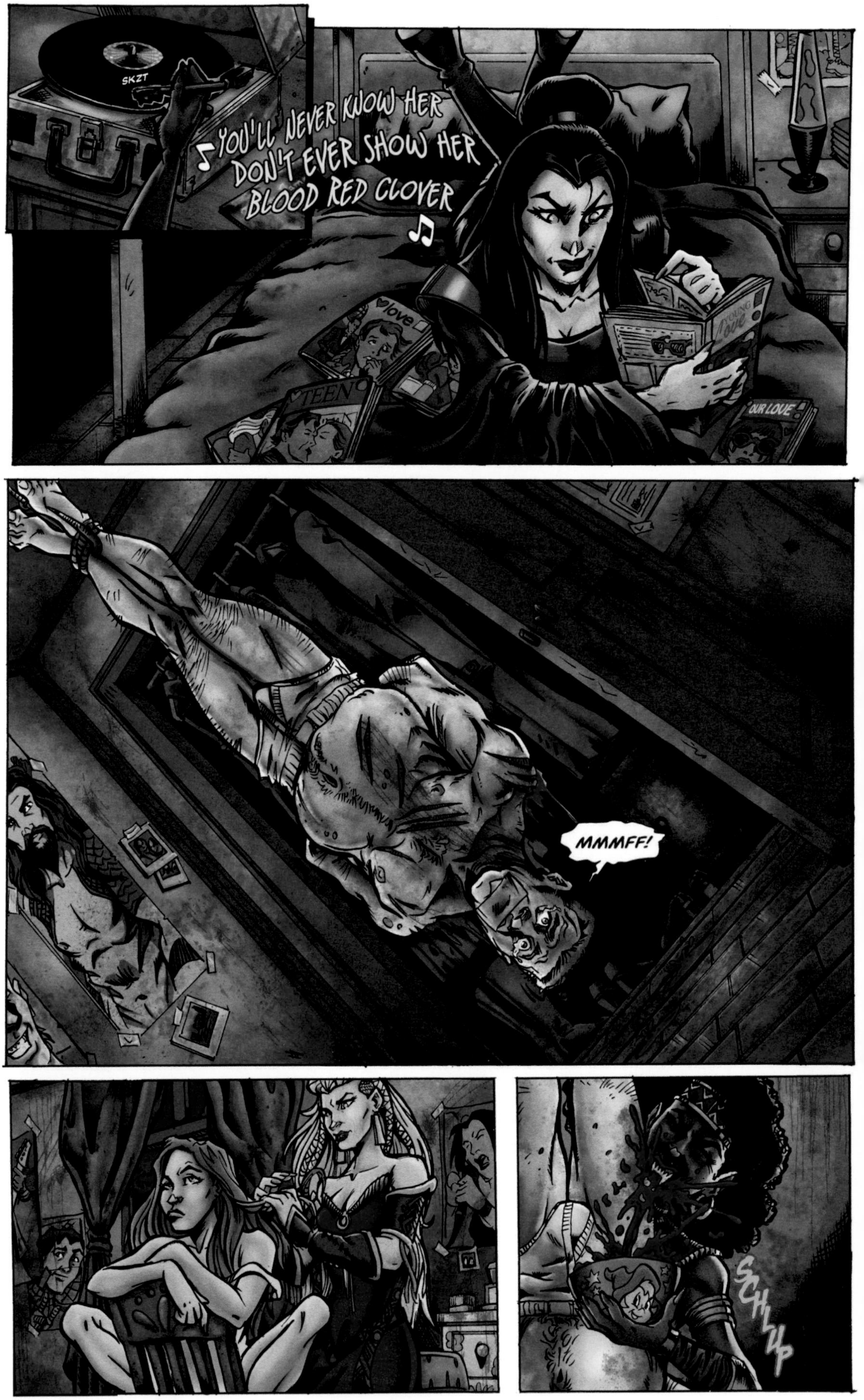
SKZT
YOU'LL NEVER KNOW HER
DON'T EVER SHOW HER
BLOOD RED CLOVER
love
TEEN
YOUNG Love
OUR LOVE
MMMFF!
SCHLUP

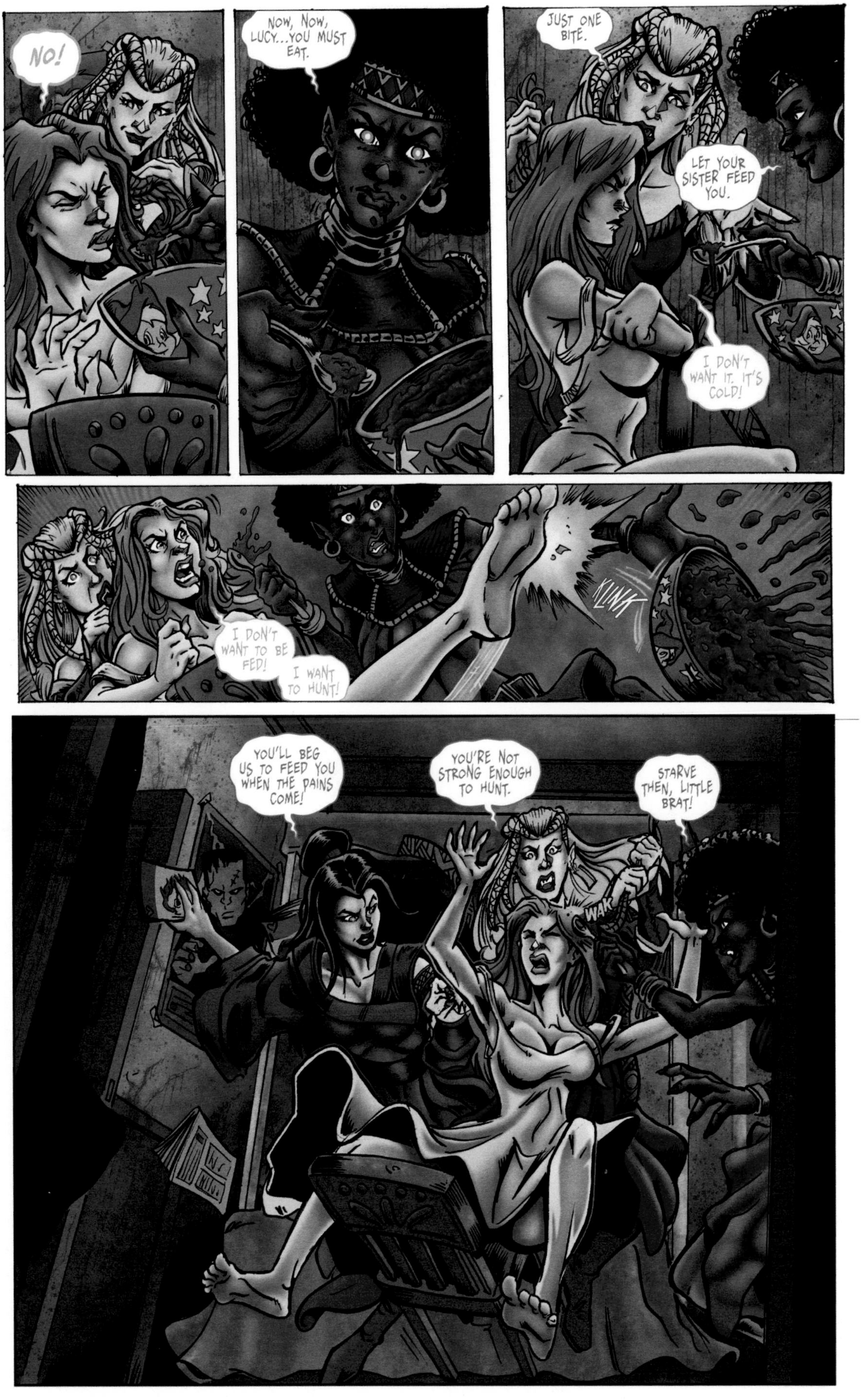
NO!
NOW, NOW, LUCY...YOU MUST EAT.
JUST ONE BITE.
LET YOUR SISTER FEED YOU.
I DON'T WANT IT. IT'S COLD!
I DON'T WANT TO BE FED!
I WANT TO HUNT!
KLINK
YOU'LL BEG US TO FEED YOU WHEN THE PAINS COME!
YOU'RE NOT STRONG ENOUGH TO HUNT.
STARVE THEN, LITTLE BRAT!
WAK

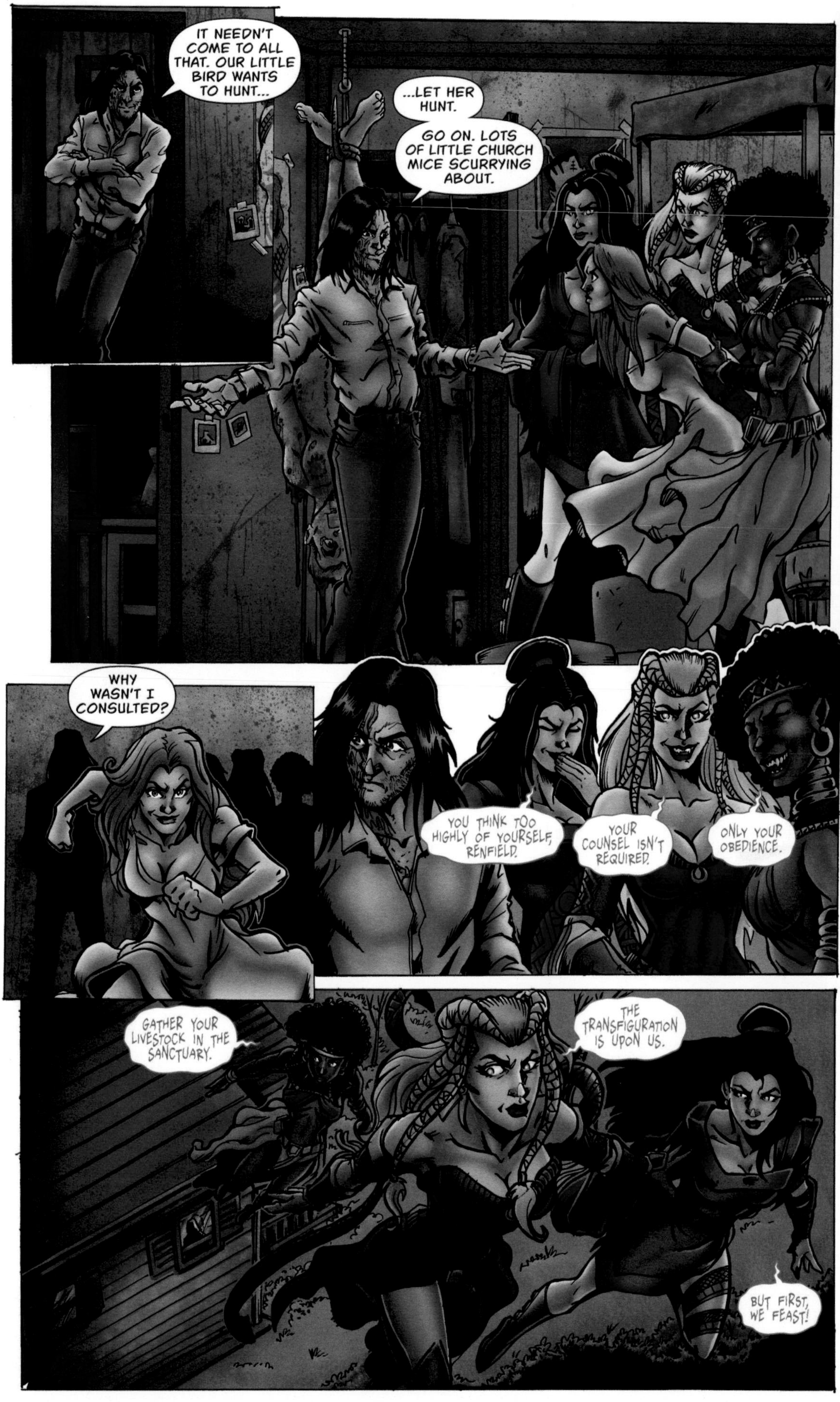
IT NEEDN'T COME TO ALL THAT. OUR LITTLE BIRD WANTS TO HUNT...
...LET HER HUNT.
GO ON. LOTS OF LITTLE CHURCH MICE SCURRYING ABOUT.
WHY WASN'T I CONSULTED?
YOU THINK TOO HIGHLY OF YOURSELF, RENFIELD.
YOUR COUNSEL ISN'T REQUIRED.
ONLY YOUR OBEDIENCE.
GATHER YOUR LIVESTOCK IN THE SANCTUARY.
THE TRANSFIGURATION IS UPON US.
BUT FIRST, WE FEAST!

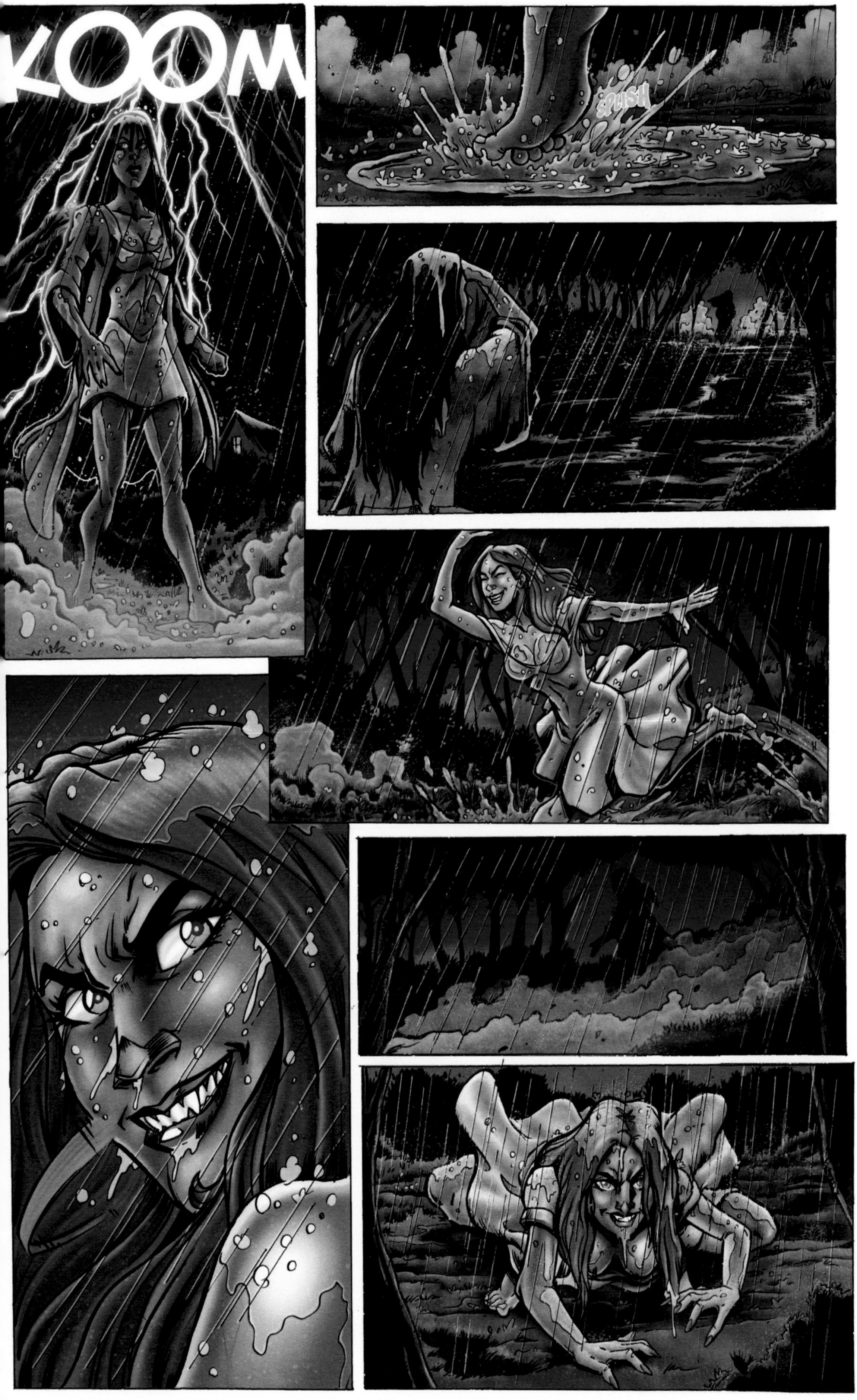
KOOM
SPLISH

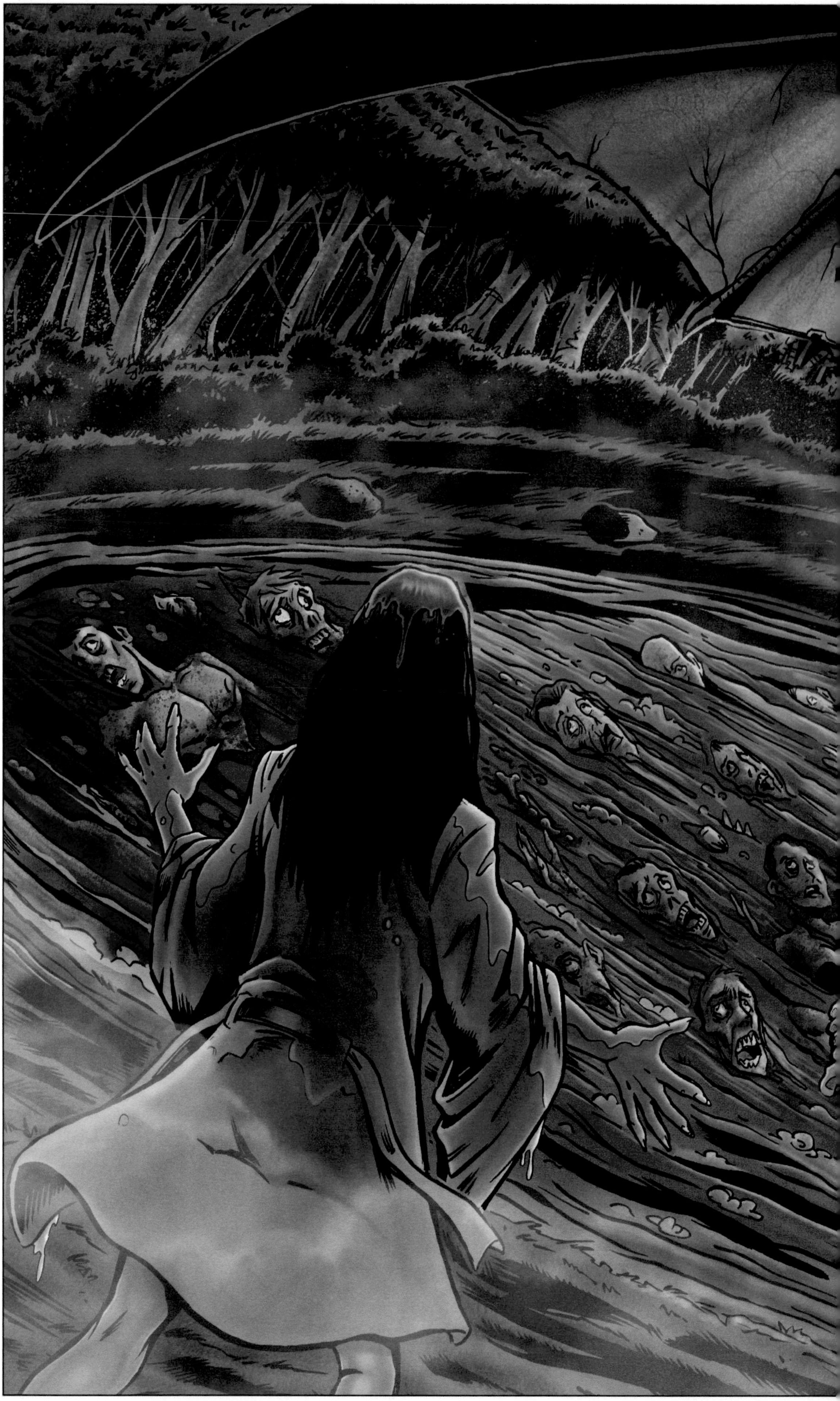

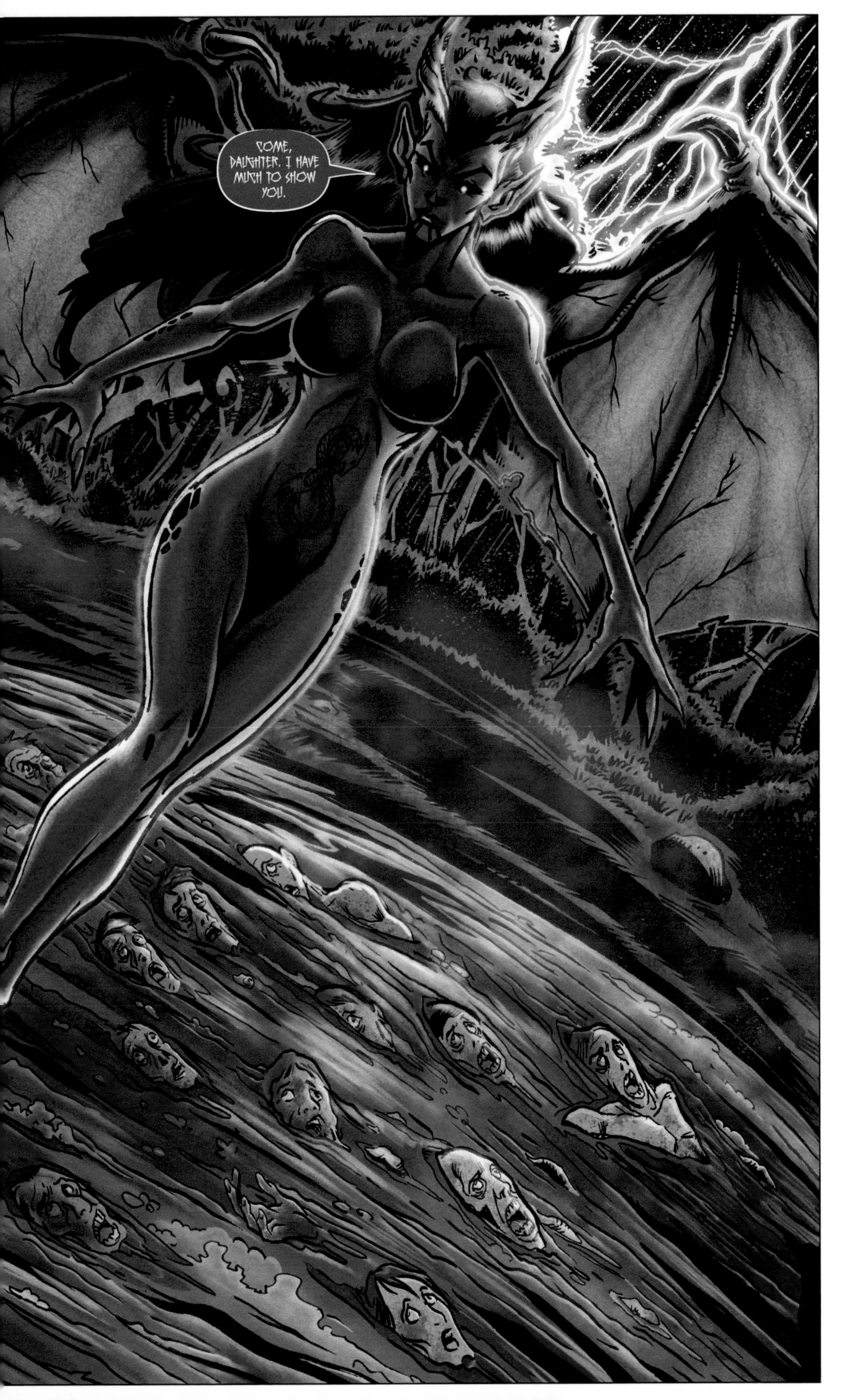
COME, DAUGHTER. I HAVE MUCH TO SHOW YOU.

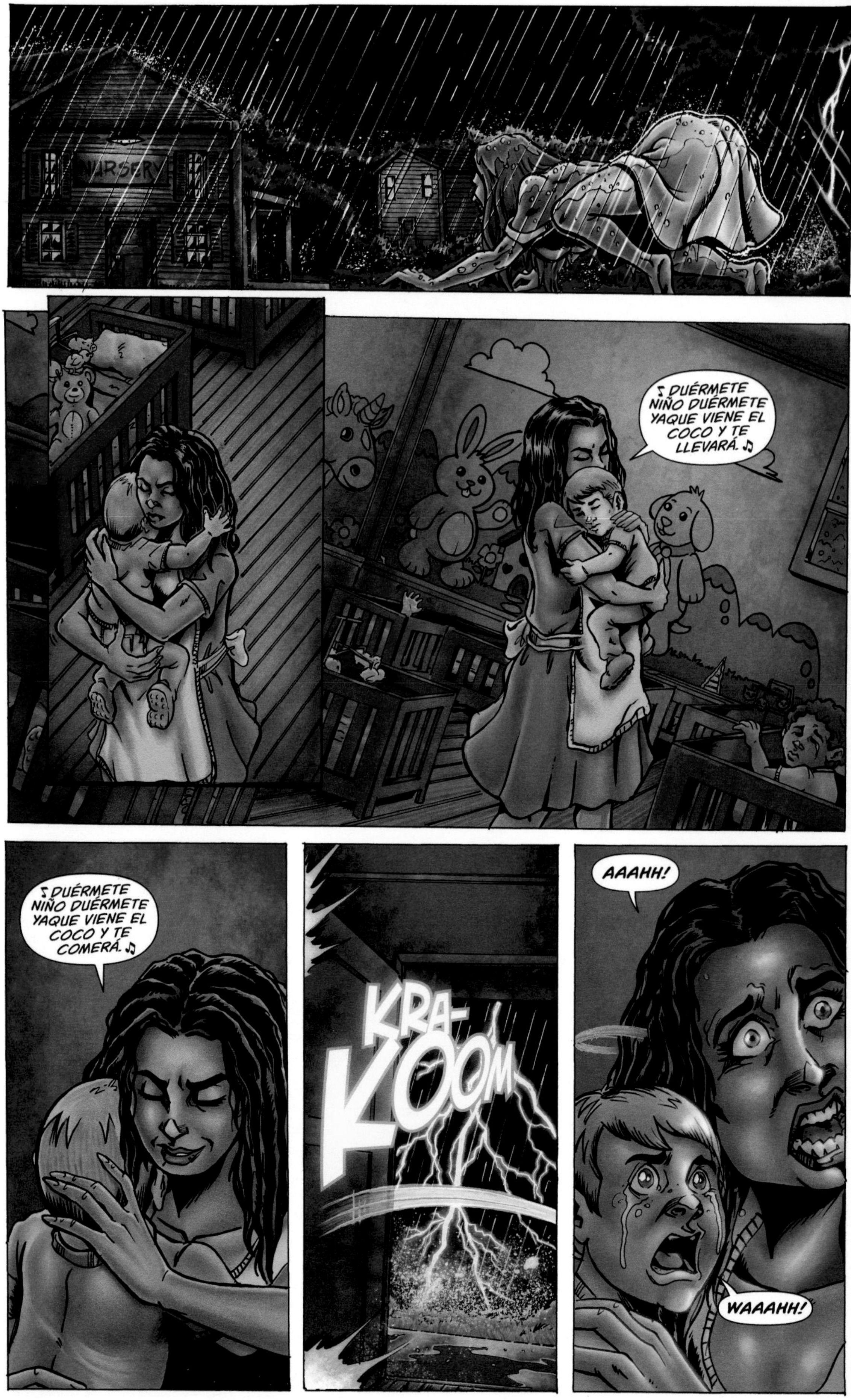
NURSERY
♪ DUÉRMETE NIÑO DUÉRMETE YAQUE VIENE EL COCO Y TE LLEVARÁ. ♫
♪ DUÉRMETE NIÑO DUÉRMETE YAQUE VIENE EL COCO Y TE COMERÁ. ♫
KRA-KOOM
AAAHH!
WAAAHH!

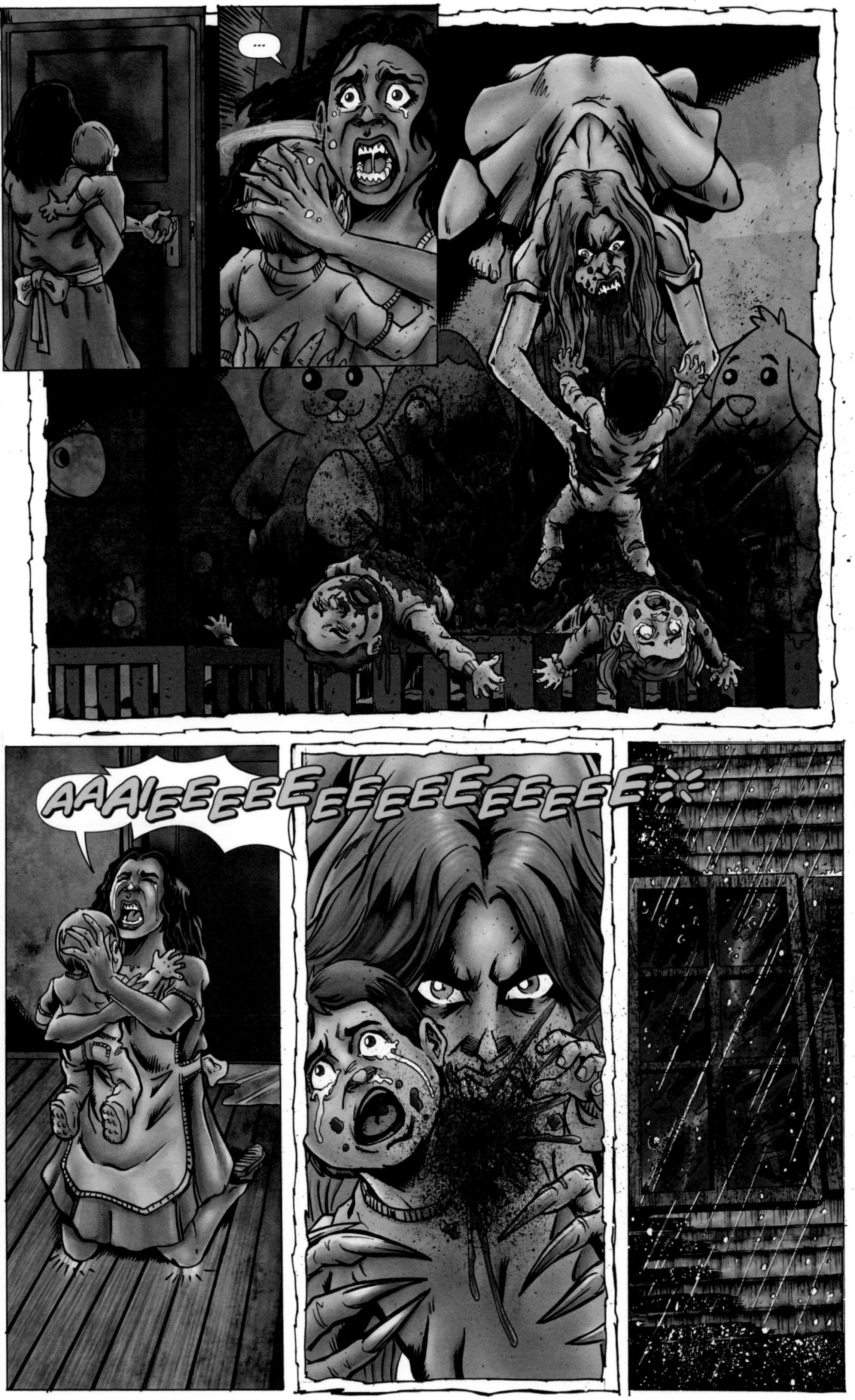
...
AAAIEEEEEEEEEEEEEEEEE--!!

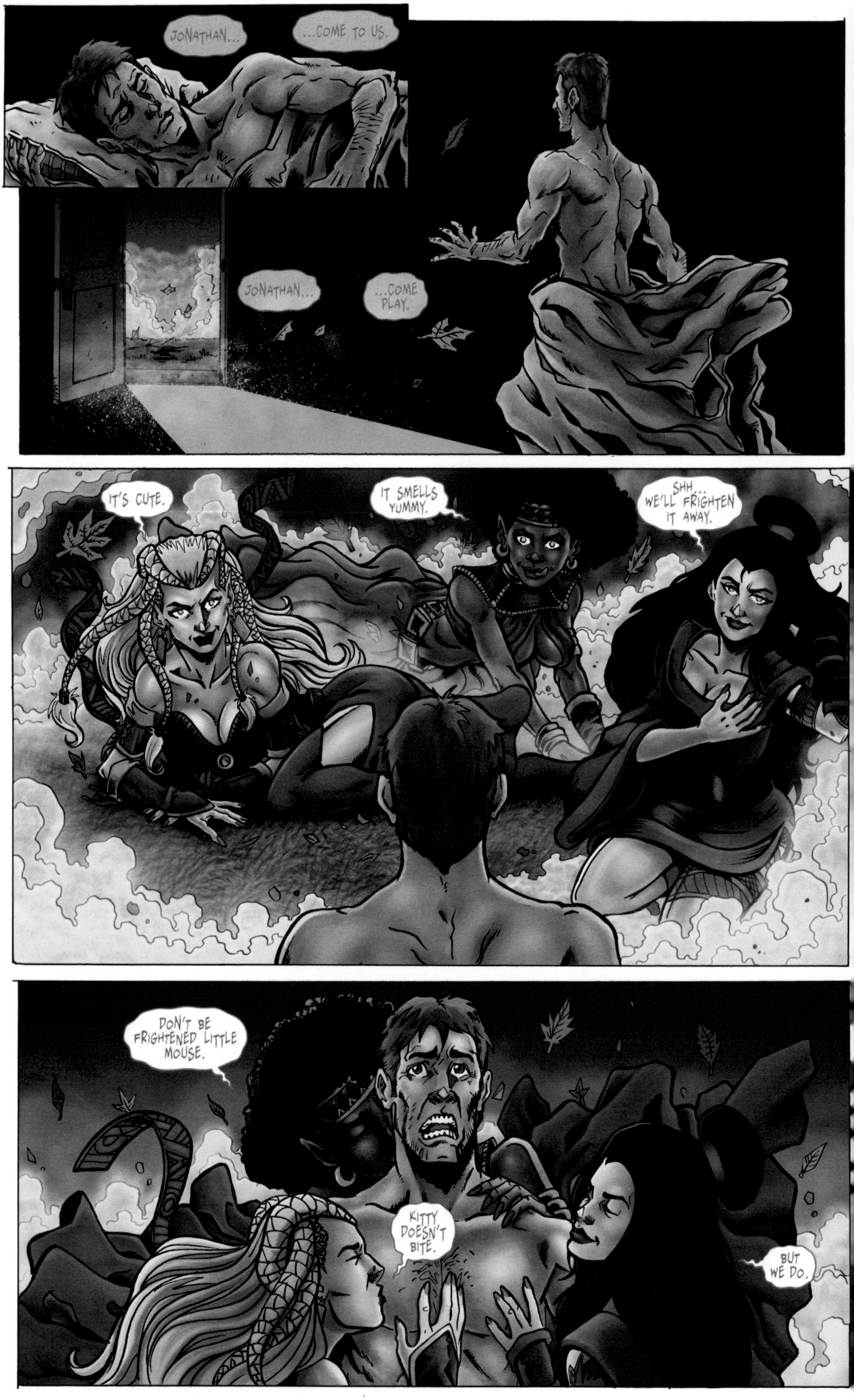
JONATHAN...
...COME TO US.
JONATHAN...
...COME PLAY.
IT'S CUTE.
IT SMELLS YUMMY.
SHH... WE'LL FRIGHTEN IT AWAY.
DON'T BE FRIGHTENED LITTLE MOUSE.
KITTY DOESN'T BITE.
BUT WE DO.

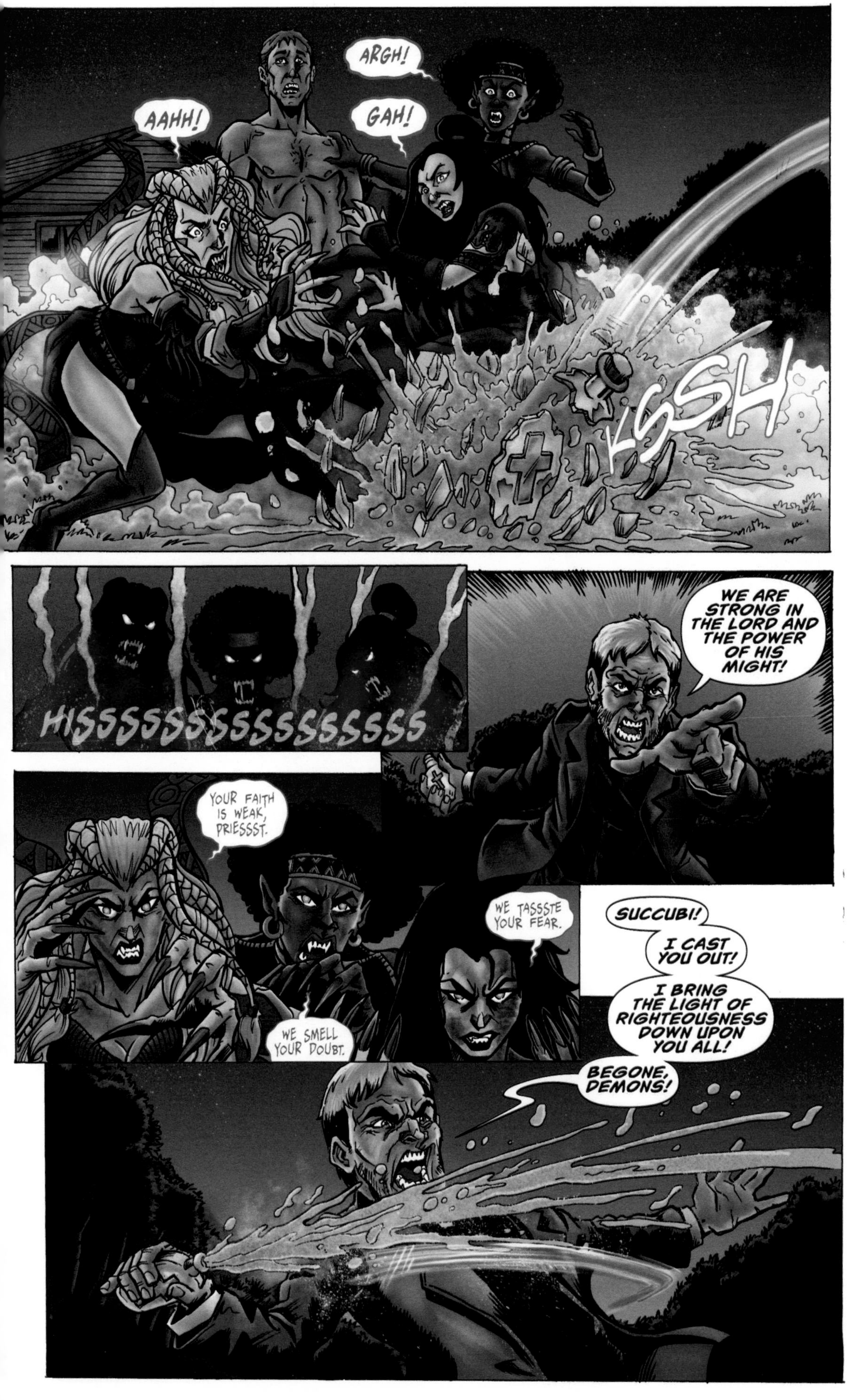
AAHH!
ARGH!
GAH!
KSSH
HISSSSSSSSSSSSSSSS
WE ARE STRONG IN THE LORD AND THE POWER OF HIS MIGHT!
YOUR FAITH IS WEAK, PRIESSST.
WE TASSSTE YOUR FEAR.
WE SMELL YOUR DOUBT.
SUCCUBI!
I CAST YOU OUT!
I BRING THE LIGHT OF RIGHTEOUSNESS DOWN UPON YOU ALL!
BEGONE, DEMONS!

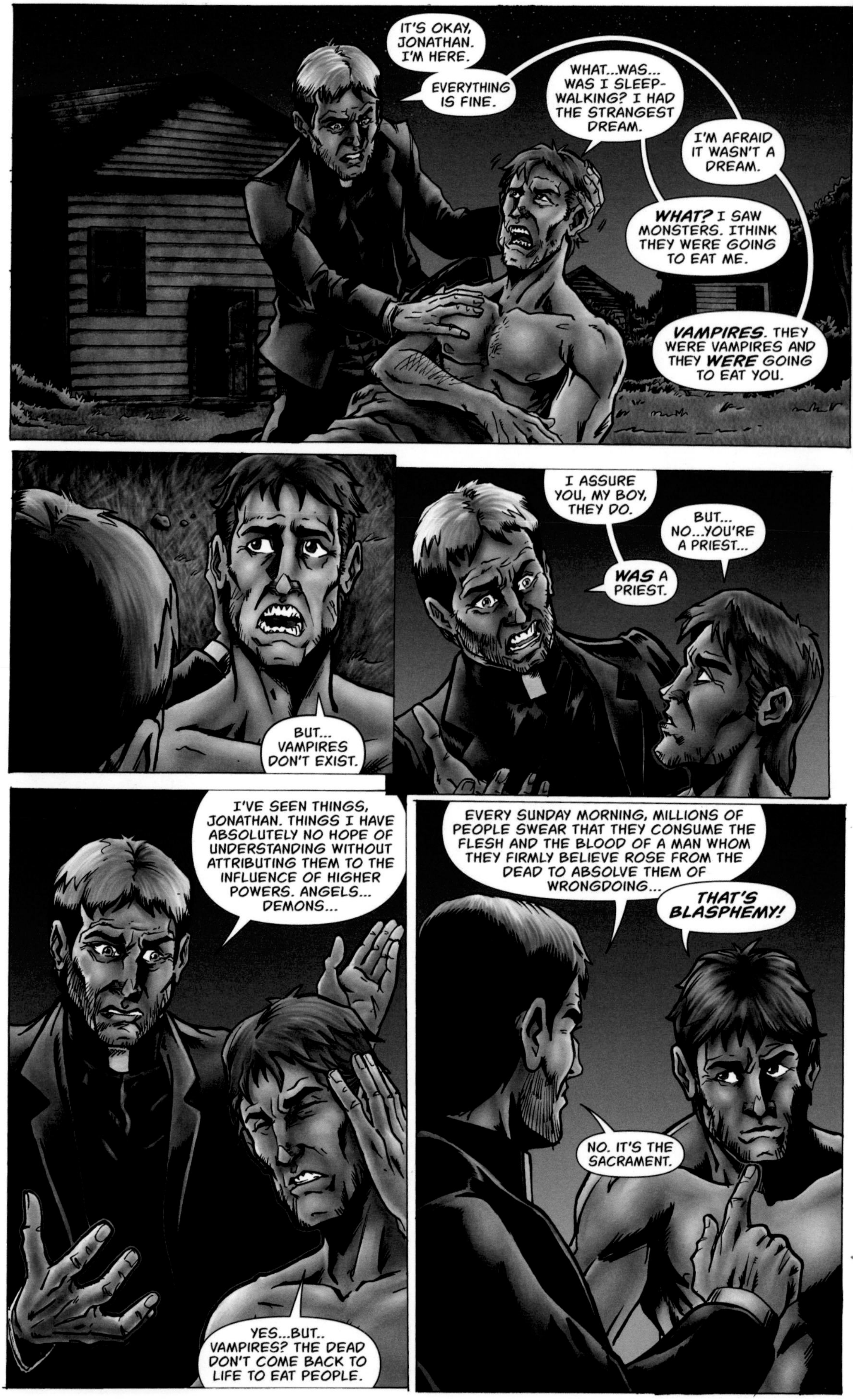
IT'S OKAY, JONATHAN. I'M HERE.
EVERYTHING IS FINE.
WHAT...WAS... WAS I SLEEP-WALKING? I HAD THE STRANGEST DREAM.
I'M AFRAID IT WASN'T A DREAM.
WHAT? I SAW MONSTERS. ITHINK THEY WERE GOING TO EAT ME.
VAMPIRES. THEY WERE VAMPIRES AND THEY WERE GOING TO EAT YOU.
BUT... VAMPIRES DON'T EXIST.
I ASSURE YOU, MY BOY, THEY DO.
BUT... NO...YOU'RE A PRIEST...
WAS A PRIEST.
I'VE SEEN THINGS, JONATHAN. THINGS I HAVE ABSOLUTELY NO HOPE OF UNDERSTANDING WITHOUT ATTRIBUTING THEM TO THE INFLUENCE OF HIGHER POWERS. ANGELS... DEMONS...
YES...BUT.. VAMPIRES? THE DEAD DON'T COME BACK TO LIFE TO EAT PEOPLE.
EVERY SUNDAY MORNING, MILLIONS OF PEOPLE SWEAR THAT THEY CONSUME THE FLESH AND THE BLOOD OF A MAN WHOM THEY FIRMLY BELIEVE ROSE FROM THE DEAD TO ABSOLVE THEM OF WRONGDOING...
THAT'S BLASPHEMY!
NO. IT'S THE SACRAMENT.

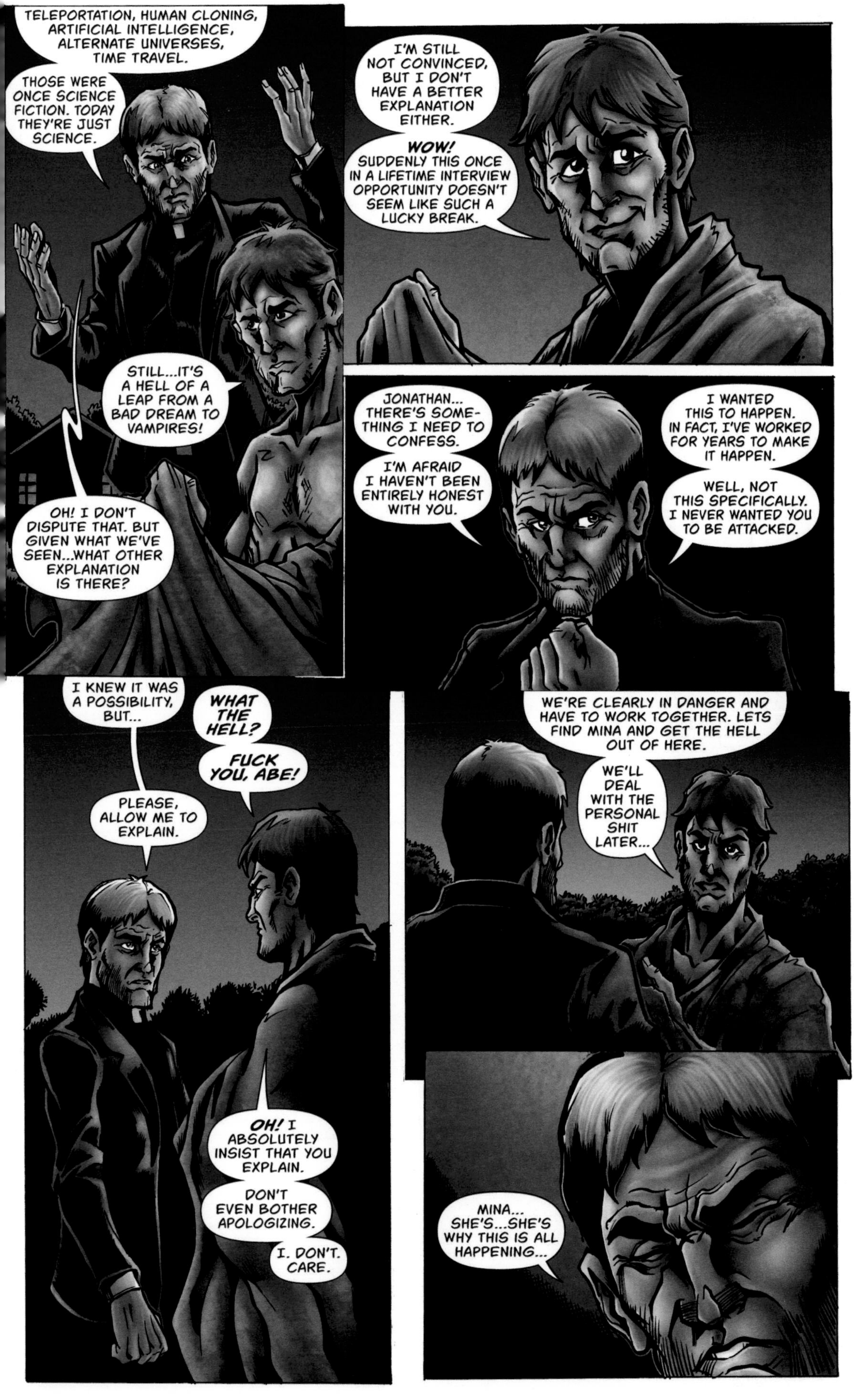
TELEPORTATION, HUMAN CLONING, ARTIFICIAL INTELLIGENCE, ALTERNATE UNIVERSES, TIME TRAVEL.
THOSE WERE ONCE SCIENCE FICTION. TODAY THEY'RE JUST SCIENCE.
STILL...IT'S A HELL OF A LEAP FROM A BAD DREAM TO VAMPIRES!
OH! I DON'T DISPUTE THAT. BUT GIVEN WHAT WE'VE SEEN...WHAT OTHER EXPLANATION IS THERE?
I'M STILL NOT CONVINCED, BUT I DON'T HAVE A BETTER EXPLANATION EITHER.
WOW! SUDDENLY THIS ONCE IN A LIFETIME INTERVIEW OPPORTUNITY DOESN'T SEEM LIKE SUCH A LUCKY BREAK.
JONATHAN... THERE'S SOMETHING I NEED TO CONFESS.
I'M AFRAID I HAVEN'T BEEN ENTIRELY HONEST WITH YOU.
I WANTED THIS TO HAPPEN. IN FACT, I'VE WORKED FOR YEARS TO MAKE IT HAPPEN.
WELL, NOT THIS SPECIFICALLY. I NEVER WANTED YOU TO BE ATTACKED.
I KNEW IT WAS A POSSIBILITY, BUT...
WHAT THE HELL?
FUCK YOU, ABE!
PLEASE, ALLOW ME TO EXPLAIN.
OH! I ABSOLUTELY INSIST THAT YOU EXPLAIN.
DON'T EVEN BOTHER APOLOGIZING.
I. DON'T. CARE.
WE'RE CLEARLY IN DANGER AND HAVE TO WORK TOGETHER. LETS FIND MINA AND GET THE HELL OUT OF HERE.
WE'LL DEAL WITH THE PERSONAL SHIT LATER...
MINA... SHE'S...SHE'S WHY THIS IS ALL HAPPENING...

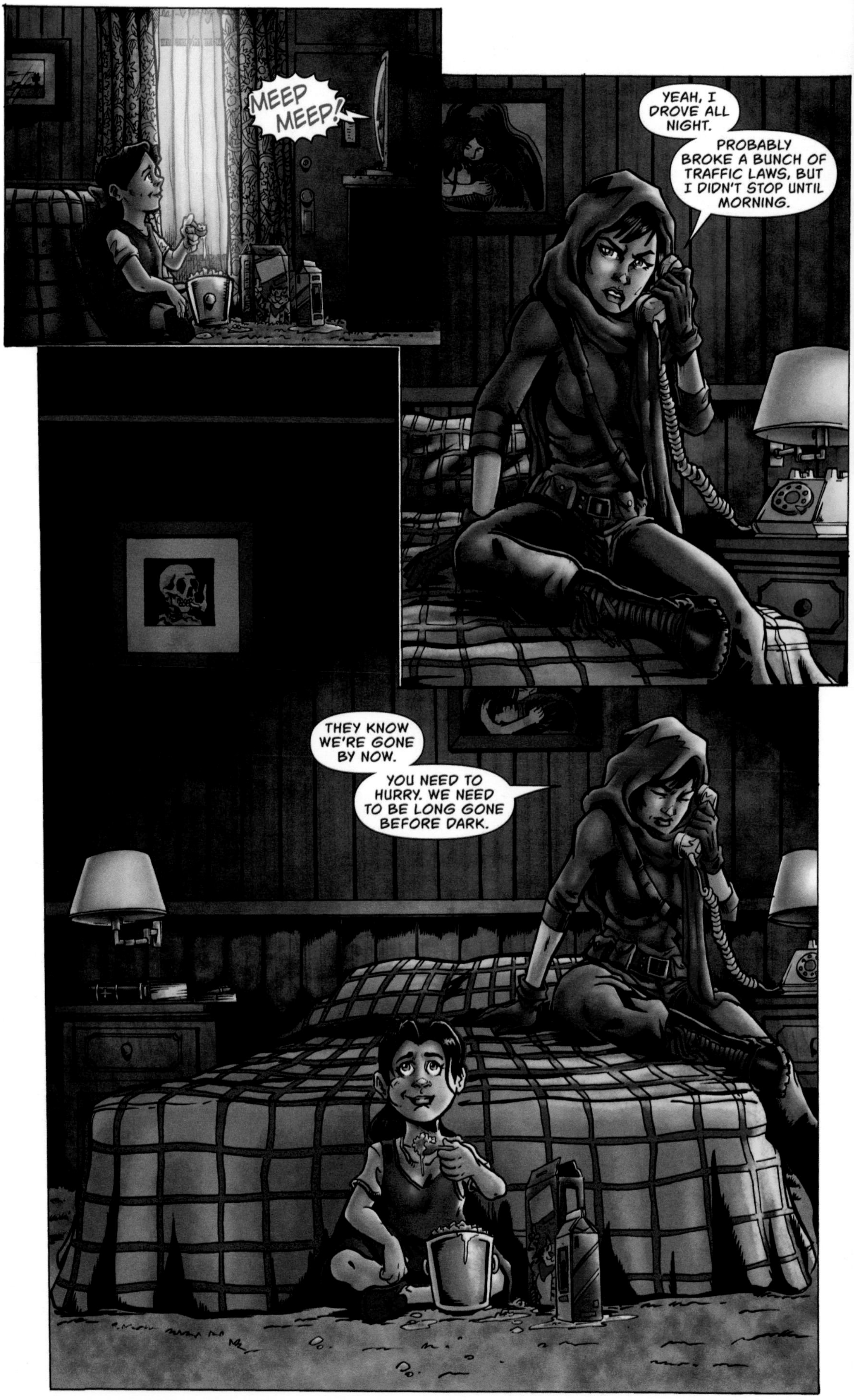
MEEP MEEP!
YEAH, I DROVE ALL NIGHT.
PROBABLY BROKE A BUNCH OF TRAFFIC LAWS, BUT I DIDN'T STOP UNTIL MORNING.
THEY KNOW WE'RE GONE BY NOW.
YOU NEED TO HURRY. WE NEED TO BE LONG GONE BEFORE DARK.

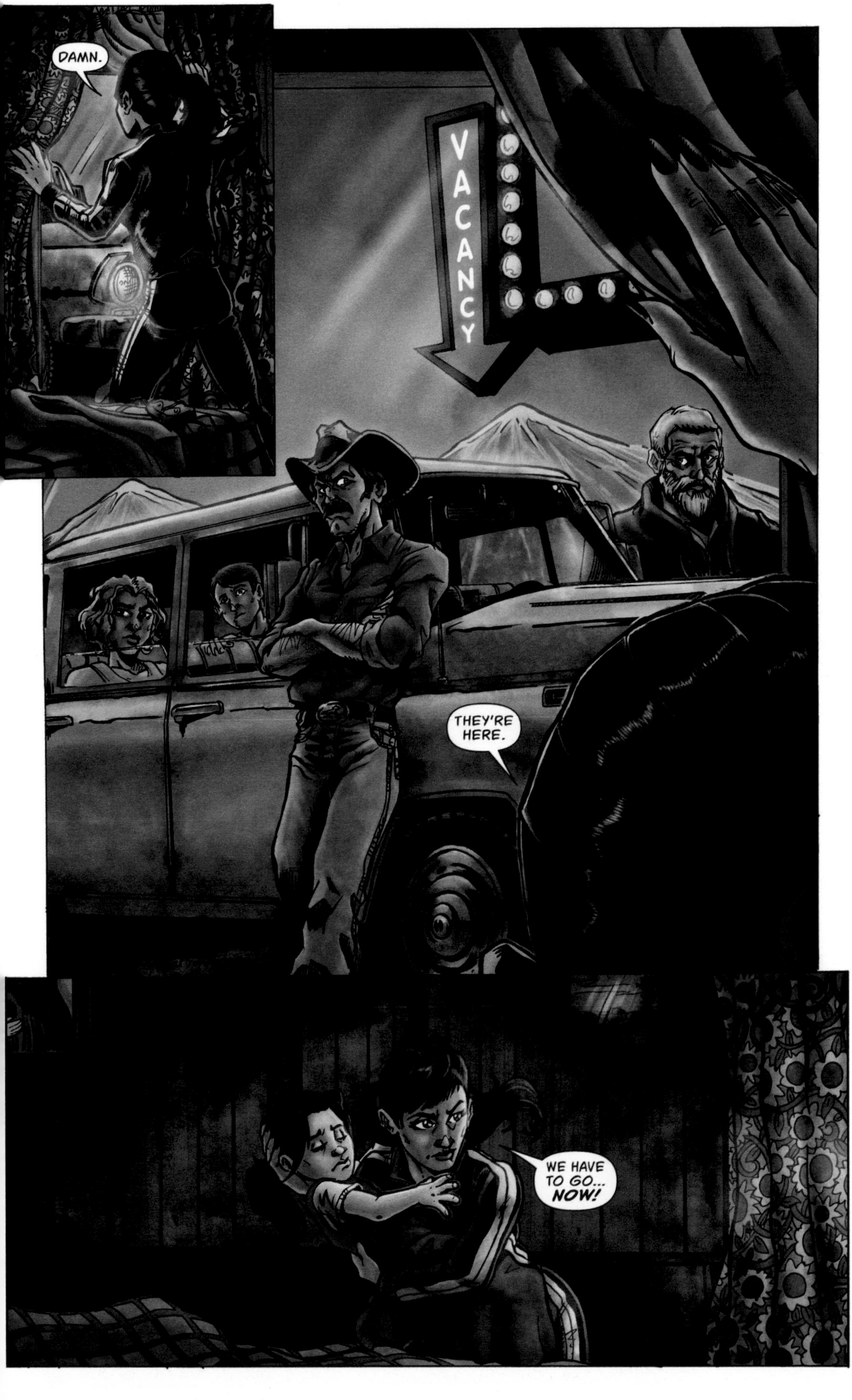
DAMN.
VACANCY
THEY'RE HERE.
WE HAVE TO GO... NOW!

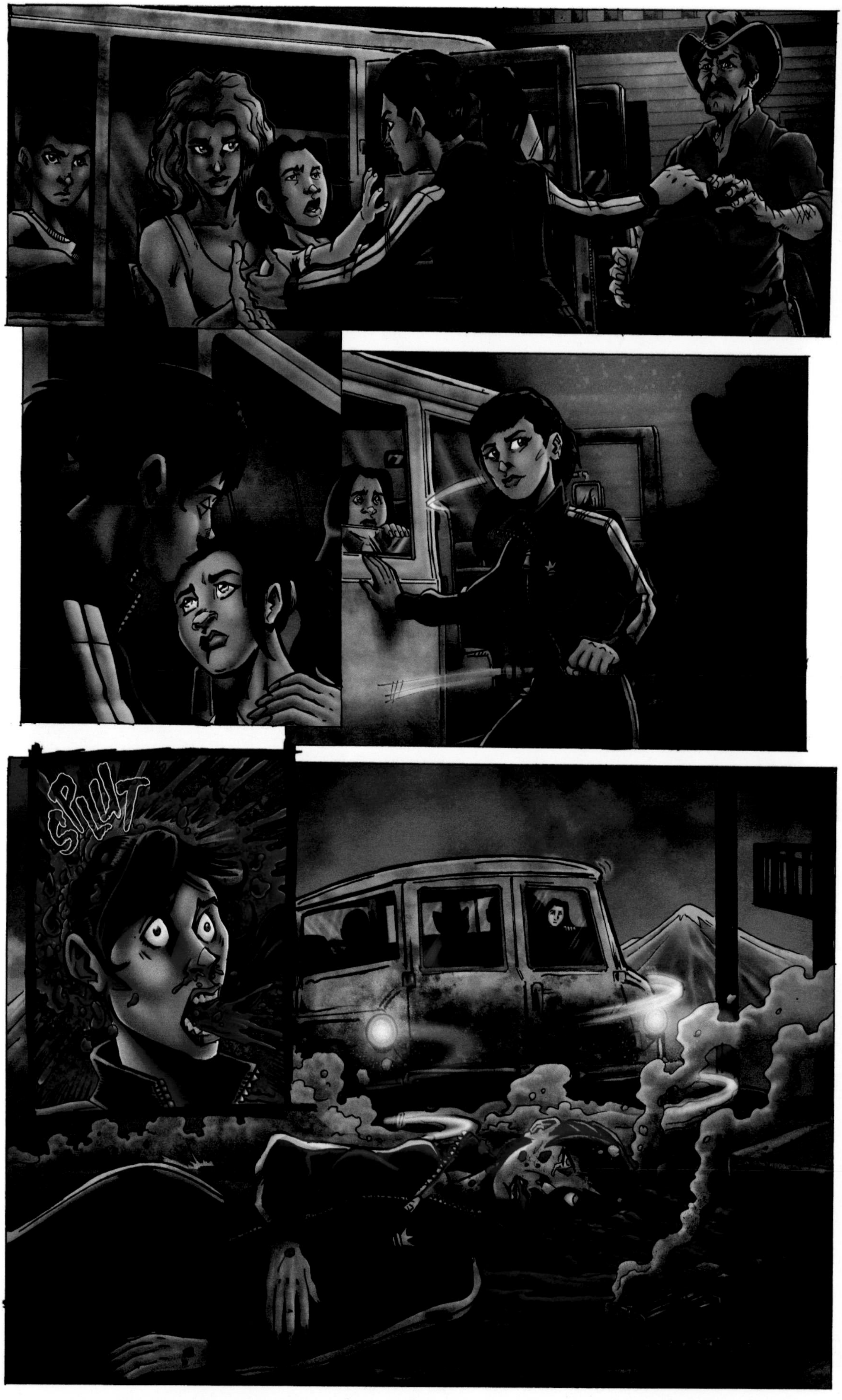
SPLUT

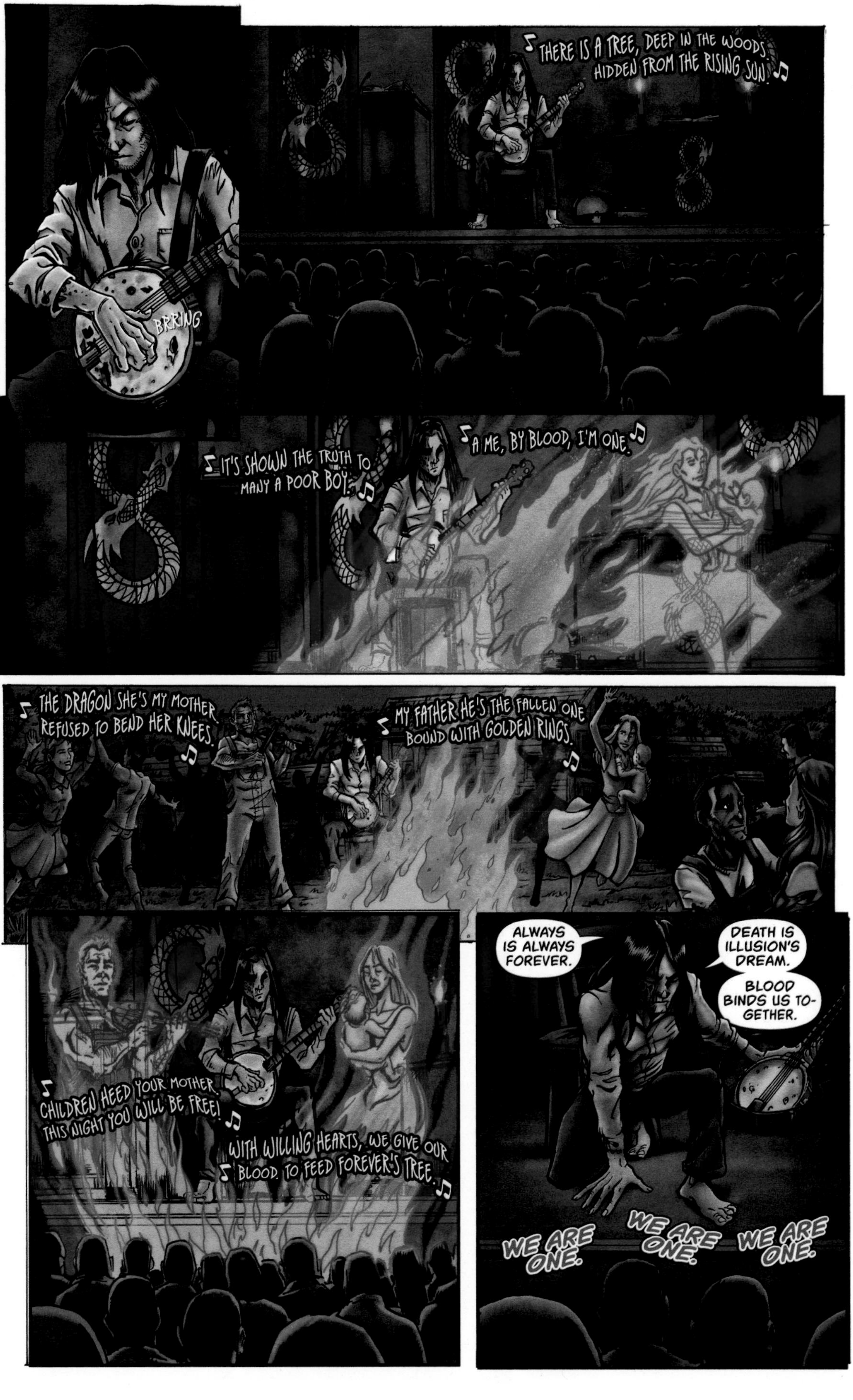
BRRING
THERE IS A TREE, DEEP IN THE WOODS HIDDEN FROM THE RISING SUN.
IT'S SHOWN THE TRUTH TO MANY A POOR BOY.
A ME, BY BLOOD, I'M ONE.
THE DRAGON SHE'S MY MOTHER REFUSED TO BEND HER KNEES.
MY FATHER HE'S THE FALLEN ONE BOUND WITH GOLDEN RINGS.
CHILDREN HEED YOUR MOTHER. THIS NIGHT YOU WILL BE FREE!
WITH WILLING HEARTS, WE GIVE OUR BLOOD TO FEED FOREVER'S TREE.
ALWAYS IS ALWAYS FOREVER.
DEATH IS ILLUSION'S DREAM.
BLOOD BINDS US TOGETHER.
WE ARE ONE.
WE ARE ONE.
WE ARE ONE.

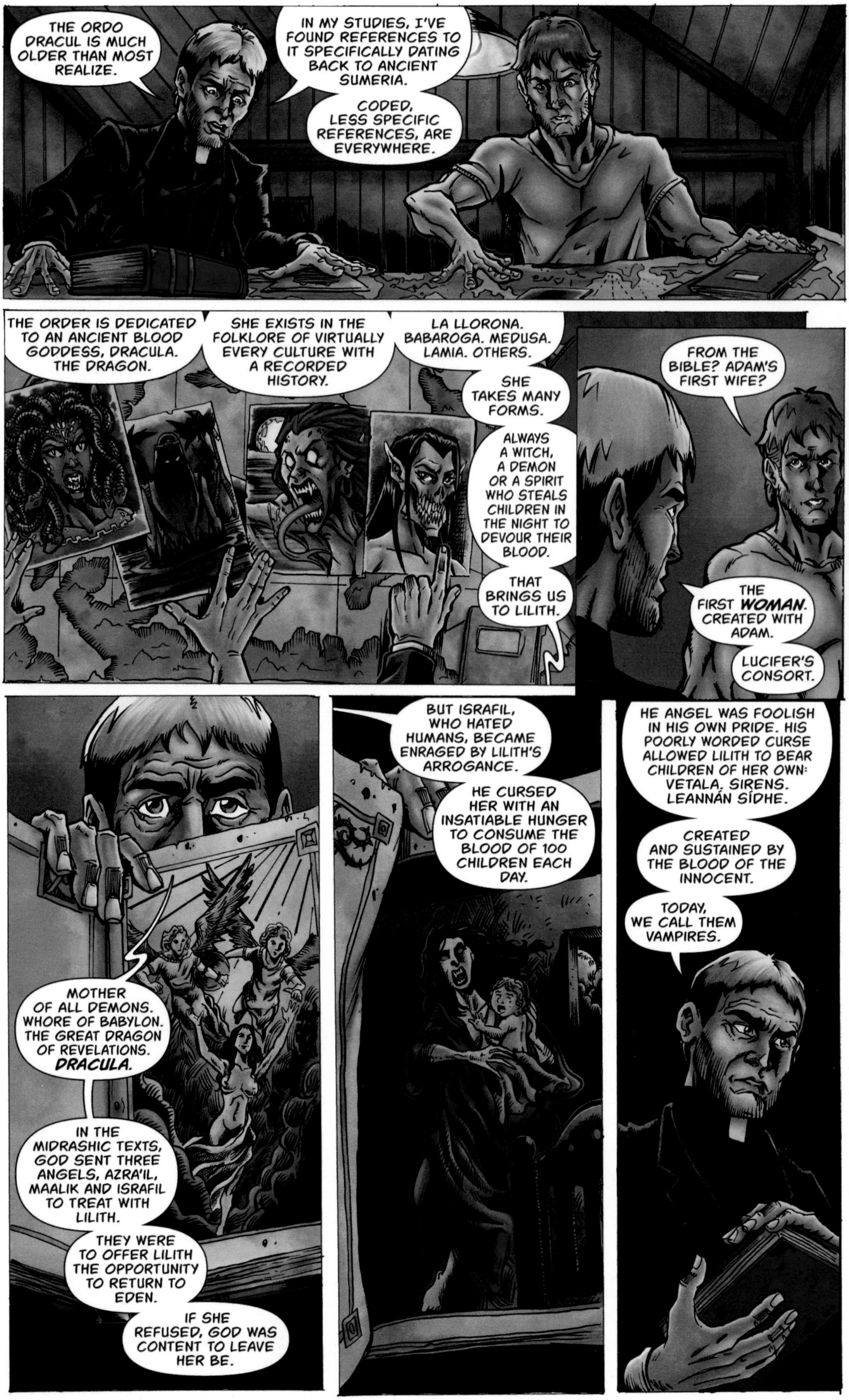
THE ORDO DRACUL IS MUCH OLDER THAN MOST REALIZE.
IN MY STUDIES, I'VE FOUND REFERENCES TO IT SPECIFICALLY DATING BACK TO ANCIENT SUMERIA.
CODED, LESS SPECIFIC REFERENCES, ARE EVERYWHERE.
THE ORDER IS DEDICATED TO AN ANCIENT BLOOD GODDESS, DRACULA. THE DRAGON.
SHE EXISTS IN THE FOLKLORE OF VIRTUALLY EVERY CULTURE WITH A RECORDED HISTORY.
LA LLORONA. BABAROGA. MEDUSA. LAMIA. OTHERS.
SHE TAKES MANY FORMS.
ALWAYS A WITCH, A DEMON OR A SPIRIT WHO STEALS CHILDREN IN THE NIGHT TO DEVOUR THEIR BLOOD.
THAT BRINGS US TO LILITH.
FROM THE BIBLE? ADAM'S FIRST WIFE?
THE FIRST **WOMAN**. CREATED WITH ADAM.
LUCIFER'S CONSORT.
MOTHER OF ALL DEMONS. WHORE OF BABYLON. THE GREAT DRAGON OF REVELATIONS. ***DRACULA***.
IN THE MIDRASHIC TEXTS, GOD SENT THREE ANGELS, AZRA'IL, MAALIK AND ISRAFIL TO TREAT WITH LILITH.
THEY WERE TO OFFER LILITH THE OPPORTUNITY TO RETURN TO EDEN.
IF SHE REFUSED, GOD WAS CONTENT TO LEAVE HER BE.
BUT ISRAFIL, WHO HATED HUMANS, BECAME ENRAGED BY LILITH'S ARROGANCE.
HE CURSED HER WITH AN INSATIABLE HUNGER TO CONSUME THE BLOOD OF 100 CHILDREN EACH DAY.
HE ANGEL WAS FOOLISH IN HIS OWN PRIDE. HIS POORLY WORDED CURSE ALLOWED LILITH TO BEAR CHILDREN OF HER OWN: VETALA. SIRENS. LEANNÁN SÍDHE.
CREATED AND SUSTAINED BY THE BLOOD OF THE INNOCENT.
TODAY, WE CALL THEM VAMPIRES.

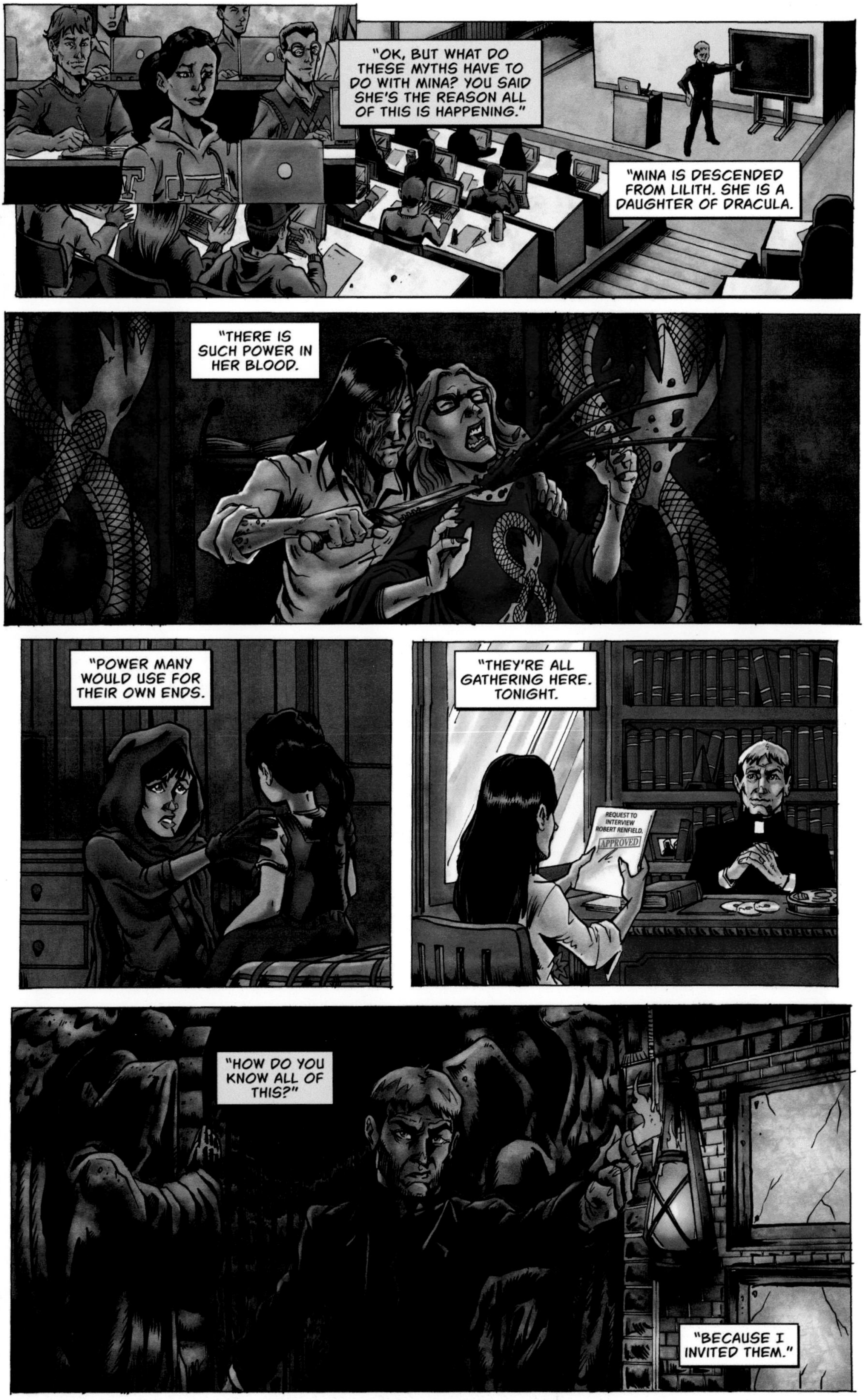
"OK, BUT WHAT DO THESE MYTHS HAVE TO DO WITH MINA? YOU SAID SHE'S THE REASON ALL OF THIS IS HAPPENING."
"MINA IS DESCENDED FROM LILITH. SHE IS A DAUGHTER OF DRACULA.
"THERE IS SUCH POWER IN HER BLOOD.
"POWER MANY WOULD USE FOR THEIR OWN ENDS.
"THEY'RE ALL GATHERING HERE. TONIGHT.
REQUEST TO INTERVIEW ROBERT RENFIELD.
APPROVED
"HOW DO YOU KNOW ALL OF THIS?"
"BECAUSE I INVITED THEM."

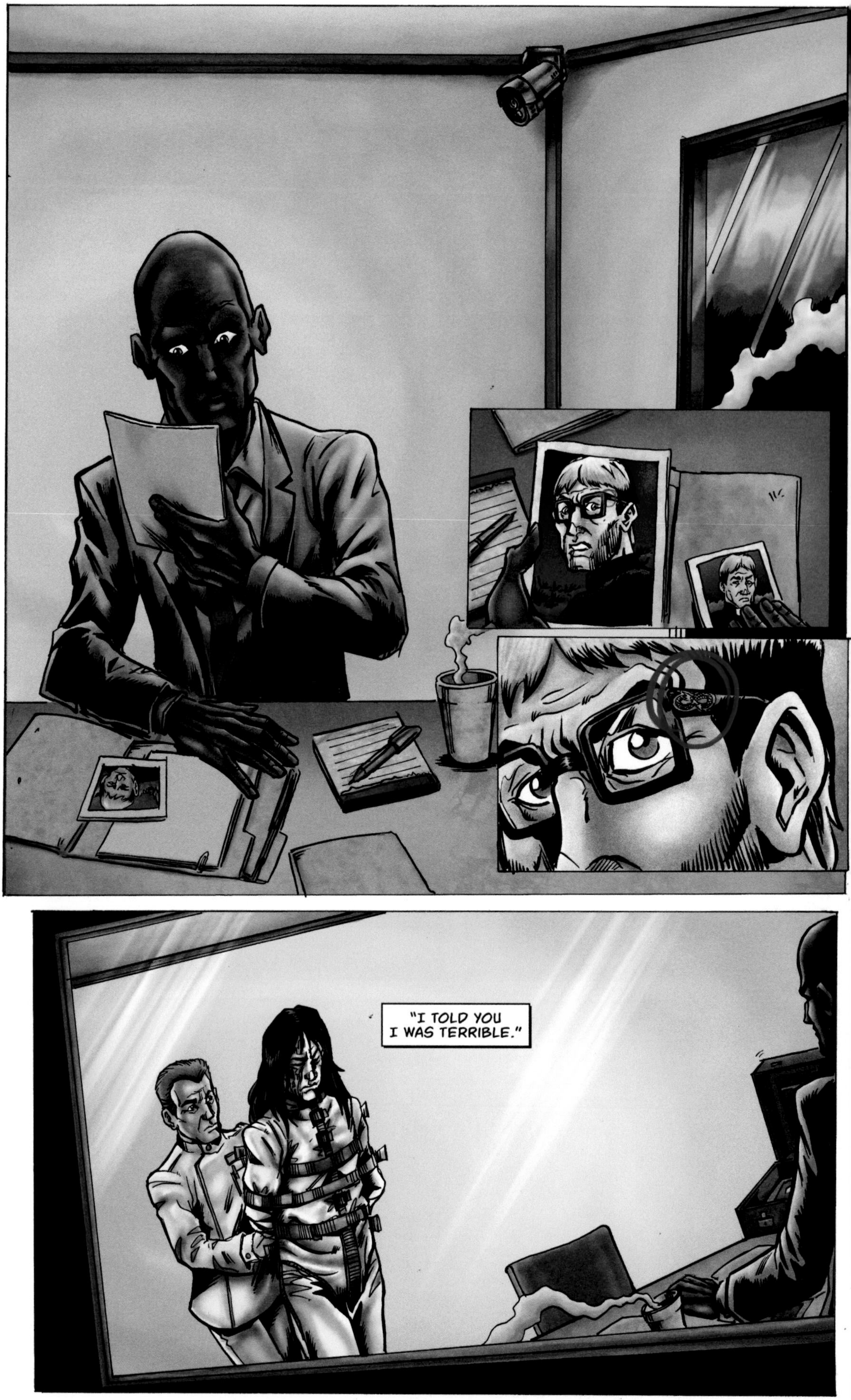
"I TOLD YOU
I WAS TERRIBLE."

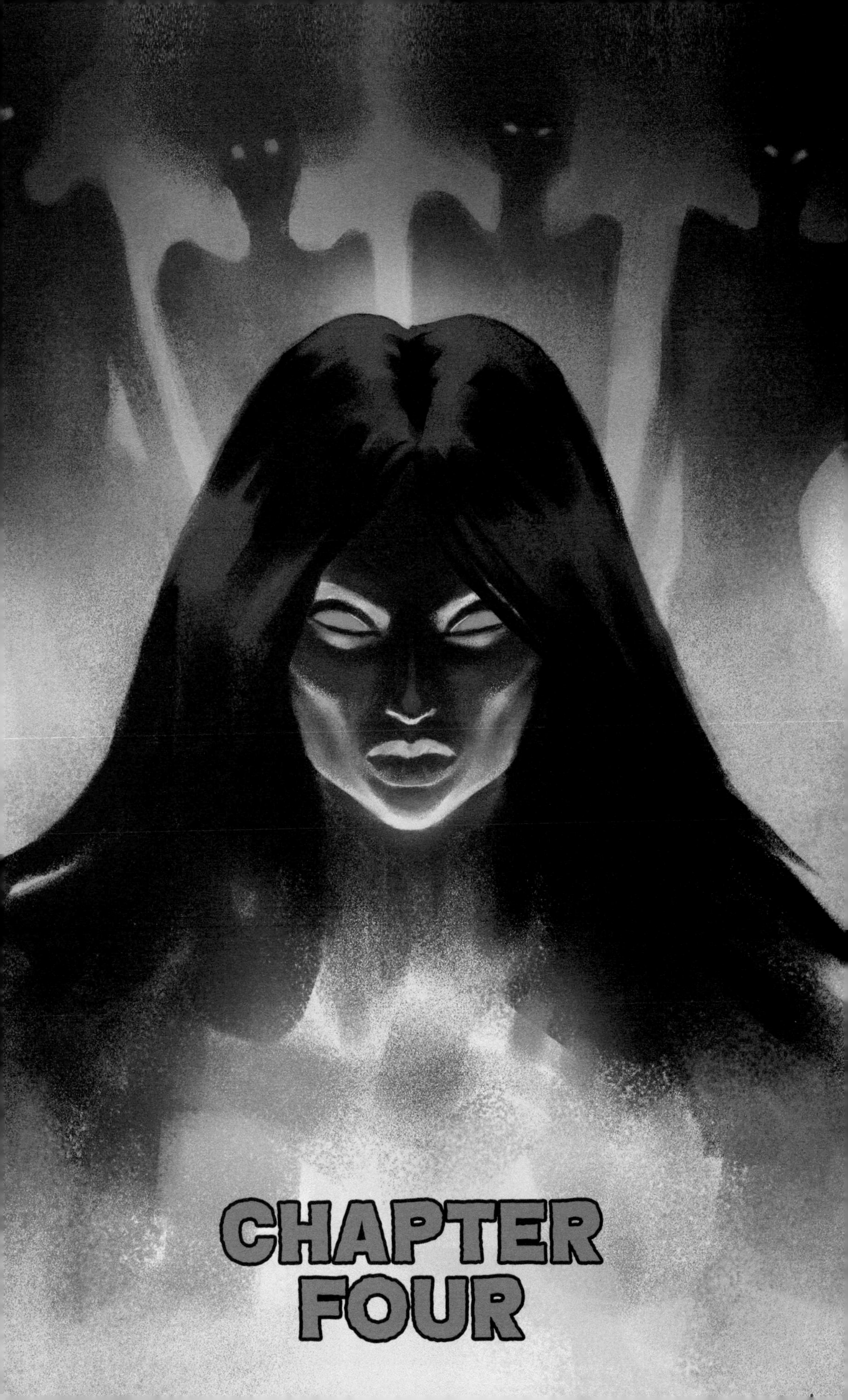

CHAPTER FOUR

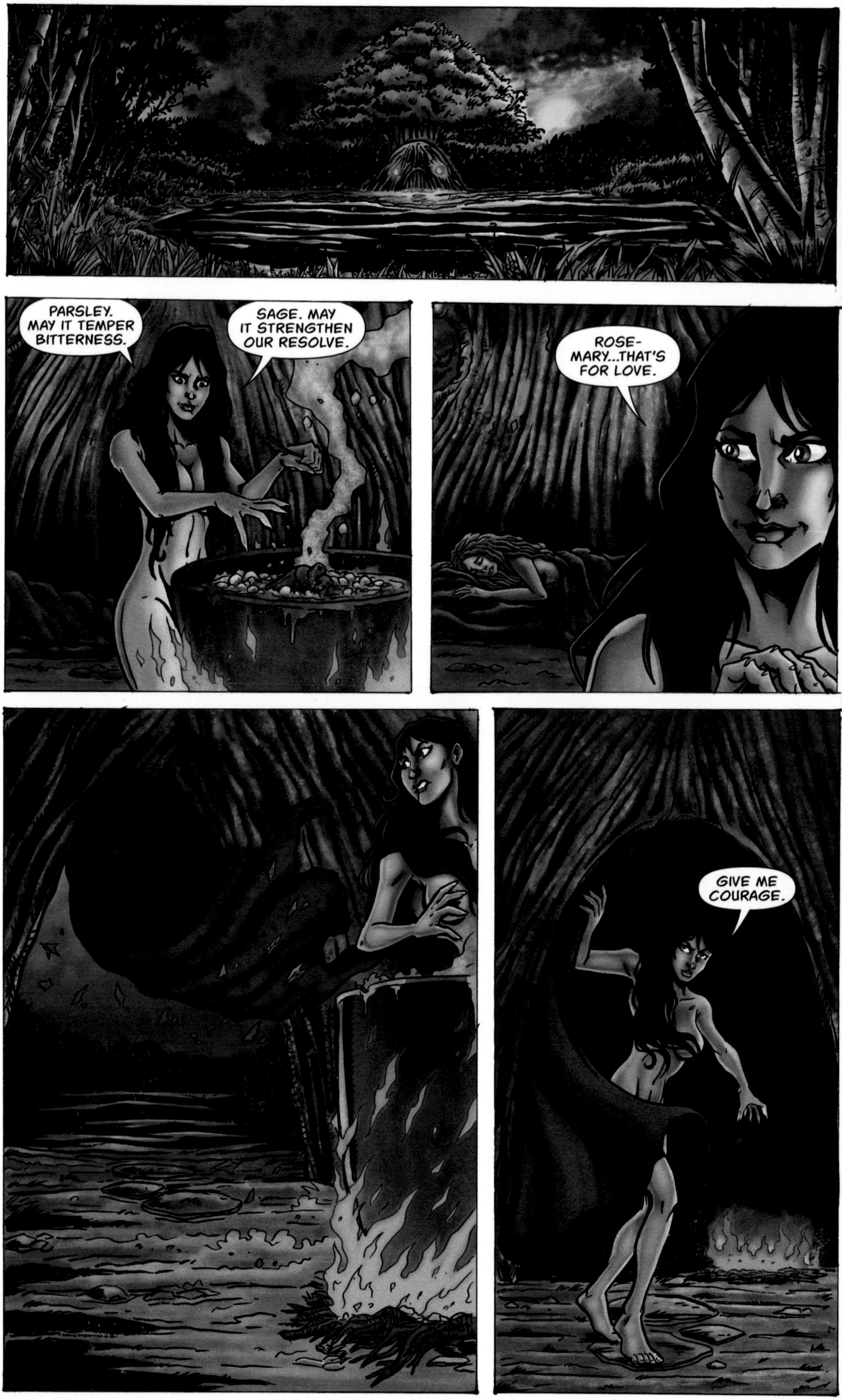
PARSLEY. MAY IT TEMPER BITTERNESS.
SAGE. MAY IT STRENGTHEN OUR RESOLVE.
ROSE-MARY...THAT'S FOR LOVE.
GIVE ME COURAGE.

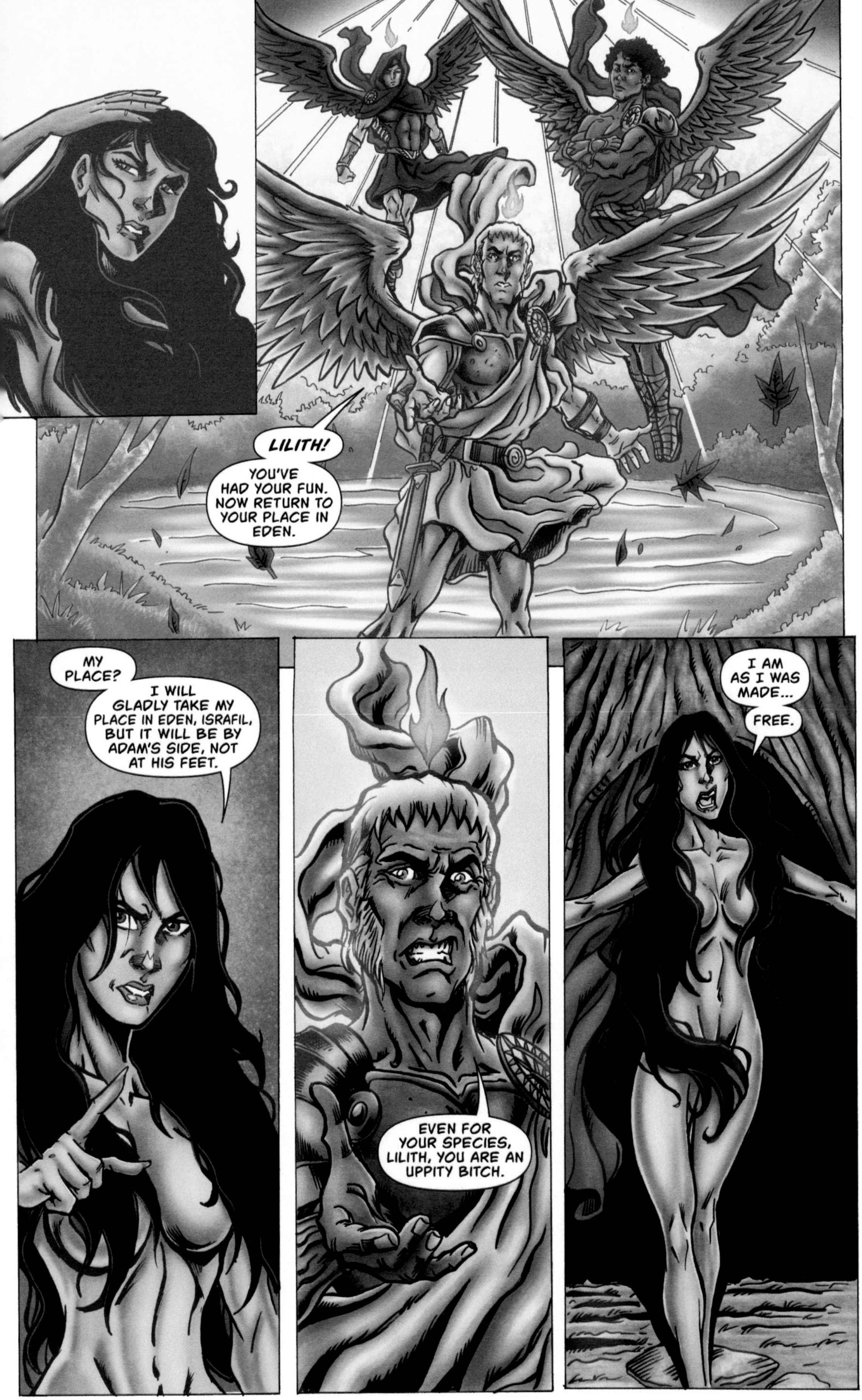
LILITH!
YOU'VE HAD YOUR FUN. NOW RETURN TO YOUR PLACE IN EDEN.
MY PLACE?
I WILL GLADLY TAKE MY PLACE IN EDEN, ISRAFIL, BUT IT WILL BE BY ADAM'S SIDE, NOT AT HIS FEET.
EVEN FOR YOUR SPECIES, LILITH, YOU ARE AN UPPITY BITCH.
I AM AS I WAS MADE...
FREE.

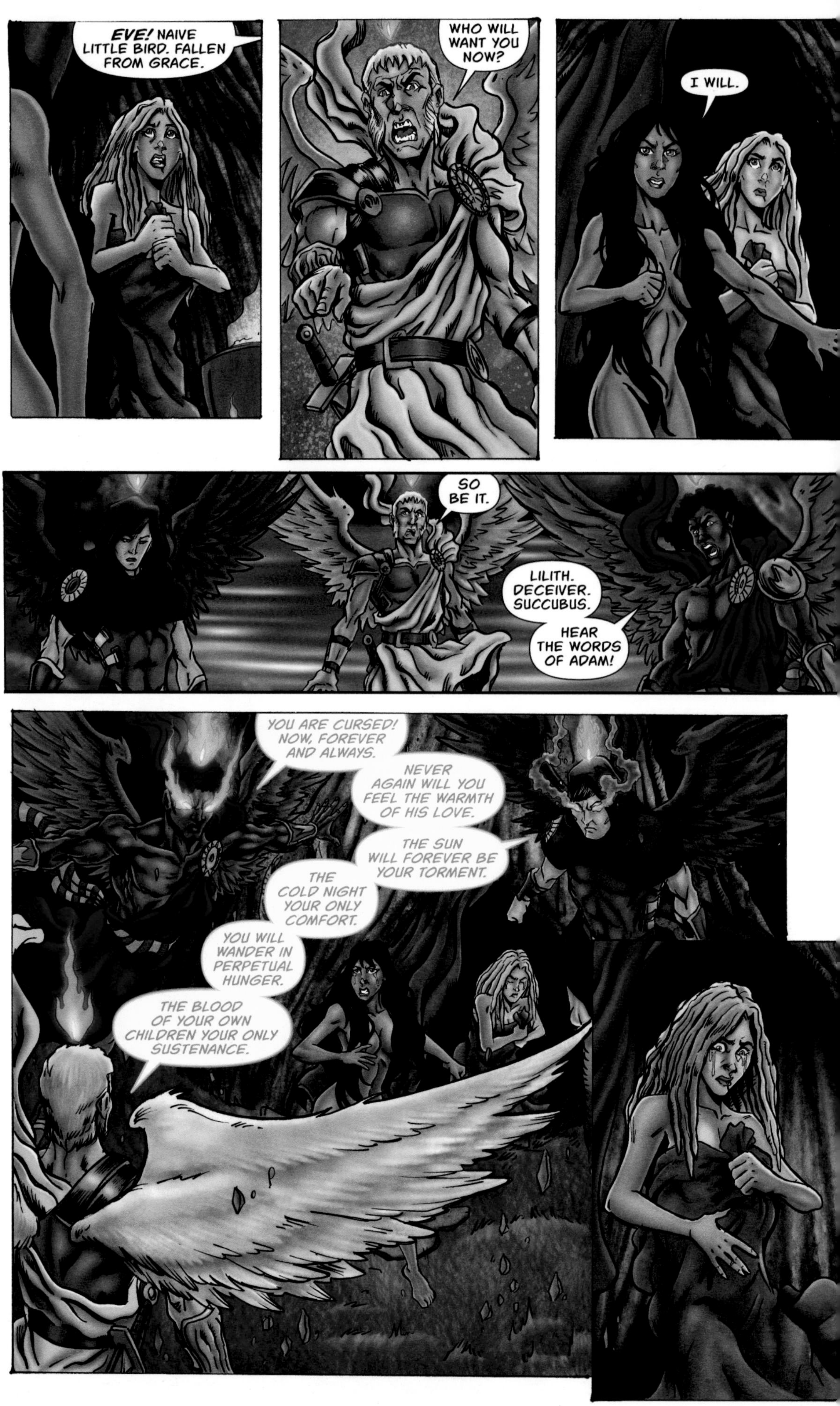
EVE! NAIVE LITTLE BIRD. FALLEN FROM GRACE.
WHO WILL WANT YOU NOW?
I WILL.
SO BE IT.
LILITH. DECEIVER. SUCCUBUS.
HEAR THE WORDS OF ADAM!
YOU ARE CURSED! NOW, FOREVER AND ALWAYS.
NEVER AGAIN WILL YOU FEEL THE WARMTH OF HIS LOVE.
THE SUN WILL FOREVER BE YOUR TORMENT.
THE COLD NIGHT YOUR ONLY COMFORT.
YOU WILL WANDER IN PERPETUAL HUNGER.
THE BLOOD OF YOUR OWN CHILDREN YOUR ONLY SUSTENANCE.

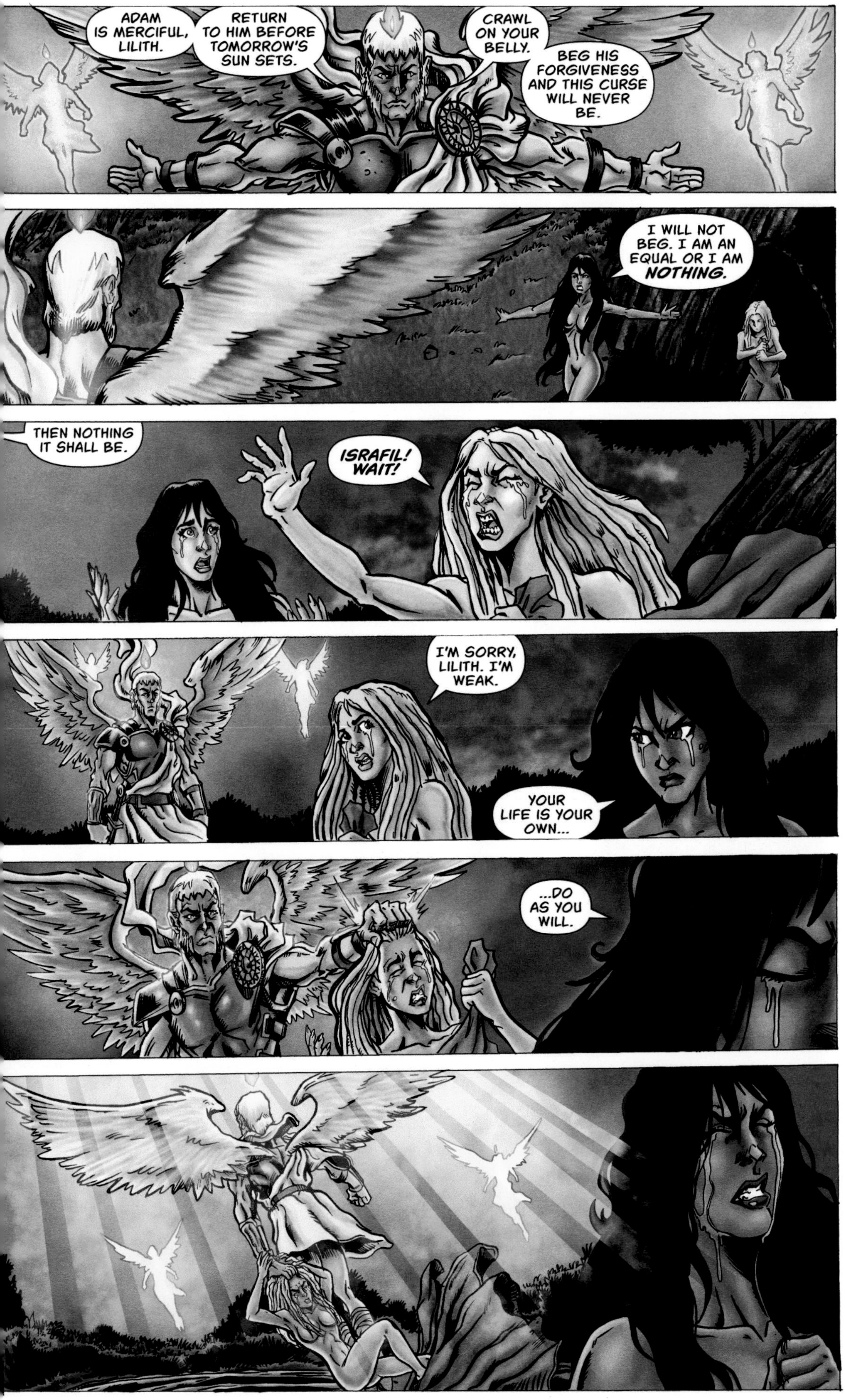
ADAM IS MERCIFUL, LILITH.
RETURN TO HIM BEFORE TOMORROW'S SUN SETS.
CRAWL ON YOUR BELLY.
BEG HIS FORGIVENESS AND THIS CURSE WILL NEVER BE.
I WILL NOT BEG. I AM AN EQUAL OR I AM NOTHING.
THEN NOTHING IT SHALL BE.
ISRAFIL! WAIT!
I'M SORRY, LILITH. I'M WEAK.
YOUR LIFE IS YOUR OWN...
...DO AS YOU WILL.

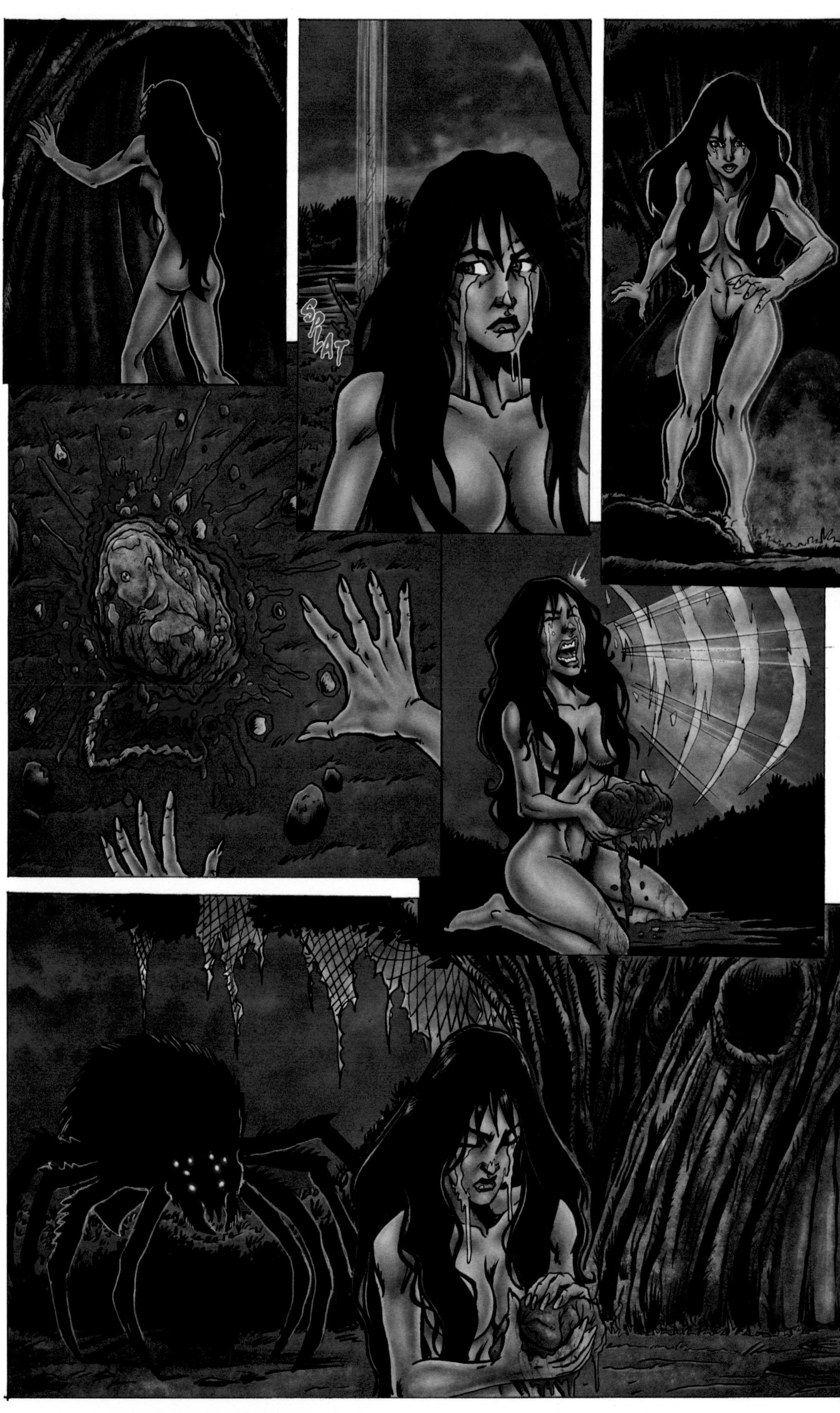
SPLAT

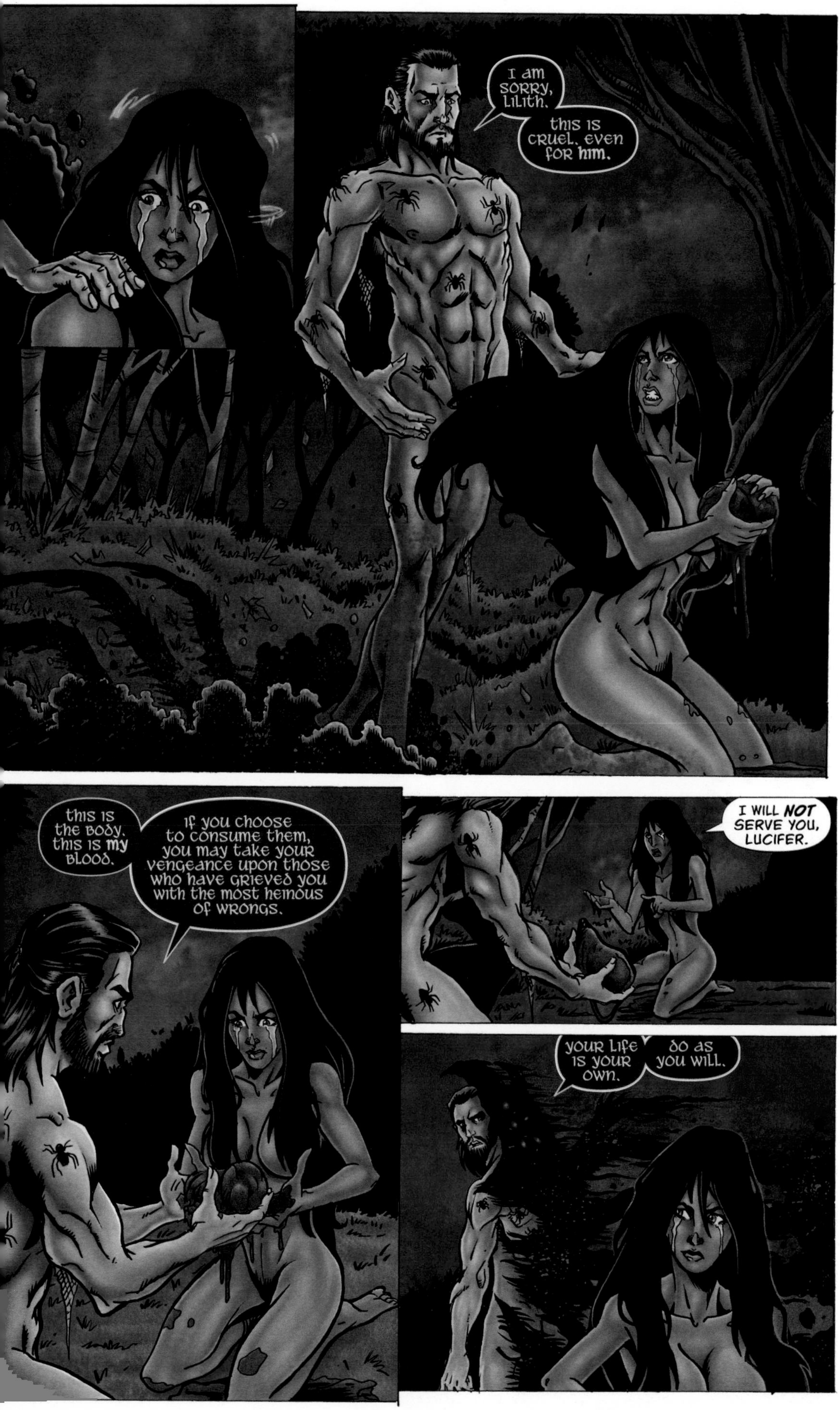
I am SORRY, LILITH.
this is CRUEL, even for him.
this is the Body. this is my BLOOD.
If you choose to consume them, you may take your vengeance upon those who have grieved you with the most heinous of wrongs.
I WILL NOT SERVE YOU, LUCIFER.
your life is your own.
do as you will.

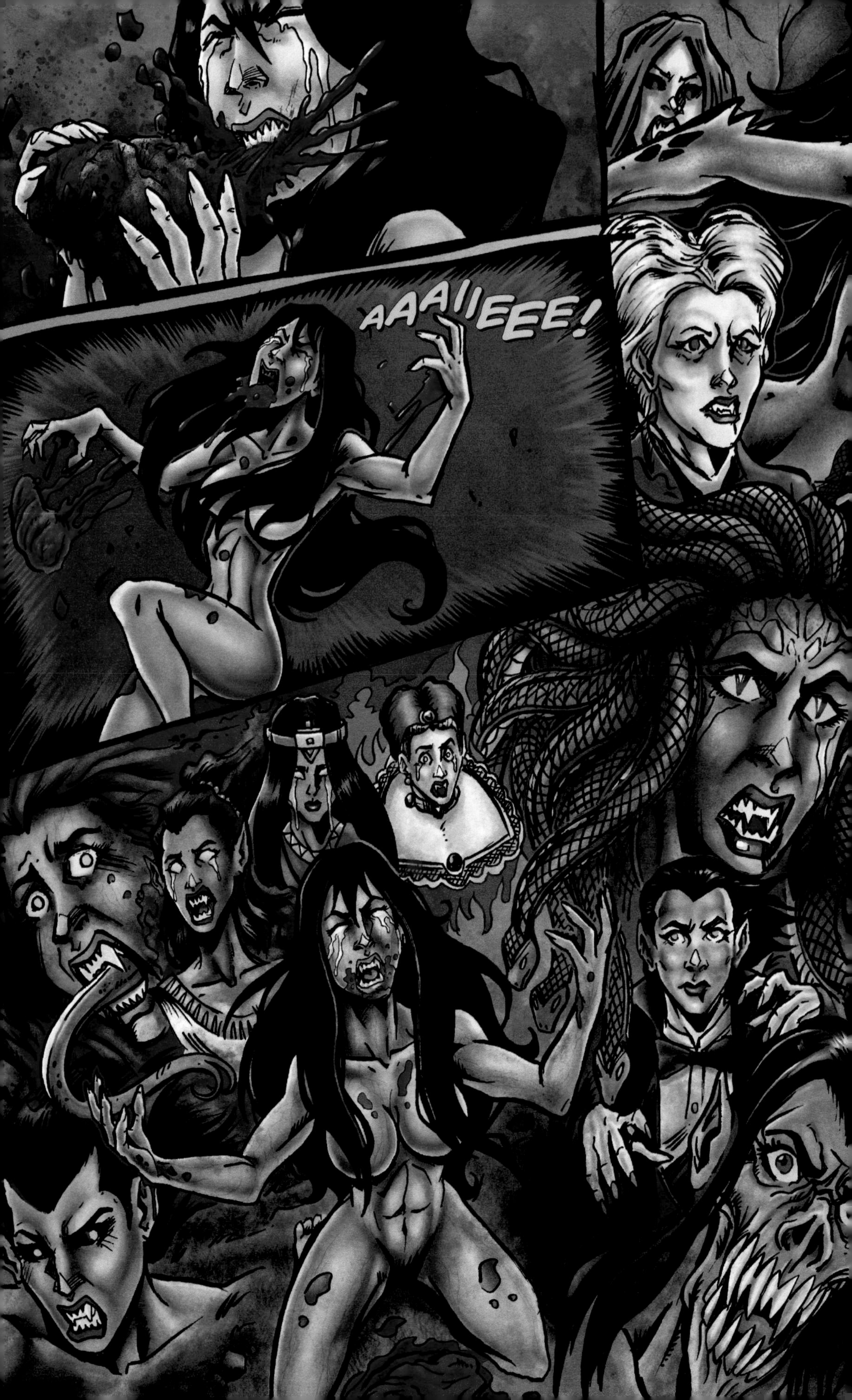
AAAIIEEEE!

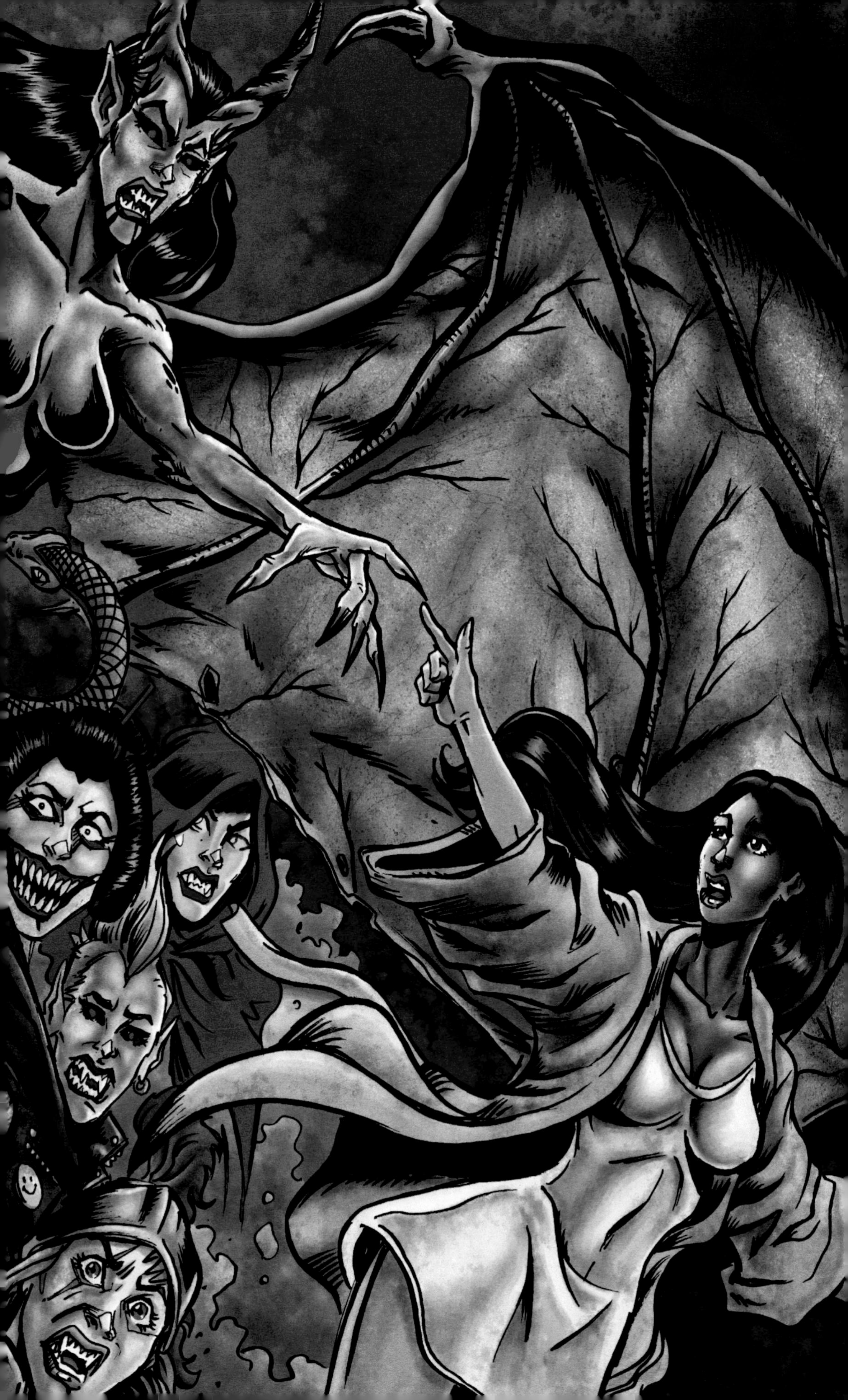

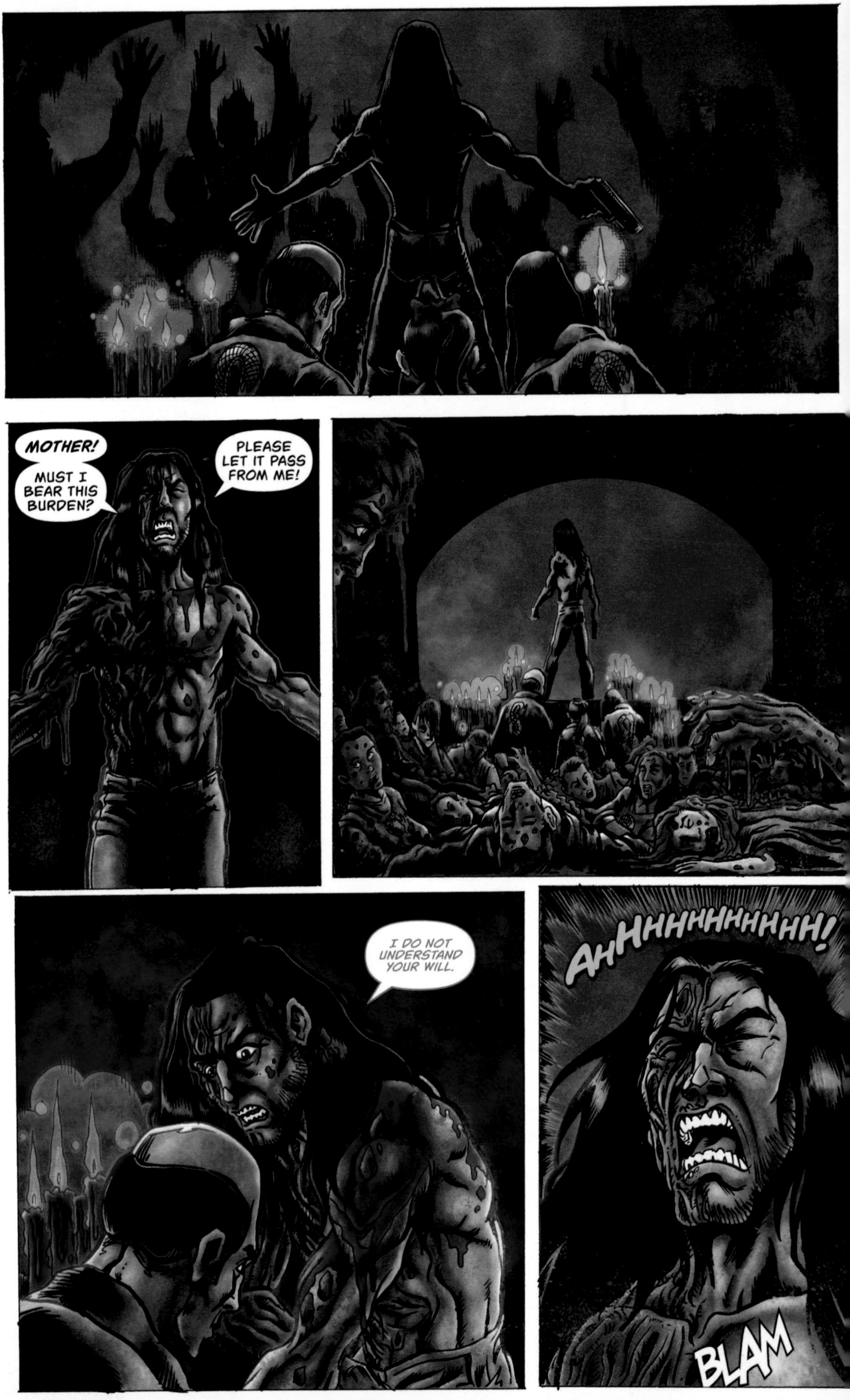
MOTHER!
MUST I BEAR THIS BURDEN?
PLEASE LET IT PASS FROM ME!
I DO NOT UNDERSTAND YOUR WILL.
AHHHHHHHHHHH!
BLAM

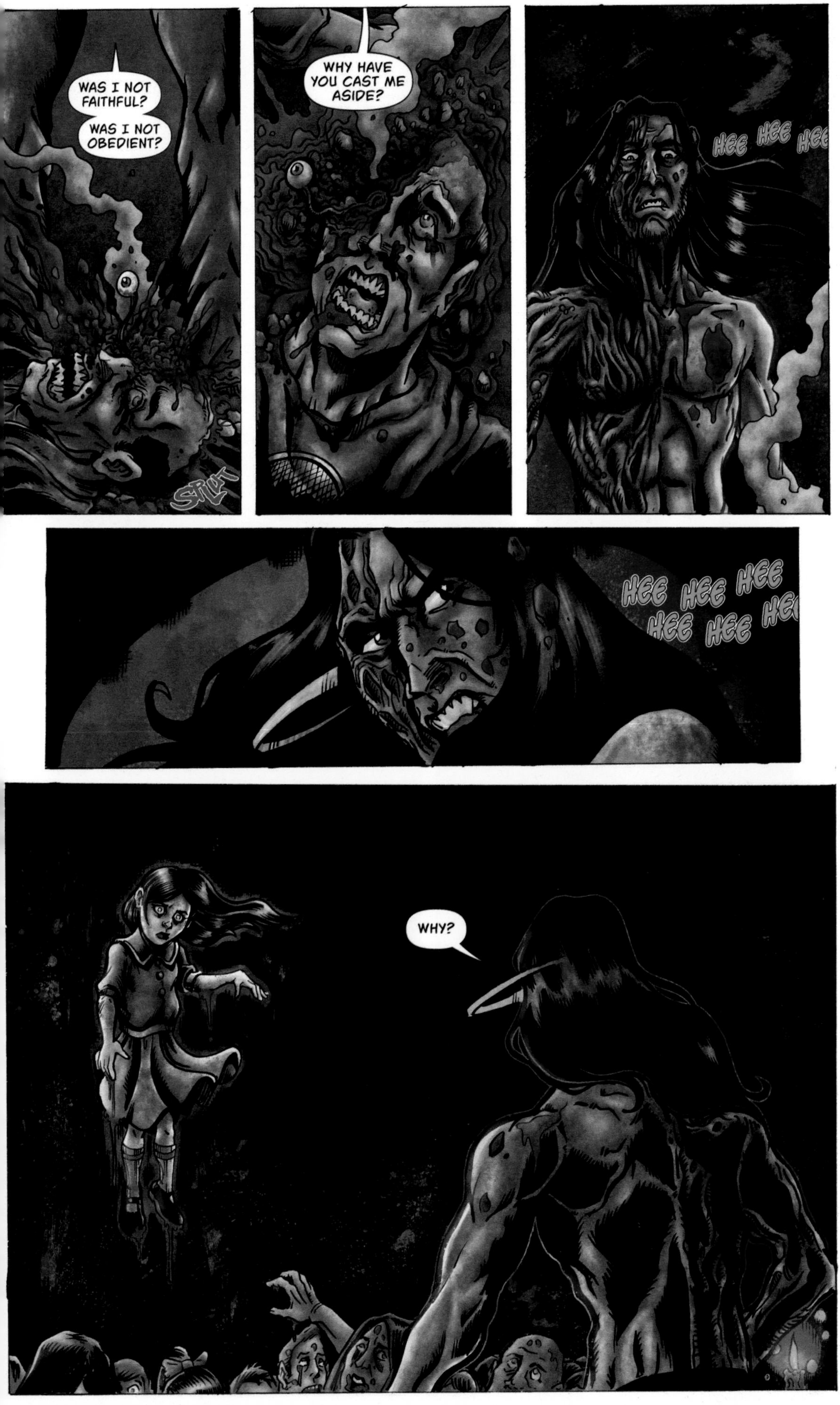
WAS I NOT FAITHFUL?
WAS I NOT OBEDIENT?
SPLUT
WHY HAVE YOU CAST ME ASIDE?
HEE HEE HEE
HEE HEE HEE
HEE HEE HEE
WHY?

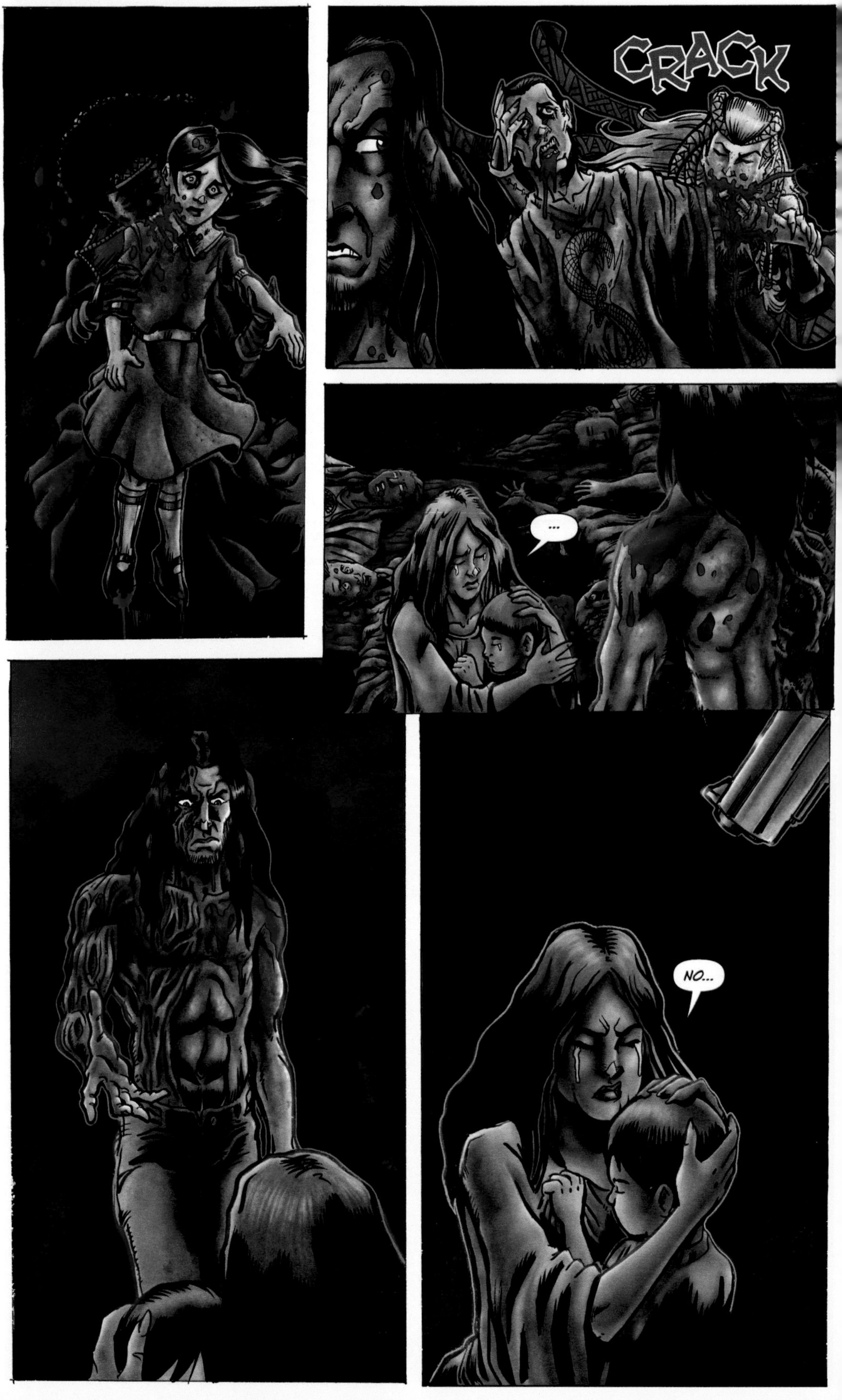
CRACK
...
NO...

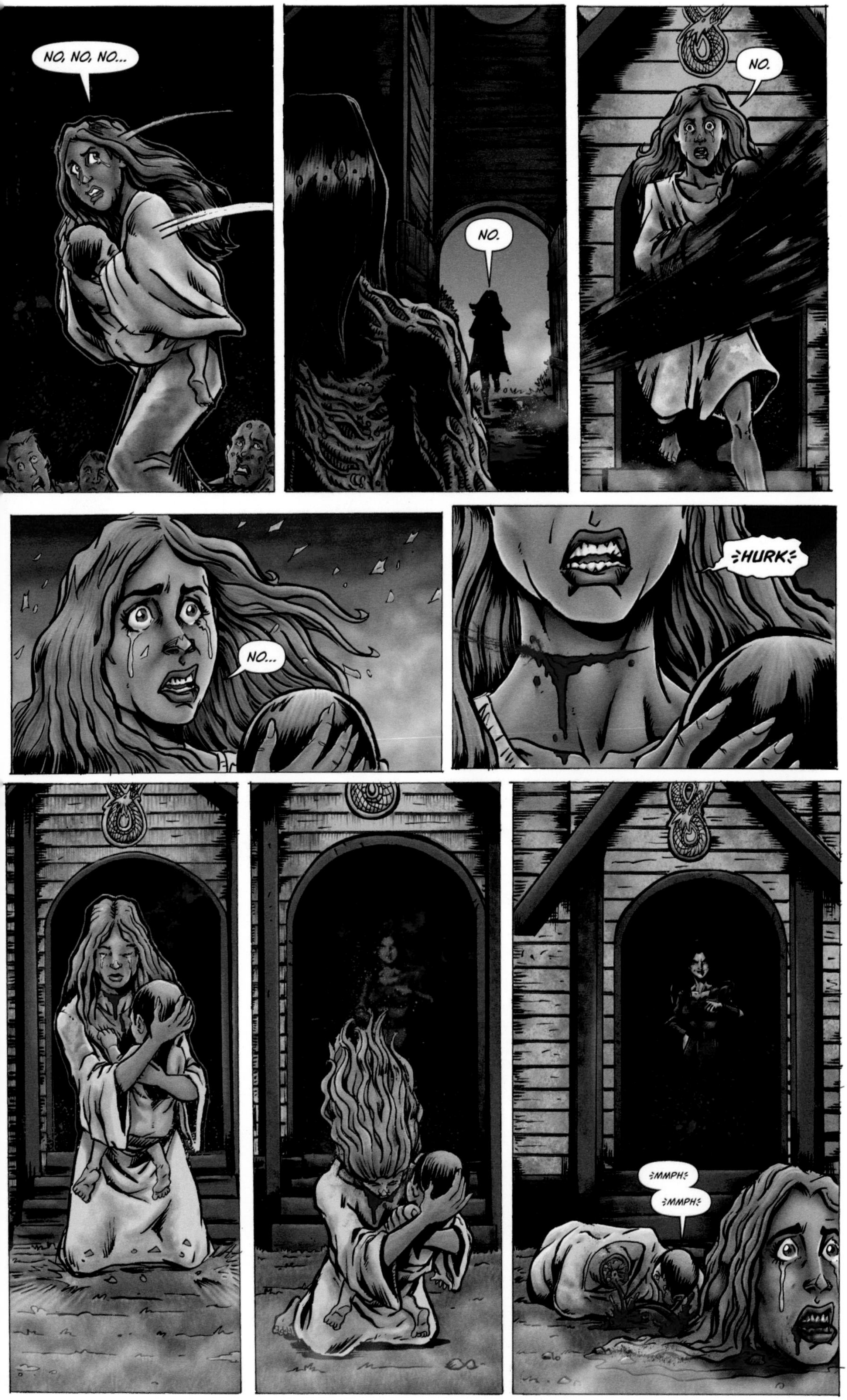
NO, NO, NO...
NO.
NO.
NO...
HURK
MMPH
MMPH

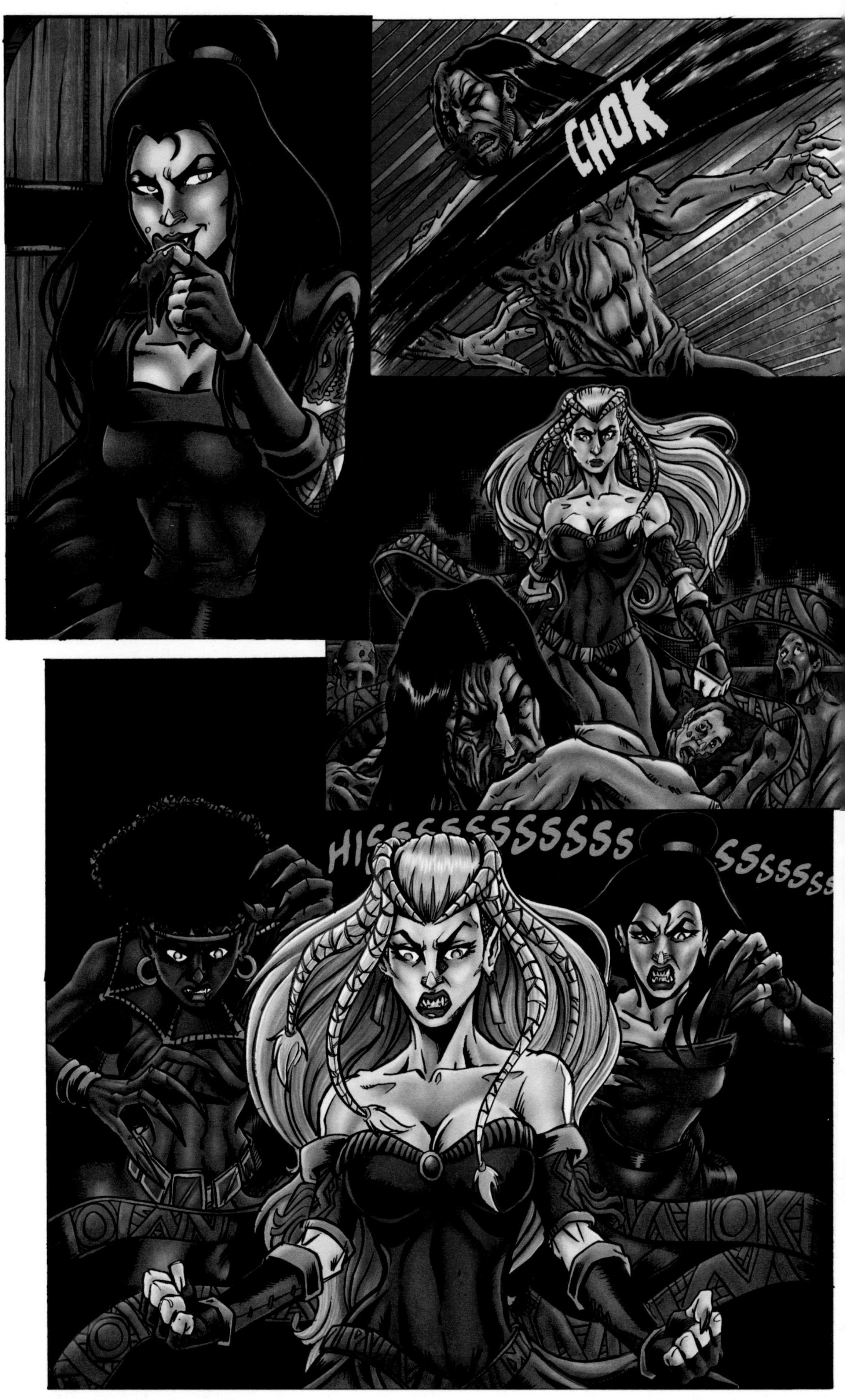
CHOK
HISSSSSSSSSSs
SSSSSSS

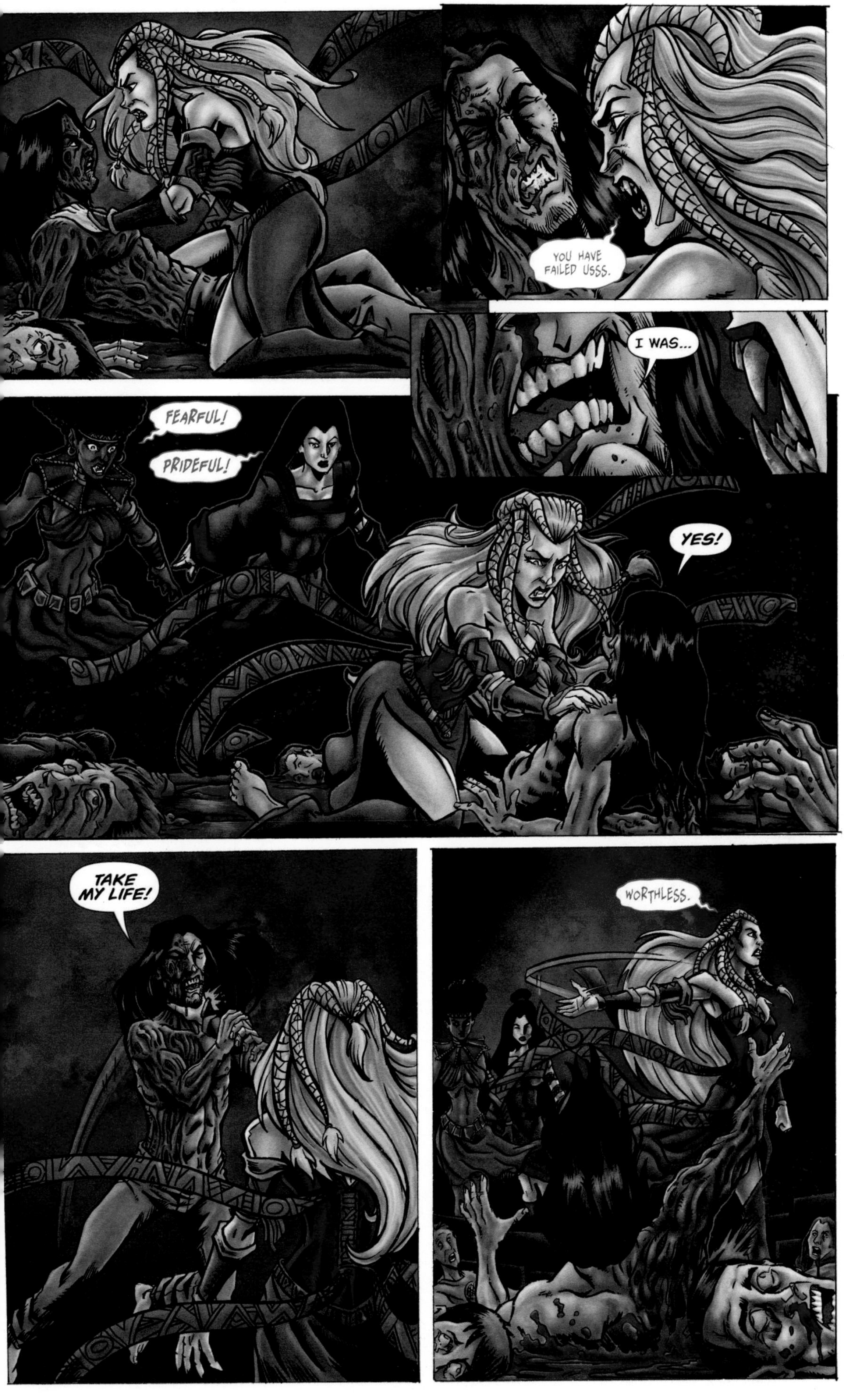
YOU HAVE FAILED USSS.
I WAS...
FEARFUL!
PRIDEFUL!
YES!
TAKE MY LIFE!
WORTHLESS.

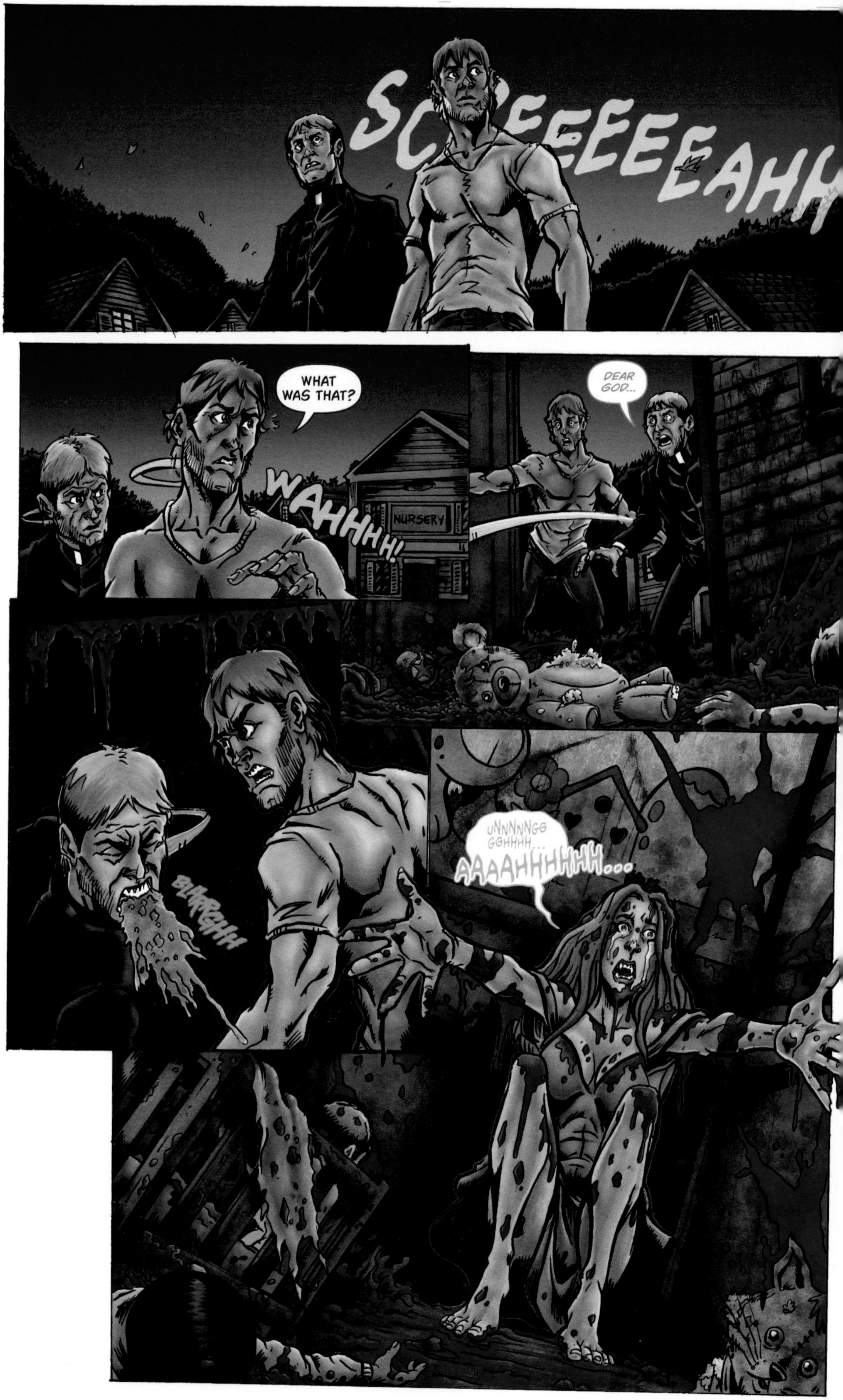
SCREEEEEEAHH
WHAT WAS THAT?
WAHHHHH!
NURSERY
DEAR GOD...
BLARRGHHH
UNNNNNGG GGHHHH...
AAAAHHHHHH...

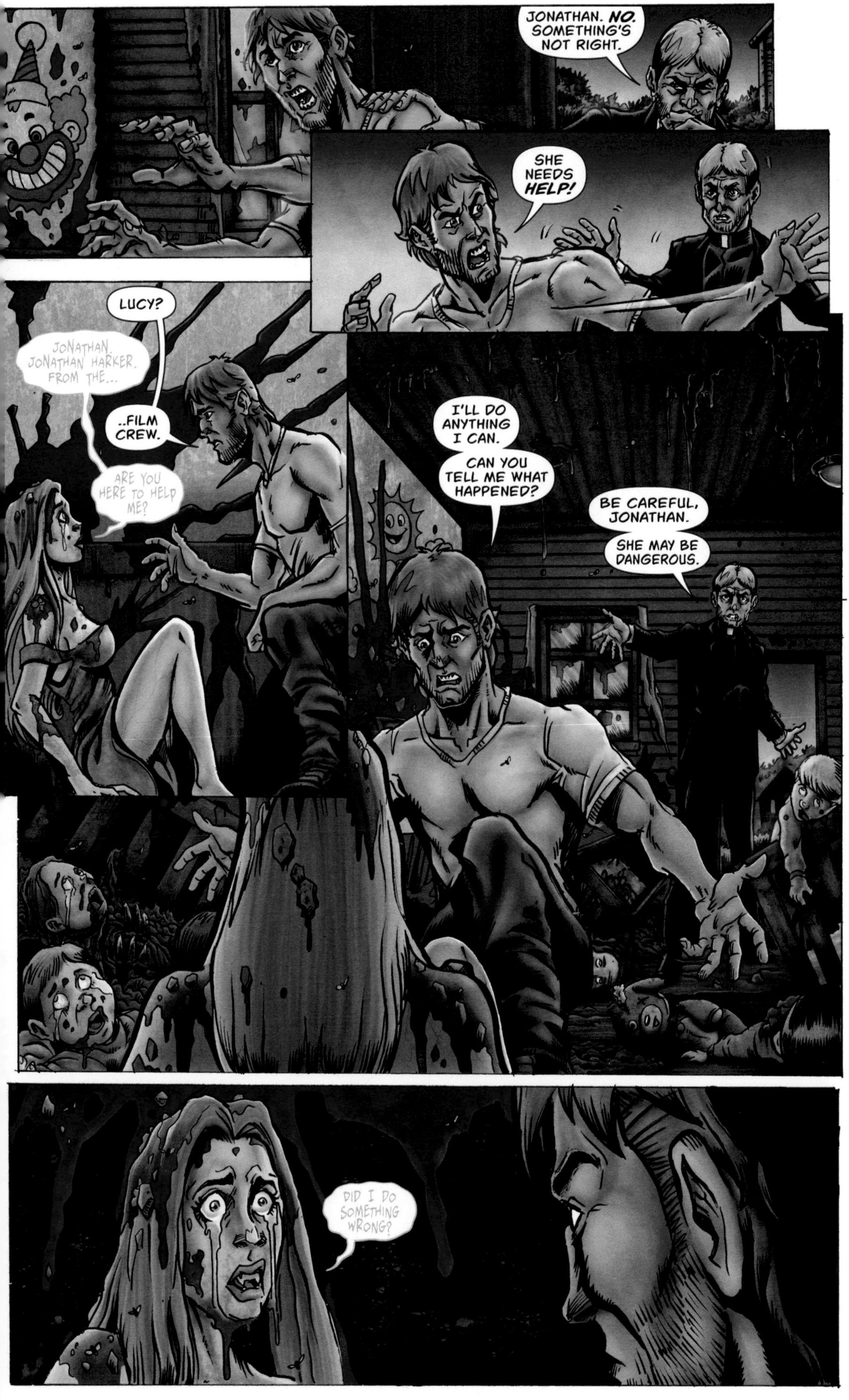

JONATHAN. **NO.** SOMETHING'S NOT RIGHT.
SHE NEEDS **HELP!**
LUCY?
JONATHAN. JONATHAN HARKER. FROM THE...
..FILM CREW.
ARE YOU HERE TO HELP ME?
I'LL DO ANYTHING I CAN.
CAN YOU TELL ME WHAT HAPPENED?
BE CAREFUL, JONATHAN.
SHE MAY BE DANGEROUS.
DID I DO SOMETHING WRONG?

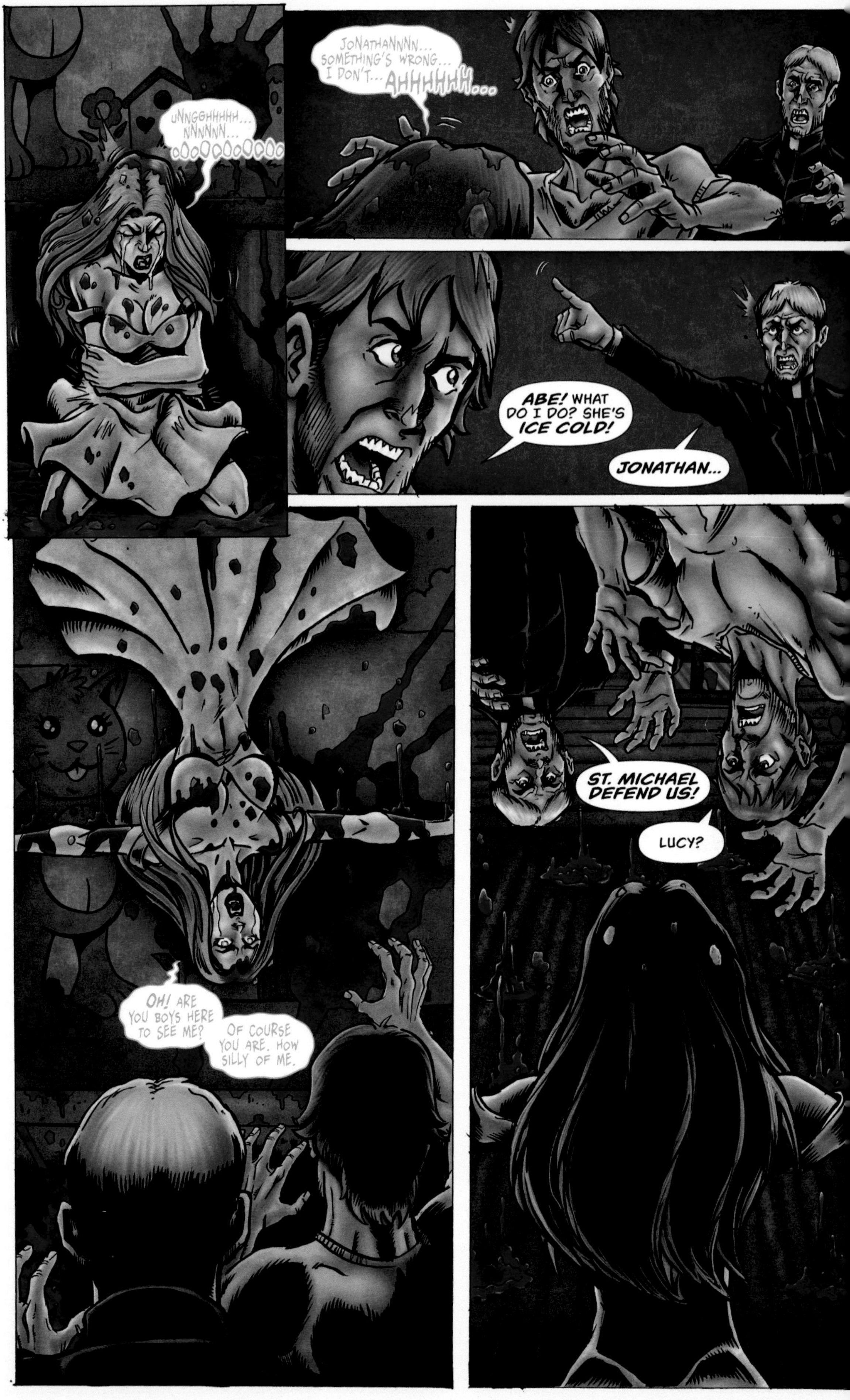
UNNGGHHHHH...
NNNNNN...
OOOOOOOOOOO
JONATHANNNN...
SOMETHING'S WRONG...
I DON'T... AHHHHHH...
ABE! WHAT DO I DO? SHE'S ICE COLD!
JONATHAN...
OH! ARE YOU BOYS HERE TO SEE ME?
OF COURSE YOU ARE. HOW SILLY OF ME.
ST. MICHAEL DEFEND US!
LUCY?

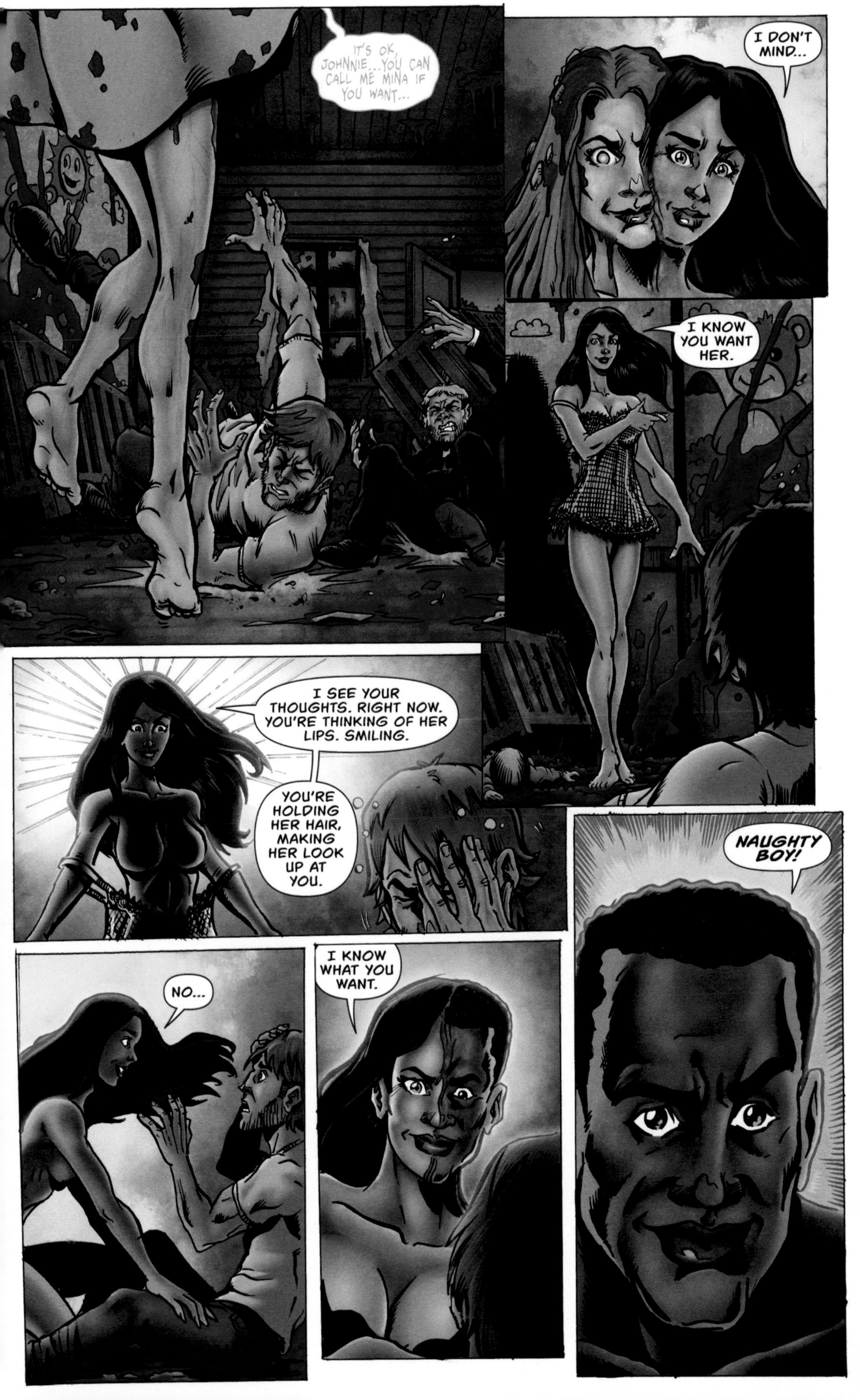
IT'S OK, JOHNNIE...YOU CAN CALL ME MINA IF YOU WANT...
I DON'T MIND...
I KNOW YOU WANT HER.
I SEE YOUR THOUGHTS. RIGHT NOW. YOU'RE THINKING OF HER LIPS. SMILING.
YOU'RE HOLDING HER HAIR, MAKING HER LOOK UP AT YOU.
NAUGHTY BOY!
NO...
I KNOW WHAT YOU WANT.

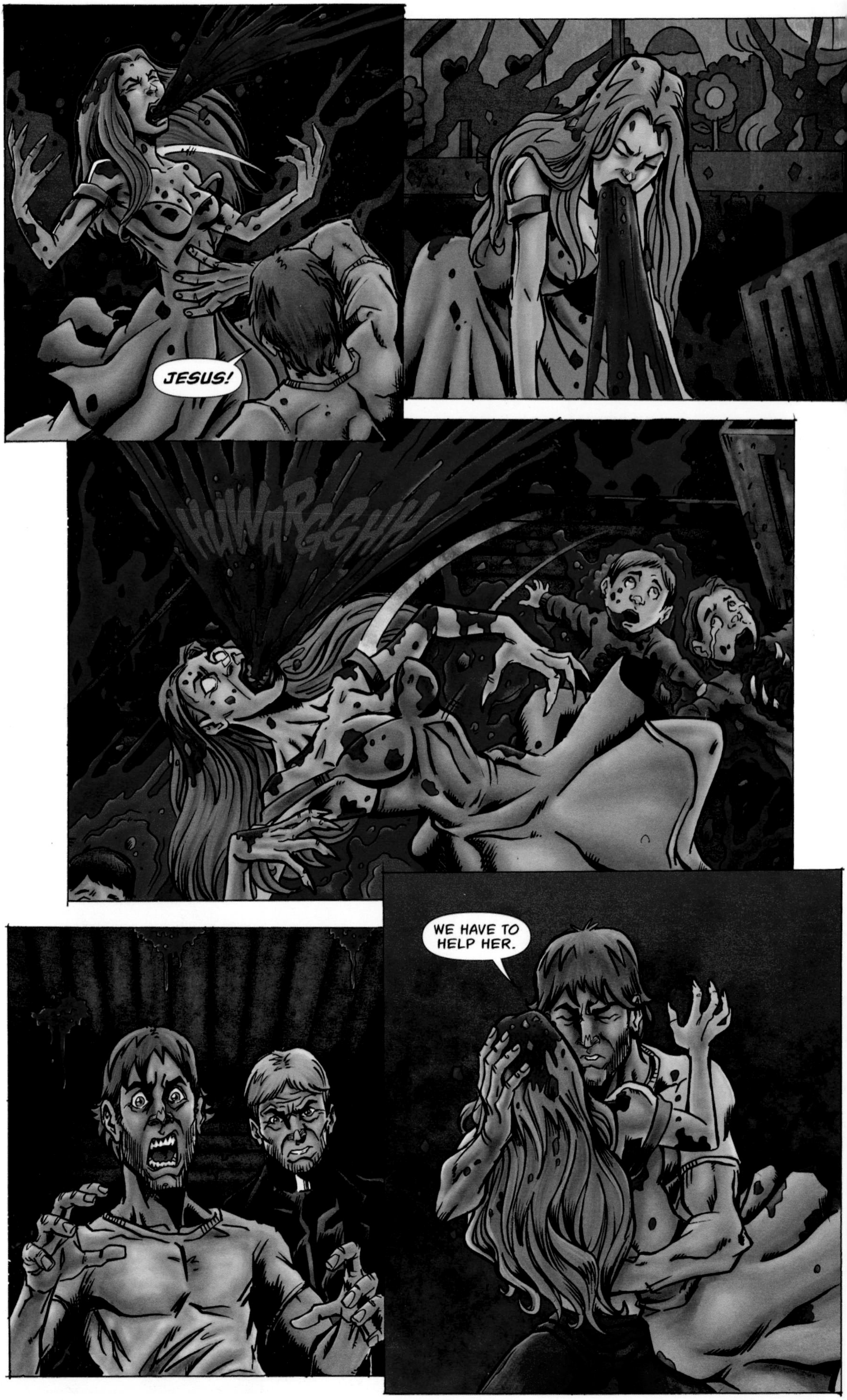
JESUS!
HUWARGGHH
WE HAVE TO HELP HER.

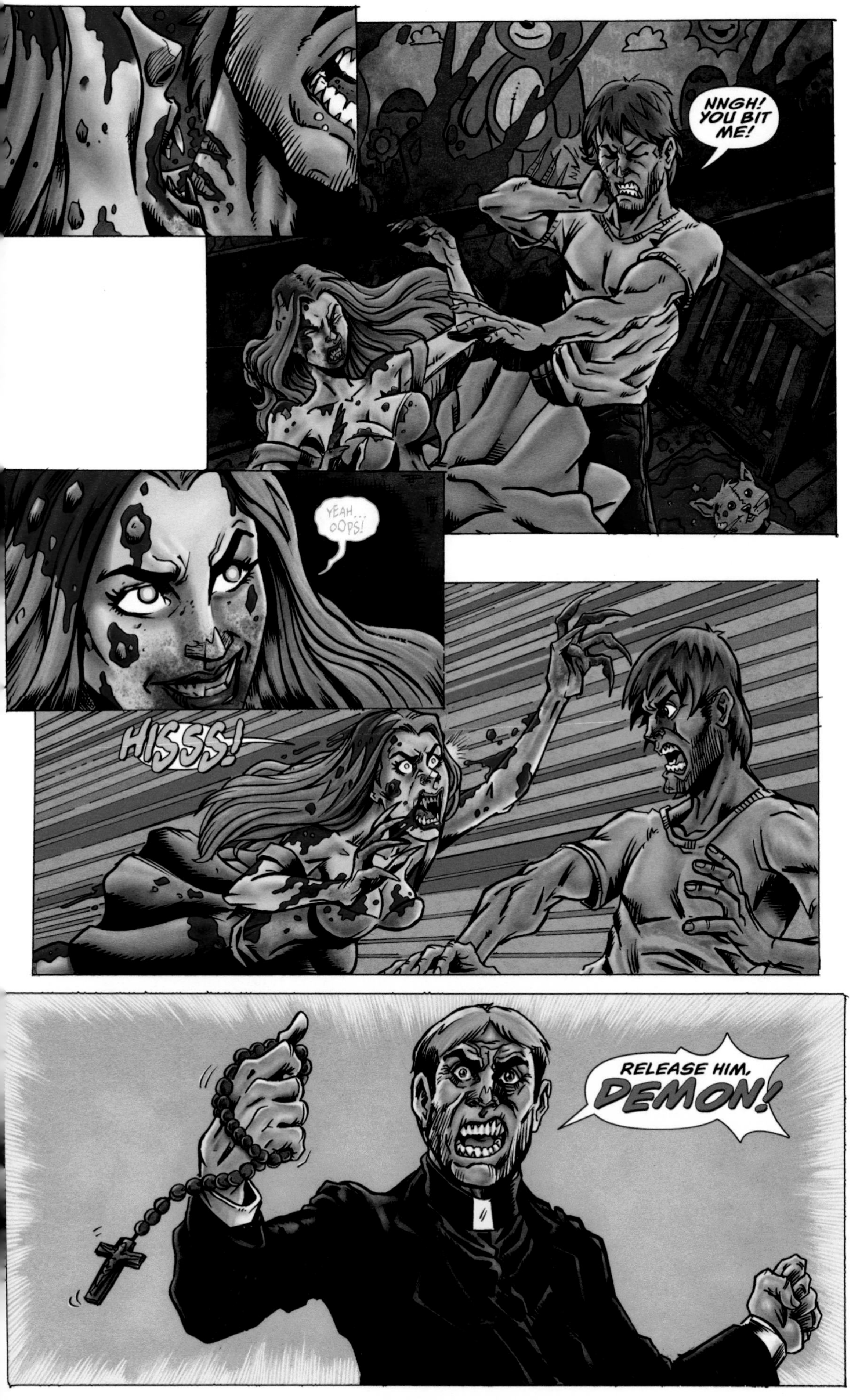

NNGH! YOU BIT ME!
YEAH... OOPS!
HISSS!
RELEASE HIM, DEMON!

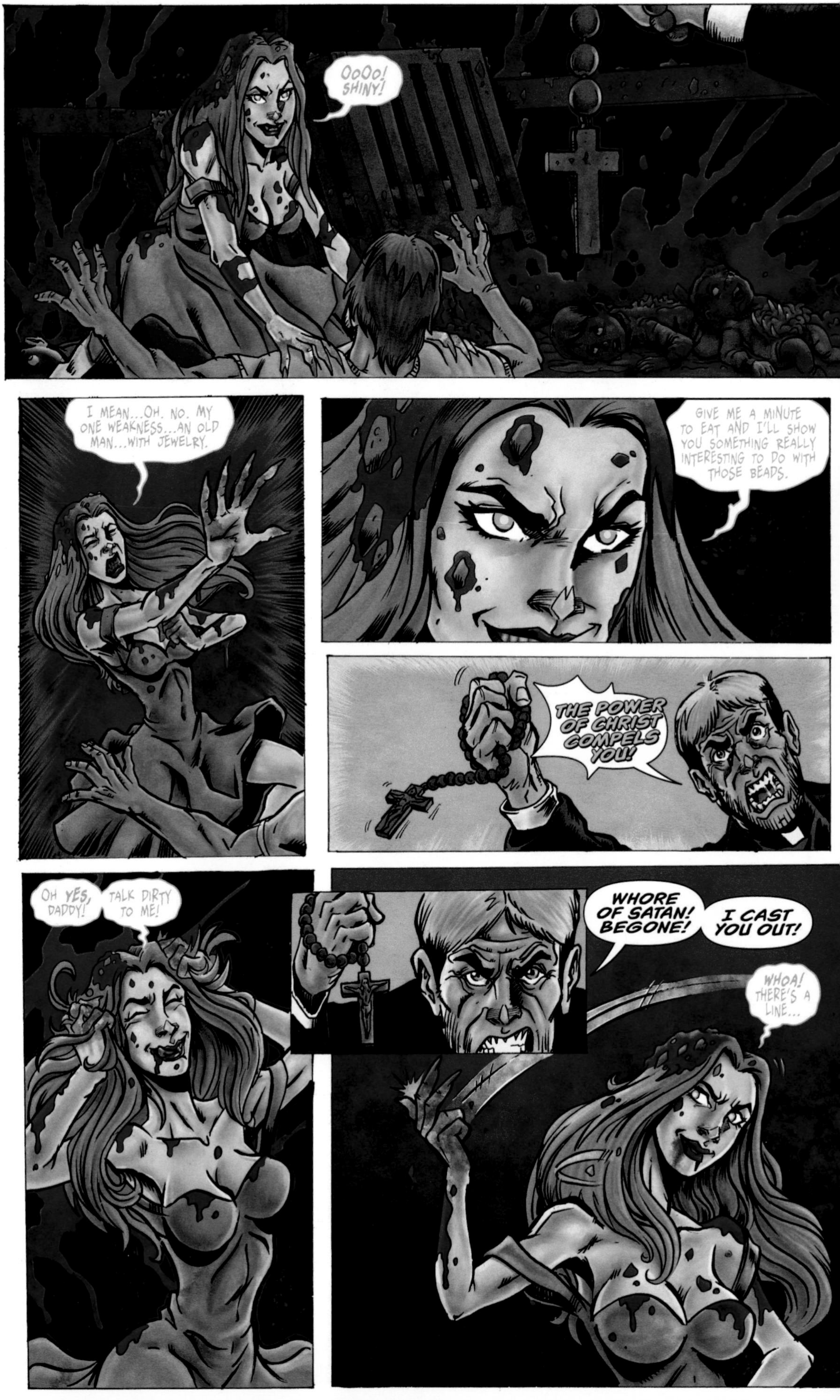
OOOO! SHINY!
I MEAN...OH. NO. MY ONE WEAKNESS...AN OLD MAN...WITH JEWELRY.
GIVE ME A MINUTE TO EAT AND I'LL SHOW YOU SOMETHING REALLY INTERESTING TO DO WITH THOSE BEADS.
THE POWER OF CHRIST COMPELS YOU!
OH YES, DADDY!
TALK DIRTY TO ME!
WHORE OF SATAN! BEGONE!
I CAST YOU OUT!
WHOA! THERE'S A LINE...

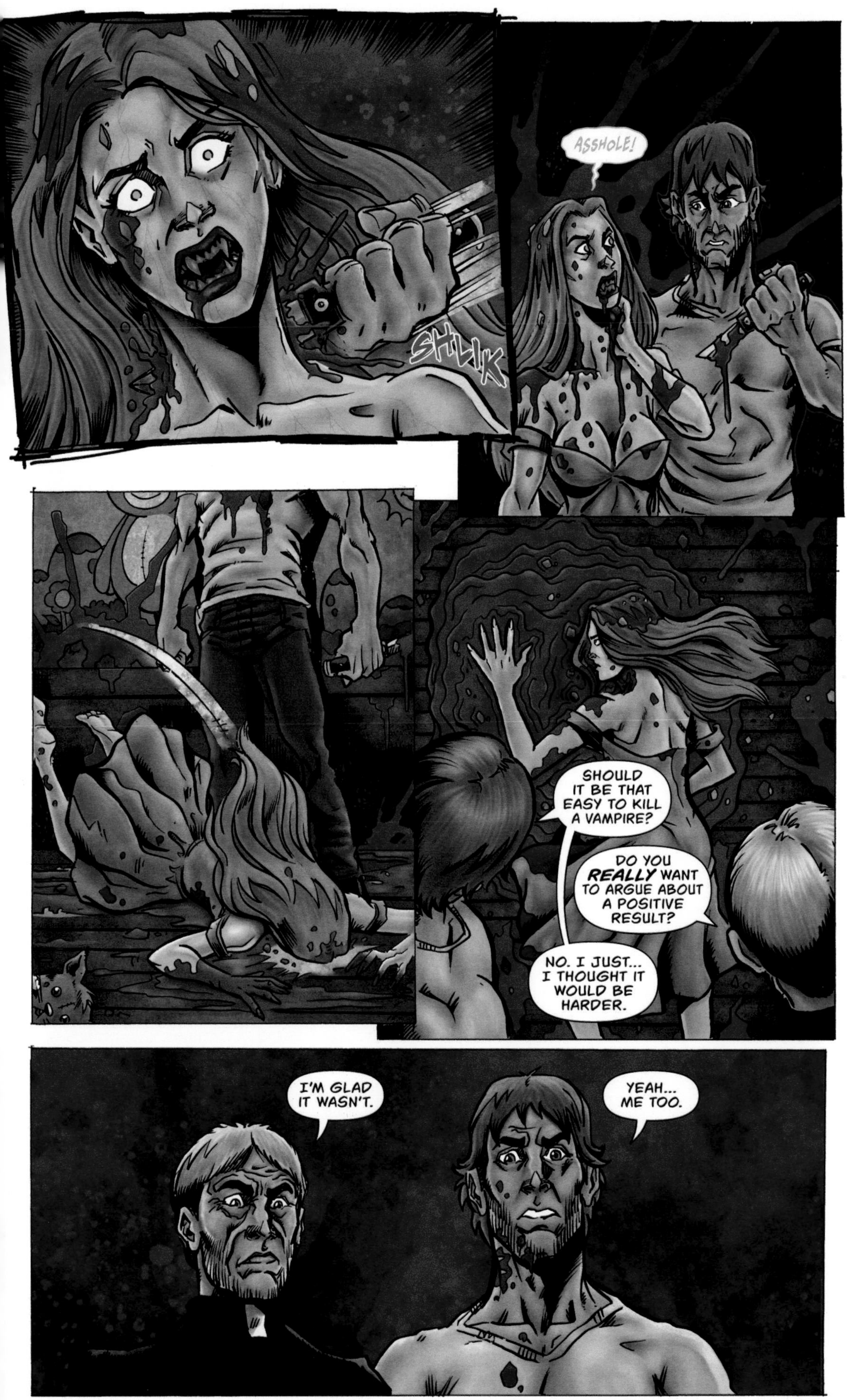
SHLIK
ASSHOLE!
SHOULD IT BE THAT EASY TO KILL A VAMPIRE?
DO YOU REALLY WANT TO ARGUE ABOUT A POSITIVE RESULT?
NO. I JUST... I THOUGHT IT WOULD BE HARDER.
I'M GLAD IT WASN'T.
YEAH... ME TOO.

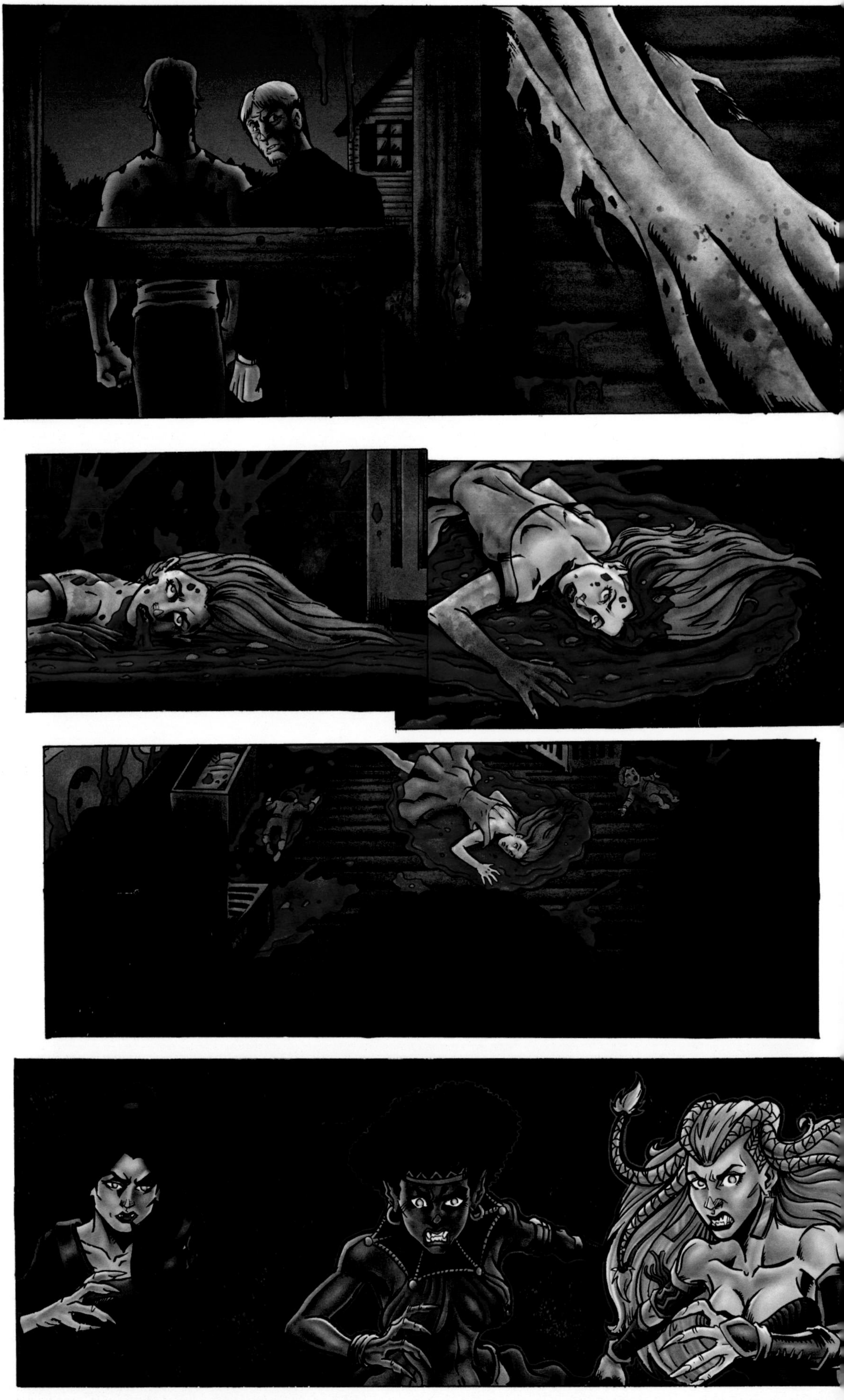

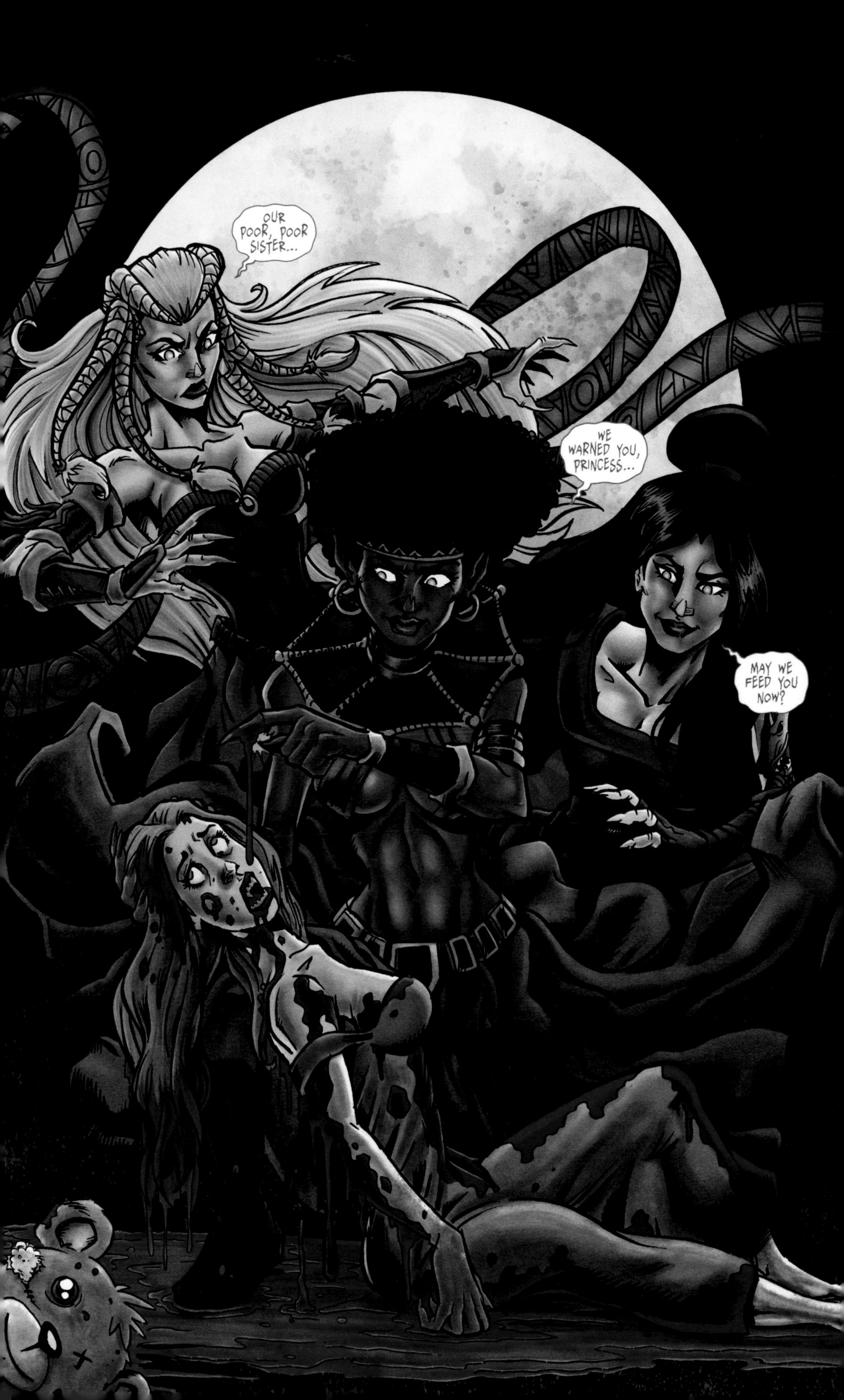
OUR POOR, POOR SISTER...
WE WARNED YOU, PRINCESS...
MAY WE FEED YOU NOW?

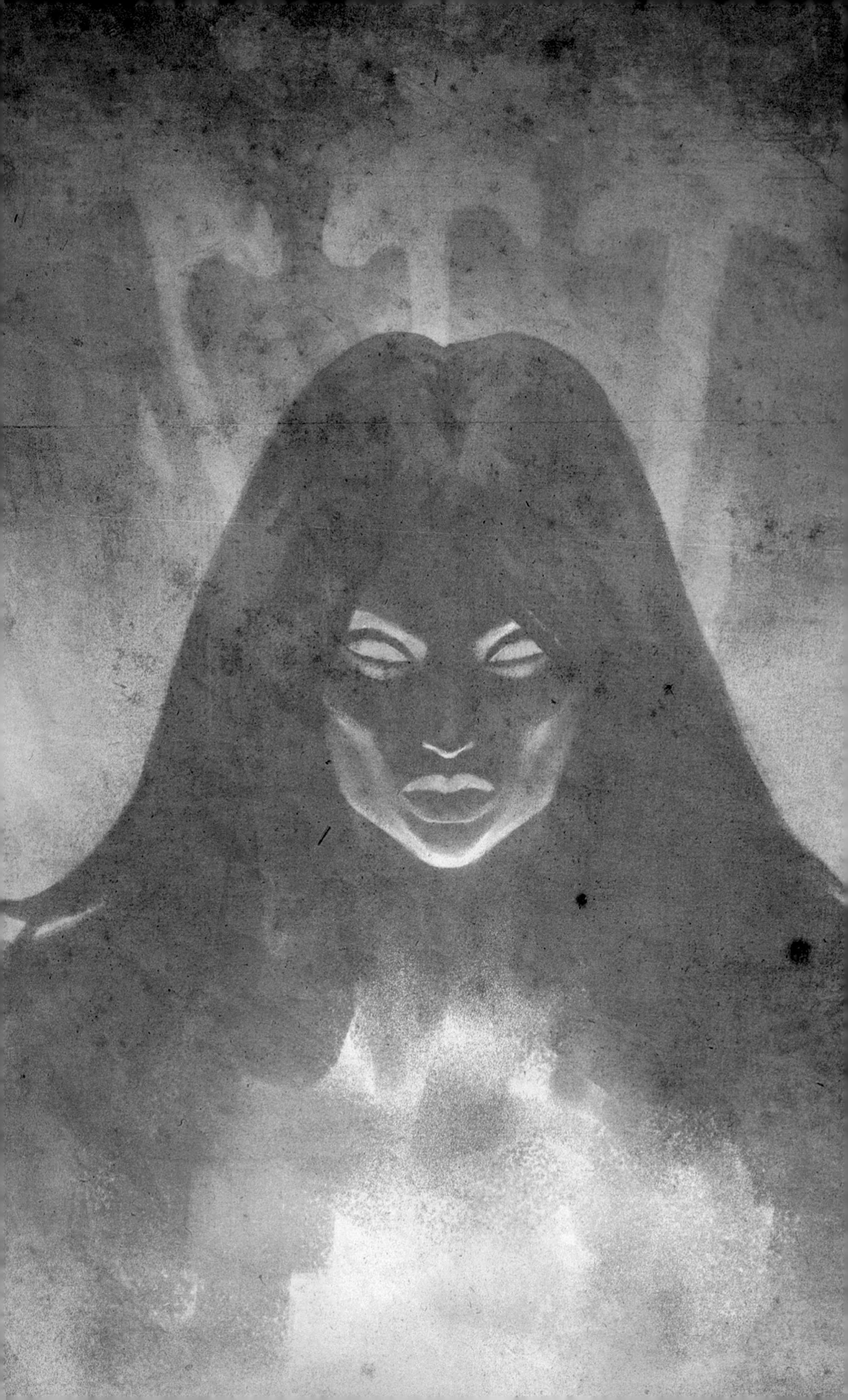

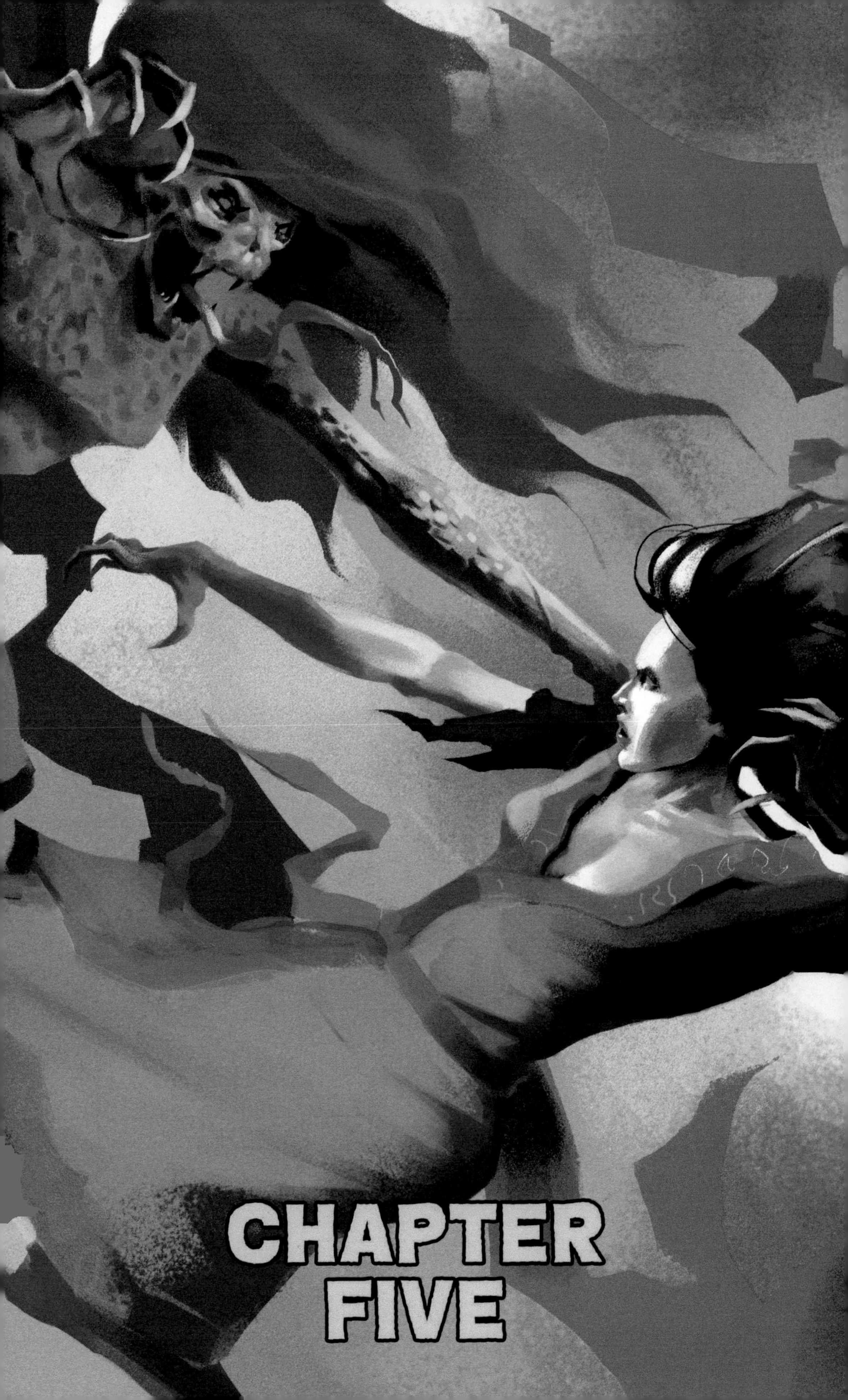

CHAPTER FIVE

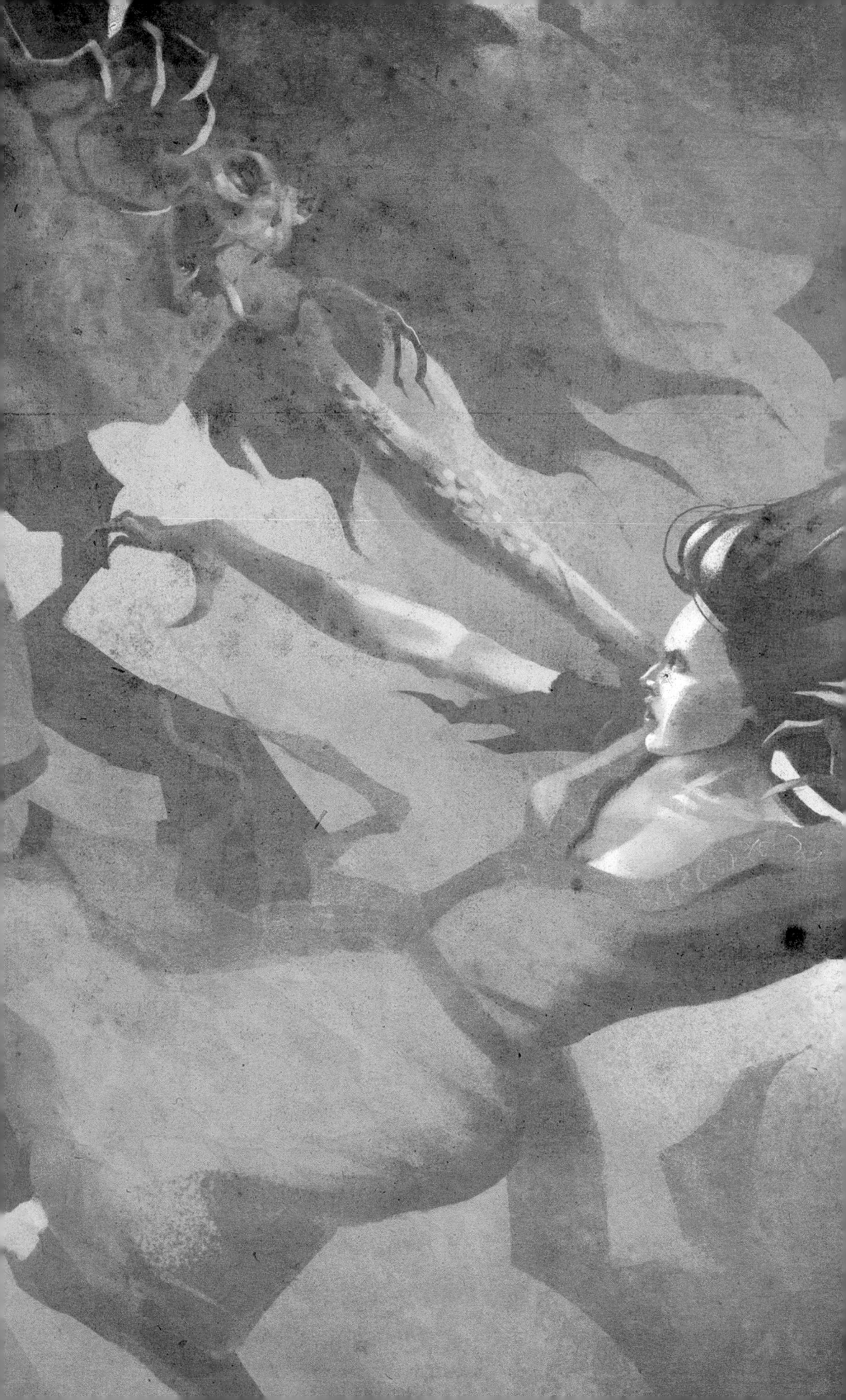

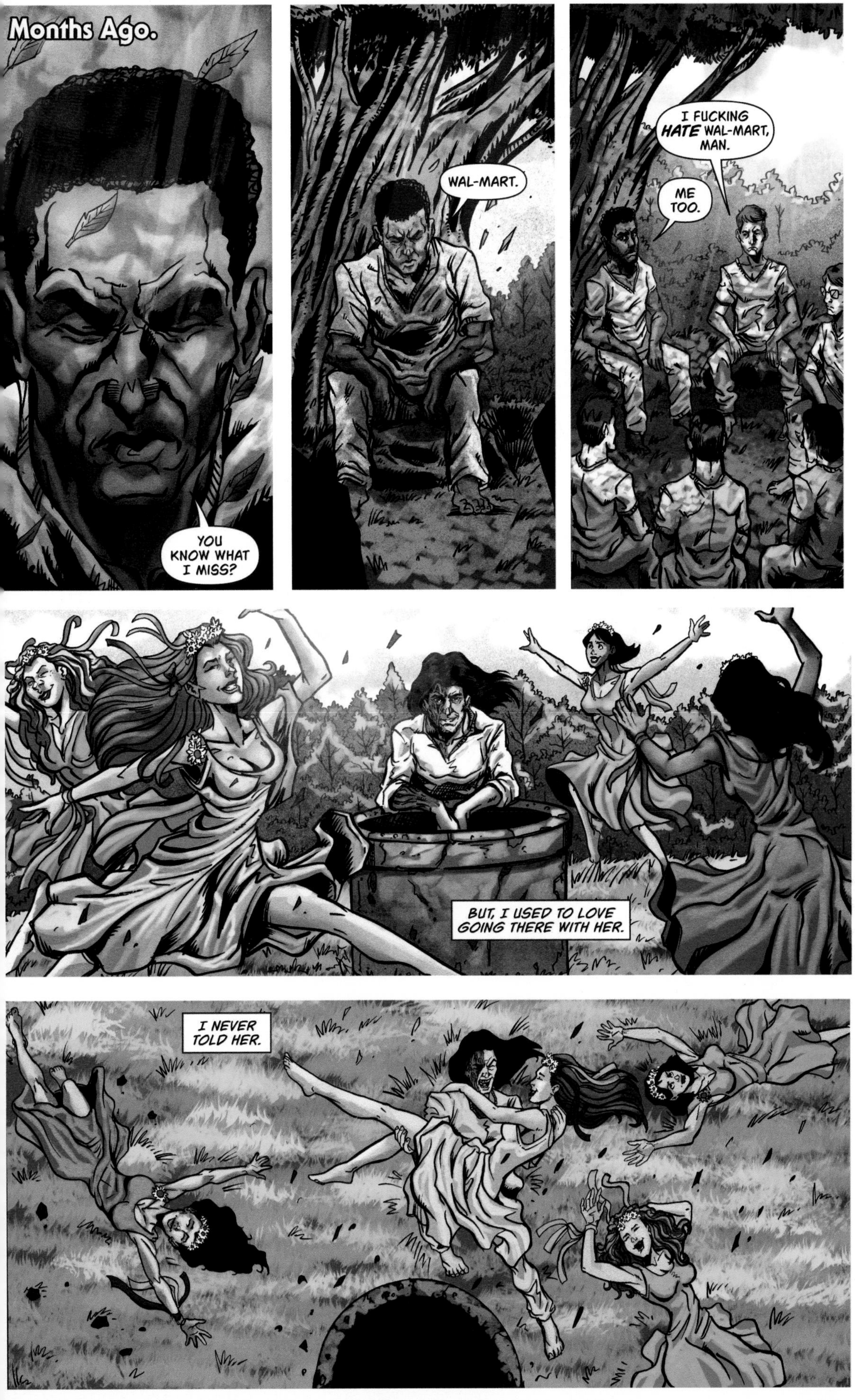
Months Ago.
YOU KNOW WHAT I MISS?
WAL-MART.
I FUCKING HATE WAL-MART, MAN.
ME TOO.
BUT, I USED TO LOVE GOING THERE WITH HER.
I NEVER TOLD HER.

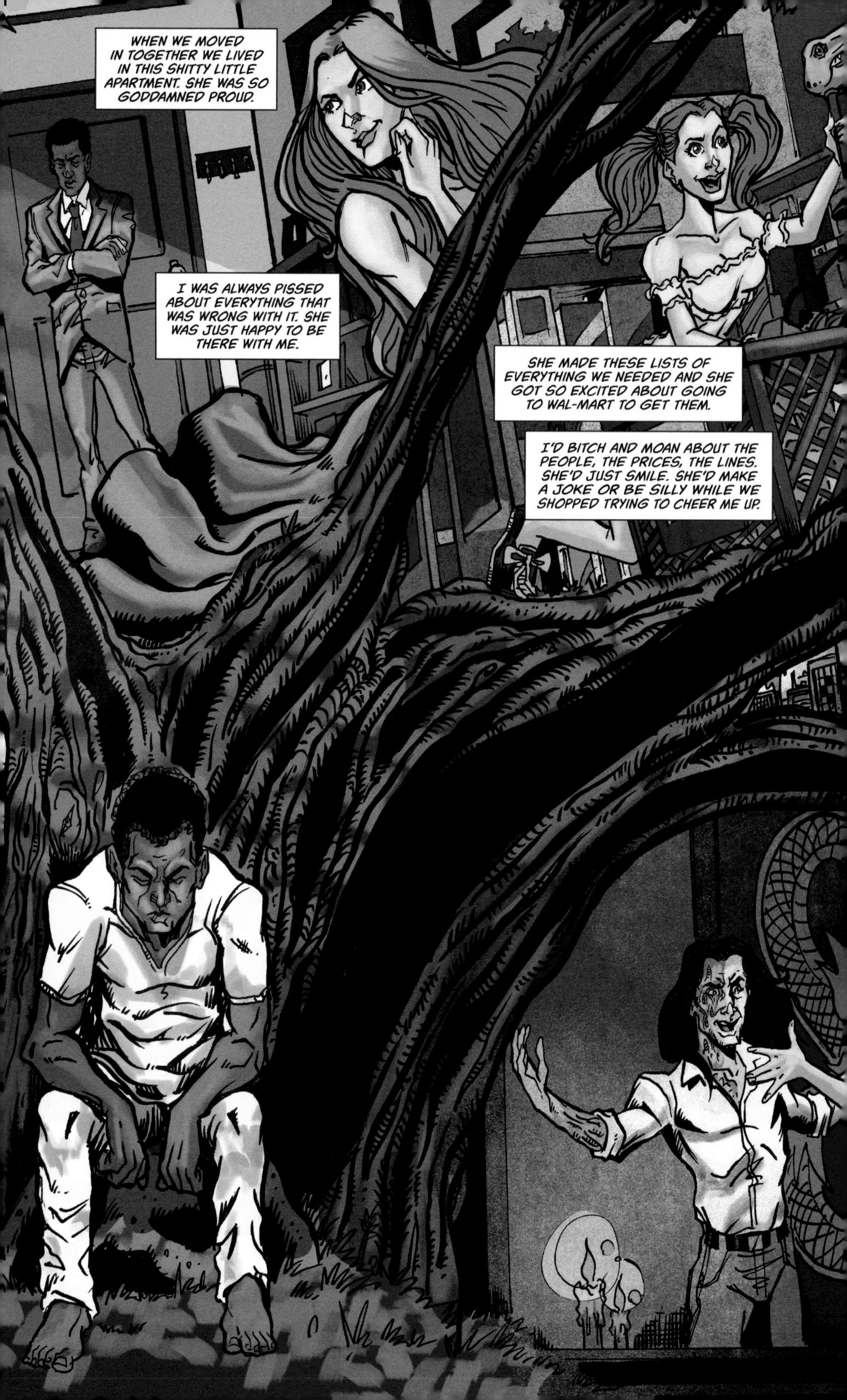

WHEN WE MOVED IN TOGETHER WE LIVED IN THIS SHITTY LITTLE APARTMENT. SHE WAS SO GODDAMNED PROUD.
I WAS ALWAYS PISSED ABOUT EVERYTHING THAT WAS WRONG WITH IT. SHE WAS JUST HAPPY TO BE THERE WITH ME.
SHE MADE THESE LISTS OF EVERYTHING WE NEEDED AND SHE GOT SO EXCITED ABOUT GOING TO WAL-MART TO GET THEM.
I'D BITCH AND MOAN ABOUT THE PEOPLE, THE PRICES, THE LINES. SHE'D JUST SMILE. SHE'D MAKE A JOKE OR BE SILLY WHILE WE SHOPPED TRYING TO CHEER ME UP.

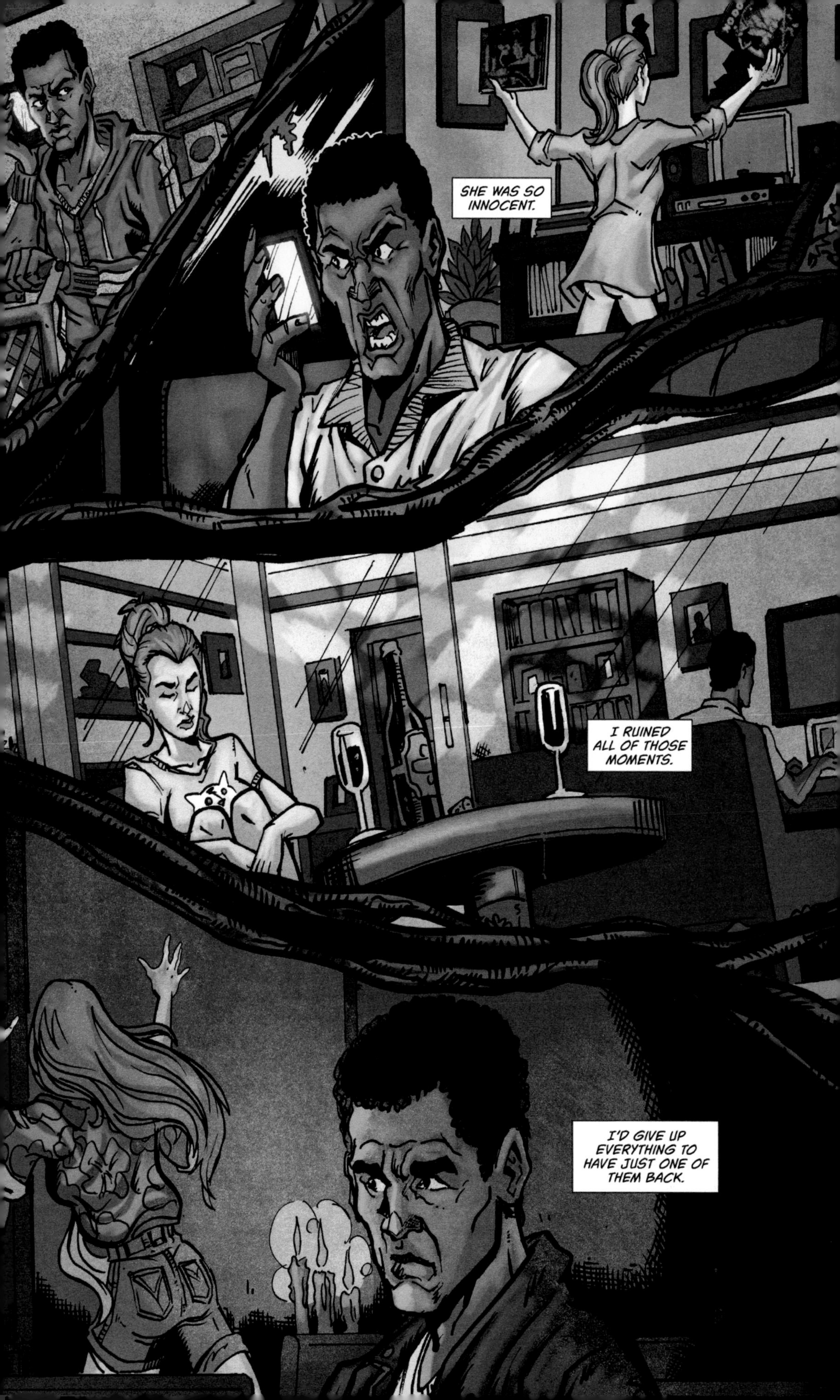
SHE WAS SO INNOCENT.
I RUINED ALL OF THOSE MOMENTS.
I'D GIVE UP EVERYTHING TO HAVE JUST ONE OF THEM BACK.

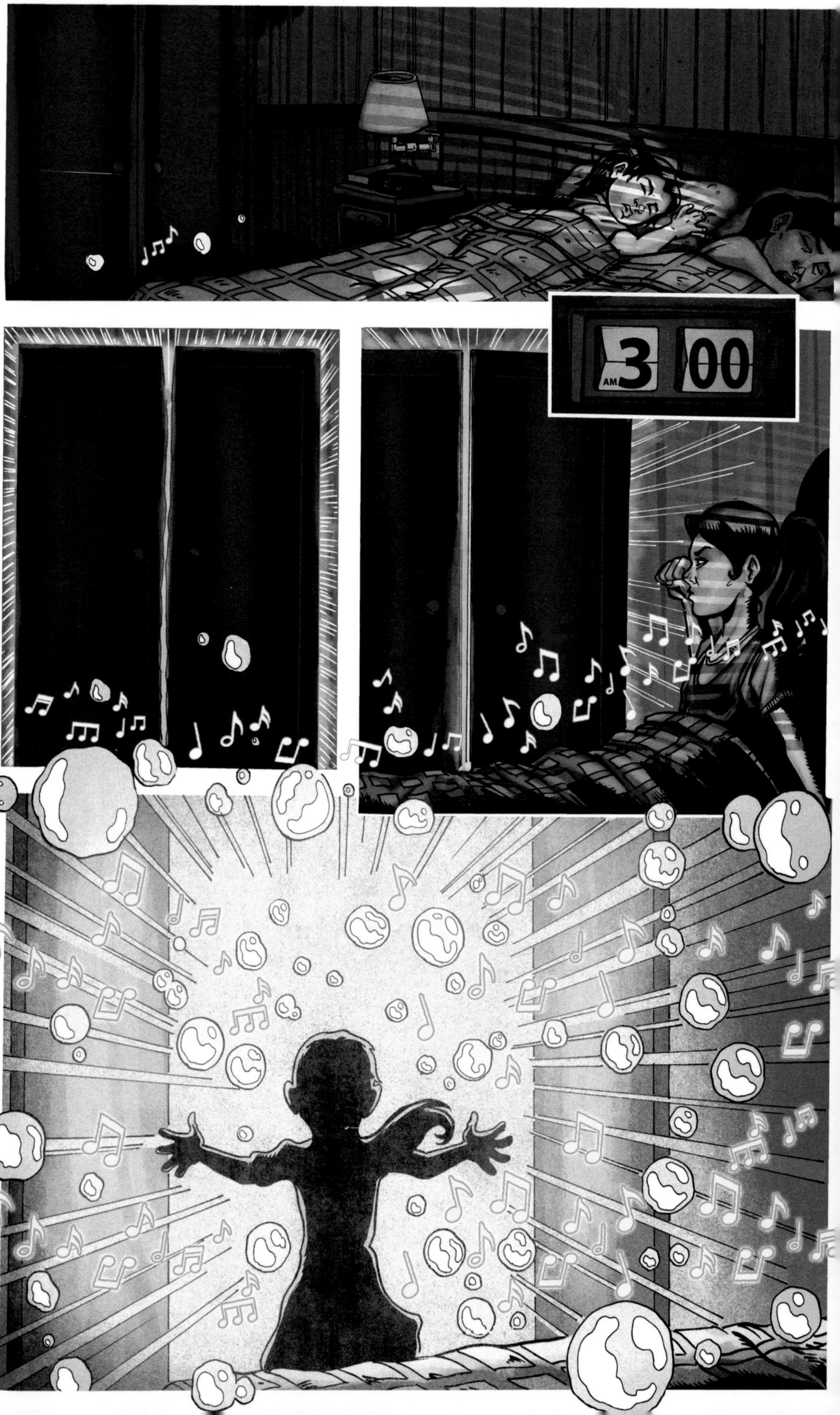

AM 3 00

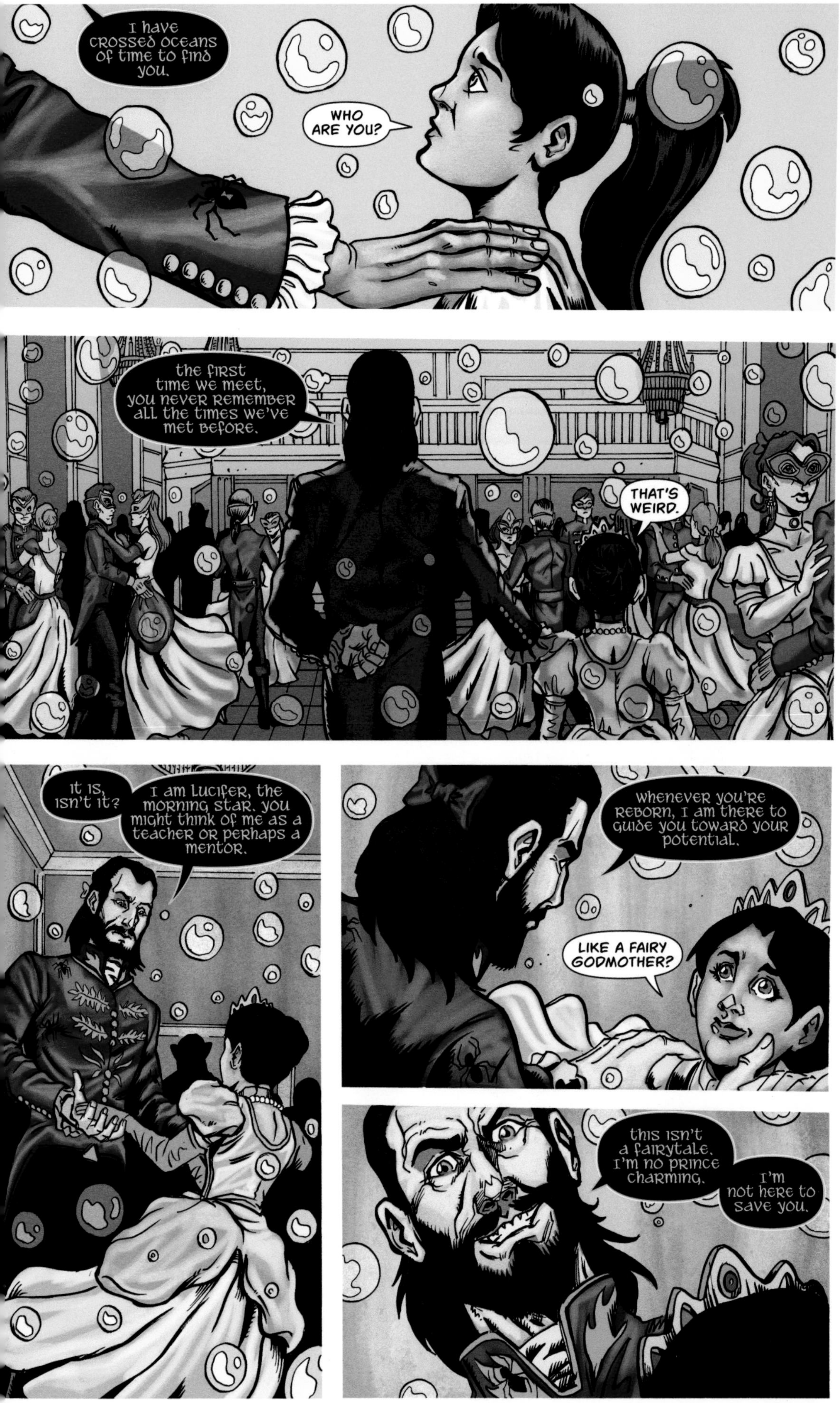
I have crossed oceans of time to find you.
WHO ARE YOU?
the first time we meet, you never remember all the times we've met before.
THAT'S WEIRD.
it is, isn't it?
I am Lucifer, the morning star. you might think of me as a teacher or perhaps a mentor.
whenever you're reborn, I am there to guide you toward your potential.
LIKE A FAIRY GODMOTHER?
this isn't a fairytale. I'm no prince charming.
I'm not here to save you.

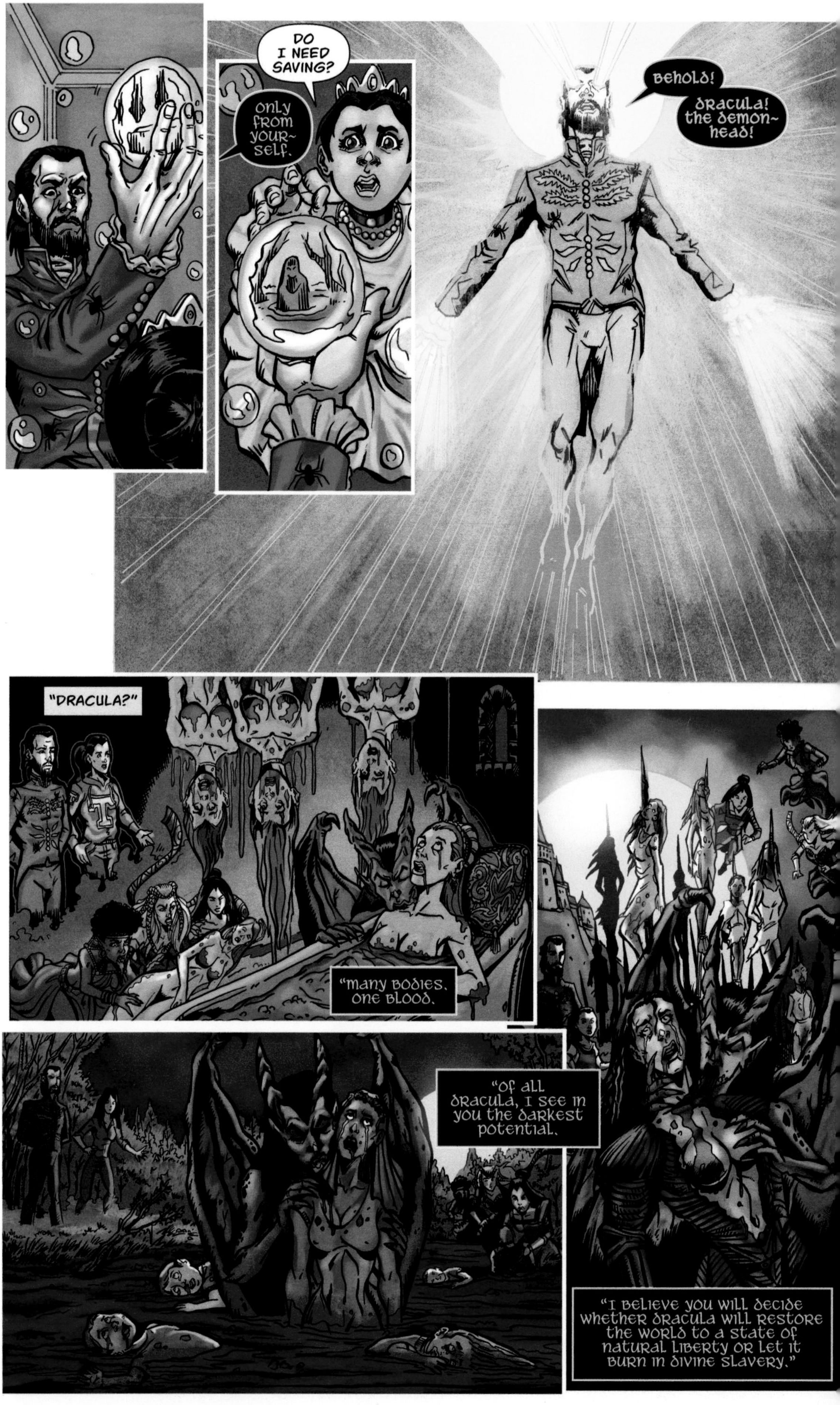

DO I NEED SAVING?
Only from your~self.
Behold!
Dracula! the demon~head!
"DRACULA?"
"Many bodies, one blood.
"Of all Dracula, I see in you the darkest potential.
"I believe you will decide whether Dracula will restore the world to a state of natural liberty or let it burn in divine slavery."

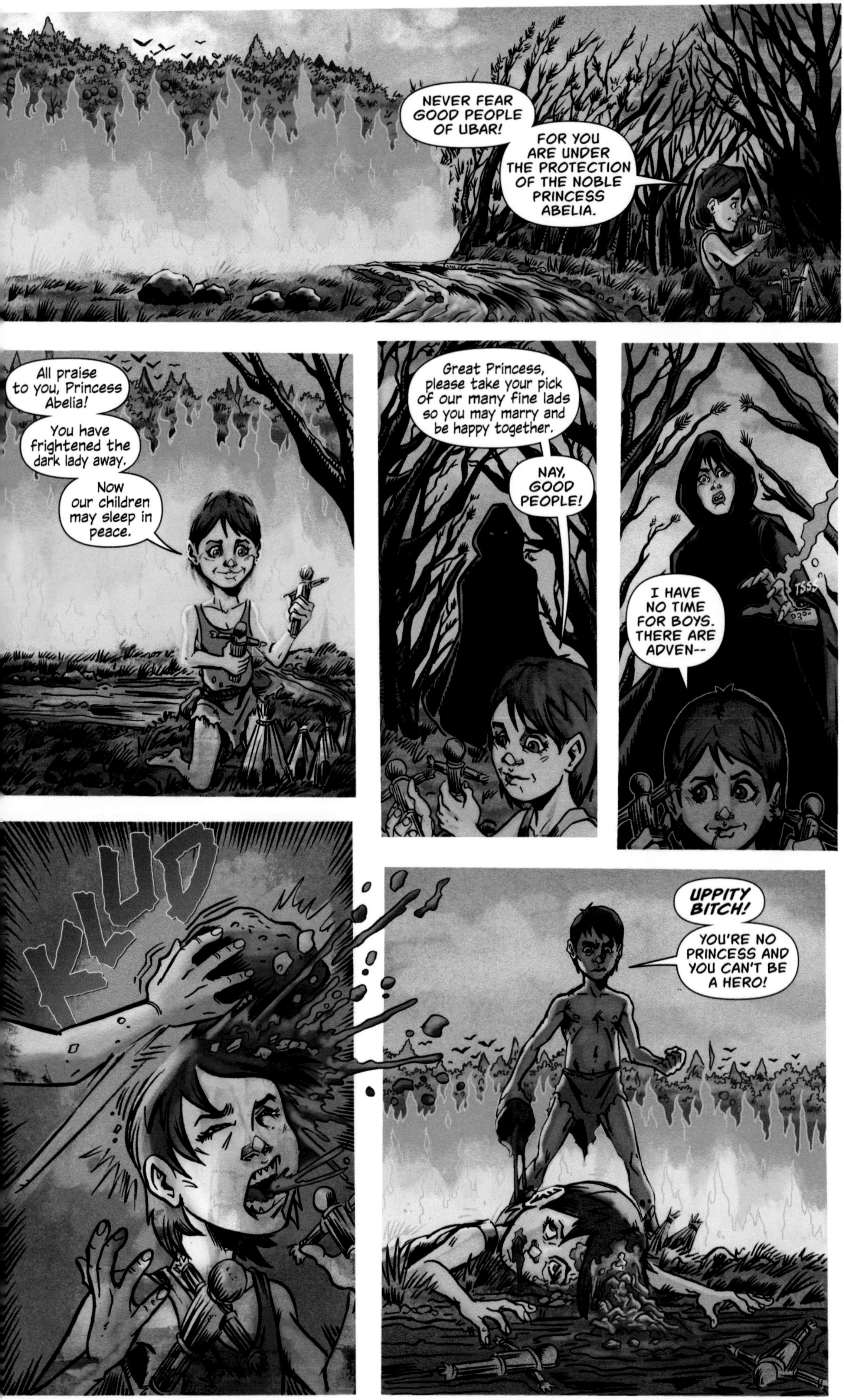
NEVER FEAR GOOD PEOPLE OF UBAR!
FOR YOU ARE UNDER THE PROTECTION OF THE NOBLE PRINCESS ABELIA.
All praise to you, Princess Abelia!
You have frightened the dark lady away.
Now our children may sleep in peace.
Great Princess, please take your pick of our many fine lads so you may marry and be happy together.
NAY, GOOD PEOPLE!
TSSS
I HAVE NO TIME FOR BOYS. THERE ARE ADVEN--
KLUD
UPPITY BITCH!
YOU'RE NO PRINCESS AND YOU CAN'T BE A HERO!

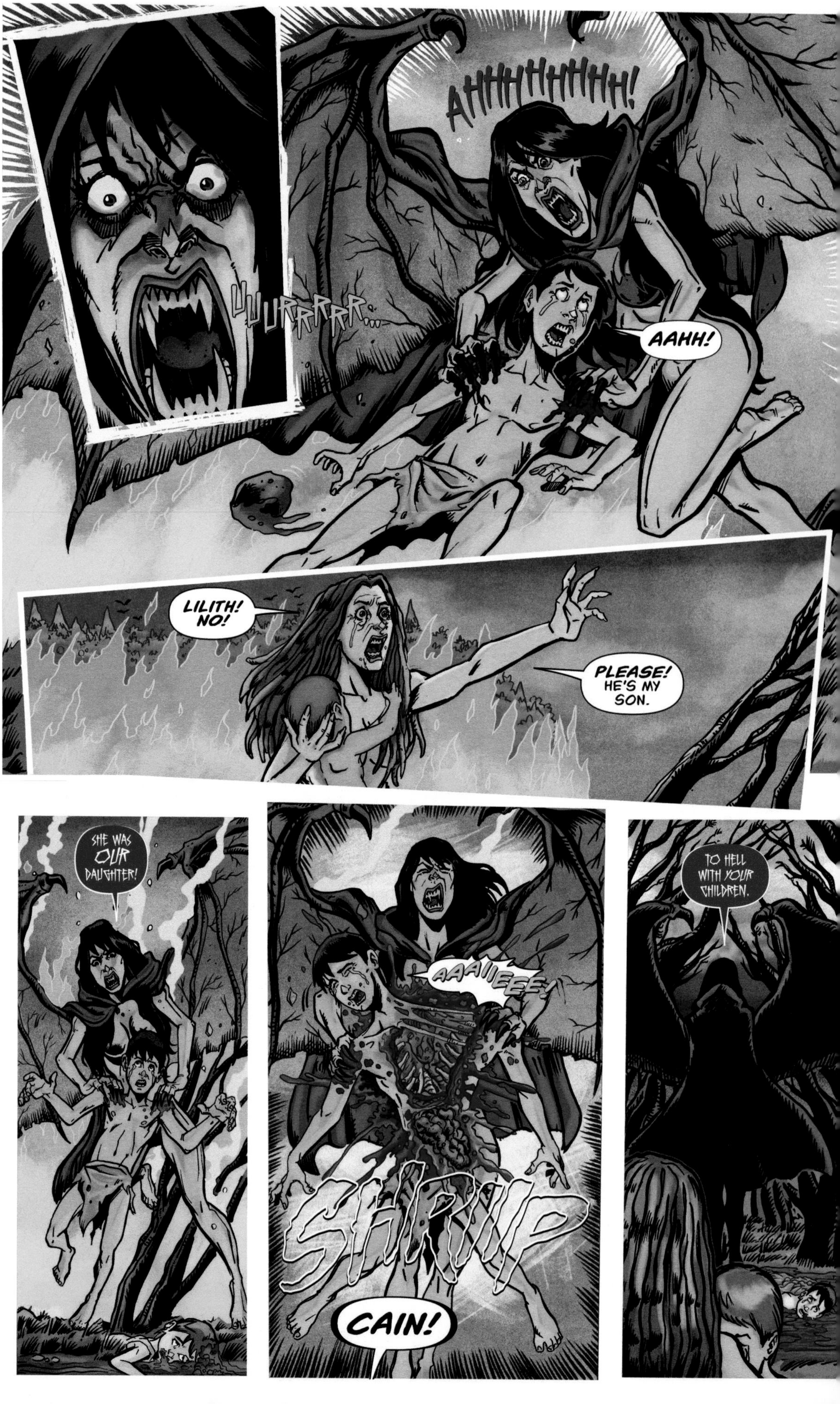
AHHHHHHHH!
UUURRRRR...
AAHH!
LILITH! NO!
PLEASE! HE'S MY SON.
SHE WAS OUR DAUGHTER!
AAAIIEEEE!
SHRUP
CAIN!
TO HELL WITH YOUR CHILDREN.

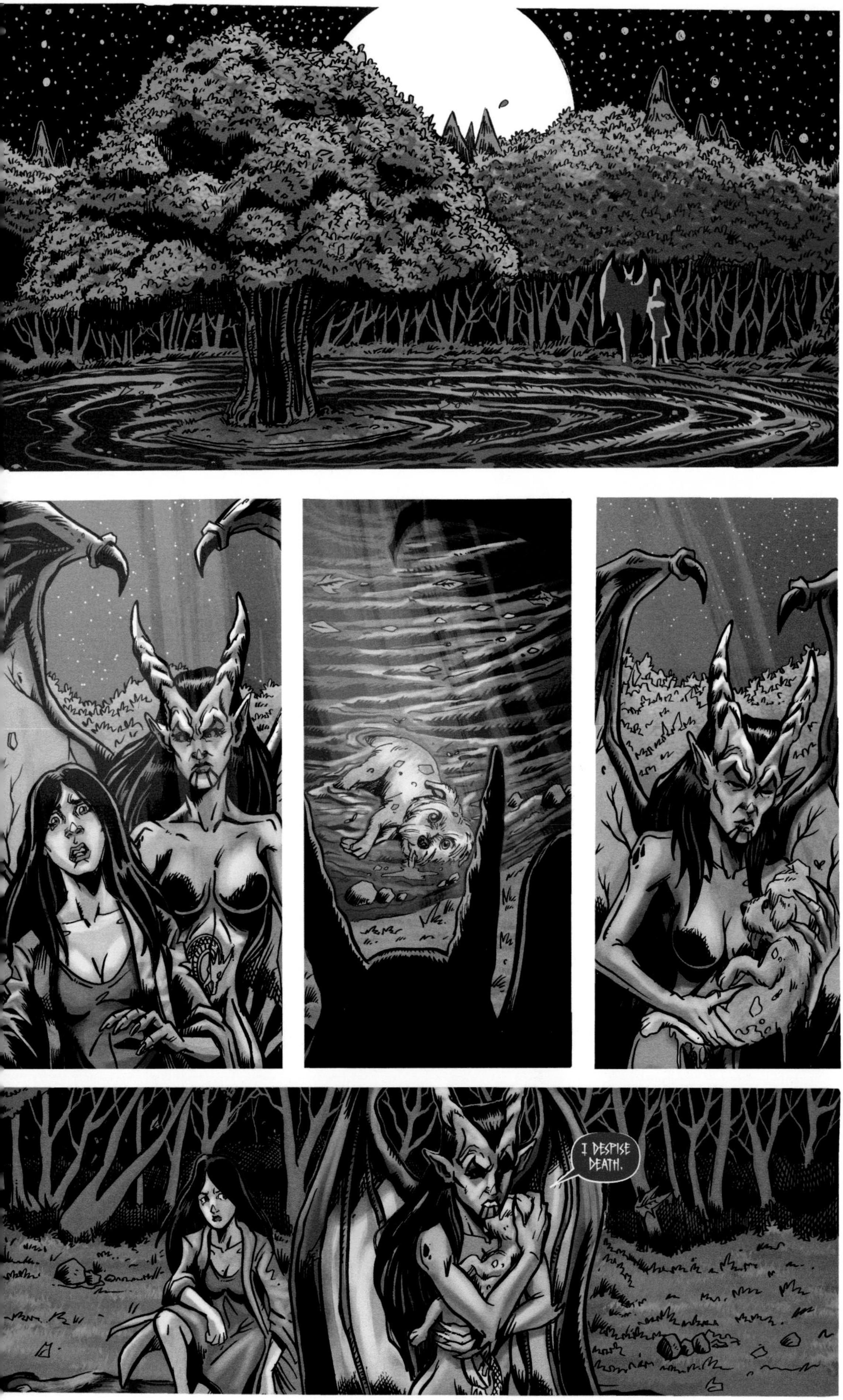
I DESPISE DEATH.

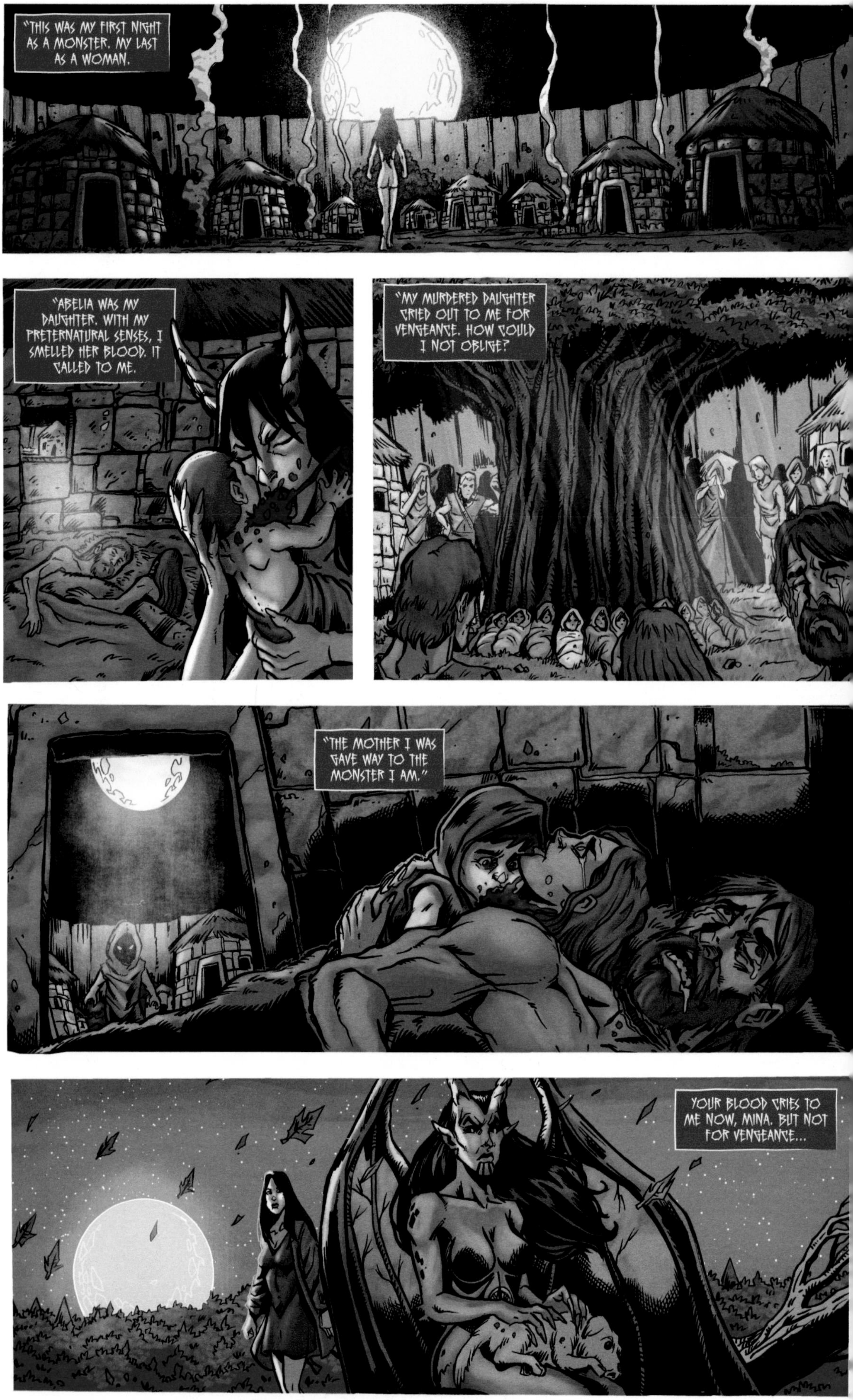
"THIS WAS MY FIRST NIGHT AS A MONSTER. MY LAST AS A WOMAN.
"ABELIA WAS MY DAUGHTER. WITH MY PRETERNATURAL SENSES, I SMELLED HER BLOOD. IT CALLED TO ME.
"MY MURDERED DAUGHTER CRIED OUT TO ME FOR VENGEANCE. HOW COULD I NOT OBLIGE?
"THE MOTHER I WAS GAVE WAY TO THE MONSTER I AM."
YOUR BLOOD CRIES TO ME NOW, MINA. BUT NOT FOR VENGEANCE...

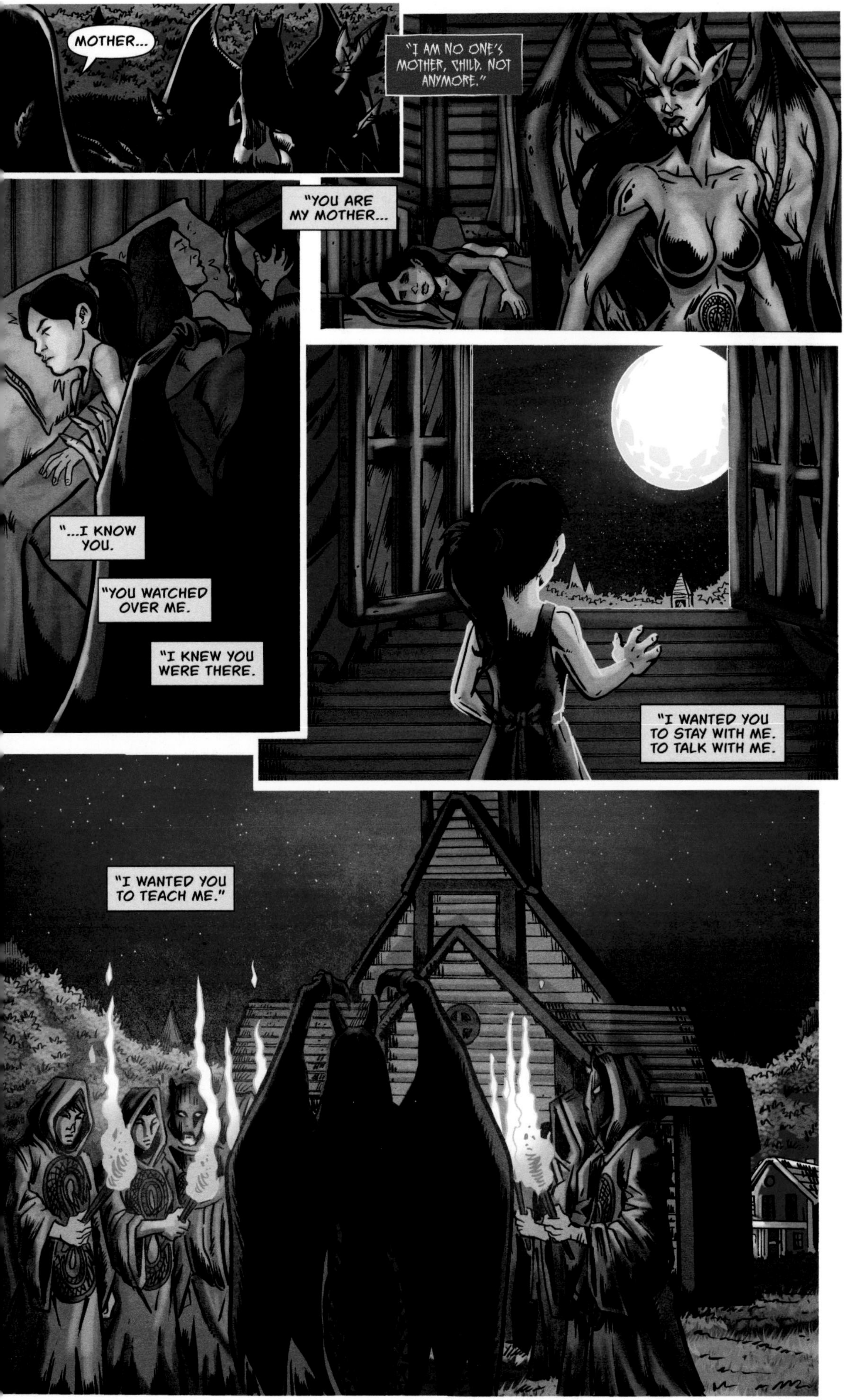
MOTHER...
"I AM NO ONE'S MOTHER, CHILD. NOT ANYMORE."
"YOU ARE MY MOTHER...
"...I KNOW YOU.
"YOU WATCHED OVER ME.
"I KNEW YOU WERE THERE.
"I WANTED YOU TO STAY WITH ME. TO TALK WITH ME.
"I WANTED YOU TO TEACH ME."

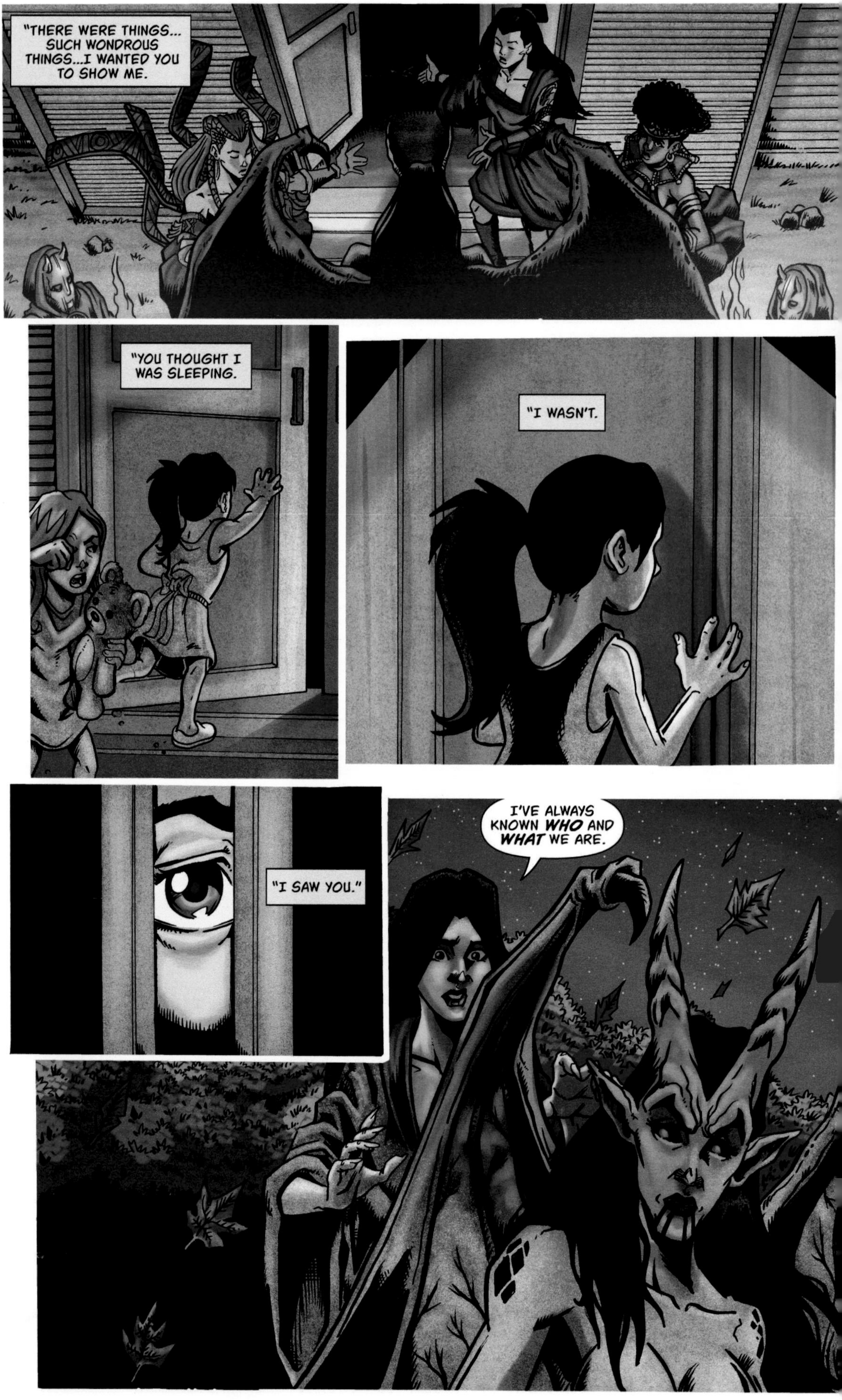
"THERE WERE THINGS... SUCH WONDROUS THINGS...I WANTED YOU TO SHOW ME.
"YOU THOUGHT I WAS SLEEPING.
"I WASN'T.
"I SAW YOU."
I'VE ALWAYS KNOWN **WHO** AND **WHAT** WE ARE.

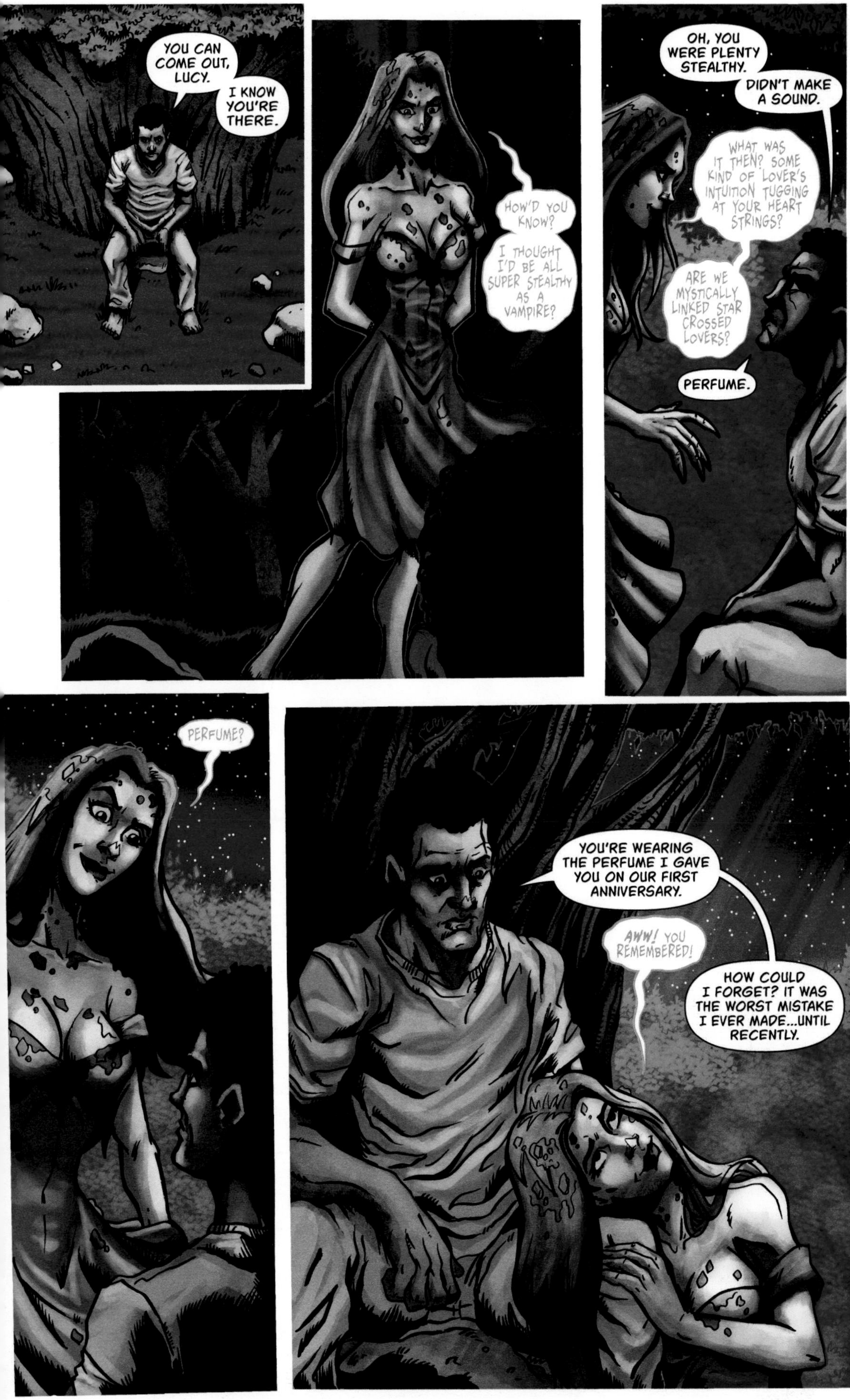

YOU CAN COME OUT, LUCY.
I KNOW YOU'RE THERE.
HOW'D YOU KNOW?
I THOUGHT I'D BE ALL SUPER STEALTHY AS A VAMPIRE?
OH, YOU WERE PLENTY STEALTHY.
DIDN'T MAKE A SOUND.
WHAT WAS IT THEN? SOME KIND OF LOVER'S INTUITION TUGGING AT YOUR HEART STRINGS?
ARE WE MYSTICALLY LINKED STAR CROSSED LOVERS?
PERFUME.
PERFUME?
YOU'RE WEARING THE PERFUME I GAVE YOU ON OUR FIRST ANNIVERSARY.
AWW! YOU REMEMBERED!
HOW COULD I FORGET? IT WAS THE WORST MISTAKE I EVER MADE...UNTIL RECENTLY.

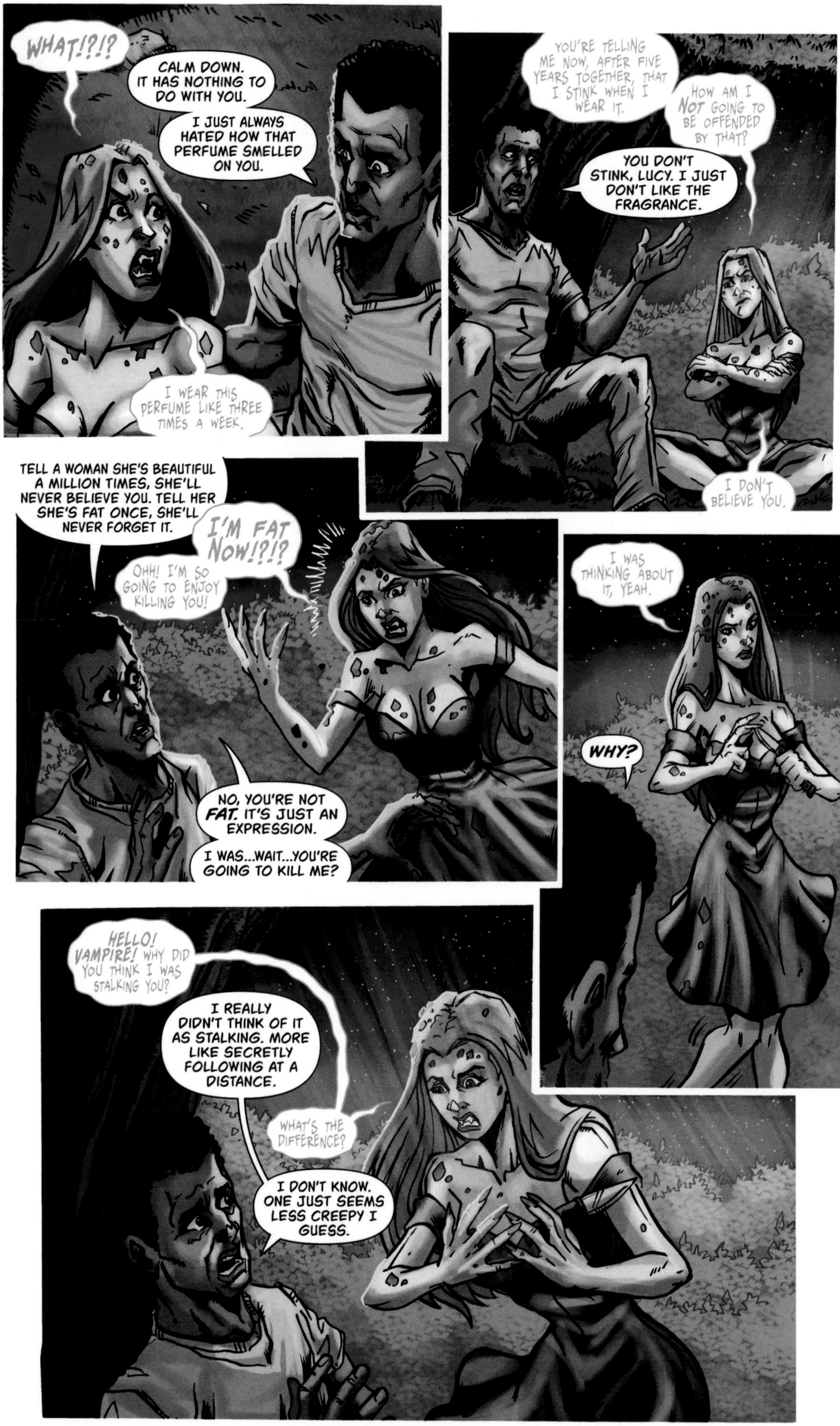
WHAT!?!?
CALM DOWN. IT HAS NOTHING TO DO WITH YOU.
I JUST ALWAYS HATED HOW THAT PERFUME SMELLED ON YOU.
I WEAR THIS PERFUME LIKE THREE TIMES A WEEK.
YOU'RE TELLING ME NOW, AFTER FIVE YEARS TOGETHER, THAT I STINK WHEN I WEAR IT.
HOW AM I NOT GOING TO BE OFFENDED BY THAT?
YOU DON'T STINK, LUCY. I JUST DON'T LIKE THE FRAGRANCE.
I DON'T BELIEVE YOU.
TELL A WOMAN SHE'S BEAUTIFUL A MILLION TIMES, SHE'LL NEVER BELIEVE YOU. TELL HER SHE'S FAT ONCE, SHE'LL NEVER FORGET IT.
I'M FAT NOW!?!?
OHH! I'M SO GOING TO ENJOY KILLING YOU!
NO, YOU'RE NOT FAT. IT'S JUST AN EXPRESSION.
I WAS...WAIT...YOU'RE GOING TO KILL ME?
I WAS THINKING ABOUT IT, YEAH.
WHY?
HELLO! VAMPIRE! WHY DID YOU THINK I WAS STALKING YOU?
I REALLY DIDN'T THINK OF IT AS STALKING. MORE LIKE SECRETLY FOLLOWING AT A DISTANCE.
WHAT'S THE DIFFERENCE?
I DON'T KNOW. ONE JUST SEEMS LESS CREEPY I GUESS.

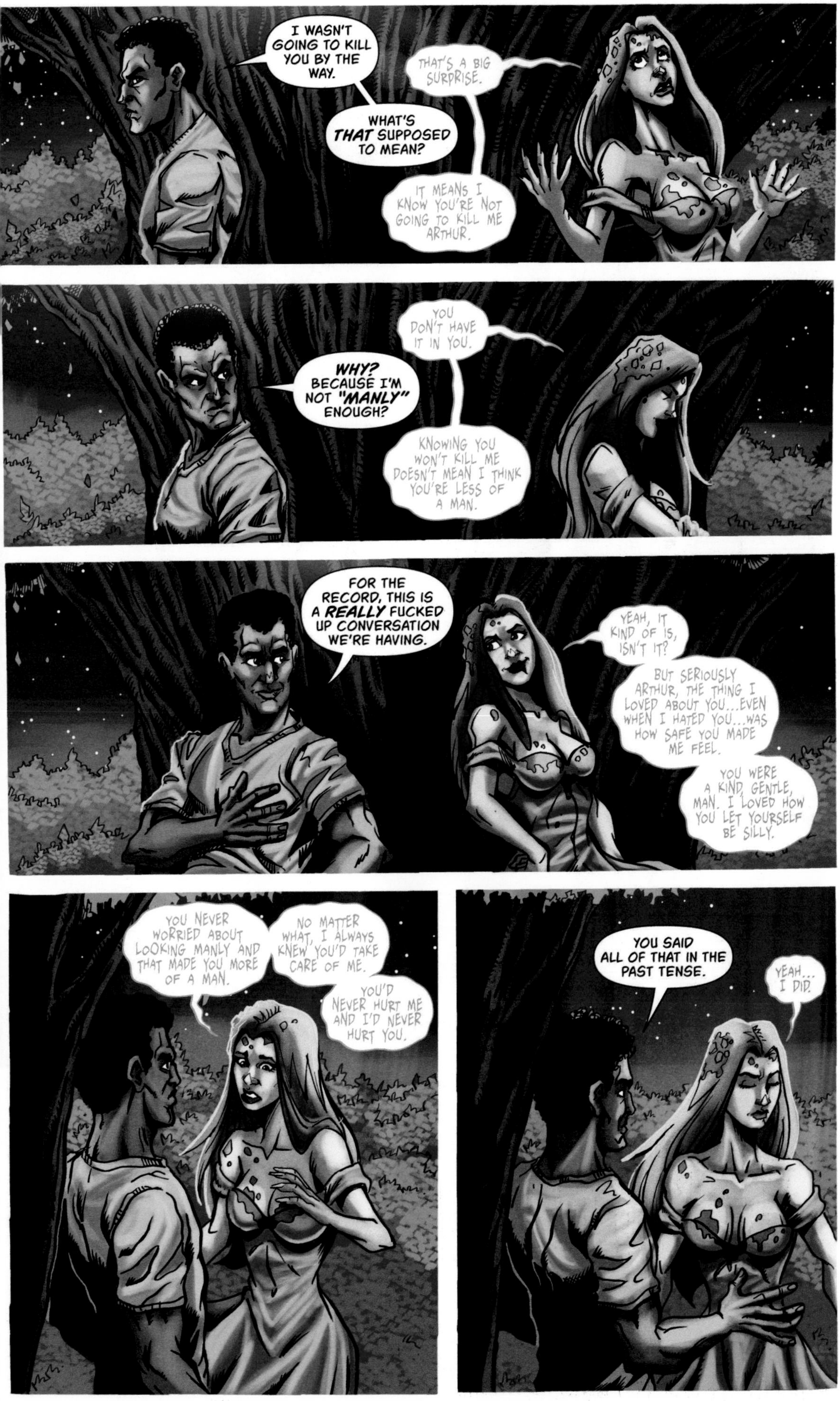
I WASN'T GOING TO KILL YOU BY THE WAY.
THAT'S A BIG SURPRISE.
WHAT'S *THAT* SUPPOSED TO MEAN?
IT MEANS I KNOW YOU'RE NOT GOING TO KILL ME ARTHUR.
YOU DON'T HAVE IT IN YOU.
WHY? BECAUSE I'M NOT *"MANLY"* ENOUGH?
KNOWING YOU WON'T KILL ME DOESN'T MEAN I THINK YOU'RE LESS OF A MAN.
FOR THE RECORD, THIS IS A *REALLY* FUCKED UP CONVERSATION WE'RE HAVING.
YEAH, IT KIND OF IS, ISN'T IT?
BUT SERIOUSLY ARTHUR, THE THING I LOVED ABOUT YOU...EVEN WHEN I HATED YOU...WAS HOW SAFE YOU MADE ME FEEL.
YOU WERE A KIND, GENTLE, MAN. I LOVED HOW YOU LET YOURSELF BE SILLY.
YOU NEVER WORRIED ABOUT LOOKING MANLY AND THAT MADE YOU MORE OF A MAN.
NO MATTER WHAT, I ALWAYS KNEW YOU'D TAKE CARE OF ME.
YOU'D NEVER HURT ME AND I'D NEVER HURT YOU.
YOU SAID ALL OF THAT IN THE PAST TENSE.
YEAH... I DID.

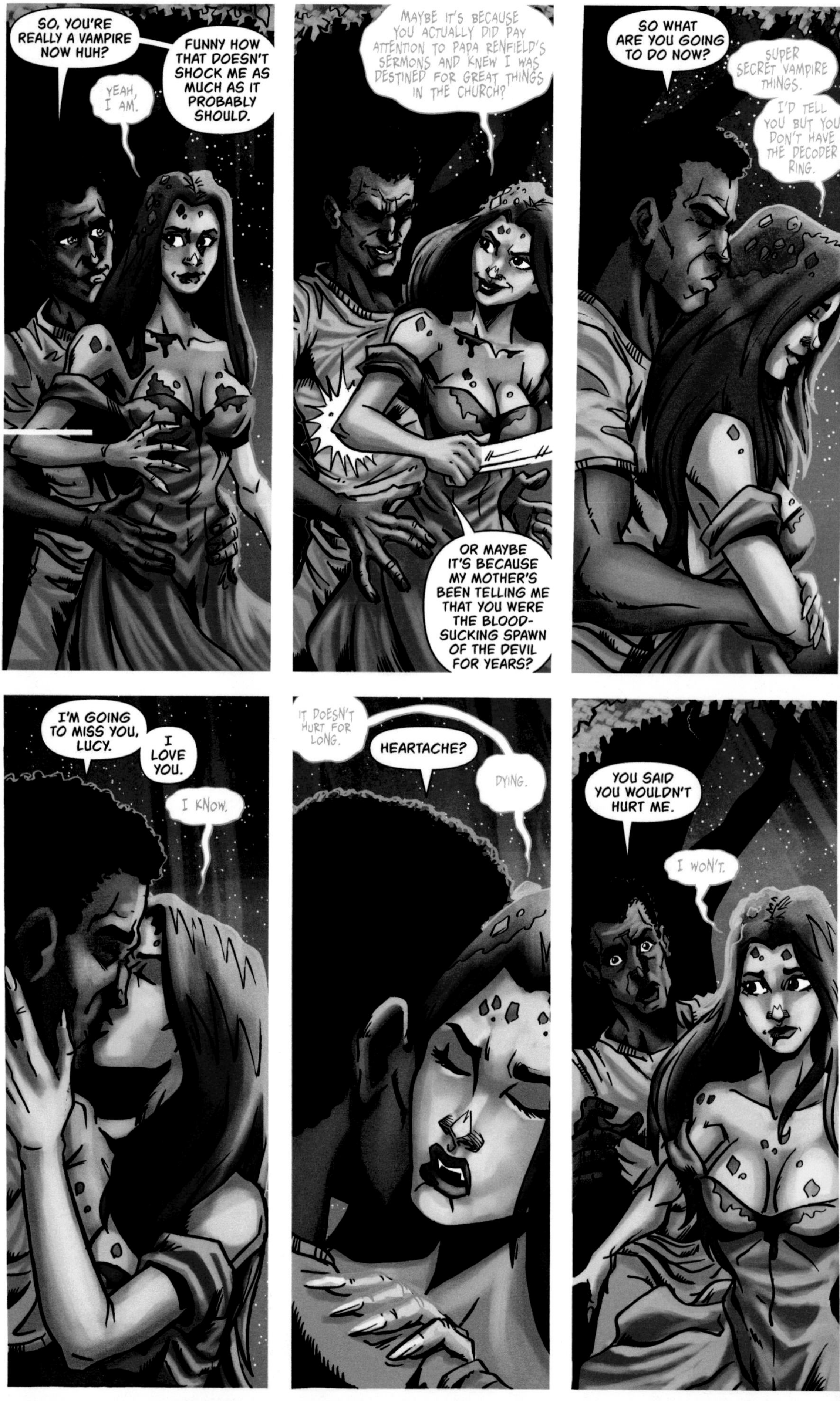
SO, YOU'RE REALLY A VAMPIRE NOW HUH?
YEAH, I AM.
FUNNY HOW THAT DOESN'T SHOCK ME AS MUCH AS IT PROBABLY SHOULD.
MAYBE IT'S BECAUSE YOU ACTUALLY DID PAY ATTENTION TO PAPA RENFIELD'S SERMONS AND KNEW I WAS DESTINED FOR GREAT THINGS IN THE CHURCH?
OR MAYBE IT'S BECAUSE MY MOTHER'S BEEN TELLING ME THAT YOU WERE THE BLOOD-SUCKING SPAWN OF THE DEVIL FOR YEARS?
SO WHAT ARE YOU GOING TO DO NOW?
SUPER SECRET VAMPIRE THINGS.
I'D TELL YOU BUT YOU DON'T HAVE THE DECODER RING.
I'M GOING TO MISS YOU, LUCY.
I LOVE YOU.
I KNOW.
IT DOESN'T HURT FOR LONG.
HEARTACHE?
DYING.
YOU SAID YOU WOULDN'T HURT ME.
I WON'T.

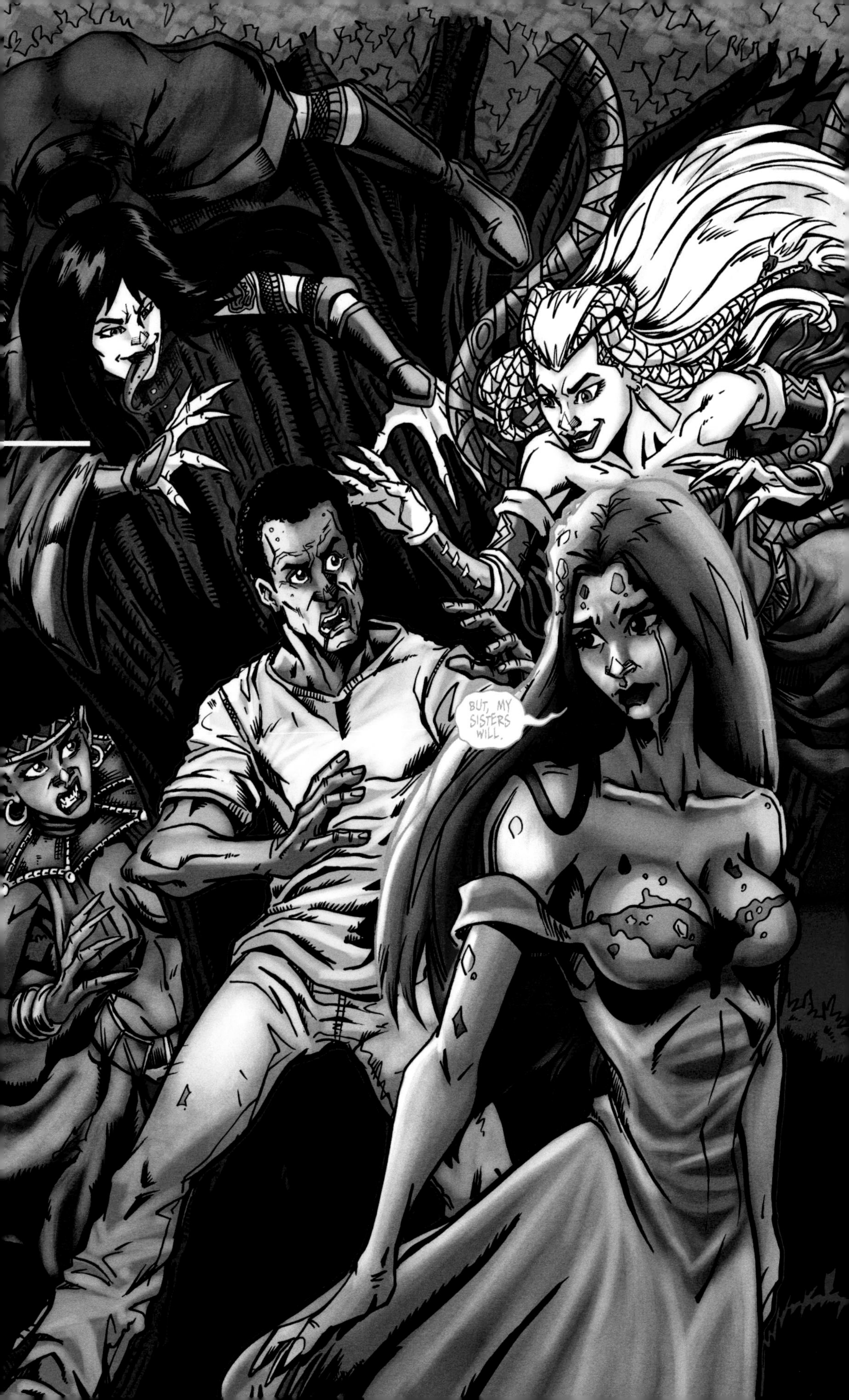
BUT, MY SISTERS WILL.

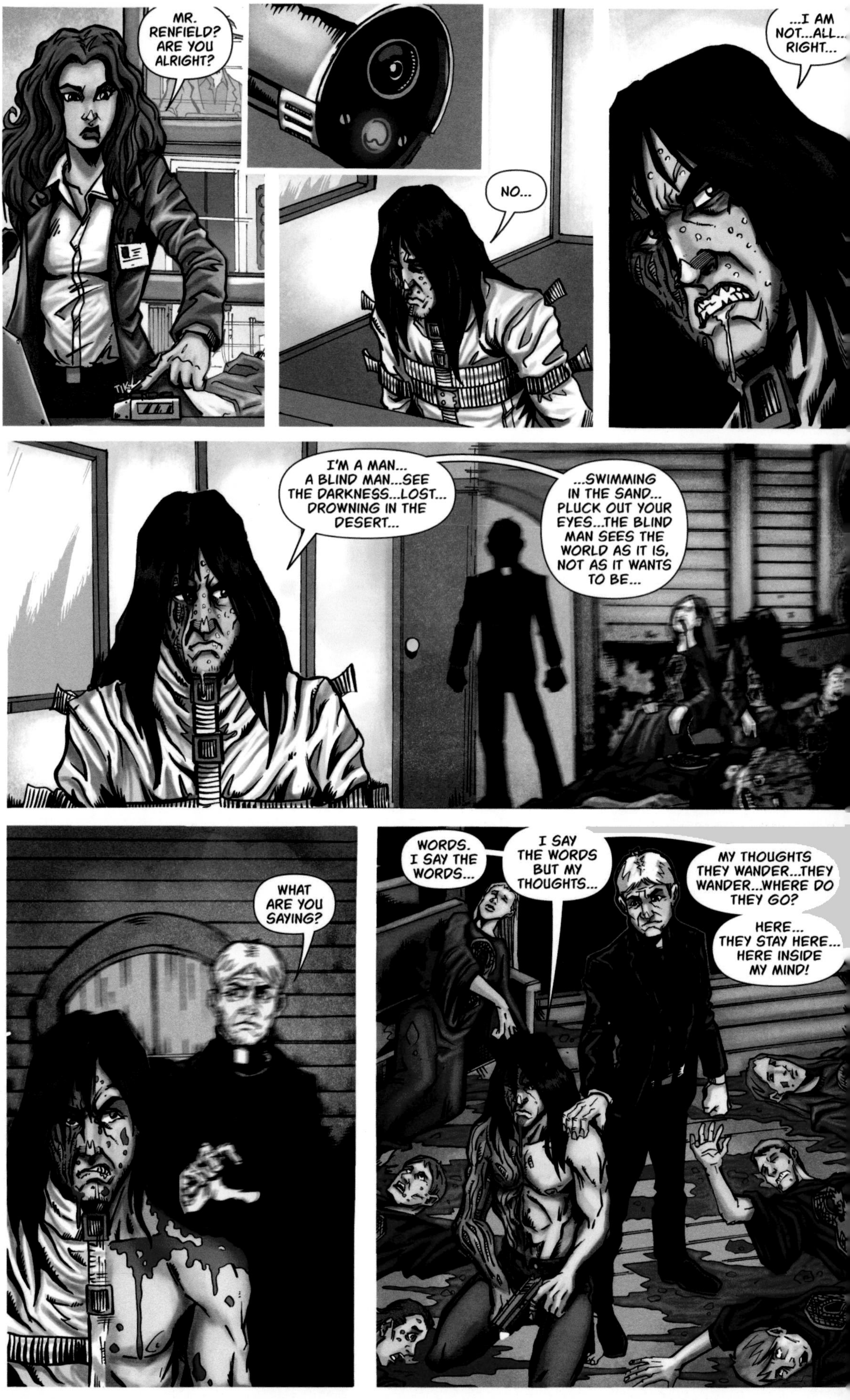
MR. RENFIELD? ARE YOU ALRIGHT?
NO...
...I AM NOT...ALL... RIGHT...
I'M A MAN... A BLIND MAN...SEE THE DARKNESS...LOST... DROWNING IN THE DESERT...
...SWIMMING IN THE SAND... PLUCK OUT YOUR EYES...THE BLIND MAN SEES THE WORLD AS IT IS, NOT AS IT WANTS TO BE...
WHAT ARE YOU SAYING?
WORDS. I SAY THE WORDS...
I SAY THE WORDS BUT MY THOUGHTS...
MY THOUGHTS THEY WANDER...THEY WANDER...WHERE DO THEY GO?
HERE... THEY STAY HERE... HERE INSIDE MY MIND!

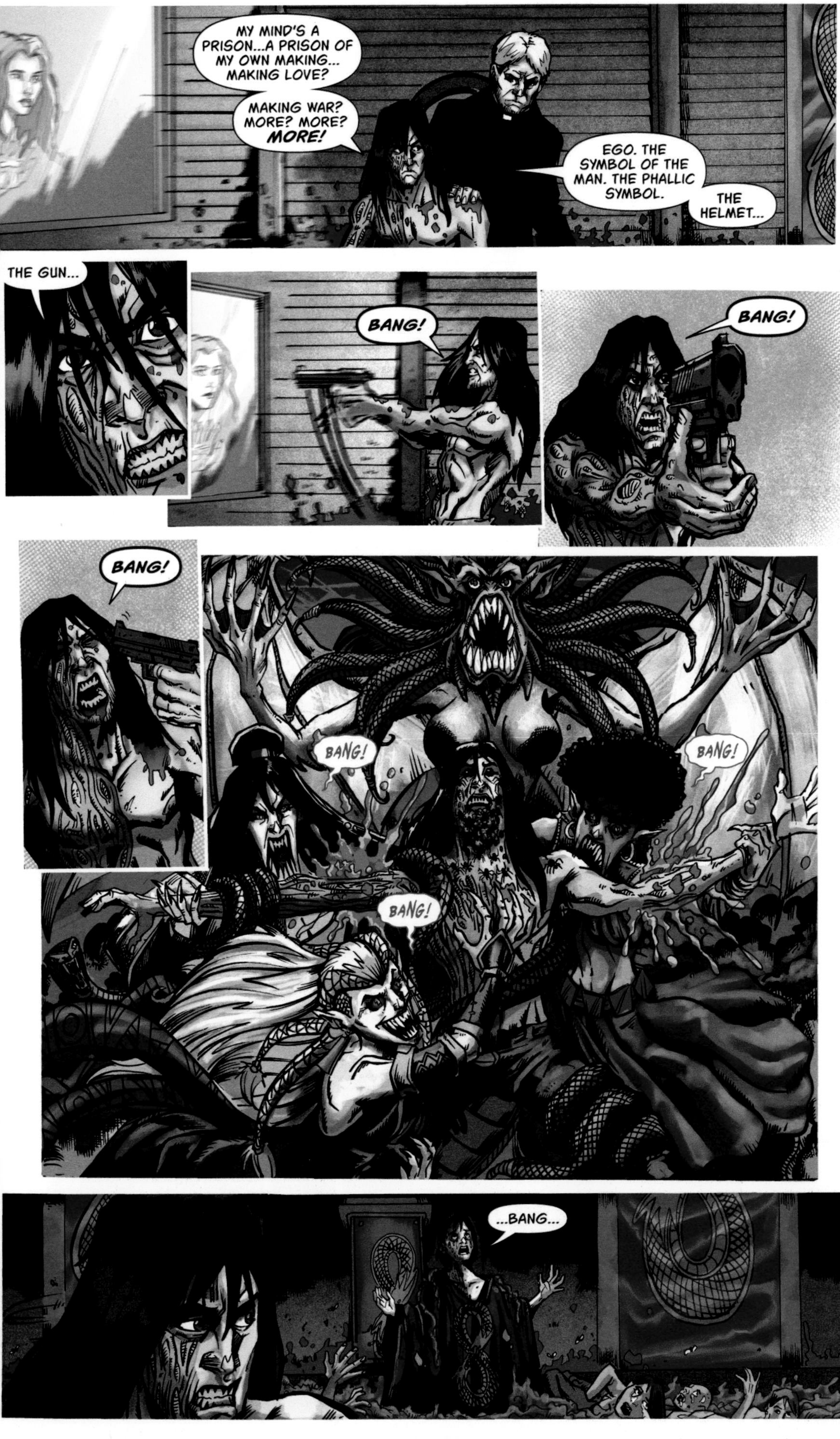

MY MIND'S A PRISON...A PRISON OF MY OWN MAKING... MAKING LOVE?
MAKING WAR? MORE? MORE? MORE!
EGO. THE SYMBOL OF THE MAN. THE PHALLIC SYMBOL.
THE HELMET...
THE GUN...
BANG!
BANG!
BANG!
BANG!
BANG!
BANG!
...BANG...

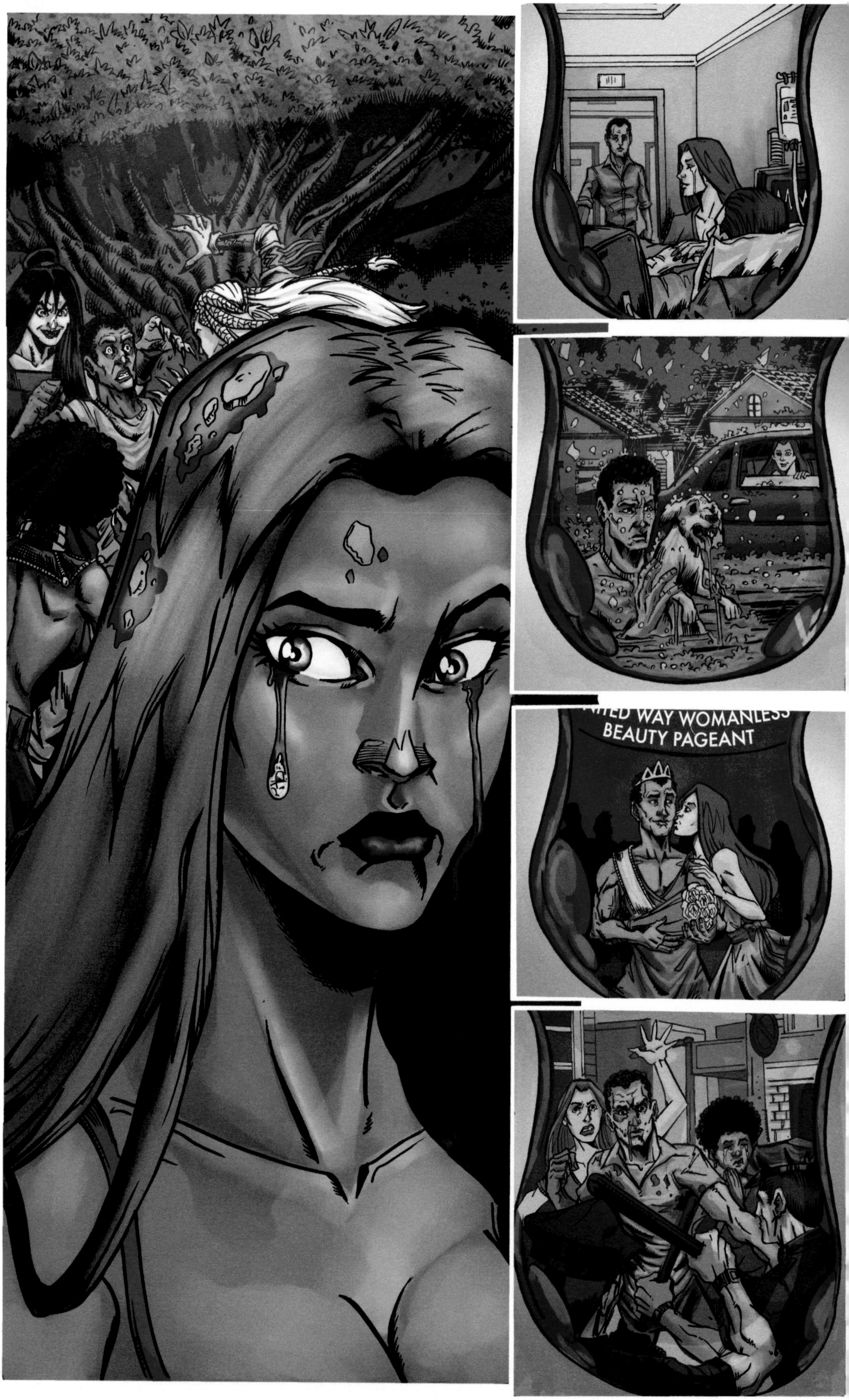
WAY WOMANLESS
BEAUTY PAGEANT

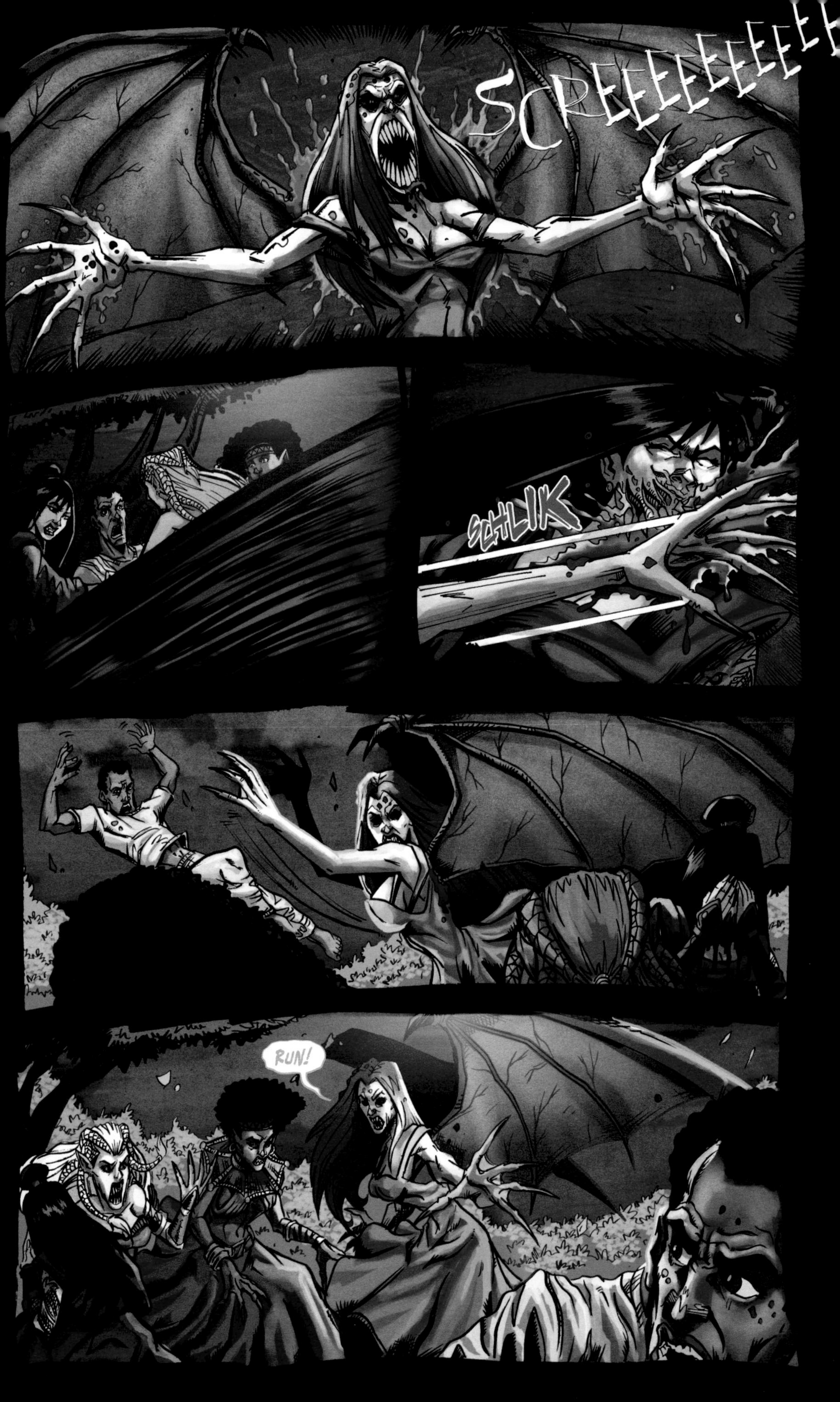
SCREEEEEEEEEE
SCHLIK
RUN!

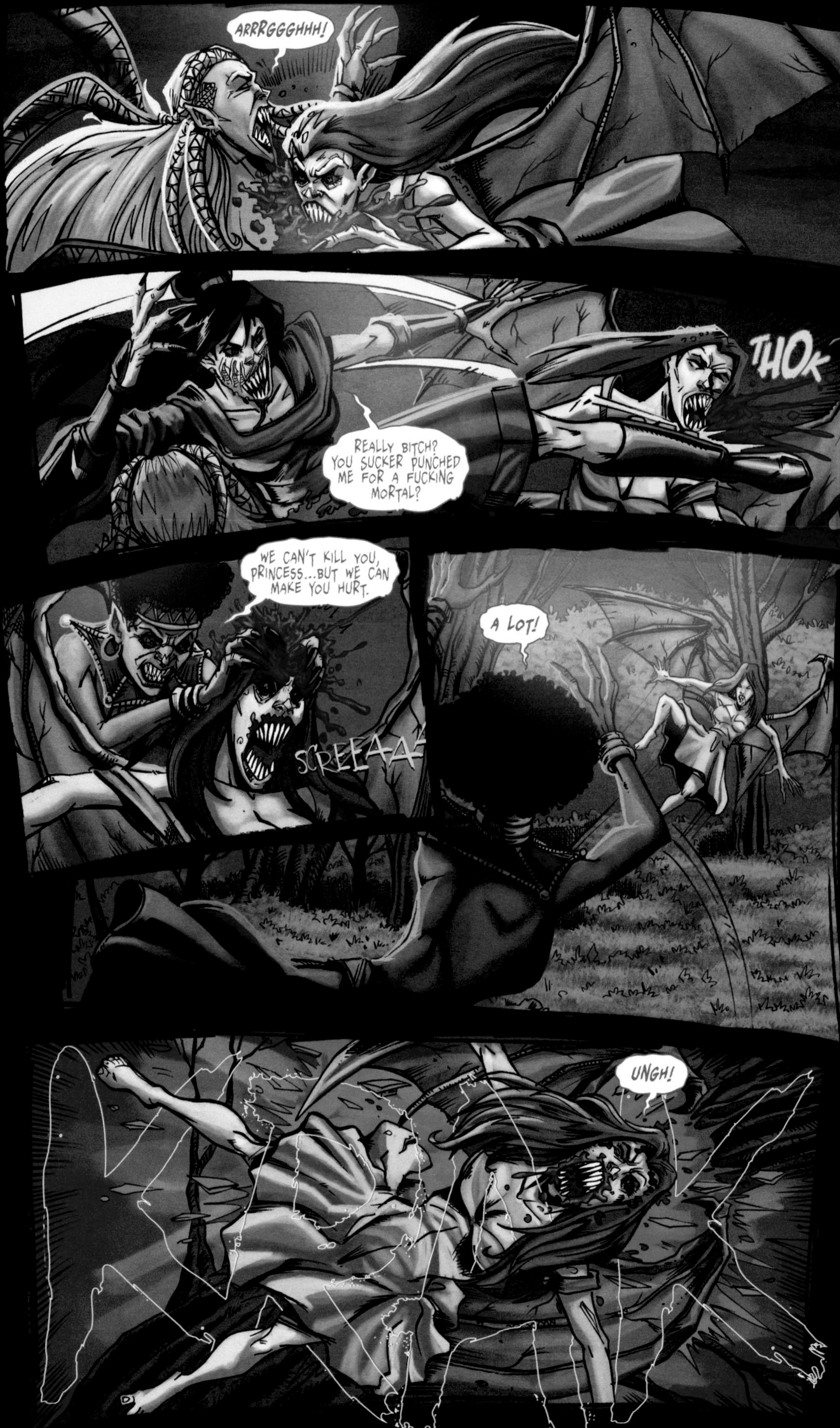

ARRRGGGHHH!
THOk
REALLY BITCH? YOU SUCKER PUNCHED ME FOR A FUCKING MORTAL?
WE CAN'T KILL YOU, PRINCESS...BUT WE CAN MAKE YOU HURT.
SCREEAAA
A LOT!
UNGH!

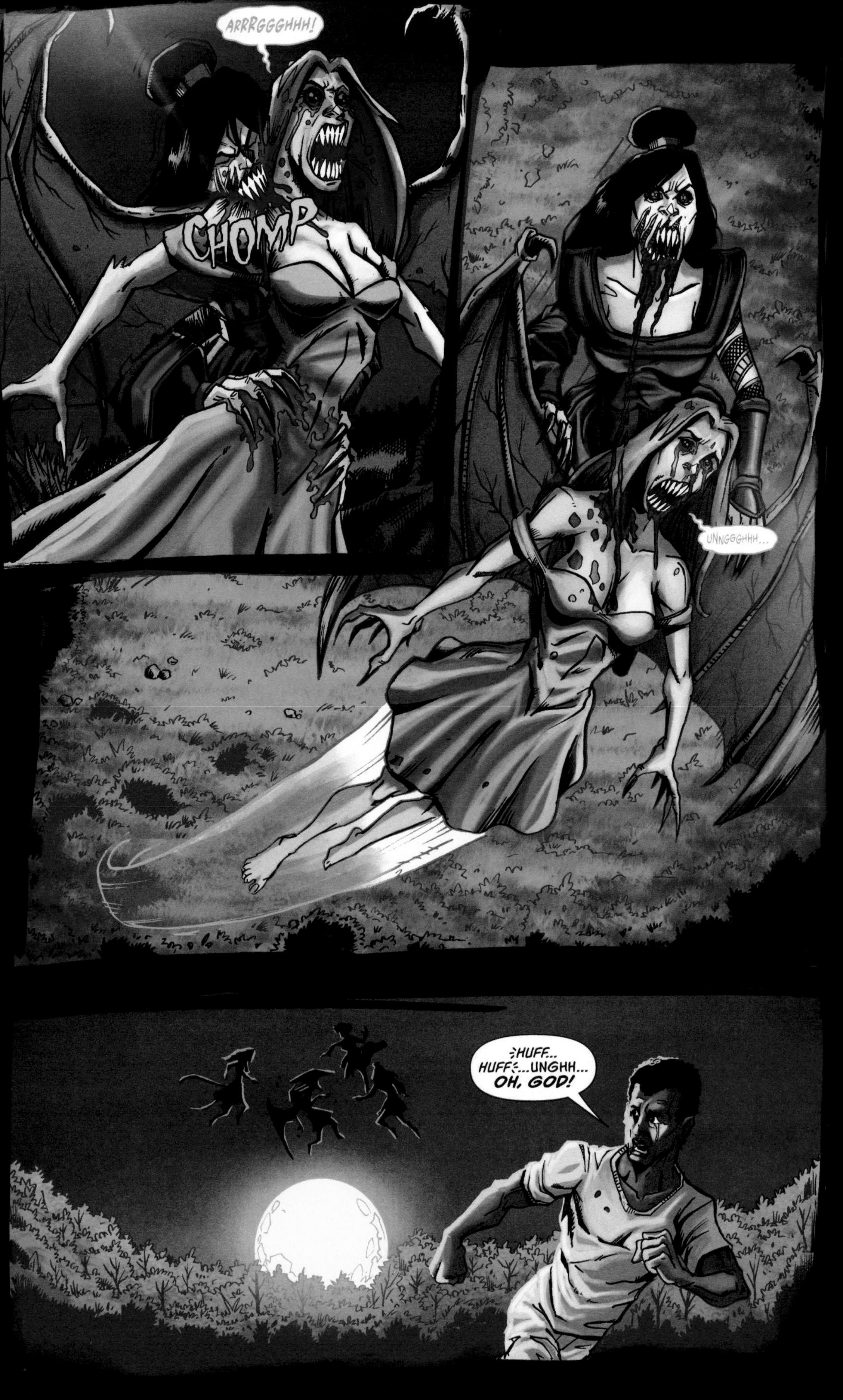
ARRRGGGHHH!
CHOMP
UNNGGGHHH...
HUFF... HUFF... UNGHH... OH, GOD!

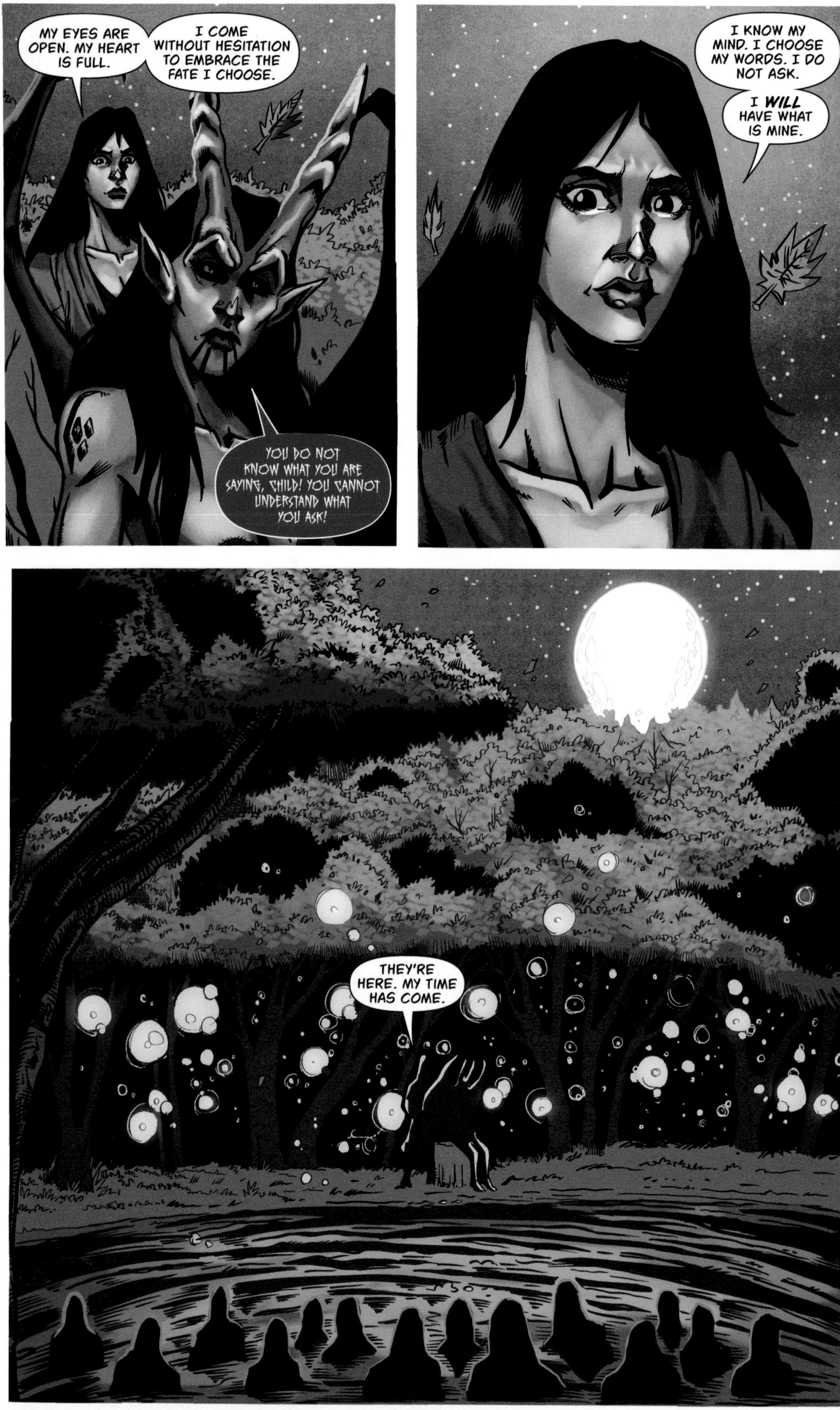
MY EYES ARE OPEN. MY HEART IS FULL.
I COME WITHOUT HESITATION TO EMBRACE THE FATE I CHOOSE.
YOU DO NOT KNOW WHAT YOU ARE SAYING, CHILD! YOU CANNOT UNDERSTAND WHAT YOU ASK!
I KNOW MY MIND. I CHOOSE MY WORDS. I DO NOT ASK.
I **WILL** HAVE WHAT IS MINE.
THEY'RE HERE. MY TIME HAS COME.

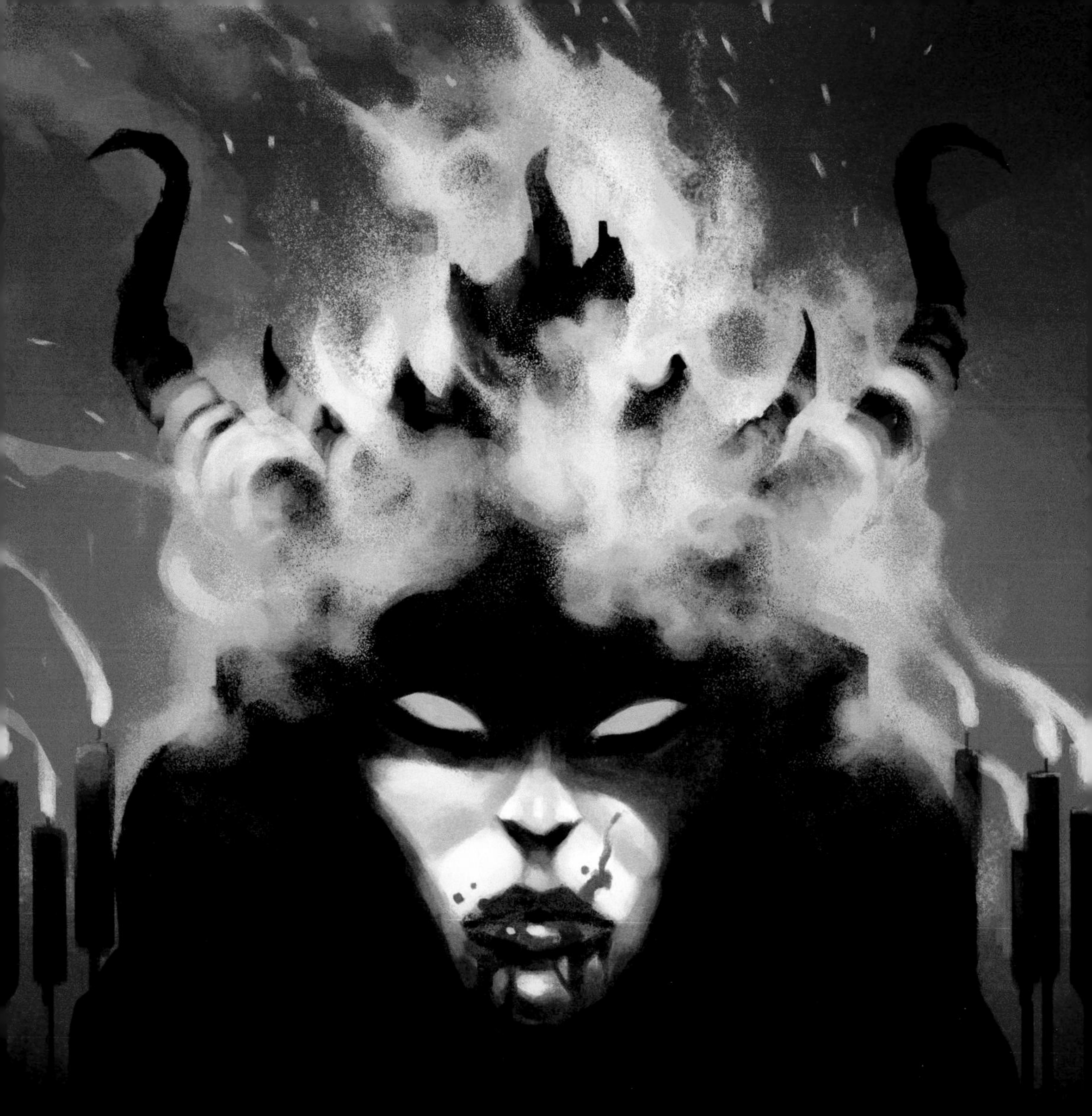

CHAPTER SIX

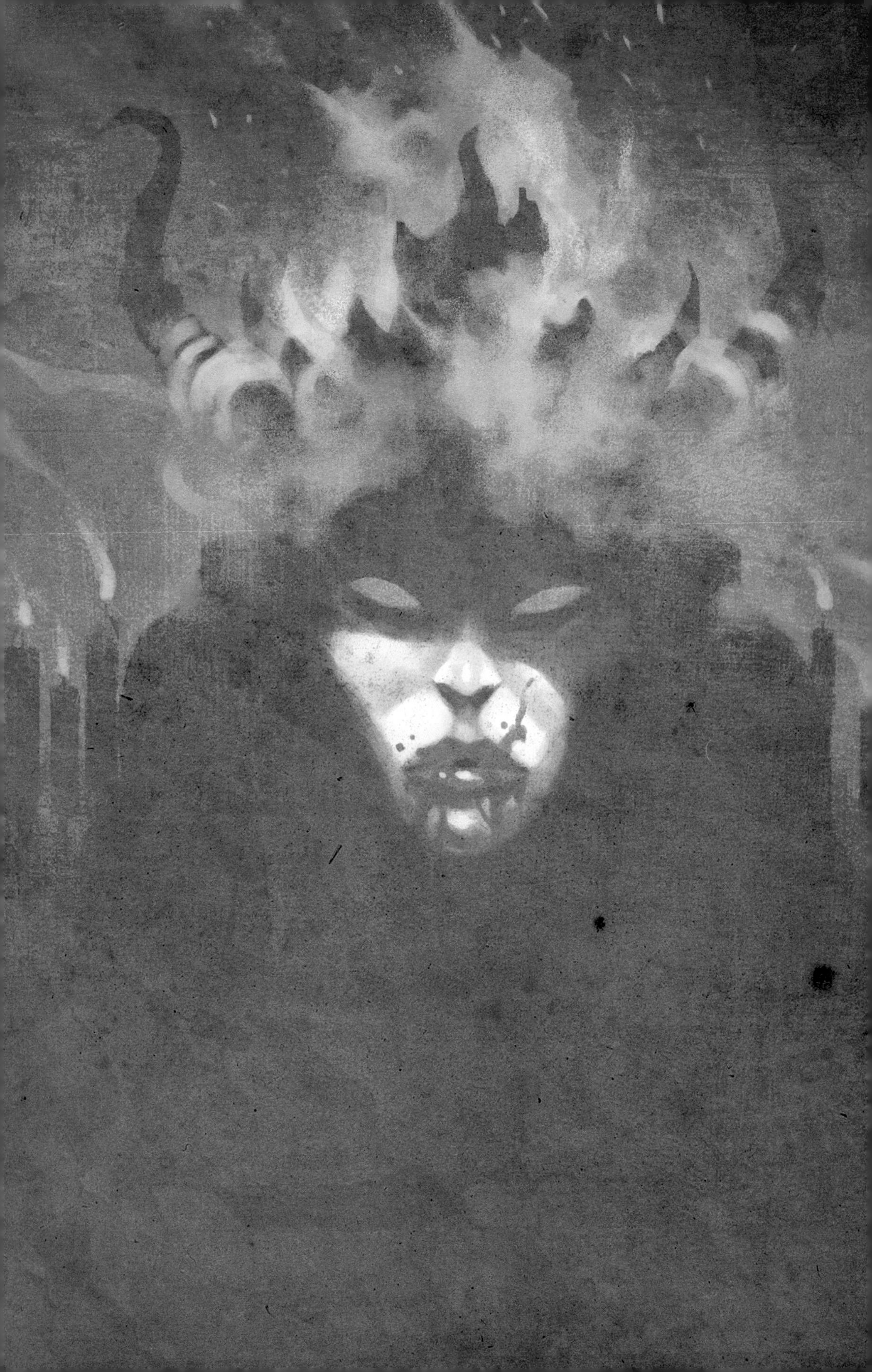

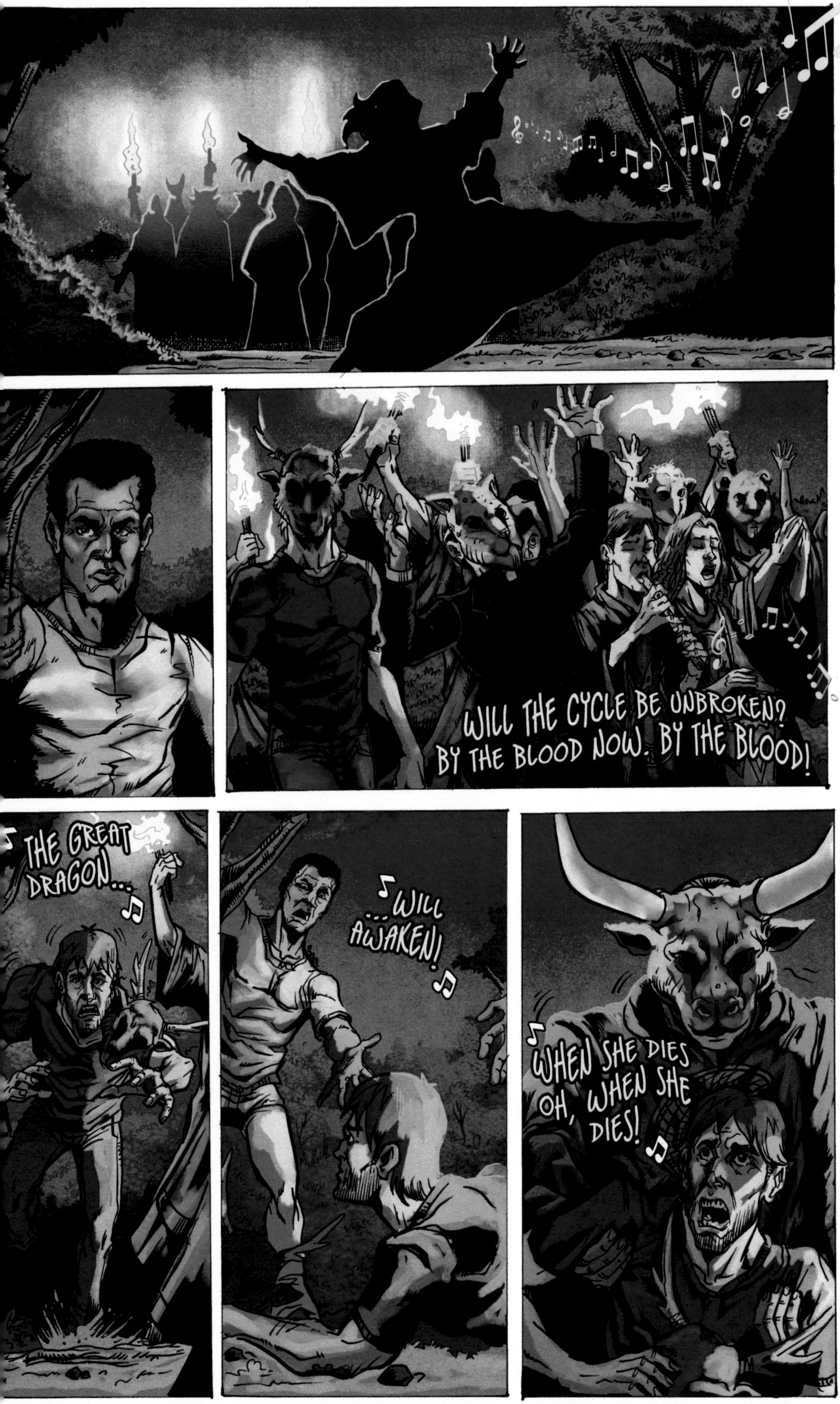
WILL THE CYCLE BE UNBROKEN?
BY THE BLOOD NOW. BY THE BLOOD!
THE GREAT DRAGON...
...WILL AWAKEN!
WHEN SHE DIES
OH, WHEN SHE DIES!

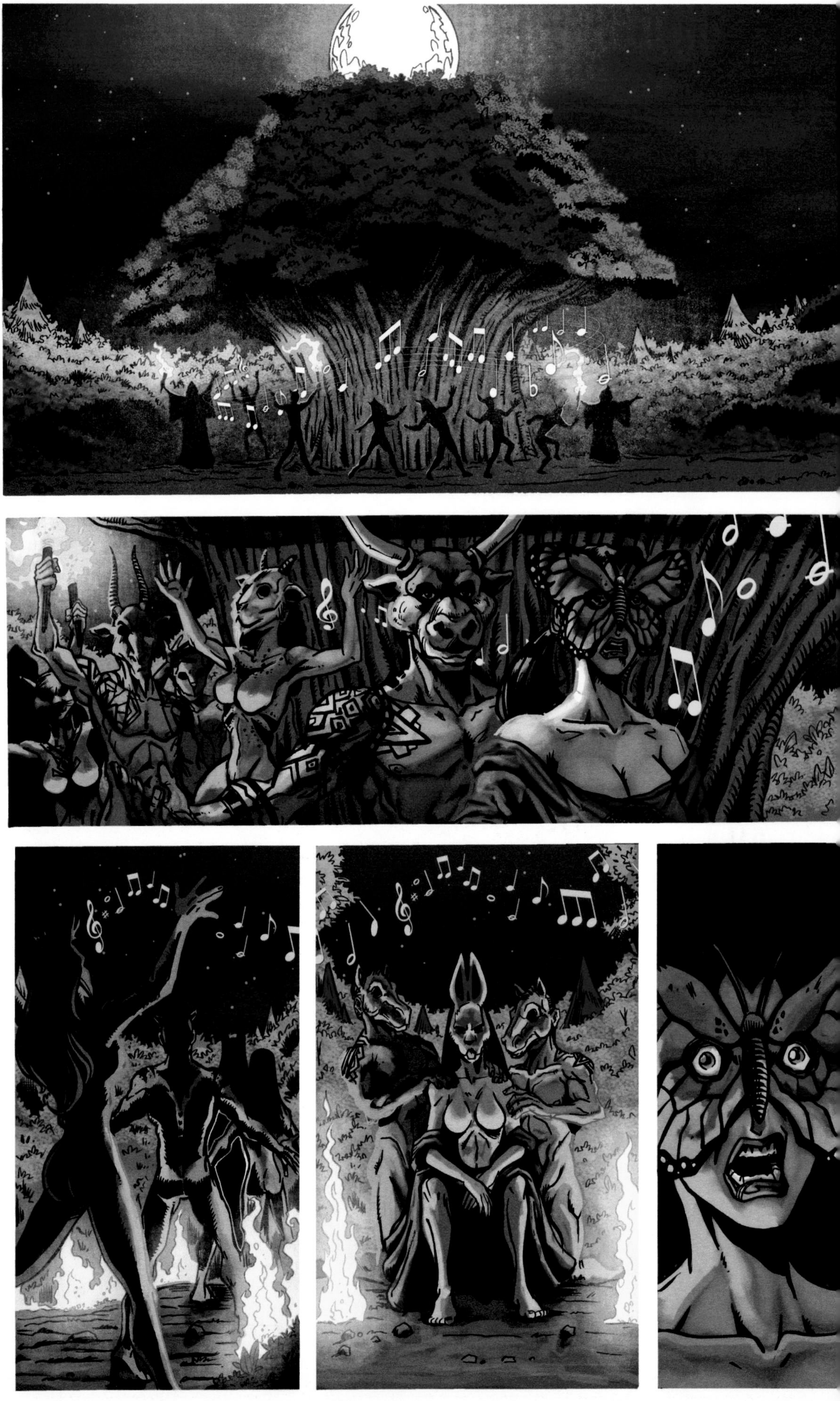

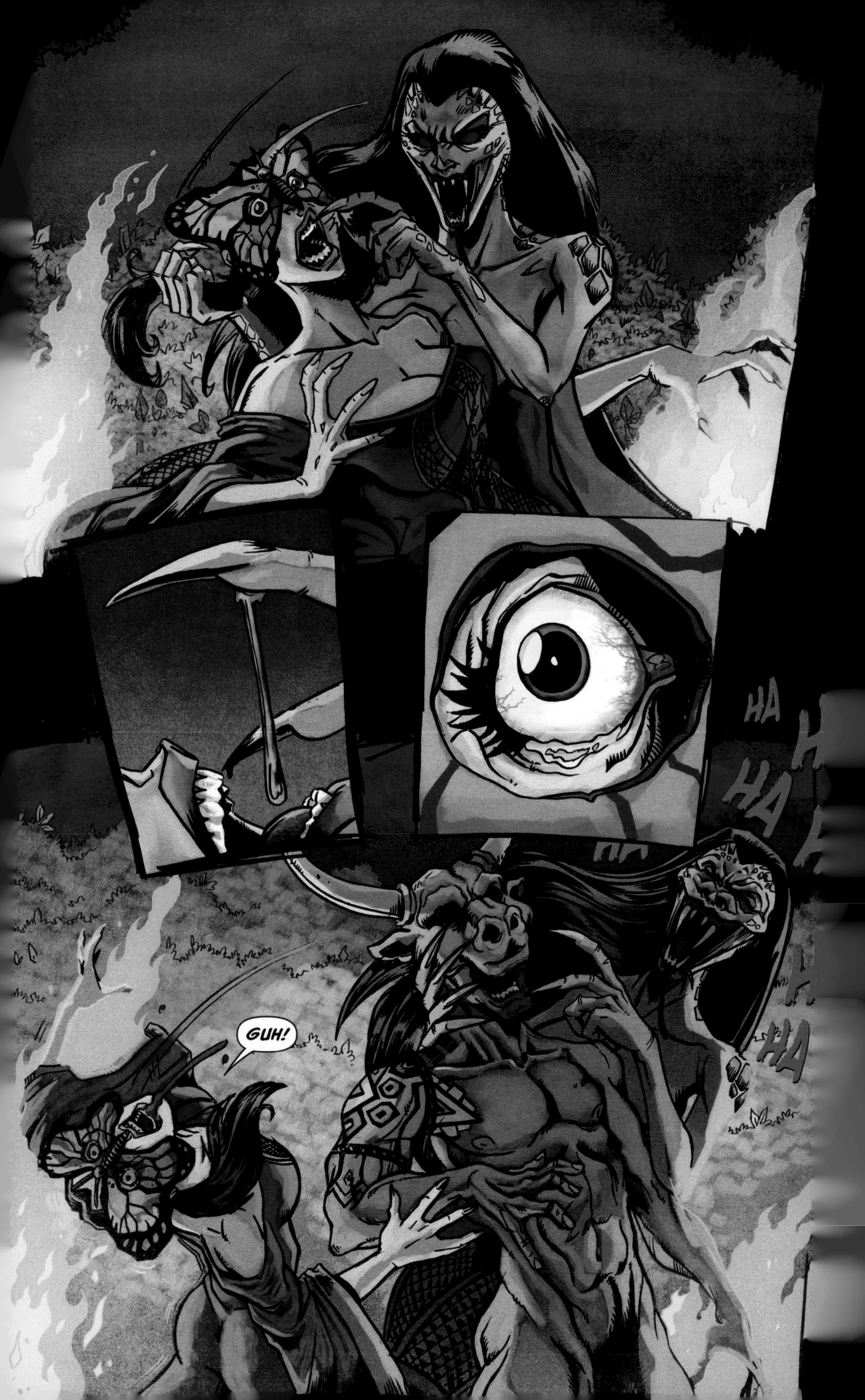
HA
HA
HA
GUH!

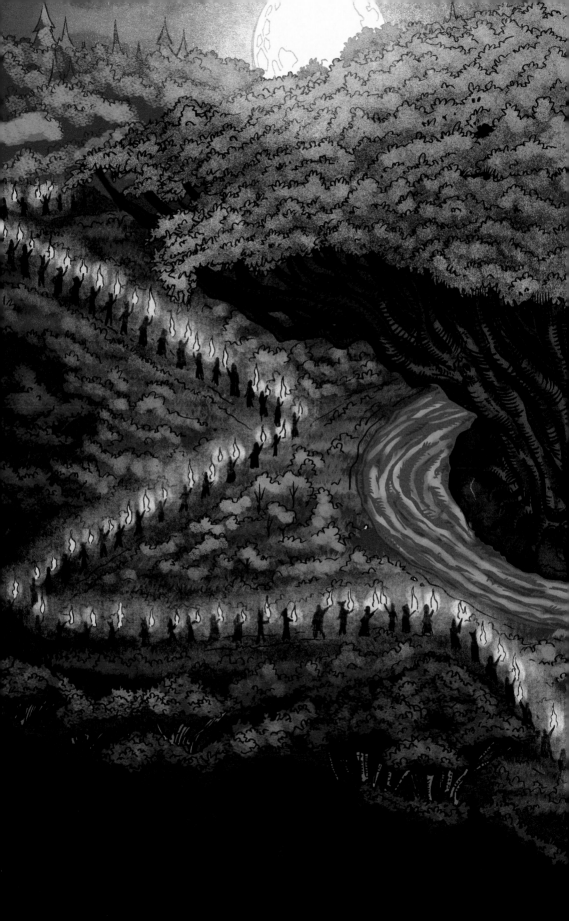

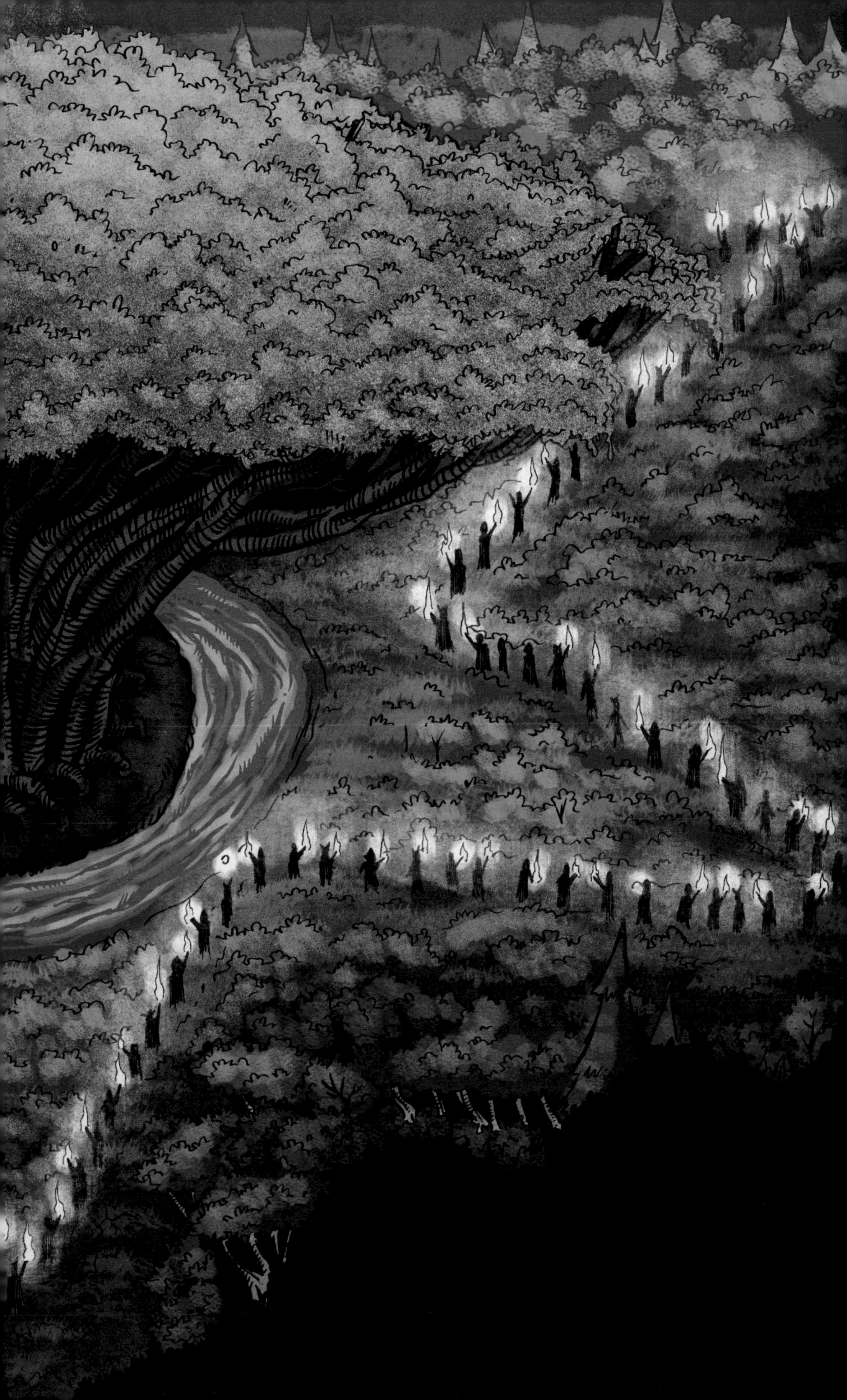

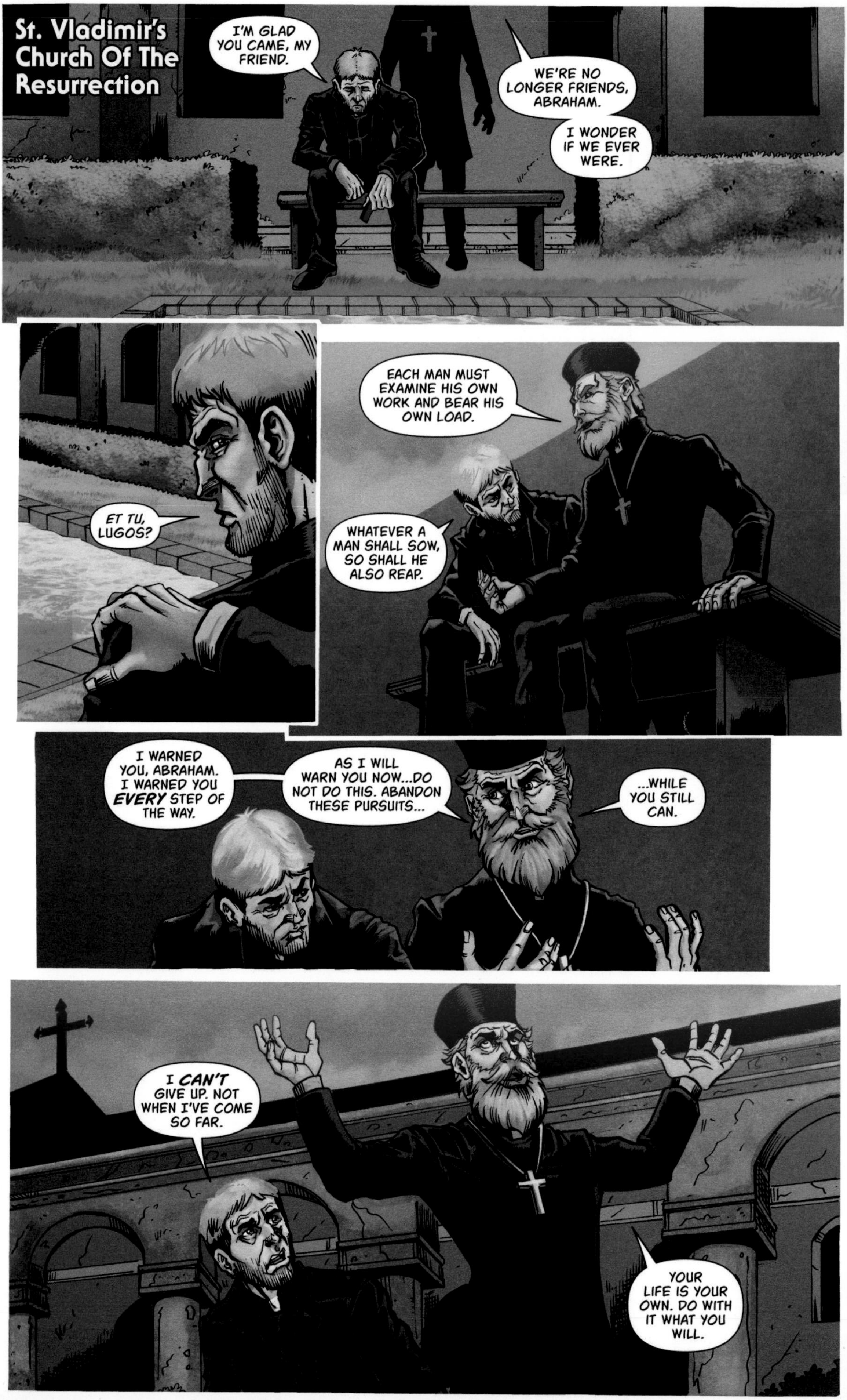
St. Vladimir's Church Of The Resurrection
I'M GLAD YOU CAME, MY FRIEND.
WE'RE NO LONGER FRIENDS, ABRAHAM.
I WONDER IF WE EVER WERE.
ET TU, LUGOS?
EACH MAN MUST EXAMINE HIS OWN WORK AND BEAR HIS OWN LOAD.
WHATEVER A MAN SHALL SOW, SO SHALL HE ALSO REAP.
I WARNED YOU, ABRAHAM. I WARNED YOU EVERY STEP OF THE WAY.
AS I WILL WARN YOU NOW...DO NOT DO THIS. ABANDON THESE PURSUITS...
...WHILE YOU STILL CAN.
I CAN'T GIVE UP. NOT WHEN I'VE COME SO FAR.
YOUR LIFE IS YOUR OWN. DO WITH IT WHAT YOU WILL.

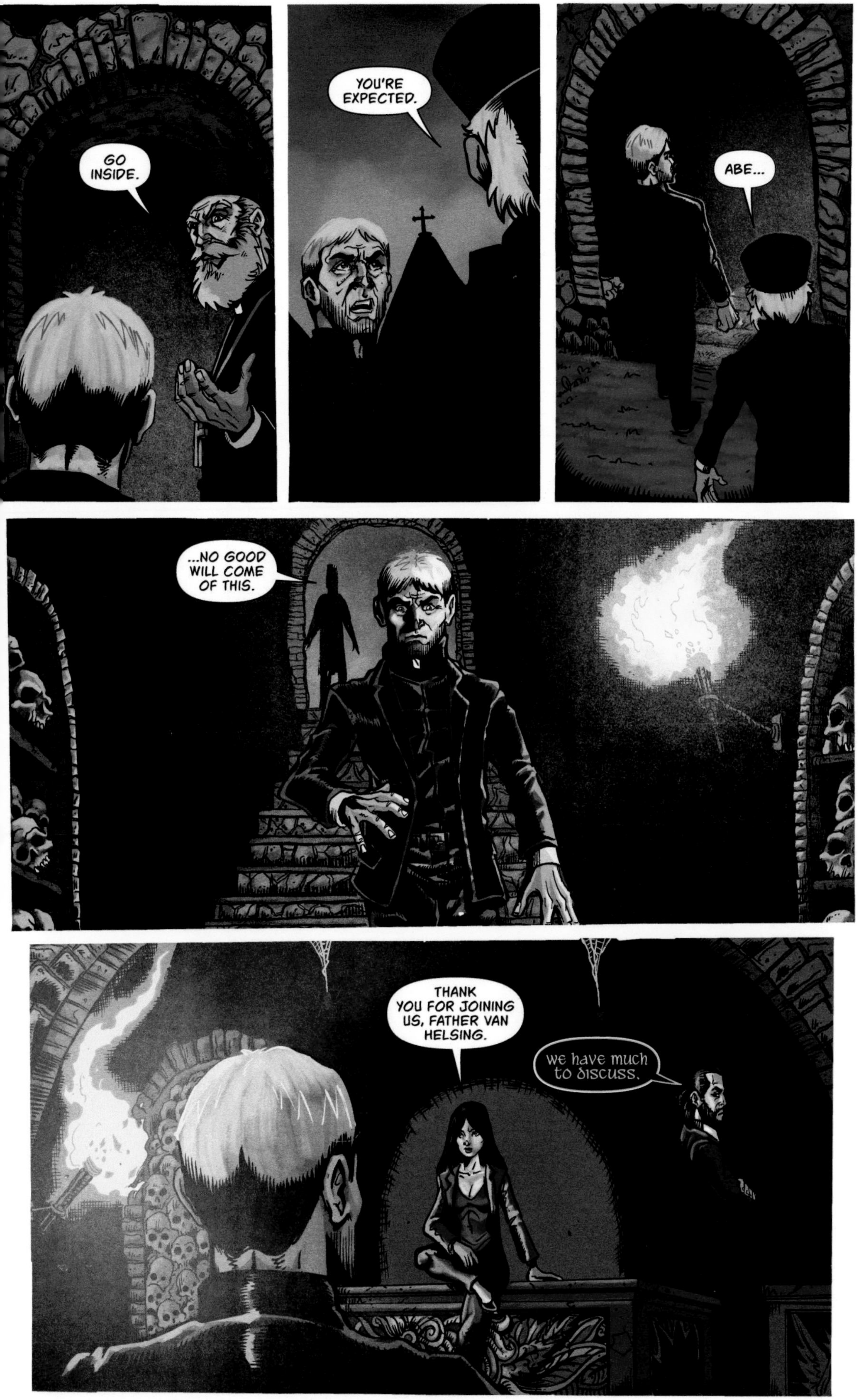
GO INSIDE.
YOU'RE EXPECTED.
ABE...
...NO GOOD WILL COME OF THIS.
THANK YOU FOR JOINING US, FATHER VAN HELSING.
we have much to discuss.

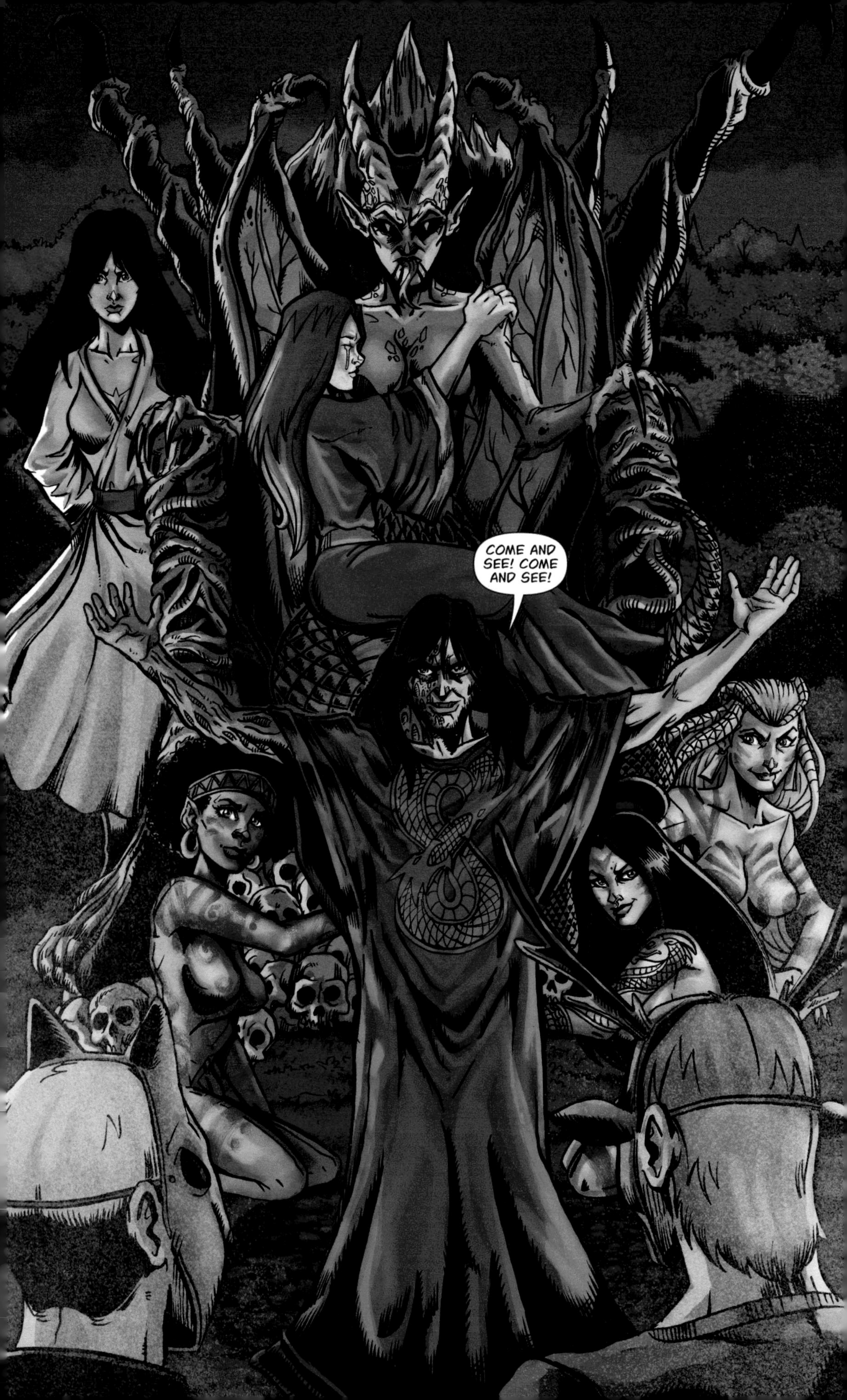
COME AND SEE! COME AND SEE!

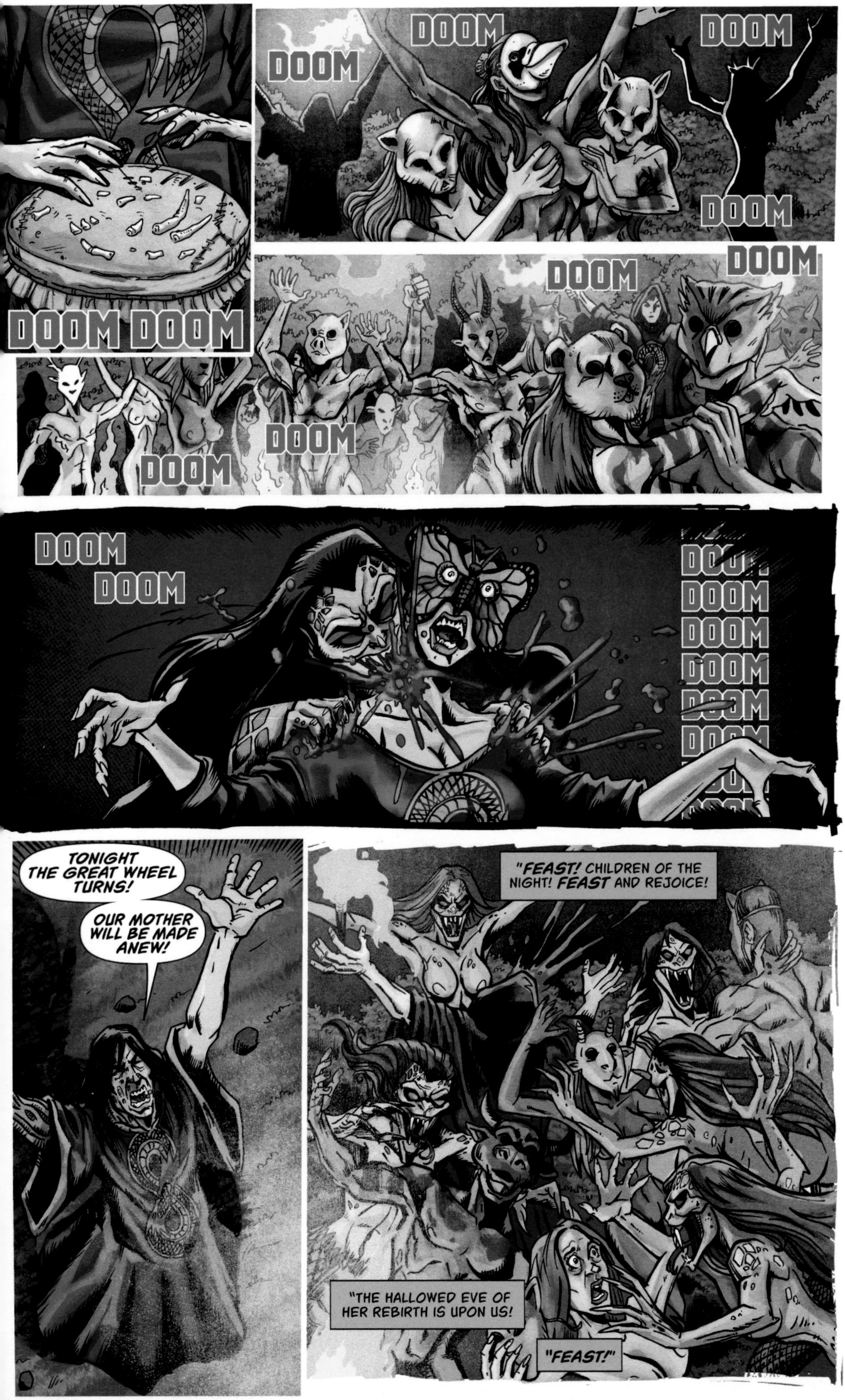
DOOM DOOM
DOOM
DOOM
DOOM
DOOM
DOOM
DOOM
DOOM
DOOM
DOOM
DOOM
DOOM
DOOM
DOOM
DOOM
TONIGHT THE GREAT WHEEL TURNS!
OUR MOTHER WILL BE MADE ANEW!
"FEAST! CHILDREN OF THE NIGHT! FEAST AND REJOICE!
"THE HALLOWED EVE OF HER REBIRTH IS UPON US!
"FEAST!"

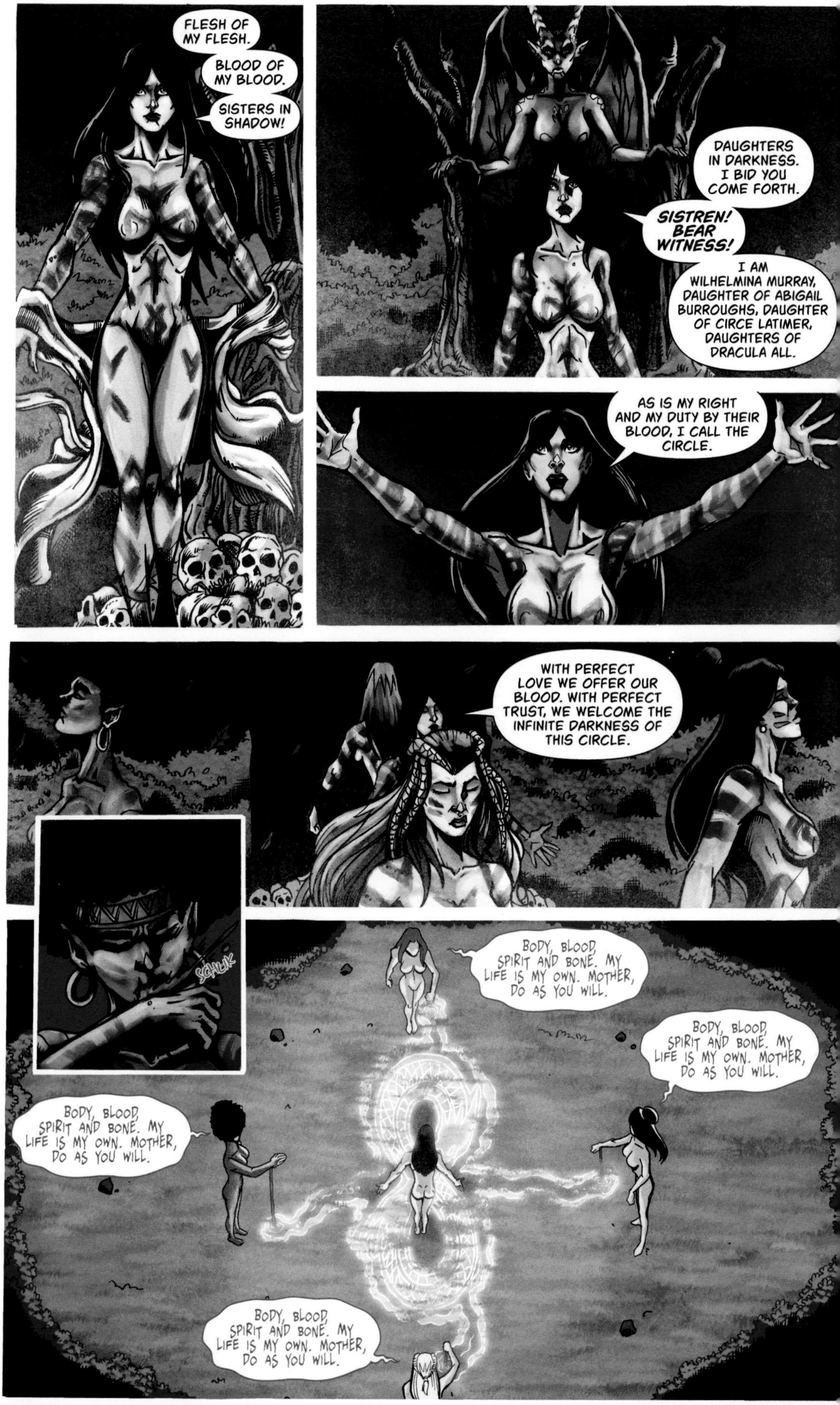
FLESH OF MY FLESH.
BLOOD OF MY BLOOD.
SISTERS IN SHADOW!
DAUGHTERS IN DARKNESS. I BID YOU COME FORTH.
SISTREN! BEAR WITNESS!
I AM WILHELMINA MURRAY, DAUGHTER OF ABIGAIL BURROUGHS, DAUGHTER OF CIRCE LATIMER, DAUGHTERS OF DRACULA ALL.
AS IS MY RIGHT AND MY DUTY BY THEIR BLOOD, I CALL THE CIRCLE.
WITH PERFECT LOVE WE OFFER OUR BLOOD. WITH PERFECT TRUST, WE WELCOME THE INFINITE DARKNESS OF THIS CIRCLE.
SCHLIK
BODY, BLOOD, SPIRIT AND BONE. MY LIFE IS MY OWN. MOTHER, DO AS YOU WILL.
BODY, BLOOD, SPIRIT AND BONE. MY LIFE IS MY OWN. MOTHER, DO AS YOU WILL.
BODY, BLOOD, SPIRIT AND BONE. MY LIFE IS MY OWN. MOTHER, DO AS YOU WILL.
BODY, BLOOD, SPIRIT AND BONE. MY LIFE IS MY OWN. MOTHER, DO AS YOU WILL.

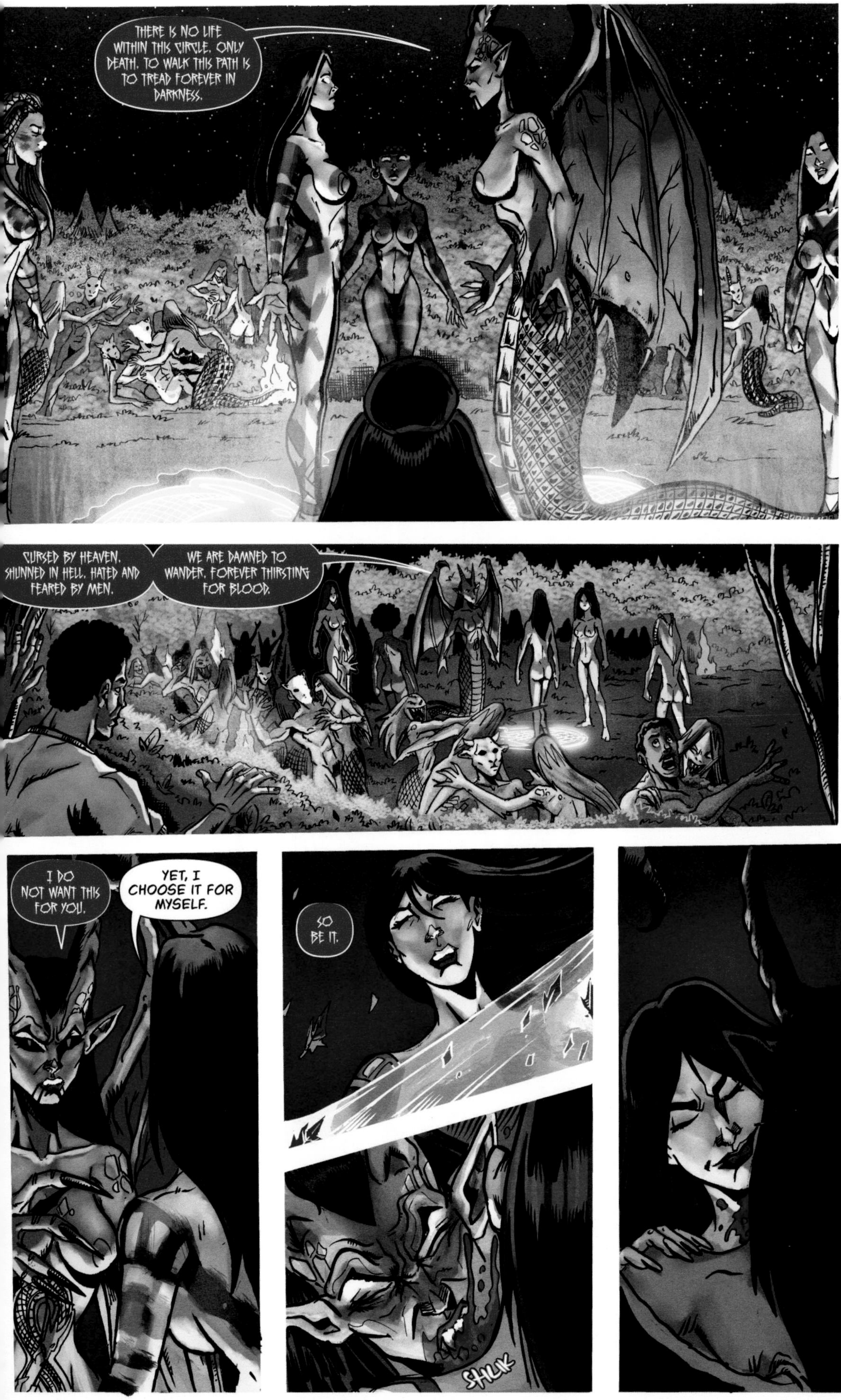
THERE IS NO LIFE WITHIN THIS CIRCLE, ONLY DEATH. TO WALK THIS PATH IS TO TREAD FOREVER IN DARKNESS.
CURSED BY HEAVEN, SHUNNED IN HELL, HATED AND FEARED BY MEN.
WE ARE DAMNED TO WANDER, FOREVER THIRSTING FOR BLOOD.
I DO NOT WANT THIS FOR YOU.
YET, I CHOOSE IT FOR MYSELF.
SO BE IT.
SHLIK

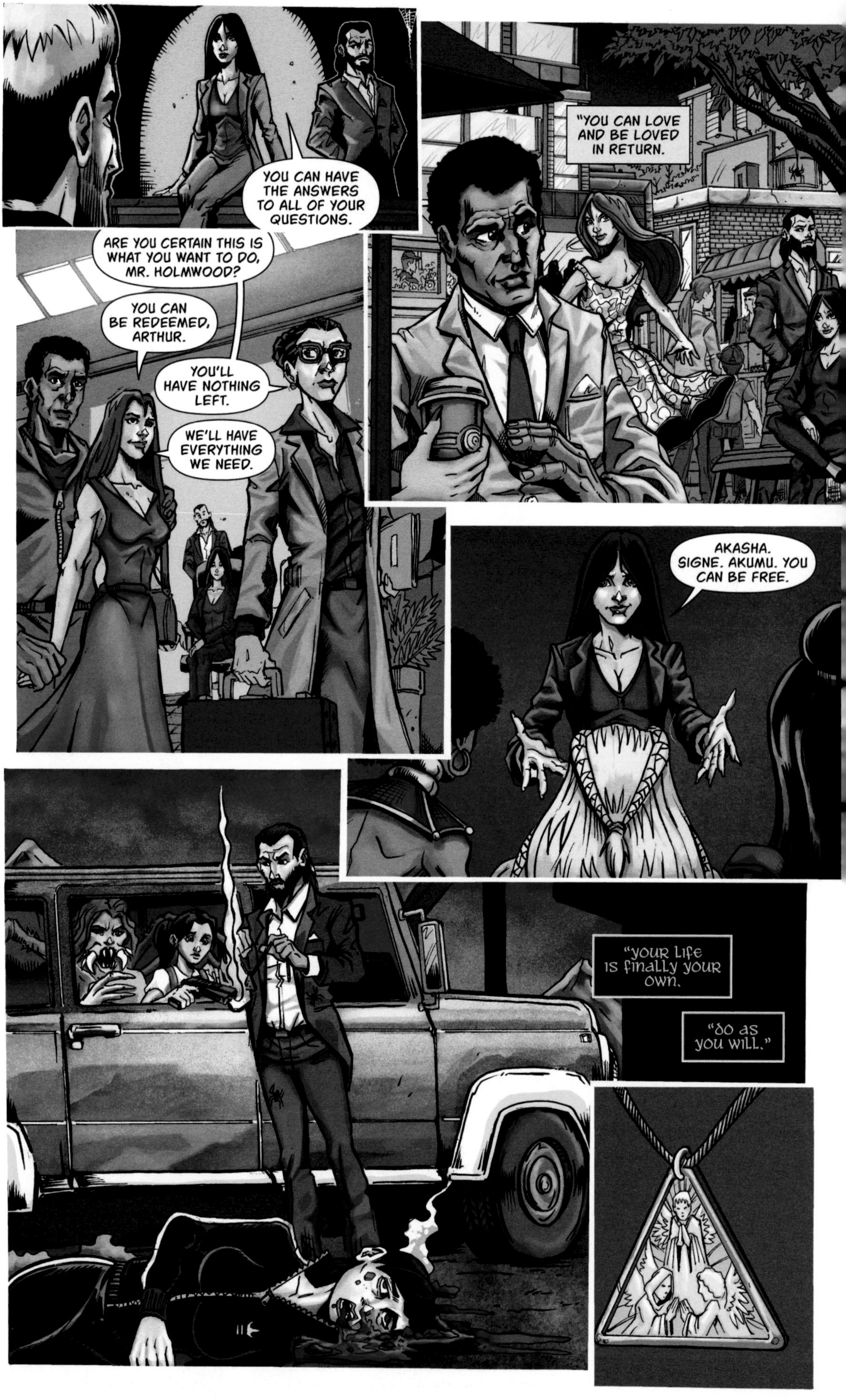
YOU CAN HAVE THE ANSWERS TO ALL OF YOUR QUESTIONS.
"YOU CAN LOVE AND BE LOVED IN RETURN.
ARE YOU CERTAIN THIS IS WHAT YOU WANT TO DO, MR. HOLMWOOD?
YOU CAN BE REDEEMED, ARTHUR.
YOU'LL HAVE NOTHING LEFT.
WE'LL HAVE EVERYTHING WE NEED.
AKASHA. SIGNE. AKUMU. YOU CAN BE FREE.
"YOUR LIFE IS FINALLY YOUR OWN.
"DO AS YOU WILL."

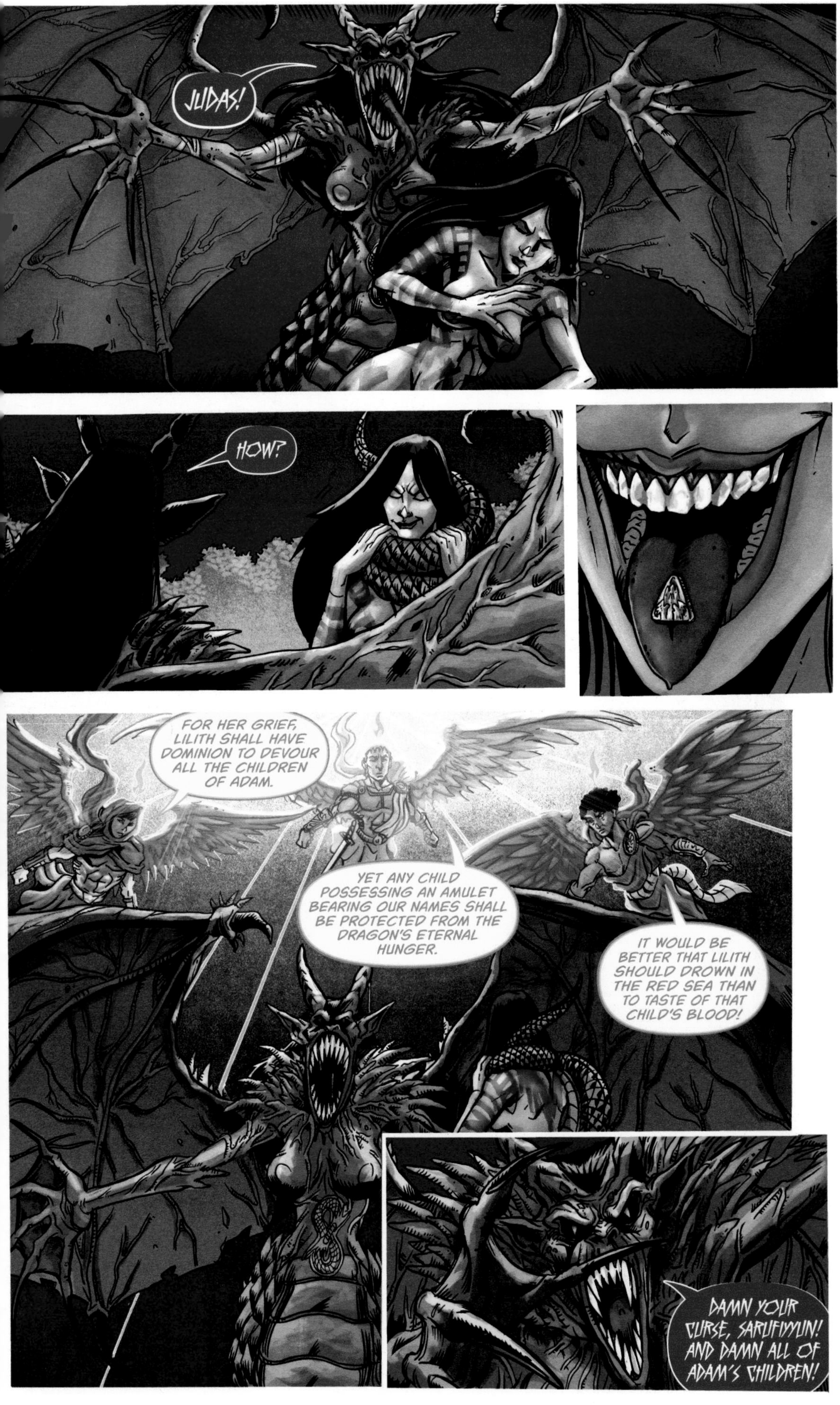
JUDAS!
HOW?
FOR HER GRIEF, LILITH SHALL HAVE DOMINION TO DEVOUR ALL THE CHILDREN OF ADAM.
YET ANY CHILD POSSESSING AN AMULET BEARING OUR NAMES SHALL BE PROTECTED FROM THE DRAGON'S ETERNAL HUNGER.
IT WOULD BE BETTER THAT LILITH SHOULD DROWN IN THE RED SEA THAN TO TASTE OF THAT CHILD'S BLOOD!
DAMN YOUR CURSE, SARUFIYYUN! AND DAMN ALL OF ADAM'S CHILDREN!

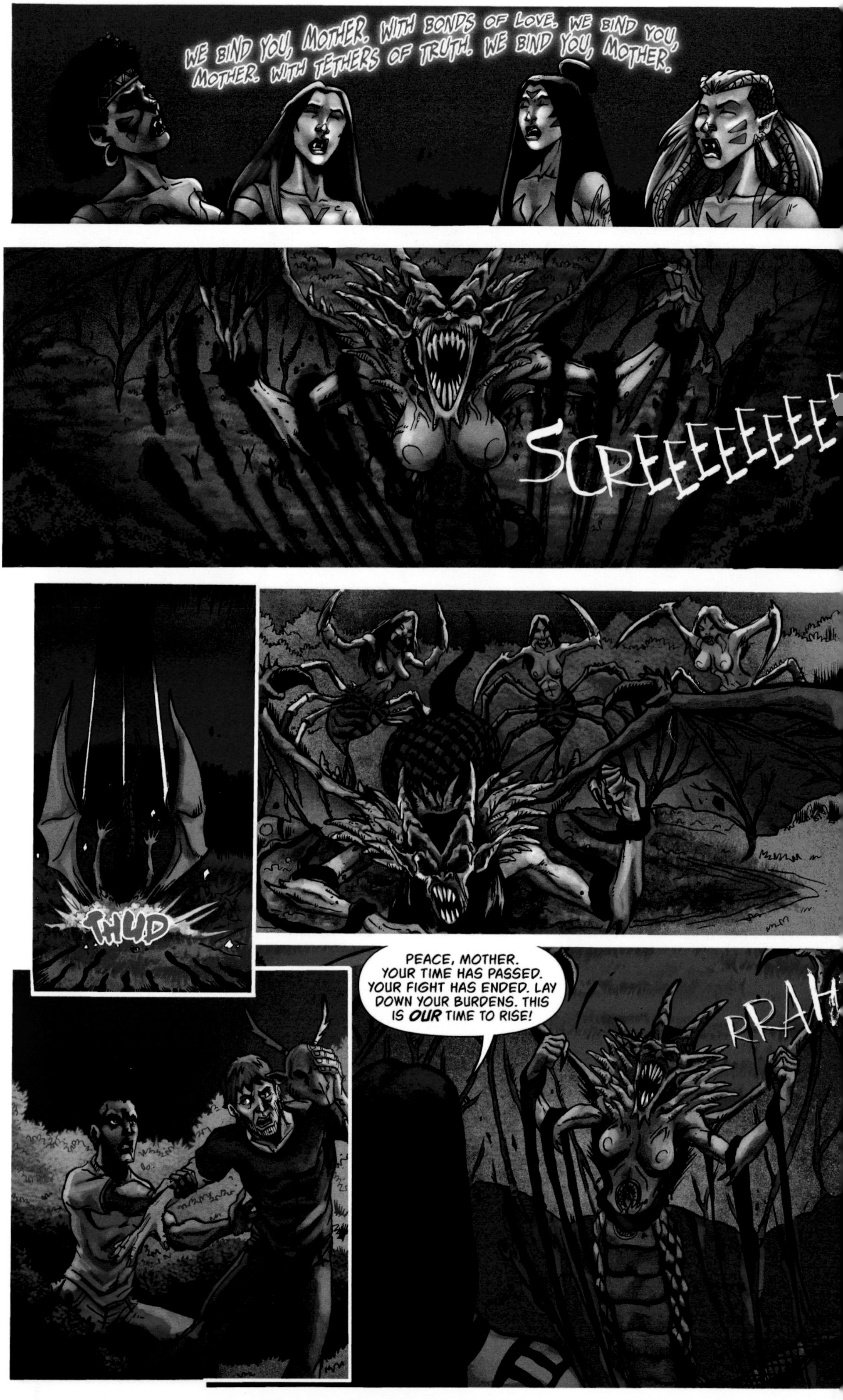
WE BIND YOU, MOTHER. WITH BONDS OF LOVE. WE BIND YOU, MOTHER. WITH TETHERS OF TRUTH. WE BIND YOU, MOTHER.
SCREEEEEEEEE
THUD
PEACE, MOTHER. YOUR TIME HAS PASSED. YOUR FIGHT HAS ENDED. LAY DOWN YOUR BURDENS. THIS IS *OUR* TIME TO RISE!
RRAH

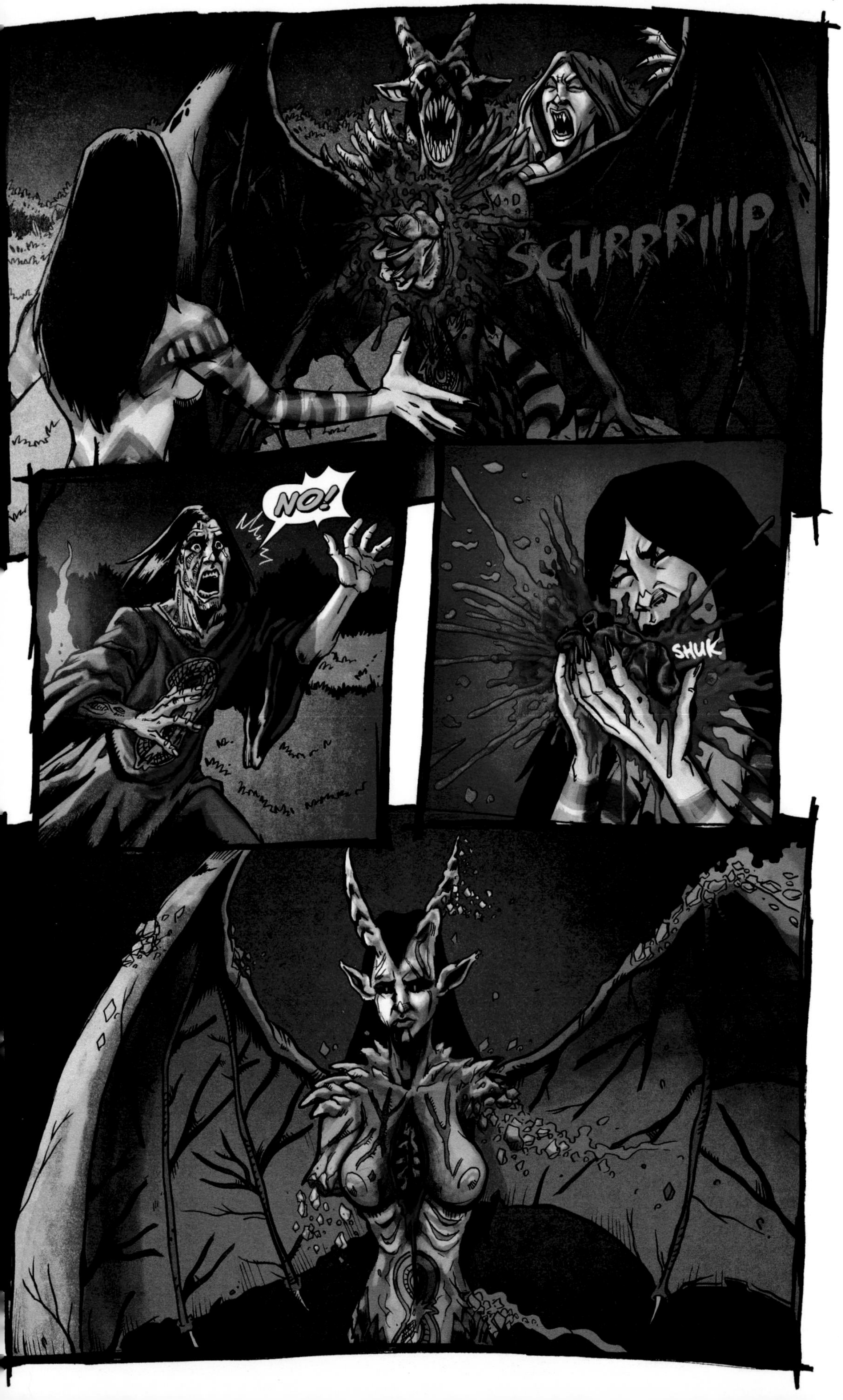
SCHRRRIIIP
NO!
SHUK

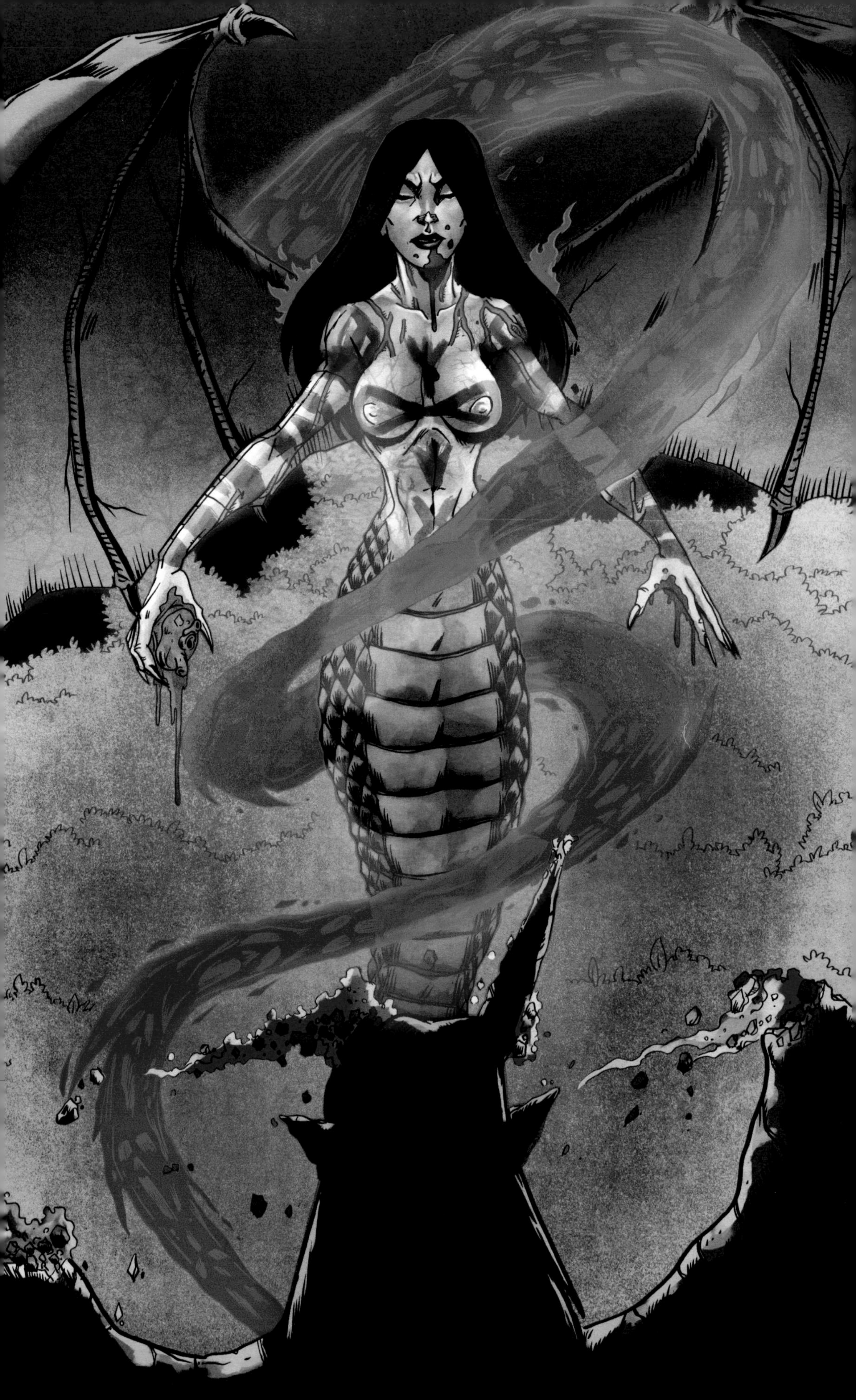

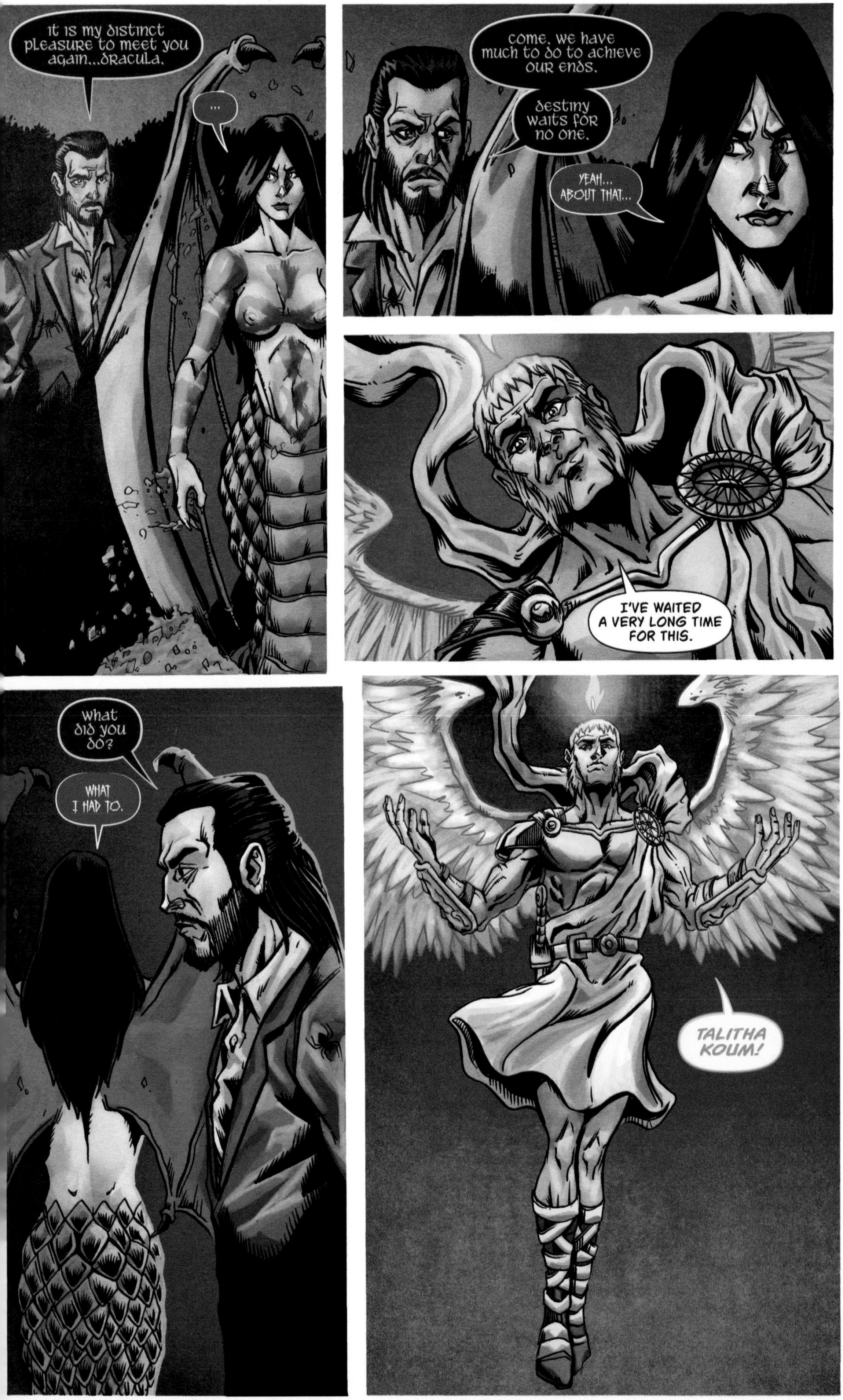
it is my distinct pleasure to meet you again...dracula.
...
come, we have much to do to achieve our ends.
destiny waits for no one.
YEAH... ABOUT THAT...
I'VE WAITED A VERY LONG TIME FOR THIS.
what did you do?
WHAT I HAD TO.
TALITHA KOUM!

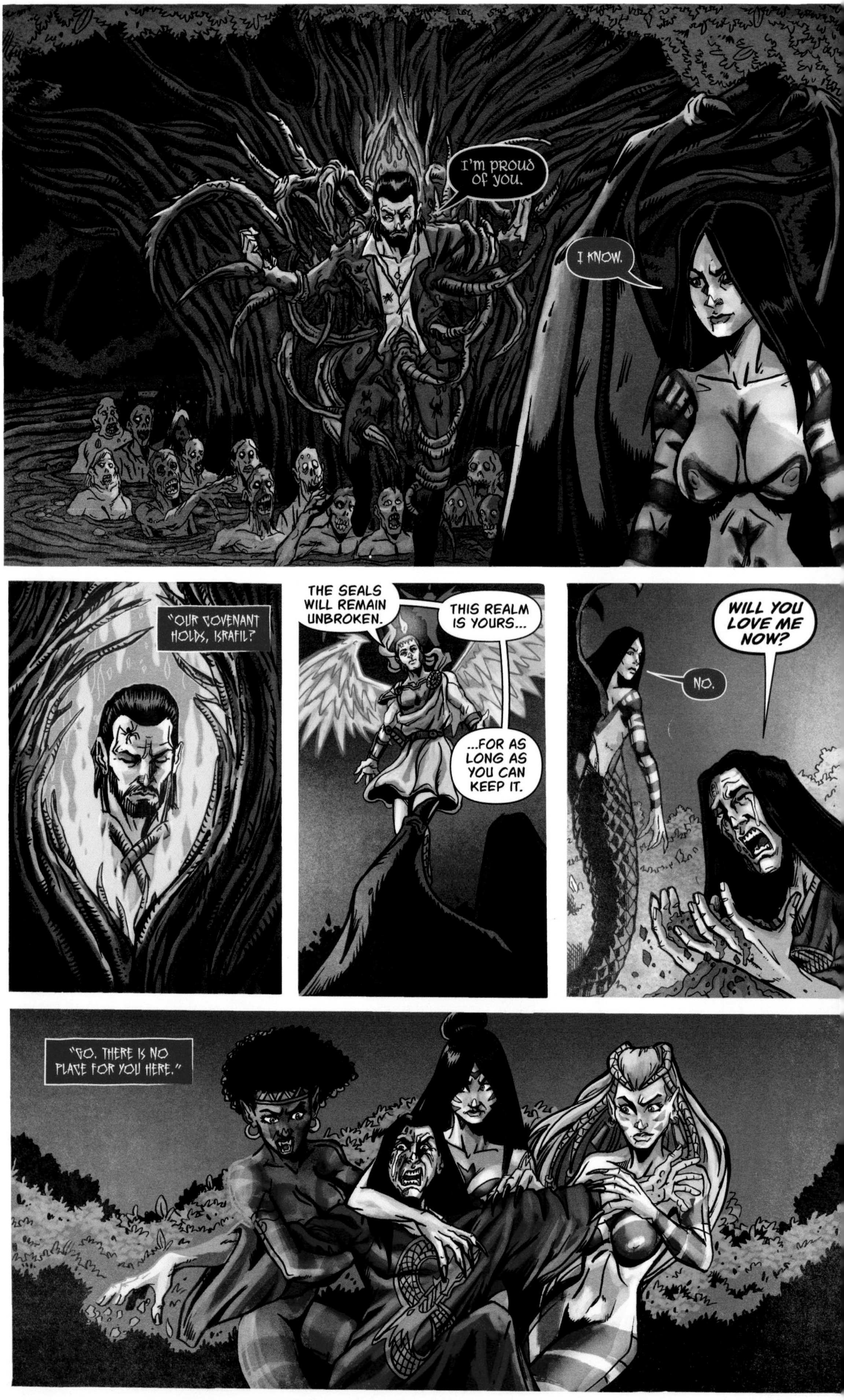
I'M PROUD OF YOU.
I KNOW.
"OUR COVENANT HOLDS, ISRAFIL?
THE SEALS WILL REMAIN UNBROKEN.
THIS REALM IS YOURS...
...FOR AS LONG AS YOU CAN KEEP IT.
WILL YOU LOVE ME NOW?
NO.
"GO. THERE IS NO PLACE FOR YOU HERE."

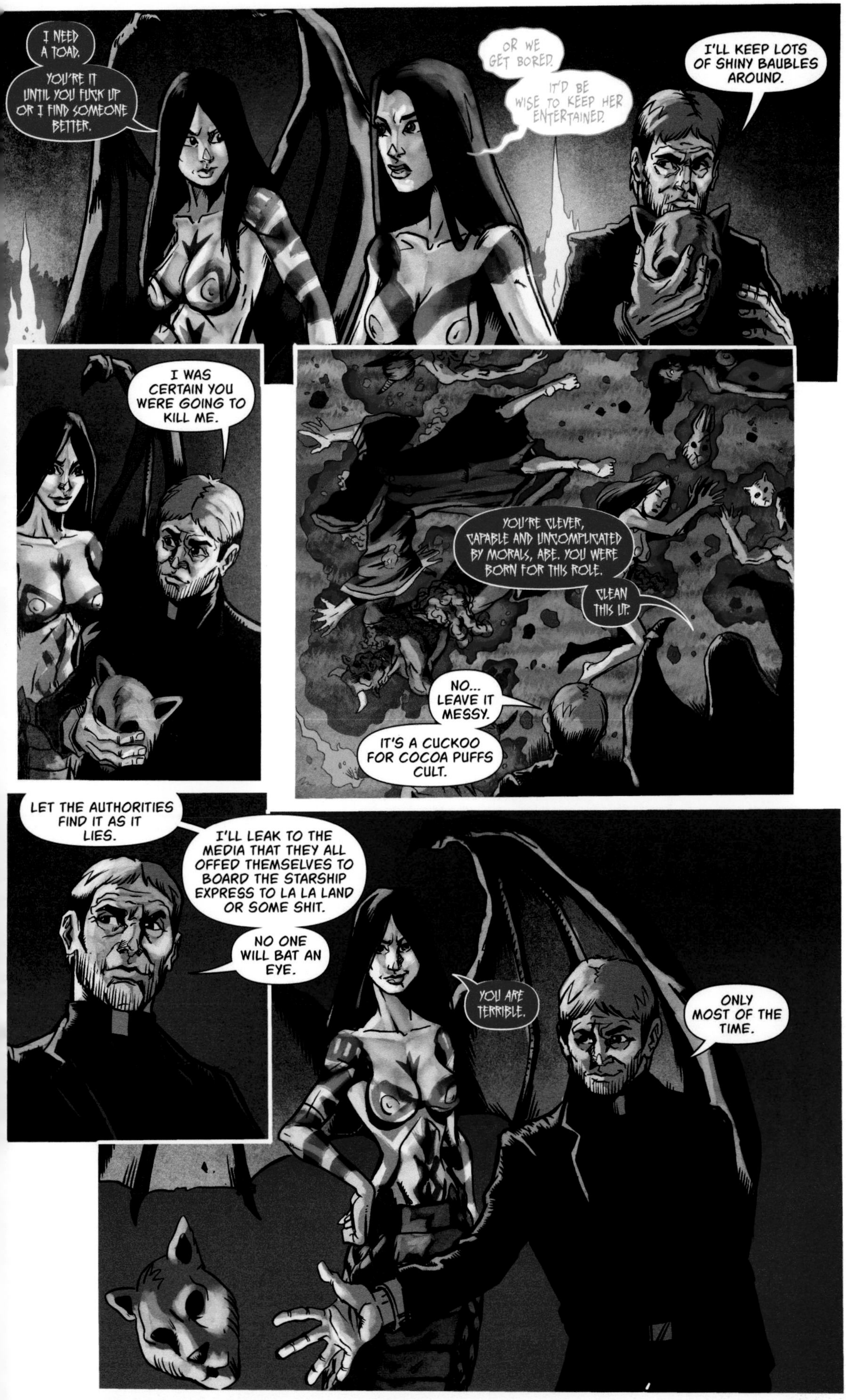
I NEED A TOAD.
YOU'RE IT UNTIL YOU FUCK UP OR I FIND SOMEONE BETTER.
OR WE GET BORED.
IT'D BE WISE TO KEEP HER ENTERTAINED.
I'LL KEEP LOTS OF SHINY BAUBLES AROUND.
I WAS CERTAIN YOU WERE GOING TO KILL ME.
YOU'RE CLEVER, CAPABLE AND UNCOMPLICATED BY MORALS, ABE. YOU WERE BORN FOR THIS ROLE.
CLEAN THIS UP.
NO... LEAVE IT MESSY.
IT'S A CUCKOO FOR COCOA PUFFS CULT.
LET THE AUTHORITIES FIND IT AS IT LIES.
I'LL LEAK TO THE MEDIA THAT THEY ALL OFFED THEMSELVES TO BOARD THE STARSHIP EXPRESS TO LA LA LAND OR SOME SHIT.
NO ONE WILL BAT AN EYE.
YOU ARE TERRIBLE.
ONLY MOST OF THE TIME.

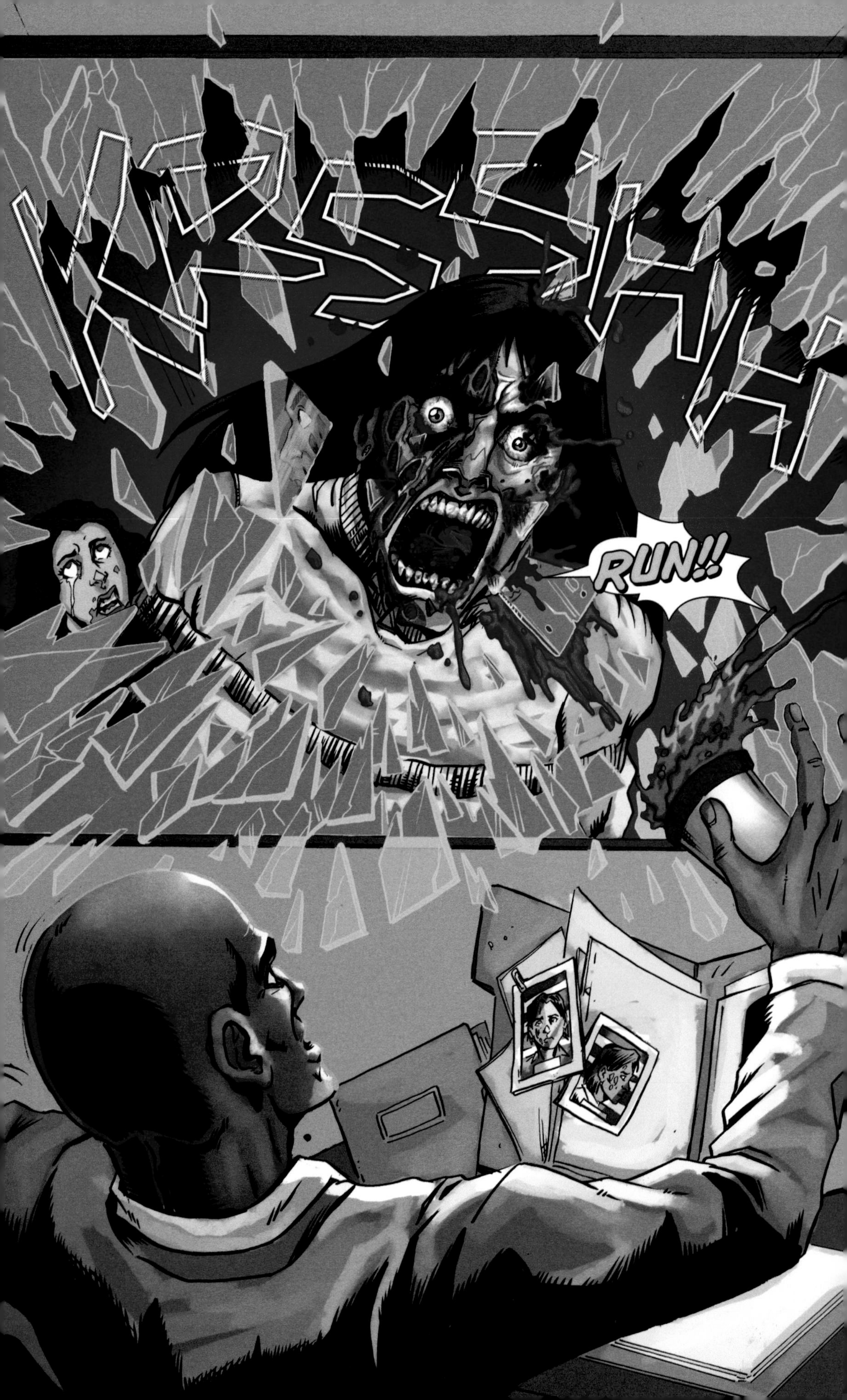
KRSSHH
RUN!!

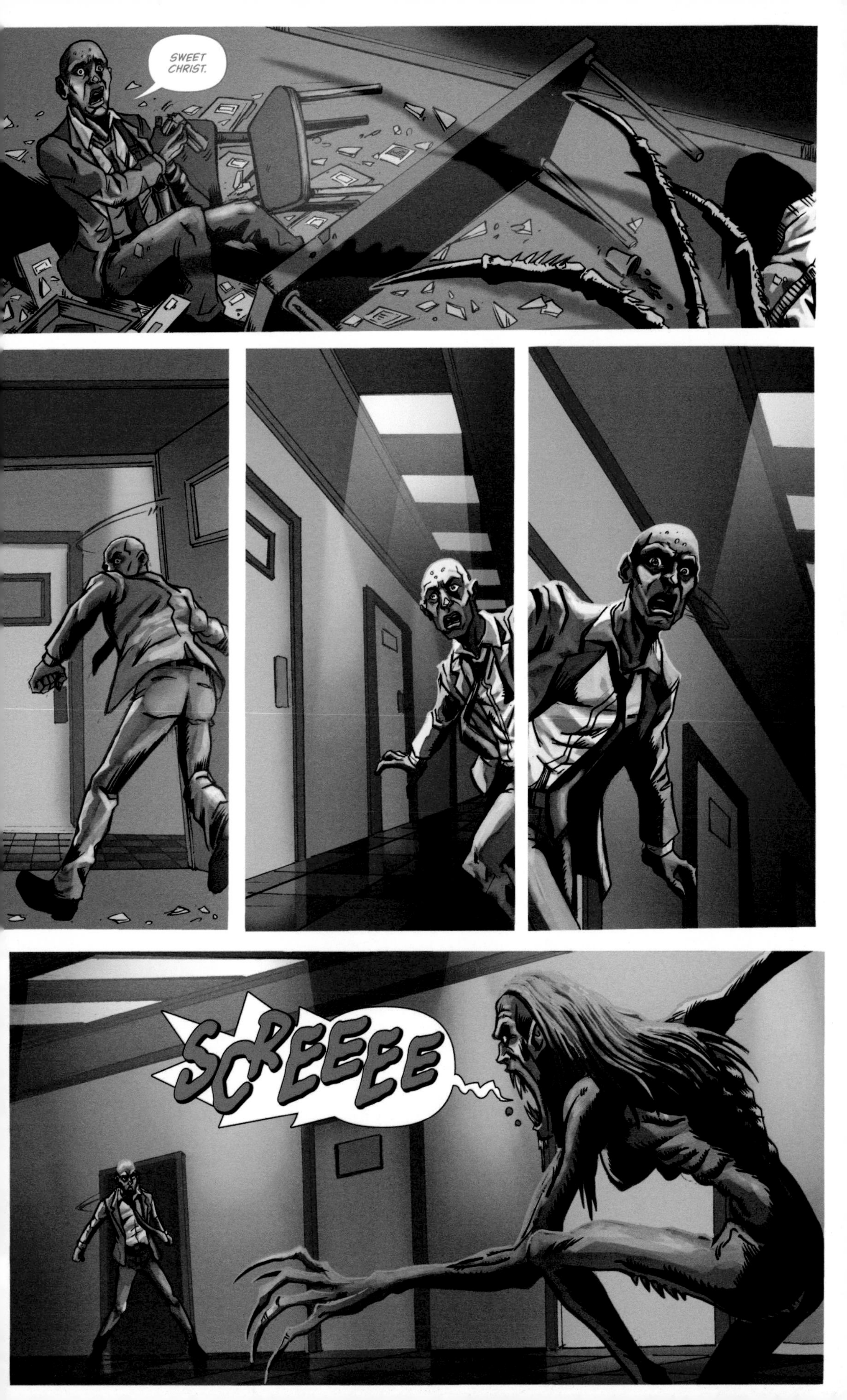
SWEET CHRIST.
SCREEEEE

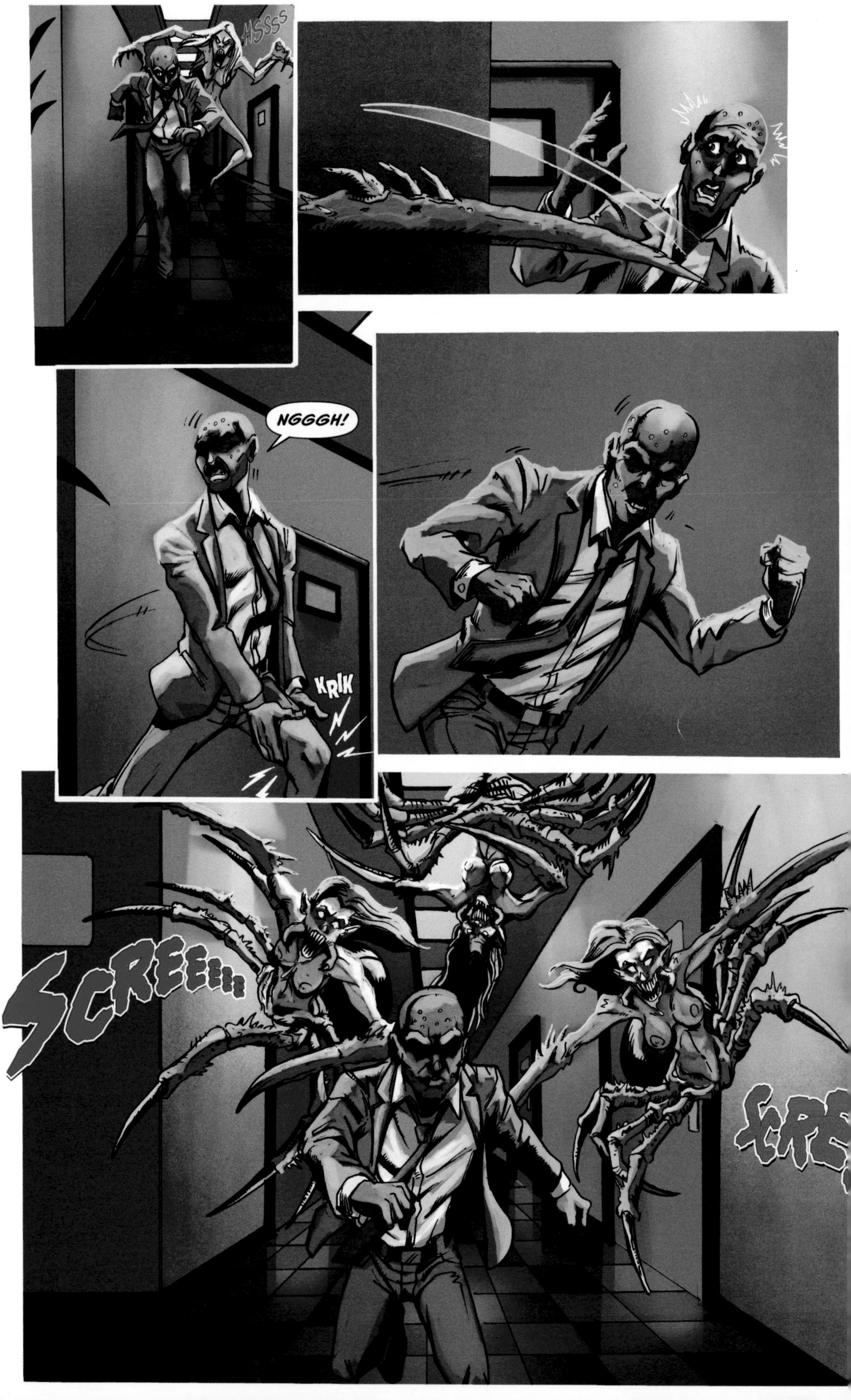
HSSSS
NGGGH!
KRIK
SCREEeee
SCRE

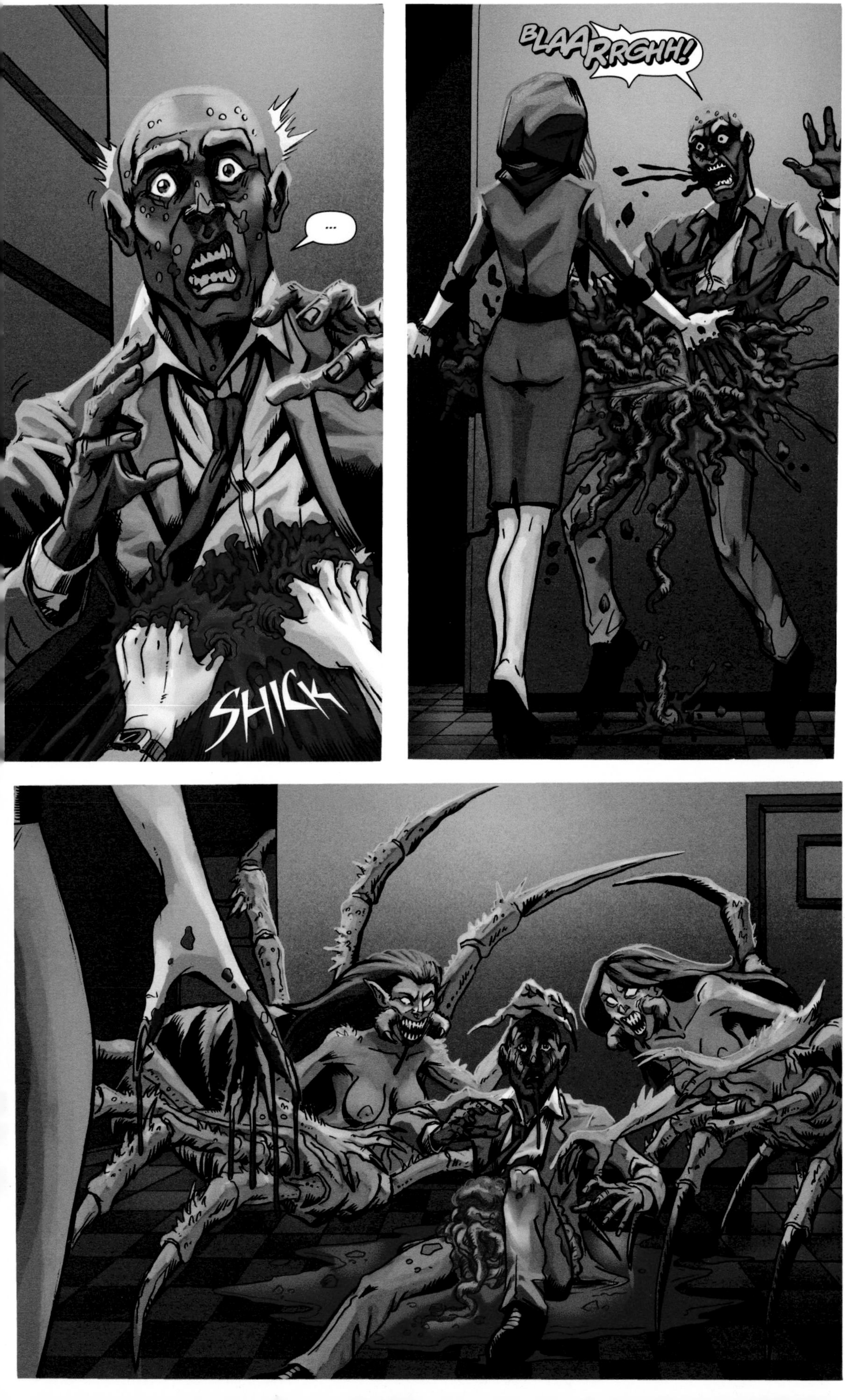
...
SHICK
BLAARRGHH!

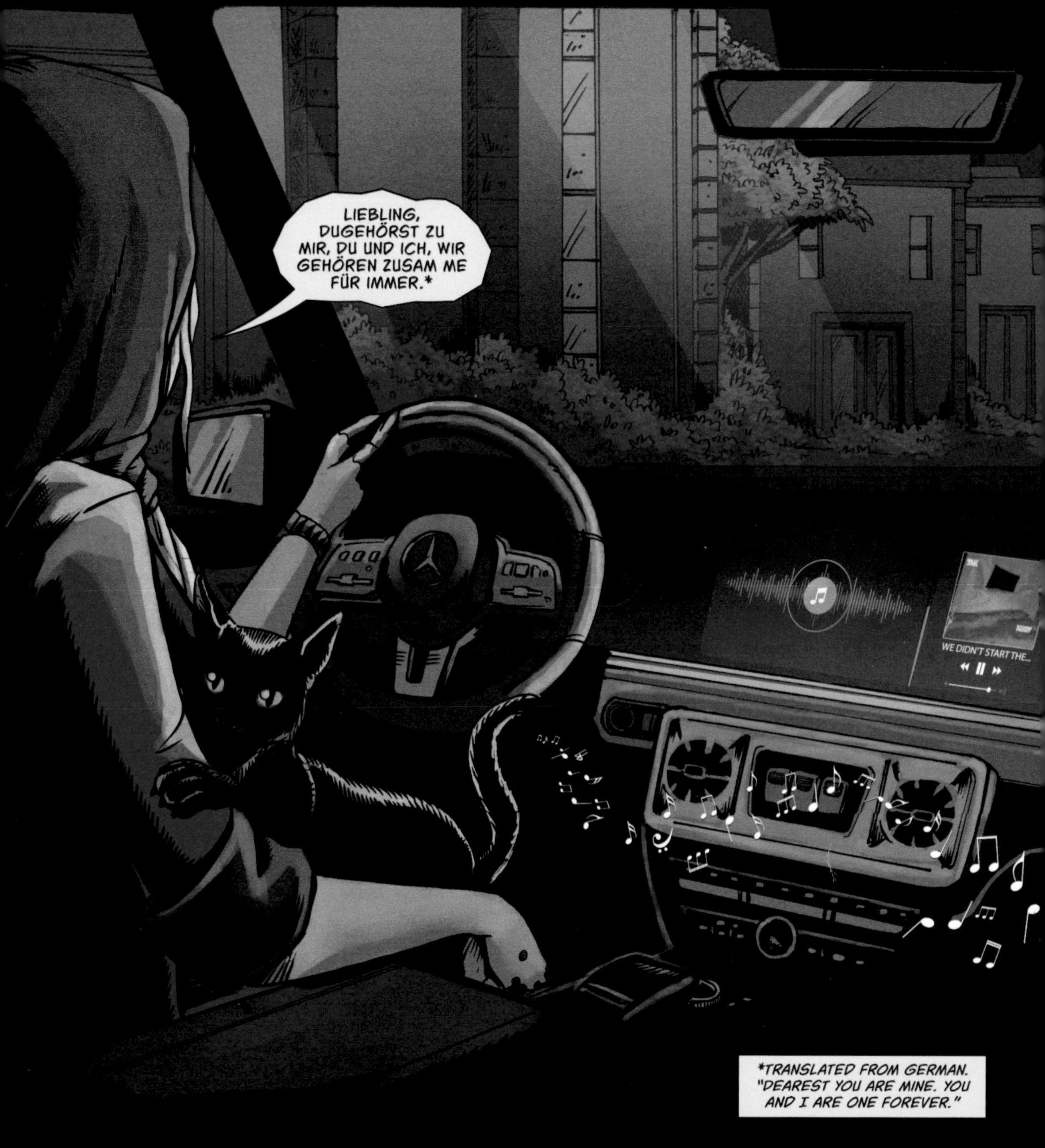
LIEBLING, DUGEHÖRST ZU MIR, DU UND ICH, WIR GEHÖREN ZUSAM ME FÜR IMMER.*
WE DIDN'T START THE...
*TRANSLATED FROM GERMAN. "DEAREST YOU ARE MINE. YOU AND I ARE ONE FOREVER."

COMING SOON:

RISE OF DRACULA

COVER GALLERY

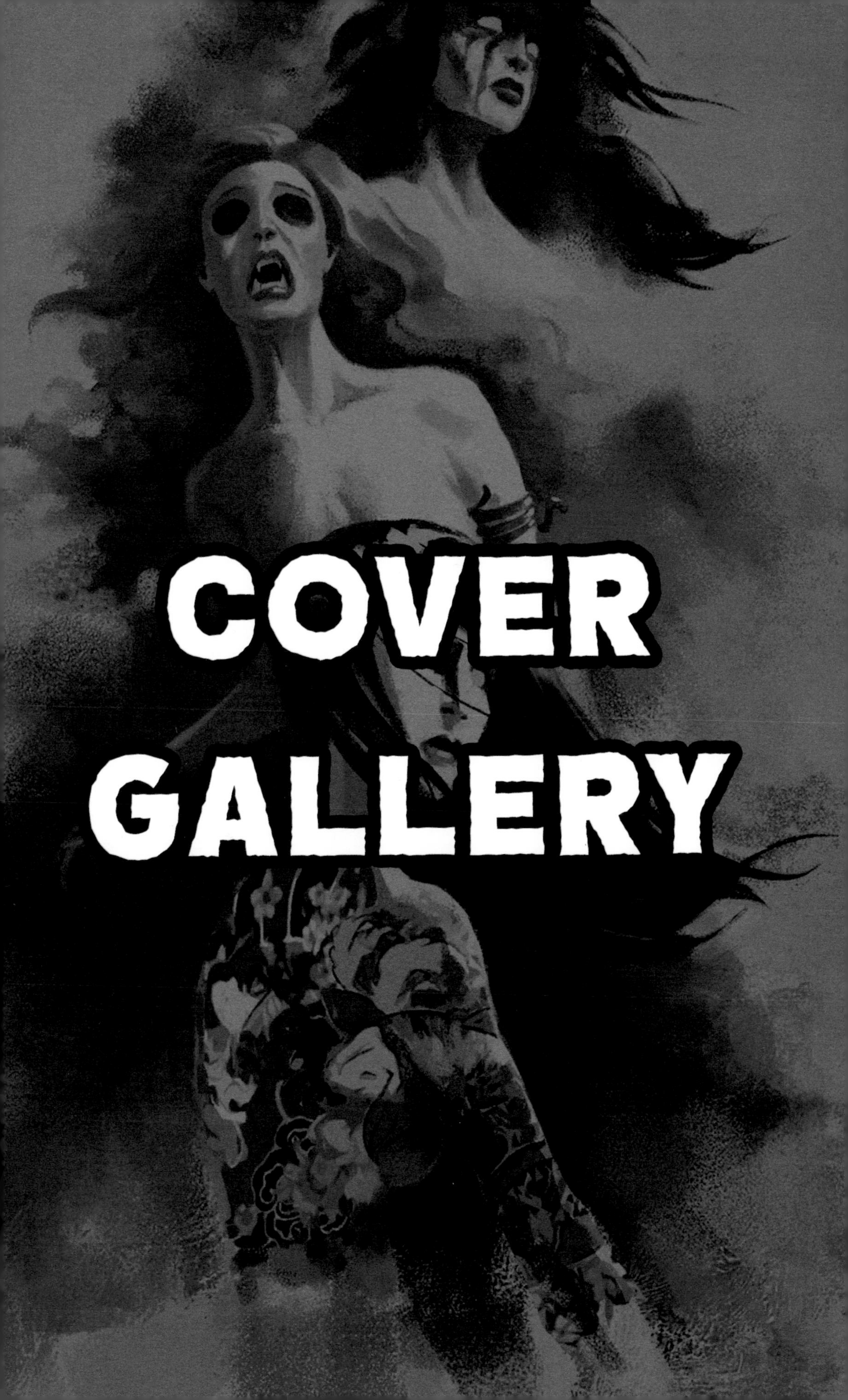

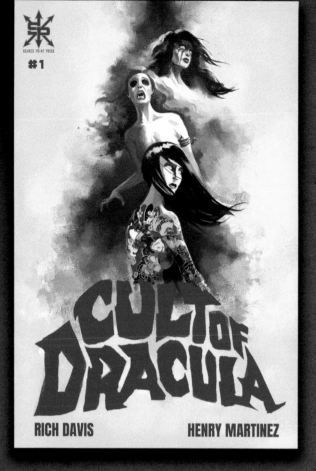

SOURCE POINT PRESS
#1
CULT OF DRACULA
RICH DAVIS
HENRY MARTINEZ

CULT OF DRACULA #1

COVER A

GYULA NEMETH

SOURCE POINT PRESS
#1
Cult of
DRACULA

CULT OF DRACULA #1

COVER B

SHANNON MAER

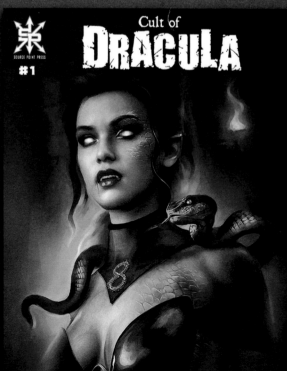

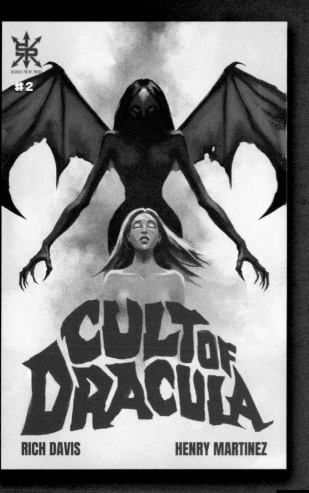

SOURCE POINT PRESS
#2
CULT OF DRACULA
RICH DAVIS
HENRY MARTINEZ

CULT OF DRACULA #2

COVER A

GYULA NEMETH

SOURCE POINT PRESS
#2
Cult of
DRACULA

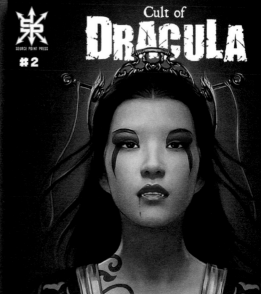

CULT OF DRACULA #2

COVER B

SHANNON MAER

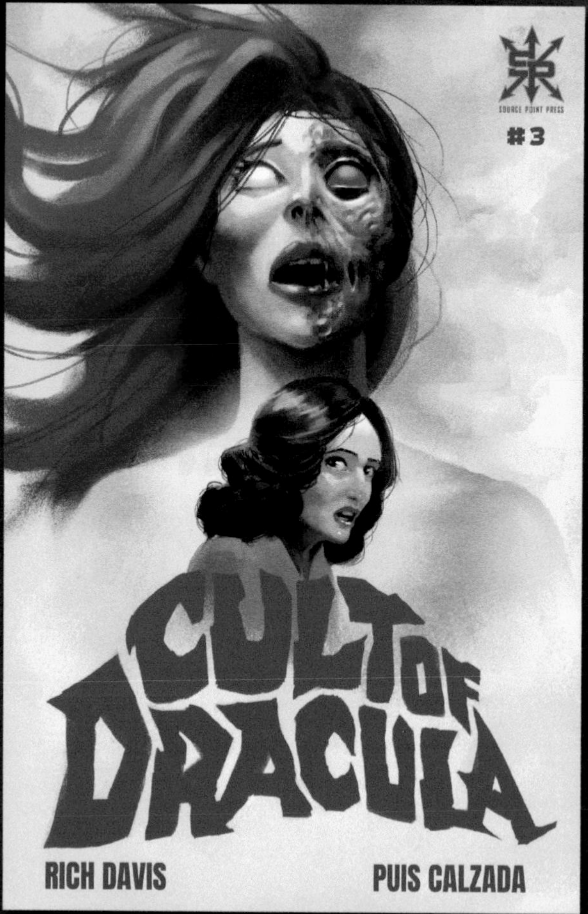
SOURCE POINT PRESS
#3
CULT OF DRACULA
RICH DAVIS
PUIS CALZADA

CULT OF DRACULA #3

COVER A

GYULA NEMETH

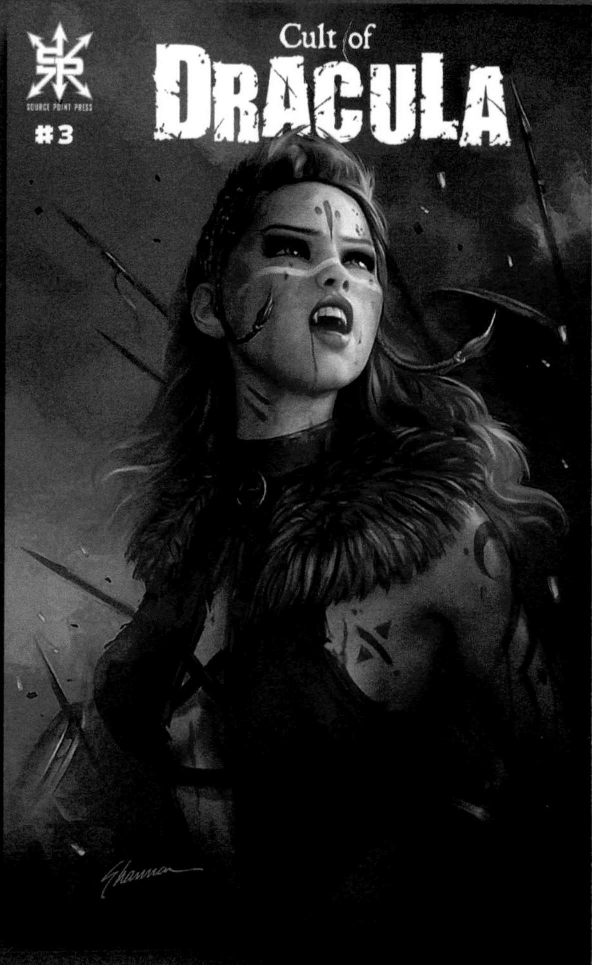
SOURCE POINT PRESS
#3
Cult of
DRACULA

CULT OF DRACULA #3

COVER B

SHANNON MAER

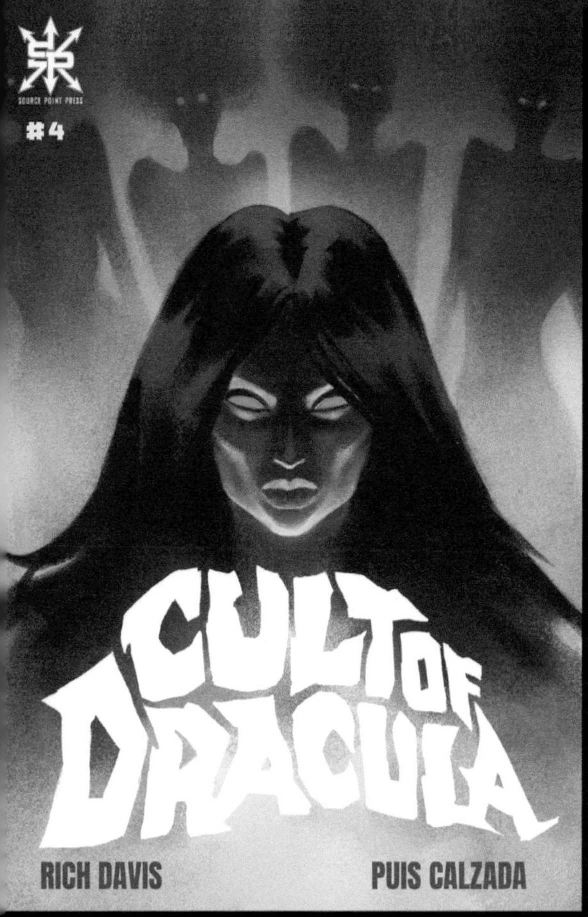
SOURCE POINT PRESS
#4
CULT OF DRACULA
RICH DAVIS
PUIS CALZADA

CULT OF DRACULA #4

COVER A

GYULA NEMETH

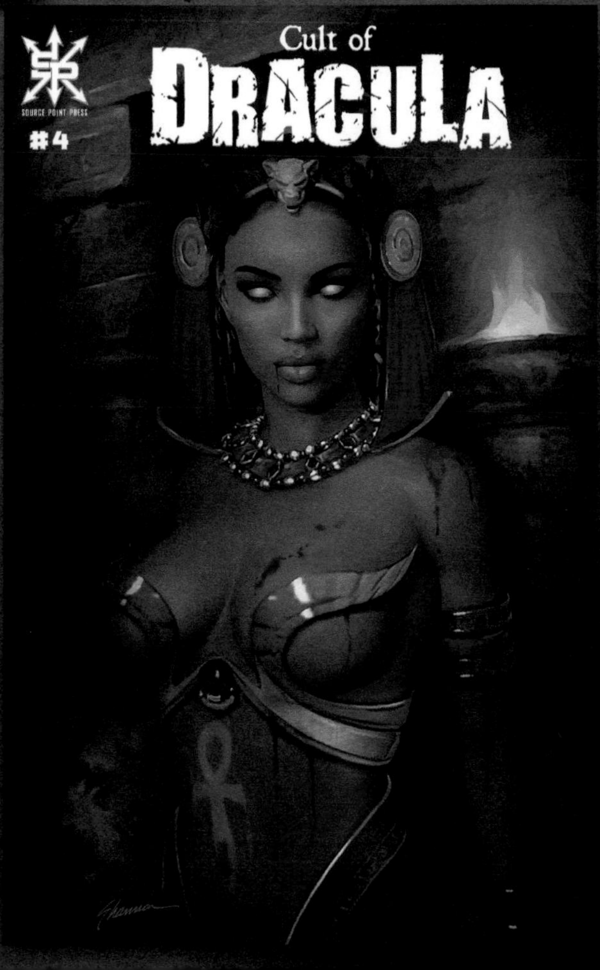
SOURCE POINT PRESS
#4
Cult of
DRACULA

CULT OF DRACULA #4

COVER B

SHANNON MAER

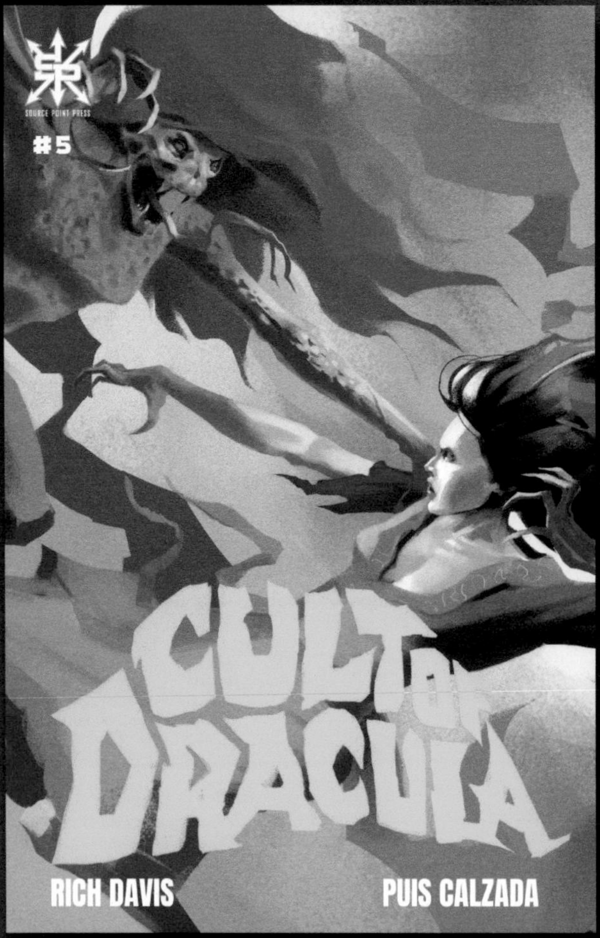
SOURCE POINT PRESS
#5
CULT OF DRACULA
RICH DAVIS
PUIS CALZADA

CULT OF DRACULA #5

COVER A

GYULA NEMETH

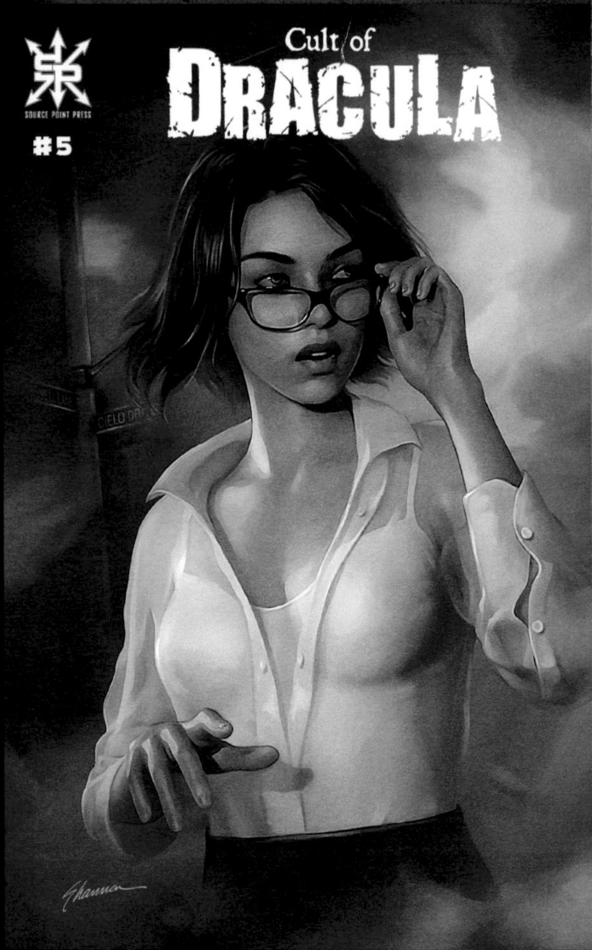
SOURCE POINT PRESS
#5
Cult of
DRACULA

CULT OF DRACULA #5

COVER B

SHANNON MAER

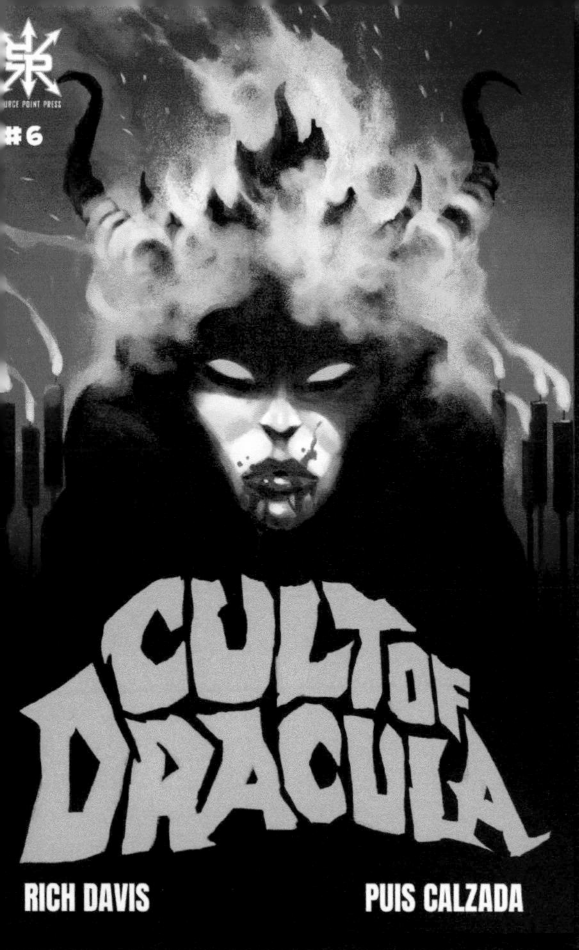

SOURCE POINT PRESS
#6
CULT OF DRACULA
RICH DAVIS
PUIS CALZADA

CULT OF DRACULA #6

COVER A

GYULA NEMETH

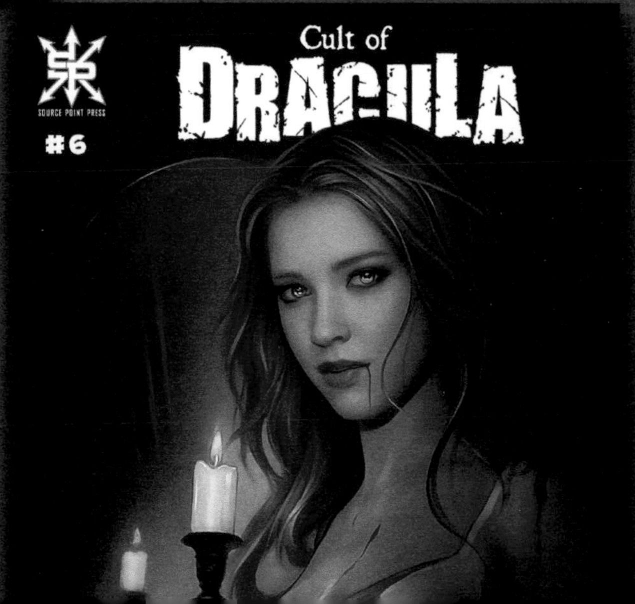

SOURCE POINT PRESS
#6
Cult of
DRACULA

CULT OF DRACULA #6

COVER B

SHANNON MAER

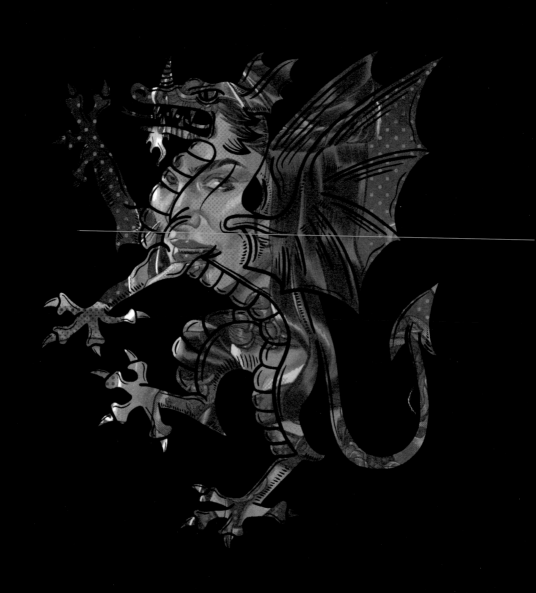